Praise for Stone Soup

So impressive and moving! A p(... tremendous gift to the world. Your story m...... tender intergenerational inspiration. You have put it together in a way that is really powerful. I'm waiting impatiently with a long list of people to send copies. Love embraces justice.

Felicia Davis, HBCU Green Fund

It is the voice and leadership of these young people in this book that will make the ultimate difference. For it is their future.

Chip Comins, American Renewable Energy Institute (AREI)

These young people in the book are the decision makers of tomorrow. Kids are poised to make better decisions than we have based on massive diverse amounts of information they receive daily. They remind me of ocean sponges filtering huge amounts of water cleaning the ocean. Kids thrive making a difference doing exactly what they are inspired to do. Our children elevate us all to higher levels of compassion and understanding. Reading the stories in this book, I'm reminded that we must watch, listen closely and learn from them, as they have from us.

Jean-Michel Cousteau, Our Future Society

Stone Soup for a Sustainable World: Life-changing Stories of Young Heroes is a thought-provoking tour of the planet and those who make a difference. Writer, Marianne Larned, carries the reader to the heart of spirited ideas and action.

Randy Hayes, Rainforest Action Network

Young people have been at the forefront of social change across the globe and throughout history, including today and here in the climate justice movement. I learn so much from so many of the leaders celebrated in Stone Soup -- their creativity, courage, and spirit to get it done without compromising joy -- that I apply in my work, leadership, and parenting of daughters growing up with so many powerful models for expressing their leadership in life.

Sarah Shanley Hope, The Solutions Project

When all seems lost, reading these stories of young people who are searching for and finding solutions makes the world a little brighter. Our planet is in good hands under the stewardship of these young leaders, and if we listen to their advice, we can help heal this world.

Dr. Sarah Oktay, Chemical Oceanographer/Field Station Director

It takes courage to face the prospect of a long future with eyes wide open -- given projections for how much change the planet will see in a young person's lifetime. How inspiring it is to read these stories of young people acting to reconcile humanity with nature -- and to do it from a place not of anger, as one notes, but of love. This book offers a balm for readers of all ages at a needed time.

Robert Engelman, Worldwatch Institute

This book is full of inspirational stories about the next generation of leaders who are passionate about our environment and oceans. Protecting our oceans, and in turn our planet, is going to require passionate leaders like these who are willing to take action. I hope that they will encourage all of us to consider what needs to be done to create a more sustainable world.

Dr. Tobias Stapleton, Blue Innovation Symposium

Every story in this book is an inspiration, and motivates me to redouble my efforts to help in the quest to save humanity -- and the Earth -- from ourselves.

Erik Assadourian, Worldwatch Institute

The collection of stories of young people from all around the world featured in Stone Soup for a Sustainable World is inspiring. It is also comforting to know that, far from being discouraged by the frankly desperate current state of the world, these young people have chosen to push aside fear, take a deep breath, and do something about it. If humanity survives, if balance is restored to our world, it is this generation we will have to thank. And we will have Marianne to thank for shining a light on their bold, brave, ingenious, and generous efforts to make our earth safe for future generations.

Janet Hulstrand, Winged Words Editorial Services

STONE SOUP

FOR A SUSTAINABLE WORLD

LIFE-CHANGING STORIES OF
YOUNG HEROES

MARIANNE LARNED

ISBN: 978-0-578-89380-8

DEDICATION
To All Young People
Imagine what it must be like to be a young person in 2021.

It's been a privilege and an honor to work alongside multicultural youth for the last 20 years. They are my teachers. I've learned so much from them as I imagine walking in their shoes. Young people are precious. They give us hope for the future.

However, it's really tough to be a young person in today's world. It's a time when they are trying to find themselves and their place in the world. But just as they are really ready to explore the world, they find themselves trapped in lockdown, not knowing when they can go out and continue their journey toward adulthood. It's hard to make any plans. They feel confused, frustrated, and lost. Sometimes they can't even imagine a future.

At the beginning of every Summit, I welcome our new youth delegates with a heartfelt apology: "I'm sorry." I *am* truly sorry that our generation has left them with such a mess. But I also tell them that we will do whatever we can to support them and give them the tools they need to plan for their lives, so that they can help their families, their communities, and our world.

Young people today are searching for ways to build a better world. They want to make a living while rebuilding the planet. While it's estimated that there will be over 10 million new jobs in the green economy, young people aren't being connected with these career pathways. Up until now climate change and sustainability solutions aren't taught in our classrooms. Schools just aren't prepared to guide them as they navigate through this 21st century. From the burdens of testing and standards, and then adapting to the new world of virtual learning during the pandemic, our teachers are stretched very thin. And given the current economy, young people are losing hope that they will be able to find a meaningful career, or even a job with a living wage. Young people of color are the most adversely affected. Our global youth are just simply trying to survive. And they are all doing whatever they can to alert us to what is really happening in the rest of the world.

Mental health is a very real problem for young people - with few available resources, especially for our multicultural youth. Counseling is expensive - so they are too often prescribed drugs to just numb their pain. And the age of 19 is when young people are at increased risk of having a psychotic break, which can permanently alter the entire course of one's life.

We are losing far too many of them. It is devasting for a family to lose a child. When my 19-year-old brother Chris died in a car accident, it shattered my family. As the youngest of 10 children, Chris was larger than life. His passing left a huge hole in my heart. As part of my own healing journey, I dedicated my first book, and the Institute's work to his memory. His spirit lives on in all the young people we work with.

In 2019, the Institute lost its first youth leader. At 21 years old, Jackie Noborikawa had her whole life ahead of her. She had traveled from her home in Hawaii to Martha's Vineyard to serve as a youth delegate to the Institute's Youth Leadership Summit. She loved New England, and chose to brave the cold winters to attend Champlain College in Vermont. Everyone was shocked at her sudden passing from colon cancer. Our young people remember Jackie as being "full of light, inspiring and spreading love to everyone she met." While in college, Jackie served as a Summit facilitator, working with our new youth delegates. She was always helpful, dependable, honest, and a true leader. "Whenever someone was upset Jackie knew how to talk to them and help them to calm down and see the bigger picture," one delegate remembers. "She was a kind and unapologetic leader who wasn't afraid to share her opinions, and yet listened to others," says another.

Young people have the energy, the desire, the will, the generosity, and the intelligence, creativity and courage to roll up their sleeves and do what has to be done to heal our world. We just have to be willing to help them do it. I'm grateful to all those who have mentored our youth over the years. Our young people need our support now more than ever. Imagine if each one of us reached out to the young people in our lives, in our communities, to lend a hand, open a door, share our gifts and skills!

I'm always touched to see just how much youth leaders care about and want to help younger people. They have a natural inclination to share what they have learned. To try to help them avoid the mistakes they have made. Help them learn how to navigate the system. And talk with them about the big questions -- about what's really important.

Whenever I'm looking for an answer to a problem, I ask the young people, what do they think? And given that the Institute's mission is to empower them, we ask, and then we really listen to them. Today I asked them why this book is important to them, and here is what they told me: "We want to be heard! This book tells the stories of young people who want to be heard. Sometimes we think we need to do big things. But if one person does just one thing, and then others join them, it starts a chain." "To bring hope and light into the world." And "To read these stories inspires people to say 'I can do it too!'"

This book is dedicated to all young people. May we listen to them. May we learn from them. May we amplify their voices. May we shine light on them and their message. May we join with them to build a more just, equitable, and sustainable world.

Marianne Larned

April 2021

TABLE OF CONTENTS

INTRODUCTION
by Ted Danson

Walking on the beach in Santa Monica with my young children, we came upon a sign: "Water polluted, no swimming." It was heartbreaking to have to explain this to them. That was in 1986. It got me questioning a lot of things.

This year Oceana is celebrating its 20th anniversary, working in 10 countries to "Save the Oceans, Feed the World." As a longtime supporter of the oceans, I'm gladdened to read so many inspiring ocean stories in this book.

Fourteen-year-old award-winning photographer Cruz Erdmann captures the beauty of New Zealand's fish and coral reefs; 22-year-old Mitzi Jonelle Ton stands with and amplifies the voices of the Indigenous fisherfolk in the Philippines; and oyster fisherman Perry Raso feeds his Rhode Island community. At 16, Trevor Tanaka got his Sustainability Resolution passed in Hawaii's House and Senate in just six months. At 19, Daniela Fernandez created the Sustainable Oceans Alliance to fund start-ups in the blue economy, and at 24, Angelique Pouponneau created the Seychelles Conservation and Climate Adaptation Fund to invest in the country's "blue future." And in Guyana, 22-year-old Benita Davis is rallying support for the Policy Forum Guyana, and the president's Green State Development Strategy.

As the son of an archaeologist and anthropologist, I grew up with an appreciation for how people leave an imprint on the Earth. These dedicated young people are a shining example of how we can imagine a more sustainable world. As an actor I've learned the power of celebrities have to amplify these important causes.

I'm impressed with the Stone Soup Leadership Institute's commitment to empowering multicultural youth to speak to truth to power, challenging their leaders to create policies to adapt to climate change realities: from depleted fish, to rising sea levels, increasing hurricanes, and coastal erosion from Newport, Rhode Island to Vieques, Puerto Rico, Virgin Gorda, BVI, Martha's Vineyard, Nantucket, the Philippines, and Sri Lanka. I'm gladdened to see these youth leaders who represented their communities at then-U.S. Secretary Kerry's Ocean Summit with leaders like Dr. Sylvia Earle, Leonardo DiCaprio, and Monaco's Prince Albert.

At U.S. Senator Whitehouse's 2021 Environmental Leadership Conference, I encouraged young people to be purposeful in their activism. Find the joy and happiness in solving these problems. Support organizations that are doing this work internationally.

Young people can create a sense of urgency that our leaders desperately need to rally the political will to ensure that these sustainable policies are implemented and legislation is quickly passed.

The scientists tell us that we only have 10 years to save our oceans. One day, I really hope my three-year-old granddaughter will be able to enjoy our oceans with her grandchildren.

I was heartened by the announcement President Biden made on Climate Day 2021: now, with new leadership, we have a chance to right this ship.

I encourage you to read the inspiring stories in this book Listen to these young people. Learn from them. Join with them. Support them. Let's get to work!

It's going to take all of us working together. The planet is counting on us, and so are our children.

SPECIAL APPRECIATION
For Walter Cronkite

"Ms. Larned, this is Walter Cronkite," said the distinguished voice on the phone. Thus began a life-changing journey.

It was just before the Bush-Gore election in 2000, and he was very concerned about the outcome. He felt strongly that the lack of an educated constituency was threatening our democracy. He thought that if people were uneducated about the issues, they would be more easily influenced by disinformation, and distracted by fear tactics. He felt a sense of urgency about the importance of educating people so they could improve their lives and the world. He invited me to his office on the 57th floor of CBS headquarters in New York City. He wanted to create a TV series based on the stories in our book *Stone Soup for the World: Life-Changing Stories of Everyday Heroes*. He believed these stories could educate people, and teach by example how they could tackle issues in their neighborhoods, have the courage to take a stand, and strive for greatness, especially against great odds.

We did many great things together. As I walked in front of him down the steep and winding stairs to the studio where we recorded his narration for our signature video *In Celebration of Heroes*, he called me his "Gunga Din," referencing Rudyard Kipling's poem about being fearless. Standing by his side, I always felt taller—and sometimes *almost* fearless.

For more than a decade Mr. Cronkite served as the Stone Soup Leadership Institute's honorary chairperson. To start, we bought the rights back for my book and got a two-book deal with Three Rivers Press/Random House; and the new edition, published in 2002, featured an introduction by Mr. Cronkite.

As the only superpower, we need to be the best country and the best global citizens we can be. That means offering a hand up to the good guys. In the last century we've shown the world how we can attack and solve perplexing problems with technology. Imagine if we were to apply that same intellectual power to solving the greatest problems the world faces – poverty, overpopulation, pollution, and medical insufficiency, as well as our dependence on nonrenewable energy resources. Now is a good time to launch a bold new national initiative. We can assure success by celebrating heroes in our midst who by their example lift up the spirit of our people. Stone Soup for the World: Life-Changing Stories of Everyday Heroes is a blueprint for building a better world. Its heroes are legendary people and ordinary folks who, by conviction, imagination, innovation, persistence, frequently hard work, and not infrequently moral or physical courage, have lifted their neighbors and their communities. They challenge each of us to respond in kind. Around the world, revolutionary forces are at work, and they have humankind's dreams on their side. It is up to us to assume leadership of this revolution, to channel it in a direction that will ensure freedom's future.

That summer we premiered our video at the Institute's Celebration of Heroes Awards Ceremony on Martha's Vineyard. And we created short videos called Hero Reports, with his iconic voice framing the videos: "The hero's journey begins with a single step. It's that moment you decide to stand up for something you believe in." Today we are keeping his spirit alive by featuring his voice in all of the Hero Reports in our social media campaign.

We relaunched the book at the Institute's Celebration of Heroes Awards Ceremony in New York City, on the first anniversary of the 9/11 attacks. At this event, Mr. Cronkite presented our Mahatma Gandhi Award to Dr. Muhammad Yunus of Grameen Bank, who went on to receive the Noble Peace Prize a few years later. Reading from the plaque that featured a quote by Gandhi's grandson, Mr. Cronkite said, "Much like Gandhi's salt march that freed India's poor, your micro-credit movement is freeing the world's poor so we can all work together to build a more peaceful world."

Upon Mr. Cronkite's passing, the Institute worked with his family and friends to honor his legacy with the Cronkite Awards, which is presented to those who have used the power of the media for positive social change. Along with his CBS colleagues Bob Schieffer and Nick Clooney, and leaders like David McCullough, Rose Styron, and Ted Kennedy Jr., we've recognized champions like Mission Blue's Dr. Sylvia Earle, filmmaker Bob Nixon, and CNN reporter and civil rights leader Charlayne Hunter-Gault, as well as the young filmmakers who produced the *Passing of the Torch* video featuring Harry Belafonte Jr. for Amnesty International's 50th Anniversary.

Widely recognized as "the most trusted man in America," Walter Cronkite was less well known as an ardent environmentalist. In fact, while he was offered the opportunity to be the first million-dollar network anchor, he chose instead to take an extended leave so he could enjoy long summers on Martha's Vineyard, sailing on his beloved *Wyntje*. Back in the spring of 1970, he had challenged his CBS investigative team to produce a series of stories about pressing environmental issues like air and water pollution, and plant and wildlife devastation from harmful industrial processes. The Emmy award-winning *CBS Evening News* segments that resulted came to be called *Can the World Be Saved?* By spotlighting these issues and introducing them into the national conversation with the urgency it required, Mr. Cronkite forever changed the way major networks treated environmental stories. Later that April he reported on the inaugural Earth Day celebration and, delivered with the same passion he had for covering the moon landing, his coverage rallied more than 20 million Americans to help launch the green movement.

Walter Cronkite would be very proud of all the great young people in this book, and grateful to the intergenerational leaders who are courageously working to build a more sustainable world. Now, at a time when journalism is being challenged on all fronts, as is the planet, we remain grateful for his leadership, and are honored to keep his spirit alive.

Marianne Larned

Stone Soup Leadership Institute

A CALL TO ACTION
#FutureGenerations

Each of the young people in this book came into this world with a mission and a purpose. Each of them has a unique story to tell about how they were inspired to change their lives, to take action, to dedicate themselves to something greater than themselves. They put a face to the reality of our climate crisis. They appeal to our collective humanity. They are intelligent, resourceful, and committed to doing whatever it takes to wake people up to the climate crisis.

Scientists have been sounding the call, but few have listened. Young people are listening. They've awakened. They are woke. They are taking action.

The Climate Clock in New York's Union Square graphically shows how many years we have to reach zero carbon emissions before locking in a catastrophic 1.5° of global warming, given current emissions trends. Seven years, now six years. Here are the facts:

- One million species (one of every eight known species) is now threatened with extinction.
- It's getting hotter: temperatures have risen 1° -- we'll hit 3° by 2200 if we don't make bold changes *now*.
- The polar ice caps are melting: since 2002, 7,900 gigatons of ice have melted from western Antarctica and Greenland.
- Sea levels have already risen 100 millimeters since 1993.
- Each year we release the equivalent of the weight of 229 million blue whales of CO_2 into the atmosphere.

It's heartbreaking to see that at such a young age, they have experienced having their dreams stolen, their future put on hold. From stolen lands and developers fracking, to ecocide with the clear-cutting of forests, and even whole islands washed away. Extreme weather from heat waves, the Arctic melting, droughts, farms turning to deserts, harvests gone; rising seas, the loss of fish, lack of food and water. And along with the ecological devastation, they are painfully aware of the intersectionality of climate change, from the effects of systemic racism to exploitation by corporate greed, to lack of courage from leaders who are striving to please lobbyists; and avoidance of these subjects from the media.

Young people are brave, honest, courageous, hardworking, undeterred -- and they are doing their part to *do something.* Conscious of their own footprints, they are eating less meat or going vegan. They are supporting each other, retweeting messages, sharing posts and images, to ensure that others will see them. But they are in danger of losing the hope of one day having a better life. We've always assumed that there would be future generations. But now?

Young people have been told to wait, but they are tired of waiting. Now is the time for their voices to be heard.

Now is the time for us to listen, and act. NOW!

****

Here are their demands:

#nomoreemptypromises: March 19, 2021Fridays for Future declared that those in power are continuing to deliver only vague and empty promises for far-off dates that are much too late. What we need are not meaningless goals for 2050, or net-zero targets full of loopholes, but *concrete and immediate action in line with science.* Our carbon budget is running out. The climate crisis is already here and will only get worse, so if we are to avoid the worst-case scenarios, annual, short-term climate binding targets that factor in justice and equity have to be prioritized by the people in charge.

The Escazú Agreement (2020). As young people, we understand the immense health crisis of the COVID-19 pandemic, which has exacerbated injustices and disproportionately harmed vulnerable communities across the world. Because of this, young people from South America, Central America, the Caribbean, and North America have come together to urge the entry into force of the Regional Agreement on Access to Information, Public Participation and Access to Justice in Environmental Matters in Latin America and the Caribbean, also known as the Escazú Agreement.

In December 2020, in preparation for COP26 in Scotland, they organized a Mock COP26 with delegations from over 140 countries, and released *Our Treaty,* which states the 18 policies they voted for. This treaty makes it perfectly clear -- they intend to keep leaders' feet to the fire!

*When day comes, we step out of the shade, aflame
and unafraid.
The new dawn blooms as we free it.
For there is always light. If only we're brave
enough to see it.
If only we're brave enough to be it.*

Amanda Gorman, "The Hill We Climb"

I
WAKE UP!
Climate Change Trailblazers

WAKE UP!
Climate Change Trailblazers

It was an honor to be invited to Greta Thunberg's first public event in the U.S. on September 9, 2019. Naomi Klein hosted a dialogue, "The Right to a Future," with Greta and other youth, including Xiye Bastida, Vic Barret, and Xiuhtezcatl Martinez. When Greta arrived on the stage, she was cheered by a standing ovation from the local students and enthusiastic Black youth from the "Compton Kidz," along with elders like Amy Goodman, Bill McKibben, and Chip Comins.

It was in that moment that I knew -- now is the time for the new Stone Soup book!

People were waking up -- finally! -- and ready to meet these brave young people who are passionately committed to waking us all up!

From the moment Greta had arrived on a sailboat in New York harbor on August 28, it was international news. On that same day the Stone Soup Leadership Institute's young people were learning to sail off the coast of Massachusetts, so they could only imagine what it must have been like for Greta to be on a sailboat in the open Atlantic Ocean for two whole weeks. Greta was their hero. They admired her courage for taking a stand against the use of fossil fuels by refusing to travel by plane. They had recently heard the 16-year-old's speech on a video at the Institute's Sustainability Summit.

Greta embarked on this journey to the U.S. to join with other climate activists and lend her star power to their efforts. Then, at the UN's Climate Action Summit, she had sounded a wake-up call, quoting the now infamous IUCN World Conservation Congress report that warned that we only had 11 years to radically change the trajectory of our planet or risk setting off a disastrous and irreversible chain reaction.

A few days later, our Institute youth joined the Global Climate Strike, the largest single-day climate protest in history. Four million people turned up to 6,000 events in more than 1,000 cities across 185 countries. Youth from around the world came together to demand urgent action to protect their future. Greta's clarion call had resonated with them:

We children are doing this to wake the adults up. We children are doing this for you to put your differences aside and start acting as you would in a crisis. We children are doing this because we want our hopes and dreams back.

Later that year, when she received recognition as *Time* magazine's Person of the Year Greta challenged the media to focus on all of the young people who are standing together with her. While writing this book, it's been an honor to connect with so many of these Climate Change Trailblazers from around the world: Jamie Margolin (U.S.), Lilly Platt (the Netherlands), Nicki Becker (Argentina), Alejandro Martinez (Spain), Joel Enrique Pena Panichine (Chile), Arshak Makichyan (Russia), Iqbal Badruddin (Pakistan), Vihaan Agarwal (India), David Wicker (Italy), Linus Dolder (Switzerland), and Jean Hinchliffe (Australia). Each of them is shining the light brightly, blazing a path, pointing the way to a more sustainable world.

But young people have been sounding the climate change alarm for decades.

Back in 1992, 13-year-old Severn Suzuki became known as "The Girl Who Silenced the World for Five Minutes" when she spoke at the UN Summit in Rio de Janeiro. "I am here to speak on behalf of the starving children around the world whose cries go unheard. I am here to speak for the countless animals dying across this planet, because they have nowhere left to go.... And now we hear of animals and plants going extinct every day, vanishing forever."

It was 1997 when Julia "Butterfly" Hill climbed to the top of a beloved ancient redwood tree to save it from being cut down by a lumber company. She had only planned to stay there a week. But once she was up there, she realized she wasn't going to come down until she had succeeded in saving that tree and the trees surrounding it. Her two-year battle was ultimately successful -- and led to her worldwide fame as an environmental activist.

In 2008, Alec Loorz became the youngest person trained by Al Gore's Climate Reality initiative. When he was just 12 years old, he'd watched the movie *An Inconvenient Truth*. "It was a turning point in my life," he says. "Before that I was aware of climate change in a roundabout way. But that made it real for me. And I wanted to do something about it."

When 14-year-old Slater Jewell-Kemker saw this same documentary, she decided to make a film about climate activists. It took her more than a decade to finish her award-winning documentary *Youth Unstoppable*.

As I was writing this introduction, I received a heart-wrenching message from David Wicker in Italy.

Time is running out, and after two years of activism, with close to no "real" and strong climate action yet, I'm afraid I'll also have to focus on what happens next: how can I help make sure people survive and people are taken care of when the worst hits us (which is already happening in some parts of the world)?

These brave young climate activists urgently need our support. NOW!

They are going to wonder why you, who had the chance to be heard, didn't speak up. It doesn't have to be that way. We could all start acting as if we were in the middle of the crisis we are in fact in. You keep saying that the children are our future, and that you would do anything for them. If you mean what you say, then please listen to us. We want you to start speaking up and telling it like it is.

Greta Thunberg

excerpted from *A Letter to Everyone Who Has a Chance to Be Heard*

Our House Is on Fire: Scenes of a Family and a Planet in Crisis

ALL HANDS ON DECK: THIS IS ZERO HOUR
Jamie Margolin
Seattle, Washington

In West Seattle, there is an urban sanctuary called Lincoln Park. With its many unique natural features, it's as impressive as any in the Pacific Northwest. With its old growth trees. Winding footpaths. Expansive views of Puget Sound. Sandy beaches dotted with glacial rocks and footprints.

It's here, in this serene setting, that Jamie Margolin likes to connect with nature, which she does often. But one day when she was walking on the beach, she saw a sign -- literally–that set her on her journey as a climate justice activist. "There was a sign that read, 'Please don't feed the seal pups.' I don't know why, but the message struck me as odd. In all the times I'd visited, I'd never seen any seal pups."

Jamie knew something wasn't adding up. But like the rest of her concerns about the climate situation, she pushed it deep down. Hoping to forget, to move on. So she kept walking. Further along the beach, another sign read, "These are the whales and porpoises that you'll commonly see around this bay."

"It was just like before. I'd never seen any whales or porpoises here. None of my friends had either. That's when I realized there's a disconnect in our way of thinking," Jamie says. "We see what we want to see, not what we need to see." She continues, "Of course, these animals were here once, when the Indigenous peoples who cared for the land lived in this region. This really got me thinking deeply about my own culture and the environment for the first time."

Jamie might have become a devoted climate justice activist that day, at age 14. But the groundwork for her activism had started long before that. Her father is a bookish man, a Reform Jewish thinker who always listens to the news. "Politics is a constant in my life," she says. "My dad is to thank for that. Believe it or not, I didn't grow up watching *Hannah Montana*. Nothing like that. For fun, we watched *The Colbert Report*. Or *The Daily Show*. Or just the plain old news," Jamie says, smiling. "This really helped shape my perspective."

Jamie's mother also had a huge impact on her world view. An immigrant from Colombia, she had grown up in poverty with six siblings and a single mother. It was a tough life. She instilled in Jamie a sense of caring about the world. Jamie credits her own resilience to the lessons her mother taught her. "It's what made me the activist I am today," she says.

Next, on a trip to Colombia to visit her cousins, Jamie had another formative experience. Her family lives near a fracking site. There, she saw rivers with dead fish in them, and polluted streams. In the city, she felt the burn of fossil fuels in the air. She knew this sort of thing was happening in the United States. But she didn't know it was happening in Colombia too. She started to see that the environment was suffering everywhere. "And our leaders weren't doing anything about it," she says.

When the night of the 2016 election came, everything changed for Jamie. "It shattered my ideal, that the good guys would always win. I decided I wasn't going to rely on party leaders to make a difference. I was going to be the one that fought for the good guys." That was the turning point that moved her from thought to action.

"I started small," she says. "First, I got involved with Plant-for-the-Planet -- which was a great introduction to the world of climate change advocacy. After that, I started community organizing. I talked to legislators and politicians, and I helped put on lobbying events for environmental legislation, from Seattle to Olympia." Jamie's journey wasn't always easy. Her rise to prominence wasn't always steady. Many times she met with forceful resistance. "In January 2017, I had my first meeting with a Republican legislator. He was quite hostile," Jamie says. "The PTA was having a rally at the same time, so it was very tense. When it came time for me to talk, the legislator cut me off and said, 'You see these people? They want money too.'"

"He was not there to actually listen," Jamie says. "If he was, he would've known that I wasn't looking for money. Still, he carried on. He pulled out a brochure on homelessness and said, 'The money you want for climate justice could be helping these kids.'"

But this is all intersectional, Jamie thought. *How come he doesn't understand? The climate crisis makes homelessness worse. It's not an isolated issue.* "I had many experiences like this, where I was just shrugged off," Jamie says. "What was even more frustrating is that there wasn't a single media article about the fight for climate justice. People weren't paying attention. So I decided, you know what? Enough is enough!"

That summer she cofounded Zero Hour, with the purpose of organizing a national youth climate march, to really get people to listen. She was ready to grow from being a local organizer to being the leader of an international movement. Jamie posted her idea for the March on social media, with an ambitious one-year timeline. At first slowly, then rapidly, the number of people who signed up from around the country grew. And one year later, as promised - on July 21, 2018 - Jamie led the first Youth Climate March in Washington DC. Thousands of young people marched on the National Mall, advocating for their right to a safe and livable future. Sister marches went on in New York City, Indianapolis, Seattle, Las Vegas, and even in Melbourne, Australia, and London. Jamie was especially grateful that the March was endorsed by groups like the Peoples Climate Movement, The Climate Group, the Alliance for Climate Education, the Citizens' Climate Lobby, the Indigenous Environmental Network, the Sierra Club, Sunrise, and the Women's March Youth Empower.

By July 2019, Jamie's efforts had expanded in a big way. Zero Hour now began to focus on increasing the voices of diverse youth in the conversation around climate and environmental justice. She organized the first Youth Climate Summit, a three-day climate justice event in Miami, Florida. All in all, the Summit trained more than 350 youth and older allies in climate justice activism and organizing. Jamie is supporting these newly-trained climate advocates to use Zero Hour's Getting to the Roots of Climate Change platform. Now those newly-trained allies serve as ambassadors, and educate their local communities about the climate movement.

For youth who want to get further involved in a community, Jamie's message is kind, and encouraging. "Growing up is hard," she says. "Sometimes it's hard to know your place in the world. So take something you are passionate about—whether that is art, performing, cooking, or robotics – and apply that same passion to a movement."

"It doesn't need to be climate justice," she adds. "Just get involved, and get informed. Use your skills and knowledge to create the change you want to see," she says, and adds, "Never be afraid to use your voice. You are never too young, or too weak."

According to Jamie, this is especially true for marginalized people, who are not used to having their voices heard. "Young women. Women of color. Queer people. It's hard out there. So let's use the tools we have to come together for a common cause. Social media can bring us together like never before. Zero Hour and the Youth Climate Movement wouldn't have been possible without it. You *can* change the world. We did!"

For adults, Jamie's advice is simple. "Stop pinning your responsibility on children. The climate crisis can't wait for my generation to fight it. By the time I'm old enough to be in a position of power, it'll be too late. The world will be on fire. 'Business as usual' isn't going to cut it this time. And words won't either. We need action. We need a major systems overhaul. And we need adults and children working together toward that goal."

Jamie pauses, and lets out a heavy sigh. After a silence, she continues, "You need to be able to look your children in the eye and say, 'I did all I could to protect your future. I fought the battle against climate change. I turned over every stone I possibly could.' Adults need to ask themselves -- and be honest -- 'Have I done all that I can for climate justice?'"

It's a big ask. But according to Jamie, it's a necessary one. "We can't just ignore it, and hope someone else will deal with it. Ensuring climate justice for future generations is an enormous task. As a country, we must all come together. As brothers and sisters together, we must have an answer to that big question. 'Have we done all that we can for climate justice?'" Jamie Margolin is counting on everyone to stand up and be counted.

To cherish what remains of the Earth and to foster its renewal is our only legitimate hope of survival.

Wendell Berry

Call to Action: Join the Zero Hour movement to demand climate action *NOW!* http://thisiszerohour.org **Buy Jamie's book:** *YOUTH TO POWER* www.youthtopowerbook.com Follow Jamie https://twitter.com/jamie_margolin

AN INCONVENIENT YOUTH
Alec Loorz
Washington DC

Young Alec Loorz was awestruck when he found himself standing on a stage with former Vice President Al Gore. "He told me he'd read my letter," he says. "That day I felt like I was in a dreamworld, on stage with my hero."

For Alec, watching *An Inconvenient Truth* when he was just 12 years old was a turning point in his life. "It gave me that spark to really take action. Before that, I was aware of climate change in a roundabout way. But that film made it real for me. And I wanted to do something about it."

When Al Gore's documentary film, *An Inconvenient Truth* was released in 2006, it created a renewed interest in the climate conversation globally – and that was his goal. The conversation around the impending climate crisis had gone stale, and needed to be reinvigorated. As a popular political figure, Gore knew he could influence change. Alec was among the countless environmental advocates inspired by the film, which to this day continues to create passionate climate activists.

From the moment Alec saw the film, he started spreading the word. Most people Alec's age weren't aware of the climate movement. "I got into an argument with one of my friends about it," he says, with a laugh. "Over time, I did a lot of research on the issues, and my own story became intertwined. I felt a sense of calling to be a part of the transition to a sustainable society."

Alec learned a lot on his own. But he knew he needed to be around top experts to really be able to make the wide-ranging impact he wanted to. So he decided to go straight to the source of his inspiration. "Mr. Gore's organization, the Climate Reality Project, had a training program. However, they had an age cutoff, and since I was only 13, I was turned down." But Alec didn't let that stop him; he worked privately, behind the scenes. "I even sent a letter to Mr. Gore, saying how I was rejected from the training, but I still wanted to be involved."

Now, standing on the stage with his hero, Alec's persistence had paid off. Mr. Gore told Alec that anybody with his passion should definitely be involved in the cause. The very next week Alec got an invitation to join the next training in Nashville, where he would become the youngest person ever trained. "That was an unbelievable three days," Alec says. At the end of the program, he was equipped with a CD full of slides and directed to go out with it, into the world.

Alec had begun his environmental journey while still in middle school, by founding Kids vs. Global Warming. He constructed signs throughout his coastal city of Ventura, California, warning about the impacts of sea level rise. News of his work began to leak out to the national press, and an intense public speaking schedule emerged. All through high school Alec was a popular speaker: he gave more than 1,000 presentations to over half a million people, most of them youth. And he received prestigious awards, including the Coretta Scott King A.N.G.E.L. Award, and the Brower Youth Award from the Earth Island Institute.

In 2010, at age 16, Alec cofounded iMatter with his mother, to support youth-centered climate action. They held the first worldwide youth climate march in 2011, with 45 countries participating. The same year, Alec and other iMatter leaders acted as plaintiffs in a lawsuit against the U.S. federal government, on the grounds that it has not lived up to its responsibility to protect the atmosphere for future generations.

"We actually made it all the way to U.S. federal court," he says, proudly. "But then the fossil fuel lobby got involved. They intervened in the case and sent some really good lawyers, and they defeated it." But, he adds, "The fact that they sent their best lawyers to shut us down showed we were considered a serious threat —and we will continue to be. While we lost that lawsuit, this legal approach goes on today. And will in the future."

Alec continued to campaign. But he knew that the movement's strategy couldn't be to just keep writing letters and having protests. "It felt like that famous Einstein saying, like we were doing the same thing over and over again and expecting different results. I got frustrated. And so I decided to go out in search of other perspectives."

Alec visited Iceland, where he walked on a glacier that scientists say will be gone in 100 years. He crossed the United States multiple times, visiting and learning from organic farming coops that have a healthy relationship with the land and their communities. He visited Indigenous people in Ecuador whose land was threatened by extractive industry.

By 2017, Alec's travels had led him to southeastern Utah. Here, at the

Bears Ears National Monument, he participated in a retreat as the Kalliopeia Foundation's Spiritual Ecology Fellow.

Bears Ears is a national monument that was established in 2016 to protect around 1.3 million acres from development. But in 2017, at the very time Alec was on retreat there, a fateful announcement was made – the protected land area was to be reduced by about 85 percent, to open up the lands to mining operations. Simultaneously, nearly 900,000 acres was to be slashed from the Grand Staircase-Escalante Monument. Being there at the time, Alec had an insight.

"If I try to identify what's missing with the movement, it's this core feature, this idea of 'us vs. them'. On one side, it's the people trying to protect Bears Ears, and on the other, it's those who see the land as a resource to exploit. Yes, we have differing viewpoints, and their actions can be damaging." He pauses, then adds. "But I don't think that the 'us vs. them' mentality will stop it. We're all just people. If we keep this kind of thinking up, we'll just be repeating the same cycles of division that got us standing on opposite sides of the issue in the first place. We're all together in this world, so we should come together and listen to one another. It's our only choice."

Alec realized that in all his travels, whether he was in Iceland, the United States, the Amazon or the Andes, there's one tried and true method to bring people together in their reverence for a land and its people – and that is through telling stories. "My work has led me to the point where I think that telling stories about places and people is the way forward. We can't approach climate change as this whole big abstract thing, where we're saving the whole wide world. It's too broad. The only way to approach the depths of this, to really change *how* we live, is to deep dive into specific spaces; and to explore the human relationship with these spaces through storytelling."

Now, through filmmaking, writing, and photography, Alec hopes to explore new ways of telling stories that can address the depth and complexity of this situation. Coupled with this change in his perspective, he also believes that more people, including more young activists and advocates, need to actually get out into the world and spend some significant time in nature, to gain a different perspective on what we really need to do to heal our planet.

"Go outside -- and keep going out," he says. "This is not emphasized enough. For anyone who wants to do this work, it's going to be difficult. It's emotional, and at times even heart-wrenching. But it's also freeing, to take a stand on behalf of something bigger than yourself. We will lose ourselves if we don't connect with the places in our world that are real, and wild, and alive."

Despite his struggles in coming to terms with what to do about such a big problem, Alec's message to youth is one of hope. "The potential of young people is greater than we realize," he says. "Sometimes we tend to think, 'We can try, but we're just kids, so no one will listen.' But I've found the opposite to be true. There's something in young people standing up and doing what they feel is right that is deeply powerful. We have this opportunity to come together in a new way. And to create the future we want to grow up into."

Alec's story of coming of age in a time of radical transition can inspire young people today. Let's start telling the stories of people like Alec, and others who have devoted themselves to fighting for our planet. It's time to let those stories help us all find ways to live lives that we can feel proud of.

I have always been fascinated with those who try to look over the horizon and see things that are coming at us.

Al Gore

Call to Action: Learn more about Alec's story and support his work at alecloorz.com And please visit the Climate Reality Project https:// climaterealityproject.org

CARING FOR THE CIRCLE OF LIFE
Lilly Platt
Lilly's Plastic Pickup
The Netherlands

Twelve-year-old Lilly Platt has a special gift. "I can tell if any animal is sad, angry, or if it wants food," she says. She loves all animals, big or small. Her favorites are snow leopards, blobfishes, and her pug puppy Mochi.

Lilly feels sad when she hears about whales dying. "When a whale eats plastic, it makes them feel full," she explains. "So then they don't want to eat food. And they die." She adds, "Whales are similar to humans, they're intelligent and they have a connection with nature. They have every single right to live on this planet."

Lilly's journey into environmental activism began with a walk she took with her grandfather one day. When she was six years old, she moved with her family from London to the Netherlands, to live on the edge of a beautiful green forest in the city of Zeist. During that 20-minute walk, Lilly was shocked to see trash everywhere: on the road, in the fields, and thrown over the fence. "It was everywhere!" she says. "At the time, I couldn't really count in Dutch, so I practiced my Dutch by counting all of these cans, bottles, and pieces of plastic. I counted 91 pieces! It opened my mind. I realized there is just so much plastic in the world."

And she decided then and there that she needed to do something about it.

A curious child, Lilly began by studying. She watched David Attenborough's documentaries, and listened to Jane Goodall's speeches. She discovered that only recently did plastics become popular, and now we are using 5 trillion plastic bags a year. Since plastics are made out of fossil fuels, they are made to last. This means that they are not biodegradable: the plastic just breaks down into smaller pieces of plastic.

Lilly was disturbed to learn from her grandfather that any piece of plastic that falls on the ground eventually makes its way into the ocean, through rivers or other waterways. And from there it makes its way into a kind of plastic soup in the ocean. In the Netherlands, rising sea levels threaten the nation's very existence. And with the Arctic ice melting, all of the plastic pieces from the earth are ending up at the bottom of the sea.

The circle of life begins with plankton, the lowest form of life on the food chain. The plankton eat microplastics, then smaller fish eat the plankton, then larger fish eat the smaller fish, all the way up to the whales. When people eat fish with plastic in their stomachs, the plastic gets inside of them too. "Once you know this, you can never un-see that piece of plastic," Lilly says. "When you pick up one piece of plastic, you might actually be saving the life of an animal."

To raise awareness, Lilly started picking up litter, and posting pictures of the trash she had collected on her Facebook page. She organized cleanups in her community, and recruited her friends to help. Together they picked up about 500 pieces of plastic a week. Since she began, they've picked up nearly 200,000 pieces. Each time Lilly takes a photo of the colored bottles, paper, and plastic, and posts it before taking it to the recycling center. Lilly's family then takes the broken electric items to be mended at the repair cafes. The move to having a circular economy is very big there!

Lilly is also campaigning to stop litter at its source. She helped get her municipality to join the Deposit Scheme Alliance for small bottles and cans. And she is now raising awareness about the harmful effects of balloons. She hopes they can be banned. "Have you ever seen the way animals suffer when they eat plastic?" she asks, and adds, "One time we saw a picture of a baby puffin wrapped in balloons, and it made me very cross." So she and her mother spoke to the local car dealer and convinced them to stop releasing balloons. And, as a youth ambassador for the Plastic Pollution Coalition she speaks about the five Rs: recycle, renew, reuse, refuse, and refill. "The refuse part inspired me to create a set of bamboo straws," she says.

After watching Greta Thunberg's videos, Lilly was inspired to organize school strikes to increase awareness of climate change. "At first lots of people didn't really know why I was doing it," she says. "Then more people started to get the message, and they started striking too."

Lilly firmly believes that environmental issues must be taught in schools. "If children learned about climate change, or about plastic pollution, and what they can do to stop it, you could build a whole generation who actually care for the environment instead of destroying it."

When Indigenous people from the Amazon visited one of her school strikes, they told her about the crisis in the rainforest. She was horrified to learn that Brazil's president was spreading fake news, saying that Indigenous people were the number-one enemy. She has proudly served on the Amazon Watch panel, to support Indigenous peoples' rights.

A frequent speaker at schools and at TEDx talks, Lilly shares her four-point plan: spot it; pick it up; put it in the bin; work to stop trash at the source by making less of it yourself. "Leave five extra minutes every day to pick up trash," she urges. "Get a bag. Get a grabber. Let's clean up the world! Who's with me?"

In 2018, Lily was voted by Onalytica as number 28 on their prestigious top 100 environmentalists list, alongside fellow activists like Leonardo DiCaprio, Mark Ruffalo, Dianna Cohen, and the Mayor of London. She also won the Green Feather from the Netherlands' Green Party, and she has been featured in *National Geographic Kids*. She is also a global youth ambassador for Youth Mundus, a youth-driven festival inspired by the United Nations Sustainable Development Goals, and a youth ambassador for Earth.org. In 2020 she was selected, out of hundreds of contenders, to speak at the first-ever virtual UN World Oceans day, along with Secretary General Antonio Guterres and other dignitaries, and she served on the youth panel there too.

Lilly travels around the world, and she cleans up plastic wherever she goes. She's been to Norway, Canada, Scotland, England, Egypt, and the Caribbean island of Curacao, where Prime Minister Rhuggenath invited her to speak, and translated her speech into Papiamento so local students could understand. She was especially happy to hear that the parliament is now planning to ban all plastic straws in Curaçao.

Even when she's speaking to world leaders, Lilly doesn't get too nervous. "I usually think about how many people are actually *doing* something," she says. "I focus on what I need to fight for."

In November 2019, Lilly had a harsh learning experience. The European Parliament had convened a climate debate in Strasbourg, France, to discuss the climate crisis. There were 751 seats, and only 28 politicians showed up. Only three of the politicians actually listened to Lilly and the other school strikers. "It showed me just how lazy some politicians can be, and how they treat climate change," Lilly says, angrily. "We really have to wake them up and get them to see that our planet is in trouble."

When you ask Lilly about her hopes and dreams, she says, "I want all world leaders to keep to 1.5 of global warming temperatures." She adds, "My hope is that people will finally realize that we should never take our planet for granted. Our planet is not a credit card, with no spending limit. Our planet is one in a billion, billion trillion. That's a one followed by 33 zeros! People really need to know that our planet is sacred, and we need to take care of it."

When asked about her message to adults Lilly says, "You have seen so many natural wonders on our planet. Now they are being destroyed. Don't you want the next generation to see the wonders you experienced? Nature is the place houses are built, and trees are grown. It has been used for thousands, if not millions of years, to give life to so many creatures on this planet."

Lilly is especially committed to giving the right to vote to the younger generation. Last year, she and her grandfather started a new tradition: he is "gifting" his vote to Lilly. When he voted in the European elections, they went together to the polling station. "I made the cross on the paper, but it was Lilly's choice that I recorded," he says. He adds, "Too much of the world is controlled by older people, whose ideas are rooted in the past and are reluctant to make any change. The future belongs to the young. They're the ones who are going to have to live it. We have to do everything we can to ensure that the voices of the young are heard, that it counts. The gift of a vote from an older person to a younger person sends a powerful message."

When Lilly attended the Ocean Heroes Boot Camp in Vancouver, she met a kindred spirit in Jamie Margolin. They had been following each other on social media for some time, and were thrilled to be able to meet in person to talk more about their mutual environmental mission.

One day she hopes to become a paleontologist, and study dinosaurs. She wants to be like her mentor and friend, Jane Goodall, to give inspirational speeches, and one day to become a famous environmentalist.

As a child ambassador for Charity Water's Project Beehives, Lilly shares a story that combines her love for animals with her passion for the environment. "Elephants were being killed by villagers for eating their crops," she explains. "So, to protect the crops—and the elephants— the people built beehives around their fruits and vegetables. Bees seek moisture, and there is lots of moisture in the trunk of an elephant! And the elephants do not want any bees in their trunks, trust me! So, they stay away."

Today's young people – everywhere I go – they're
so excited and empowered. We're listening to
their voices.
That gives us a reason to hope.

Dr. Jane Goodall

Call to Action: Join with Lilly to Recycle, Renew, Reuse, Refuse, and Refill. Refuse to use plastic. Pick up trash. Follow Lilly: <u>Lillys Plastic Pickup @lillysplasticpickup</u>

CLIMATE MOVEMENTS IN A DIGITAL WORLD
Iris Zhan
Fridays for Future Digital
Maryland

Iris Zhan was in the third grade when she first learned about the climate crisis and about how the earth is suffering. "When our teacher told us about global warming and climate change, it really took a toll on me. I wondered, how can we have such a huge problem, and no one is doing anything about it?" She turned over the problem in her mind all night, and in the morning she went to school ready to learn more about what she could do to solve it. But the next day, her class was already moving on to another subject. "We were presented with the reality of our dire situation, and just like that, that was the end of our climate education."

But Iris wasn't about to stop there: she wanted to find a way to make an impact on this climate crisis outside of the classroom.

She began spending countless hours after school, educating herself on the myriad issues related to climate justice. She devoured news articles, read scientific papers, and perused social media for trending stories, so she could learn about the people involved in fighting for climate justice, and the issues she needed to understand. Over time, she became a self-taught expert on many environmental issues–but she struggled with trying to figure out what to *do* with all of her knowledge. "I was just a young girl trying to find a way to take on these gigantic issues," she says. "A lot of the time I felt really alone."

The 2016 election was a turning point for Iris: she decided that no matter how hard and long the journey for climate justice was, she was going to take up the mantle for the youth of her generation. "The climate situation had become so urgent that I realized I had to take the energy I was putting into pursuing my environmental interests, and shift into action."

Iris quickly realized that she couldn't take on these massive environmental problems alone. So she attended a local green festival that was being held near her home in Howard County, Maryland, and she began networking with local environmental groups, clubs, associations, and grassroots organizations. This led to some minor community organizing efforts with Less Plastic Please, Citizens' Climate Lobby, and the River Hill Watershed Committee.

It was a start, but Iris knew there was a bigger mission in store for her.

While organizing with these various communities, one thing stood out to Iris -- all of these groups were adult-led. There was little or no youth engagement in Howard County on environmental issues. Through HoCo Climate Action, she learned about the work of Jamie Margolin and Zero Hour, and she understood her calling at once: she decided to begin organizing the youth of Howard County, and to create a supportive community for dealing with issues of climate justice. "Learning about Jamie and what she was doing online -- and with the Youth Climate March -- was so inspiring," she says. "There was nothing like that here."

The fact that it was a young *woman* leading these events was inspirational for Iris on a whole different level. "I said, you know what? If Jamie can get out there and lead a climate march, why can't I?"

And so she decided to take the lead. She started by creating Sunrise Movement Howard County—a local chapter of the Sunrise Movement. Sunrise is a national youth-led movement that supports the Green New Deal, and works to make climate change a priority issue for legislation.

As an introvert, it wasn't easy for Iris to be such a visible leader in this way, but she knew it was something her community desperately needed. "To really achieve change, we needed more people on board in my community. And we needed the youth to be visible. Relying on adult-led organizations to bring young people in was not going to be effective. These issues are going to affect the youth the most, so I saw the importance of taking the initiative."

Iris began leading climate marches, walkouts, strikes; and she lobbied frequently in her hometown. She was so successful that she became a trainer for Sunrise on a national level, educating other youth leaders around the country on climate issues.

She also cofounded Fridays For Future Digital (FFFD), to expand digital climate protests worldwide. "It started as just one sign each week, a sign that had a message in support of climate justice. But the more people began to join the movement, the more complex it became. Before we knew it, we were international. It was amazing!" She adds, "We wanted to take real digital actions to make change, and we did. We're proud of that." To date, FFFD has partnered on digital events with Polluters Out, Extinction Rebellion, and Re-Earth Initiative to bring youth activists of all backgrounds together in support of climate justice for all.

FFF Digital is now focused on increasing impact and accessibility in the climate movement by providing local groups with the resources and skills they need to create awesome digital campaigns. Through directly organizing with local groups, they hope to bring new people into the movement, raise awareness of climate justice and science issues, and put pressure on institutions to change.

Iris has been an effective youth organizer, but her success didn't come easy. There were lots of struggles along the way. She hopes to be able to provide some guidance for youth who are just entering this space, so they know what they are up against. "It's important that other youth who want to get involved with cause-related work understand that adversity is part of the journey," she says. "All you can do is try to innovate, solve problems, and build communities along the way. And when you get through to the other side -- which you will -- you will be glad you took on the world."

For youth leaders, peer pressure can be a tough issue to deal with. At the onset of her journey, few of Iris's peers understood what she was trying to do with her climate justice activities. "I got a lot of criticism from the kids at my school who didn't get what climate justice was all about. Sometimes I even heard mumblings from the adults. I definitely didn't get the support I thought I would. But once you grow a little, you will see that those jeers are so small when compared to the scale of the climate crisis."

Working heavily in the digital arena, there are also some bullying issues that Iris has had to learn how to deal with. "The biggest issue climate activists face online are the trolls. Insults about your looks. Your race. Your gender. It can be pretty toxic stuff. But you know you are having success when people waste their time trying to come at you online," she says, with a laugh. "The internet allows for such amazing community building, like the community we've built with FFFD. It can be hard at times dealing with that darker side of digital engagement, but there's no point in listening to the negativity. We have to let the good shine through."

In the future Iris wants to work on strengthening the communities that support the climate justice movement. "I've met some of my best friends building communities that do good. And I hear from people all around the world every day about how I've impacted them. It makes me want to create more communities, and I want the people and the networks to become even stronger." She believes that they will be, when all people are given the tools and access to contribute equally to the community and the movement. "Everybody can play a part," she says. "And it takes all kinds of people. For instance, I'm an introvert. I'm socially awkward. And I'm not a great public speaker. But that doesn't mean I don't lead, just because I don't fit the traditional description of a leader. The point is, it doesn't matter who you are or what you look like. If you can light the fire in somebody, that person will live an inspired life because of you."

The countless numbers of youth activists across the world that have been inspired by Iris are working hard now, to ensure that we will have a brighter future ahead.

It is my mission to change the world. I'm not kidding: Make no small plans, dream mighty things. I feel if we get enough people engaged in climate change, we will get enough people to change the world.

Bill Nye

Call to Action: Learn how to take digital climate action to the next level with Iris at Fridays for Future Digital (FFFD) https:// fffdigital.carrd.co and learn more at digital.fridaysforfuture.org To get involved with Sunrise Movement, and/or to start a Sunrise hub, go to sunrisemovement.org. Find out what's happening in your local community, and if there isn't anything, take the initiative to start it yourself!

HOPE FROM THE ENDS OF THE EARTH
Joel Enrique Peña Panichine
Chiloe Protegido
Chile

Joel Peña remembers the first time he felt a real connection to the ocean. As a child he would join his grandfather on his two-week fishing expeditions along the coast of Chile. One day, as the boat was pulling away from the wharf and into the ocean, a dolphin swam by. It came so close to the boat that Joel could practically reach out and touch it. "How wonderful!" he shouted. Now he's 20 years old; but still, every time he sees a dolphin, Joel says, "It reminds me of my connection to nature."

Joel grew up in the southeastern part of Chile, in two different regions that experience climate extremes. Until he was eight years old, his family lived in Chaiten, a small town of about 4,000 people. Then in 2008, the eruption of a long-dormant volcano forced them to flee. They ended up on the island of Las Islas Chiloe, on the edge of Patagonia, often called "the end of the earth."

The big island of Chiloe is like something out of a dream: colorful houses rise up on stilts in the water along the shore. Behind them are lush, green forests. Here, about 40,000 people live in an area of just under 4,000 square miles.

As a curious child, Joel began exploring the incredible biodiversity of the island. On Chiloe, the animals have to adapt to the extreme conditions, which makes them remarkably diverse, and unique. There's the *pudu*, the world's smallest deer; and the *monito del monte*, a marsupial the size of a mouse that exists only in Chile and Argentina. In the summers, magnificent blue whales -- the world's largest mammals -- migrate through the coastal waters of southern Chile. "We live in a place that's so privileged with biodiversity," Joel says. "There are tons of beautiful species, and flowers too. You start to internalize that nature."

Over the years, Joel has seen how human activity is causing harm to some species, and throwing off the balance of the ecosystem. The Chilean dolphin, which so inspired Joel when he was a kid, is listed as "near threatened" by the International Union for the Conservation of Nature. Today, only about 5,000 Chilean dolphins remain in the wild.

For years, the population of dolphins off the coast of Chile has been cut down by overfishing, and pollution from ships carrying heavy containers filled with industrial goods.

As is the case for the Chilean dolphin, for many of the marine and terrestrial animals that live in Chile climate change is not even the greatest threat to their livelihoods. Humans are. And for Joel, the only way to save the wide diversity of animals that have made the extreme southern coasts of Chile their home -- regardless of whether they live on land or in the sea -- is through education, on both a local and a global scale.

That's why Joel has made it his life's mission to bring global awareness to the environmental and human forces threatening biodiversity in Chiloe. He's also committed to educating his local community. "People just aren't aware about their impact, or about how to take care of their environment," he says. "We want people to understand, and to really dig down to see the roots of the problems."

Joel is the perfect emissary for his island community. Like much of the local population of the Islas Chiloe, Joel comes from a Mapuche Indigenous background. He knew that in order to have the biggest impact, he would have to speak with Indigenous leaders in each of the main cities and towns on the Big Island (Isla Grande). But he also knew he would have to bring his message to a global audience.

That is why in 2019 Joel joined the Chilean branch of the global Fridays for Future movement. In December he represented his people at the COP 25 Conference in Madrid. There he joined with other youth leaders to call on world leaders to do much more to protect marine ecosystems and respect human rights. He was critical of his own country, where the economy has been prioritized over the well-being of its people: where even basic goods like water aren't free, but have been privatized.

Returning from Madrid, Joel was inspired to found his own nongovernmental organization, along with 15 other young conservationists. They call it Chiloe Protegido (Chiloe Protected), and they have developed creative ways of speaking to the local populations about how they can work together to protect the island's biodiversity.

They've organized beach cleanups to remove plastic from the beaches. To offset the loss of the island's one animal rehabilitation center, which is no longer active, they're planning a training program to prepare aspiring conservationists to treat wounded or sick animals. And they developed a phone app called DóndeLaViste? (Where Did You See It?)

that allows users to describe the wildlife they encounter in their daily lives, both on land and at sea.

But increasingly, Joel is focusing his efforts on marine conservation. Inspired by Sylvia Earle's Mission Blue, through which ocean "hope spots" are selected to be protected, Joel wants to create a global youth movement aimed at protecting the oceans.

For Joel, human activity is just one threat to marine ecosystems. Warmer ocean temperatures, which lead to ocean acidification, have a devastating impact on species like whales and dolphins. And the algae that blooms in warmer waters leads to a phenomenon called *marea roja,* or red tide, which can be deadly for marine animals.

There are other silent killers too, like radar waves from boats that disrupt the migratory and communication patterns of whales. More than three-quarters of the blue whales that die don't end up washing up on shores, meaning that the death toll is probably a lot higher than we know.

The challenges can seem enormous, but Joel knows that he doesn't have to tackle them all on his own. "At Chiloe Protegido, we work together, at sea and on the earth. It's not only me," he says. "We founded an NGO because in the end it's not about the work of one person, but of many. I don't want to be the only protagonist."

As for his own future, Joel is eager to go to university to study conservation. He sees the work he's done so far as just the beginning; and he recognizes the need for swift action from young people around the world to protect the oceans. "I am seeing young people from every community taking up the banner in one way or another, and pushing for the changes that we need to protect the oceans," he says. "It's something very, very fundamental to all of us." From the depths of southern Chile, he hopes their united voices will strike a chord that is heard -- and responded to -- on a truly international level.

People ask: Why should I care about the ocean?
Because the ocean is the cornerstone of earth's
life support system, it shapes climate and
weather.
It holds most of life on earth. 97% of earth's
water is there.
It's the blue heart of the planet - we should take
care of our heart. It's what makes life possible
for us.

Sylvia Earle

Call to Action: Protect our oceans and find ways to help sustain marine life. Follow Joel at https://twitter.com/joelpanichine

HOPE SPRINGS FROM DOWN UNDER
Jean Hinchliffe
Australia

In Sydney's inner city, Jean Hinchliffe was safe from Australia's raging bushfires -- but not free from their impact. The sky over her home was a mixture of brown and gray smoke. The air was thick with particulate, and had been at various times throughout the bushfire season of 2019-2020. The world watched in horror, most people powerless to do anything. Some celebrities gave money. And firefighters came from all over to fight the fires.

Thankfully Jean, a 15-year-old youth climate activist, didn't lose anything precious, like so many others had. "I've been fortunate, but I know so many others who haven't been," she says. One of her fellow activists was evacuated shortly before her 18th birthday party. "By the end of the night, their home was destroyed. It just goes to show that when dealing with the climate crisis, things can change in a flash."

Sadly, Australia has become a tinderbox. The last devastating outbreak of bushfires began in September 2019, and lasted for months. This is mainly the result of increased temperatures, a severe drought, and the inability to fight fires by "backburning" in these conditions. Almost all of Australia was affected, with fires raging across the country, including in Tasmania. Roughly 72,000 square miles of land were impacted, and there were at least 34 reported deaths. Worst of all, the ongoing toll on families, local economies, and the climate, will not be fully realized for years to come.

When Jean started her work in activism, at the age of 13, she didn't expect to be championing the fight for climate justice. In fact, at first she was involved fighting for justice in an entirely different area. "In Australia, we had a campaign for marriage equality. I saw an ad on Twitter asking for volunteers. As a believer in the cause, I joined. I handed out pamphlets and flyers, and made cold calls to people. We ended up with a strong win for the Yes side. It was empowering, knowing I had been involved in that win. Even if I only shifted a few votes, my voice mattered."

It was then Jean realized the impact that youth could make. She immediately got involved with other young people and activist groups, including the #StopAdani campaign.

#StopAdani was protesting the construction of the Adani coal mine in Queensland, which was to be the largest coal mining operation in the southern hemisphere. It would impact the environment in a variety of ways. The mining site overlapped with one of the last remaining habitats of the endangered black-throated finch. There would be an inevitable cost to Australia's coral reefs as well, since most of the coal would be shipped near the reefs on its way out of Australia to be used by developing countries. It would also *increase* carbon emissions at a time when people all over the world were demanding that leaders work to transition *away* from coal and carbon-based economies.

So far, activists in Australia and abroad have been able to keep the mine from opening, by protesting the banks, insurers, and ancillary businesses that are supporting Adani. "#StopAdani was a great point of mobilization for lots of people, and it was a huge success," Jean says. "Sometimes these issues seem difficult to understand, or far away. But this one was very local, which made it easy for the average Australian to get behind."

Around the time Jean was involved with #StopAdani, a friend of hers sent her a link to the School Strike 4 Climate website in October 2018. This movement had three main demands for the Australian government: no new sources of fossil fuels; transition to fully renewable energy by 2030; and the creation of a just transition plan for workers currently employed in the fossil fuel industry.

"At that point, few people knew about what Greta Thunberg was doing," Jean says. "But in Australia, the youth were inspired. In Castlemaine, a small town near Melbourne, a few girls who read about Greta in *The Guardian* took up the cause. They knew they had to bring this message to Australia somehow and were in the process of organizing a strike in their capital city, Melbourne. I sent them an email, saying I want to make this happen in in my capital city, Sydney. I got their support, which was great, but it was also a lot of pressure. I'd never done anything on this scale! We decided that we wanted to make a *big* impact, and instead of having a series of small strikes, we decided to unify strikes across Australia. And leading up to November 30, 2018, we started getting a little traction."

Ultimately, what pushed the planned school strikes into the mainstream was Prime Minister Scott Morrison. He had responded to the students' concern by saying, "The children should be in school, learning about Australian history." **Not** participating in activism.

"His response was indicative of the larger problems our government won't tackle. It even became a tagline among many young activists. Right there, our strike exploded. We were covered by national and international media, which actually unified our events in a way that we wouldn't have been able to do on our own. As a result, the turnouts were just staggering. In Sydney, we had anticipated we'd get 1,000 people, if we did well–but we had a turnout of 5,000 locally, and 15,000 nationally."

And it didn't stop there. Their next strike was set for March 15, 2019. This strike had a turnout of 150,000 people in Australia, with over one million striking in support internationally. Then in September 2019, they held their largest strike ever. "When I walked past the news agency that week, the headline said *What do teachers think about the climate strike?* It wasn't explaining the climate strike. It assumed by now everyone already knew. Less than a year prior, we didn't even exist. But on September 20, we held the largest climate mobilization in Aussie history. 80,000 people showed up in Sydney, 300,000 joined nationally, and approximately 7 million internationally. I co-emceed the Sydney strike and gave a speech to the crowd. It was unbelievable!" She pauses, and smiles. "Much easier than delivering a presentation to an English class of 25."

When Jean spoke that day, the passion of the youth in the audience energized her, and her message was enthusiastically received. "This is not an inner-city issue, or a greenie issue. This is not a young person's issue or a wealthy person's issue. This is an *everybody* issue. We are the majority. *And we demand change!*" she shouted, to a gallery of cheers from the crowd.

It was a major victory for the youth climate movement in Australia, and beyond.

At just 16, Jean is still in high school. She is like many of her peers in some ways, and different in others. She is certainly wise beyond her years. Outside of school, she has taken up various interests, such as acting, and has excelled in that field as well. Currently, she has a starring role in the Australian series *The Unlisted*. In time, she hopes to have her acting work influence her activism, and vice versa. Most importantly, she wants to use any platform she has to continue urging youth to stand up for causes they are passionate about.

For those who want to get involved, Jean has an inspiring message. "It can be intimidating to join a rally with 80,000 people. Or maybe it feels like it's for experienced people with qualifications you don't have. But that's not the case. Everyone is here to help you learn and grow. Take the leap. You are so much more powerful and have so much more influence than you could ever imagine."

The conversation about the climate crisis has become global and now involves all age groups. But Jean feels there are ways to improve the dialogue. "Often, when people talk about the climate crisis, they talk about how it's an issue that doesn't discriminate. How it impacts everyone equally. That's not quite true. It's often people in the countries that emit the least amount of pollution who will be feeling the impacts of climate change more than other places. Australia has been on the frontlines recently, and it's been a wakeup call to what we've been neglecting to confront for so long. So it's up to us, we who are more aware now, and who have a voice, to ally with those who are most impacted. They are often given less of a voice, and they rarely have their stories told."

Jean doesn't know what her next project will be. She does know that she will continue to campaign for the climate, in one way or another. And that's a very good thing. With Jean, and other youth like her leading the charge, there's hope for a better world.

I believe that education is all about being excited about something. Seeing passion and enthusiasm helps push an educational message.

Steve Irwin

Call to Action: Learn more about School Strike 4 Climate https://www.schoolstrike4climate.com

LUNA
Julia Butterfly Hill
California

Ever since she was a child, Julia Hill has had a deep connection to nature. Her father was a traveling minister, and she and her family would go around the country in a camper and stay at campsites. When she was a young girl, one day they were hiking through the beautiful mountains of Pennsylvania, when a butterfly landed on her finger. She stopped to admired its beauty and then continued hiking -- but the butterfly stayed with her, resting on her finger. "Since then, butterflies have always come to me during times of need," Julia says. "Sometimes in reality, and other times in visions and dreams."

Ever since this childhood encounter Julia was gifted with a new name: Julia "Butterfly" Hill. Eventually her family settled in Arkansas, where she graduated from high school and became a restaurant manager. Her life seemed to be going great, but then, when she was 22, Julia survived a horrible car crash. That experience changed her outlook on life. "The crash woke me up to the importance of the moment," she says. "I wanted to do whatever I could to make a positive impact on the future."

Julia first entered the ancient redwood forests in the small community of Stafford, Washington: and she was instantly overwhelmed with the beauty and spirituality of the place. She had learned that these redwood trees were being cut down for timber by a company called the Pacific Lumber Company. "When I found out that they were being destroyed, I knew that I had to do something to try and protect them," she said.

"Luna" was a beautiful, majestic tree that had stood high atop a steep ridge for 1,500 years and was 180 feet tall. The branches of this tree had grown in curves and twists, which was probably what saved it from the chainsaws in the first place: when the trees of the area were cut down for timber, the mills couldn't handle such an unevenly-grown tree.

But now the famous tree was marked with blue paint, tagging it to be cut down in December 1997. And people were protesting: activists were taking turns staying in the trees, to keep the chainsaws from cutting them down. The organizers were looking for someone willing to spend more than just a couple of hours: they wanted someone to stay a full week in one of the trees. "Nobody else would volunteer," says Julia. "So they had to pick me."

Ever since she was a child, Julia has stood up for what she believes in. When she was attacked by a group of teenage boys in the parking lot of a fast-food restaurant, she knew she had to press charges, even though she also knew she would have to face them again, in school. This experience taught her that there is no backing down from what you believe to be right.

And Julia was convinced that cutting down these ancient trees was very wrong. "How can we cut something like this down, and not think that we're affecting something much deeper than ourselves?" she says.

And so, on December 10, 1997, Julia began her attempt to save Luna. She and a crew of eight fellow activists hoisted provisions to the top of the tree using a pulley system. "After an hour and a half, we got the last of the provisions up. By then it was midnight. Finally, I was able to put on the harness and ascend Luna. It seemed an exhausting eternity before I reached the top," she remembers. "When I finally got to the top, I untangled myself from the harness and looked around for a place to collapse." Then she looked around at what would be her home for the next week -- the 6-by-6-foot platform where she was to live -- and she prepared her first meal on a little camping cooker.

But once she was in the tree, Julia realized that she was fighting for something much bigger than the survival of a single tree. "From up there, I was able to see everything we stand for, and everything we struggle against every single day," she says. "I could see the beautiful forests stretching out; I could see snowcapped mountains in the distance; I could even see the ocean."

Whenever she would look out at the ocean, she would also see the Pacific Lumber mill, the very factory that was planning on cutting down the tree that she was living in. Looking out at all that natural beauty, Julia made a decision. "I had to give my word to Luna, and to the forest; to myself, and to the world," she says. "I decided I wouldn't come to the ground again until I had done everything I possibly could to make the world aware, and to bring about some change."

On her little platform 180 feet above ground, the days turned into weeks, and the weeks turned into months. But Julia had given her word that she wouldn't come to the ground until the redwood trees were safe, and she intended to keep her promise. Meanwhile, all around her, the logging continued.

"There were miles upon miles of clear-cuts, as far as the eye can see," she says. "During the time I was up there more and more trees were destroyed, until eventually I was surrounded by clear-cuts." Sadly, today, only about 5 percent of the historic redwood forests remain.

While living in the tree, Julia reflected on her traumatic childhood experiences. She was used to overcoming obstacles, and she was willing to make sacrifices. Local people from environmental organizations jerry-rigged a pulley system to deliver food and water to her. In winter, to keep warm she wore two pairs of socks, two pairs of thermal pants, and wool pants, with ski pants over that. She also wore two thermal T-shirts, a sweater, two windbreakers, and a raincoat. "I was getting close to being as wide as I am tall, but it worked," she says, laughing. To warm up she would prepare hot tea on her little gas stove.

Besides the cold, Julia had to deal with harassment by Pacific Lumber. For them, she was a serious problem, interfering with their ability to finish their job. So they tried various methods of getting rid of her: they posted an eviction notice at the bottom of the tree, and they even flew helicopters close to the platform where she was living, hoping that the wind from the rotor blades would blow her out of the tree. But Julia stayed put. She lived on the top of that tree for 738 days.

"This old growth forest that is being cut down won't come back," Julia says. "If we hadn't protected Luna, this world would never again have a Luna."

The clear-cuts around Luna were causing other environmental problems too. After cutting all of the trees in an area, the loggers would burn the soil using chemicals. And without the trees to hold the topsoil, rain would wash the earth downhill, causing chemical-infested mudslides. The chemicals then ended up in the streams and rivers, causing irreversible damage to the environment.

In 1999, after two years of living in the tree, an agreement was finally reached with Pacific Lumber. The lumber company agreed that Luna and all trees within a 200-foot buffer zone around it would be preserved. And they had raised $50,000 in donations to finance research about sustainable forestry at Humboldt State University.

On December 18, 1999, Julia climbed down the tree and, for the first time in more than two years, set foot on the ground. She had become a symbol for tree lovers everywhere, and a world-famous activist. She began giving radio and television interviews, through which she educated millions of people about the fate of the redwood forests, and the dangers of deforestation. As schoolchildren around the country, moved by her story, reached out to her, she told them how they too could get involved. She was nominated as one of the most admired women in America by a famous American magazine She traveled around the world sharing her experience, and continuing her activism for the environment. She even was invited to address the United Nations. And she wrote a book, *The Legacy of Luna.* "I really hope that people can learn from my experience," she says. "I hope they don't have to walk into a clear-cut area of a forest themselves to be motivated to do something about it."

Today, Luna is still standing tall, on its high ridge, overlooking the forests of northern California. and the small community of Stafford. The residents there call the tree "the Stafford Giant" because of its majestic size. Its twisted branches still rustle in the wind and, thanks to Julia, they will continue to do so for many years to come.

Julia has retired from public life. But her legacy lives on through the Circle of Life organization she founded, to inspire and activate people to live in a way that honors the diversity and interdependence of all life. Their motto is "We are the ancestors of the future. What do you want your legacy to be?"

Go look into a child's eyes, and know that the simplest sacrifices you make today can be the greatest gift for their future.

Julia Butterfly Hill

Call to Action: Learn more about the forests in your area and find out what steps are being taken to protect them. Join together with other activists to educate your fellow citizens about the importance of our forests, and find ways to help sustain them! http://www.circleoflife.org

PLANT-FOR-THE-PLANET
Felix Finkbeiner
Germany

Felix Finkbeiner was standing behind the stage at the United Nations. He was about to speak in the UN General Assembly Hall, on the very podium that is normally used by the presidents, prime ministers, and chancellors of the world. "I was incredibly nervous," Felix says. "Right before I went on stage, I just wished I was in school." That is quite an unusual wish for a 13-year-old.

In the audience was a woman who was very special to Felix. Her name was Wangari Maathei. She was an environmental activist, and the first female professor in the East African nation of Kenya. For the past 30 years, she had worked together with local communities to plant 30 million trees in African countries. "These trees had provided many women with their own income for the first time, and protected the soil from erosion. But they also store carbon," Felix says. "Every tree extracts CO2 from the atmosphere."

When Felix was five years old, he had gotten a present that he really loved. It was a stuffed animal, a polar bear that was almost as big as he was at the time. When, four years later, he had to give a presentation in elementary school about the climate crisis, he immediately realized the gravity of the situation: because he knew that polar bears were being threatened by rising temperatures and melting snowcaps.

For his presentation, he tried to learn about possible solutions to the climate crisis. That is when he first read about Wangari Maathei. Inspired by the work she was doing planting trees in Kenya, at the end of his presentation Felix came up with a proposition for his classmates: "Let's plant one million trees in every country on earth!" he said. That was in 2007, and it was the beginning of his organization, Plant-for-the-Planet.

A couple of weeks after his presentation, Felix and his classmates planted their first trees. Two local journalists reported on the event, and other schools heard about it and decided to join in. "Someone built a little website for us," Felix remembers. "It was basically a ranking of who had planted the most trees."

Soon more schools joined the effort, and it became a competition: and one year later the students had planted 50,000 trees. After three years they hit one million! That is how Plant-for-the-Planet started to grow.

New studies show that planting trees is the most effective way to absorb the harmful greenhouse gas CO_2 from the atmosphere. "Trees are fantastic, because they are the only machines we have that can absorb the CO_2 we emit," Felix says. "Every tree that we plant absorbs about 10 kilos of CO_2 per year."

With our current levels of emissions, that means that we have to plant a lot of trees. And that is why Felix came up with a very ambitious goal: he and his organization, Plant-for-the-Planet, are mobilizing the world to plant and restore a trillion trees.

A trillion is a thousand billions -- an almost unimaginable number.

But planting such a large number of trees is not only good for the climate: it has other positive effects too. "When we plant trees, it helps to slow down desertification; it protects biodiversity; and it creates jobs," Felix says.

Trees that are planted in tropical regions are particularly helpful. They grow much faster than in other parts of the world, so they can absorb more CO_2, and they can do it sooner. The tropical regions of Latin America, Africa, and Southeast Asia also have the greatest amount of potential area for planting new trees.

And so, in March 2015, Plant-for-the-Planet started planting trees in the Yucatan peninsula, in Mexico. Each tree they plant can absorb up to 200 kilos of CO_2 in only two decades -- and they have already planted more than 6 million trees. Their ambitious goal is to plant a million additional trees every year, and to look after each plant, to make sure that it is thriving. Of course, they need a lot of workers for this project. "In Yucatan we are already the biggest employer," Felix says, proudly.

According to a new study by scientists at ETH University in Zürich, Switzerland, there is plenty of available space on the earth for planting trees. In fact, they have calculated that the amount of available space is equal to an area as big as the United States of America.

"All around the globe, there are large areas that can be reforested," Felix says. "Of course, global reforestation is not the only solution to the climate crisis." Another important factor, he says, is educating young people to stand up for themselves and argue for the importance of fighting the climate crisis. "So we began to offer academies," Felix says. "The core idea is: we teach each other."

In the academies, children learn how to give speeches and, of course, how to plant trees. To date, Plant-for-the-Planet has organized more than 1,600 such academies, and trained more than 91,000 children and youth in 75 countries. "Whoever dares to, later gives speeches to entrepreneurs, governments, and other children, to get them on board," Felix says.

Of course, planting a trillion trees is a very ambitious goal. That is why Felix, along with other Climate Justice Ambassadors from the Plant-for-the-Planet academies, decided to work together to come up with innovative ways to do this. "What would Wangari Maathai do today, to connect people who want to plant trees around the world?" they asked themselves. And the answer they came up with was that probably she would develop an app.

Their idea was simple: just like when Plant-for-the-Planet first started, and schools had competed with each other to see who could plant the most trees, they decided that people worldwide should be able to share their tree-planting successes with each other.

"So in 2019, we launched our Plant-for-the-Planet app," Felix says. "It's amazing how much people like it, and how many people use it to plant trees! Today there are more than a hundred tree planting projects on the app. But we want to have hundreds."

Of course, Felix and his fellow activists are fighting against time. Every year, the world is losing around 10 billion trees per year. "Deforestation is the worst in Brazil, Indonesia, and Malaysia," Felix says. And while there are positive trends in Malaysia and Indonesia, the current government of Brazil has actually *weakened* many of the protections of the Amazon forest. "Still, in principle we're making progress when it comes to the protection of our forests," Felix says.

"There are many reasons to be disappointed when it comes to climate policies," he says. "But slowly we *are* moving forward. It is a very important step that with the Paris Climate Agreement we now have a common goal, and all of the countries have made clear what their contribution will be."

It is projects like Felix's that have raised global awareness of the importance of trees in the fight against climate change. To date about 14 billion trees have been reported to the tree counter; and they now have 75,000 members. "Planting trees is the easiest thing that we can do to alleviate the climate crisis, and everyone can contribute," Felix says.

Before she passed away in 2011, Wangari Maathai had started the One Billion Trees Campaign. Now it is up to the next generation to continue her legacy. "We took it to the next level," says Felix. "It is now the One Trillion Trees Campaign. I will definitely continue to work on this project. We still have a long way to go, to get to one thousand billion trees."

When we plant trees, we plant the seeds of peace and hope.

Wangari Maathai

Call to Action: Help save the world, one tree at a time. Download the Plant-for-the-Planet app, and share your stories! Stop talking. Start planting! Follow Felix Finkbeiner on Twitter @FelixFinkbeiner and www.plant-for-the-planet.org

SAVVY SOCIAL MEDIA INFLUENCER
STRIKES FOR OUR FUTURE
David Wicker
Italy

David Wicker remembers as a child playing in hip-deep snow in the foothills of the Alps near Turin, Italy. Now the 18-year-old is worried. "This year, it didn't snow even once," he explains. "Winters hover around 25 C (77 F), which is just hard to comprehend."

Born in the countryside outside Turin, David grew up with rivers running through lovely farmlands, and views of the snowcapped Alps. His rural upbringing gave him a deep sense of responsibility for protecting its natural beauty. Agricultural regions like his in Northern Italy are suffering some of the greatest negative impacts of climate change. "With the reduced snowpack, we are susceptible to droughts," he says, "We're facing serious situations, especially in our agricultural areas."

Northern Italy's farms are famous for producing the luscious tomatoes used in its tasty pasta sauces and pizzas. In the next few decades, this whole region is at risk of having a sustainable source of drinking water. "50 percent of the ice is already gone from the glaciers in the Alps," David says. "And 70 percent of that 50 percent has thawed in just the last 10 years. If it keeps up at this pace, we won't have a reliable source of water in the future. And the North is the most populated region of Italy. It's a scary thing to consider."

In high school, David had learned about climate change. So he was shocked to see that Italy's leaders weren't doing anything about it. That's when he started looking for youth leaders who were changemakers in their countries.

"I saw Greta's speech to the European Parliament, and I thought, this girl my age is speaking in front of all of our European leaders. I was so inspired. I immediately started learning about #FridaysForFuture. Then one day I said, okay, let's try it!"

For the first Friday event David's parents didn't allow him to attend. "'You're not skipping school to go on the street with some strangers,' they said. In the beginning, they weren't so sure about what I was doing," David explains. "They thought I was wasting my time, instead of studying and pursuing hobbies." But after they saw his dedication, they changed their minds. "By the second week, I was able to convince them," he says. "Now they are both a part of #ParentsForFuture, the parents' side of the movement."

A few weeks later, as David marched down the streets of old Turin, he was amazed to see the gathering masses of people. His #FridaysForFuture group had chosen Piazza Vittorio as their meeting spot. Turin's largest piazza, it can hold 100,000 people. Suddenly, their forward progress was stopped in its tracks. "We struggled to get past all the people," David says. "It was full by the time we arrived. I couldn't believe it!"

Along the way, their march was stopped again by an energetic group of young people: and for a moment, it was a somewhat tense situation. But quickly David realized that they were not being slowed down by detractors, but by a swelling crowd of unexpected supporters – tens of thousands of them! No one, including himself, could believe so many people had gathered to support this cause.

"When we arrived, the entire plaza was filled up, just like the streets. Can you imagine? To think that we were able to achieve that much support, and raise that much awareness. We were just a group of 30 young people or so, and we had brought 150,000 people into the streets of Turin, in solidarity with our cause."

What David's success story really proves is the power that tech-savvy youth can have in the environmental conversation. David is a programmer and skillful social media campaigner, both skills that have enormous potential for any movement trying to gain traction in the internet age -- particularly when they have the underlying support of innovative organizations like #FridaysForFuture.

From his position as a social media influencer, David joined with other youth leaders in creating a global awakening to our climate emergency. These dynamic youth leaders immersed in technology are reaching out with this urgent message -- and coming together to wake us all up. Thanks to youth leaders like David, Greta, and others around the world carrying the #FridaysForFuture banner, the school strike movement spread out across the globe, with millions of people participating in the Global Strike on September 20, 2019.

Shortly after, in November 2019, Italy became the very first country to require all students to learn about climate change. "It's about time,"

David says. "It's a start. Once young people learn, we can get them to take action."

For youth who want to get involved in a climate cause, David has some suggestions to help them navigate the obstacles they will surely face. "I think it's important to send a message that they should never give up the fight. When you're in a movement like this, and the message is critical, it can be very stressful. It's common among activists to experience an overwhelming sense of wanting to give up. I myself have had many moments of frustration where I've thought, 'Nobody cares about the climate emergency. The politicians don't care. I should just give up.' But it's in these moments most of all when we must support one another. The future can only be saved in the present. Coming together as a supportive community is the most effective way forward."

In fact it's the urgency of the climate situation that can often be the hardest thing to get across to other young people. "It's fundamental that we start acting now. But our institutions are lagging. So it's important for us to keep up the pressure, and introduce new levels of awareness to those in charge who aren't acting, or who don't feel the urgency of the situation that we do."

David is also setting his sights on bridging the knowledge and priorities gaps between generations in this community. "The older generations pioneered the climate movement in Italy, so there is much to learn from them. But there are also a lot of new and exciting ideas coming from the youth movements–and urgency is the most visible. A lot of older people haven't thought about the climate crisis the way we have. They don't think this situation is going to affect them as immediately as we believe it is going to–but in fact, older people can be more susceptible to the immediate effects of climate change in many ways." David fears for their future. "Older people are really more susceptible to the effects of climate change," he says. "This year alone, because of the heat waves, Turin had more than 4,000 deaths. Most of the people who were affected by the heat are older people. It really shows how our climate emergency affects everyone; so we should come together across groups to fight this battle."

David also thinks it's essential to educate the older community about the connection between climate action and social justice, which is central to making a positive change. "It's up to us as youth, who are more versed in these things, to clarify a major component of our activism: climate justice doesn't mean anything without social justice. If we don't recognize that by now, then we have already failed." He pauses, then adds, "It's not a fight between us and somebody else. It should be an effort fought by all humanity together. For our own survival. Lifting up one group, or race, or demographic, doesn't mean we are making an enemy of the others. That sort of thinking must be left in the past. It's not productive at all. Helping anyone is helping everyone. Together is the only way through this climate emergency; together to a brighter future."

Today David is preparing for college. After a rigorous selection process, he was accepted to United World College (UWC) Atlantic. "It's a hope for me to build a path toward a career in which I might be able to help concretely on the adaptation to the climate crisis," he says. He just received the news that there were no available scholarships for Italian students for UWC Atlantic. He's now hoping to find benefactors and sponsors to support his dreams. From his position as a savvy social media influencer, he has already greatly amplified the global awakening to our climate emergency, especially among youth. The more dynamic youth leaders we have immersed in technology, the more rapidly we can increase the reach of this urgent message -- and through coming together find better solutions.

You never change things by fighting the existing reality. To change something, build a new model that makes the existing model obsolete.

Buckminster Fuller

Call to Action: Follow David: https://twitter.com/davidwicker hf https://www.facebook.com/dhf.wicker https://www.instagram.com/davidwickerhf/ Fridays for Future's website: https://www.fridaysforfutureitalia.it/

SMALL PEOPLE CREATING BIG CHANGES
Asha Kirkpatrick
Petitiongirls.com
United Kingdom

Ten-year-old Asha and her eight-year-old sister Jia were watching their favorite program on TV: *The Orangutan Jungle School*. This show tells the stories of the orangutans and their caretakers in the world's biggest rehabilitation center for the species, on the island of Borneo.

The sisters were learning a lot about orangutans from the show: how they learn new skills, how they behave, and of course why they had ended up in a rehabilitation center. The answer to that question was that many of the apes had been orphaned when their natural habitats were destroyed, because rainforests are being cut down for palm oil production.

"We started looking into it. We didn't think it was that bad at first; but then we realized it's a big problem," Asha says. "It causes so much deforestation!" Jia adds.

To their dismay, Asha and Jia noticed that palm oil was in the chocolate that they had gotten their mother for her birthday, and in almost everything they liked to eat. And that is no surprise: palm oil is now the most used vegetable oil in the world, and the demand for it is continuing to rise. On the island of Borneo, where the sisters' favorite TV show is produced, since 1973 16,000 square miles of rainforest have been destroyed to make more room for palm oil production.

"It is mainly the orangutans' forests that are being cut down," says Asha. "And not a lot of wildlife can live in the agricultural palm trees, because it is not as diverse as the usual trees."

Palm oil is not only used in chocolate of course: it is also used in the production of breads and sweets, biofuels and cosmetics, ice cream and soap. And when the girls had done some more research, they found another product that uses palm oil: their breakfast cereal, which is produced by Kellogg's.

"It's ironic how it is a cereal brand for children, but they're cutting down the rainforest as well," says Asha. They found a report by the environmental organization Greenpeace that listed companies whose practices were particularly harmful to the environment: it included Pepsi and Nestlé -- and also Kellogg's.

So, together with their mom, they decided to take action. They started a petition on change.org, calling on Kellogg's to stop destroying the rainforest for palm oil.

"We love orangutans," the petition reads. "And we were really upset when we saw that the numbers of orangutans that are being killed and orphaned every year are being increased by companies who want cheap palm oil; it has to stop now!"

The sisters sent their petition to friends and family, and they gathered about 10 signatures on the first day. "It was a really slow start," Jia says. But luck was on their side.

Around the same time, a UK supermarket called Iceland teamed up with Greenpeace to create a TV ad about palm oil, but it was banned for breaching political advertising rules, and an uproar followed. "After that, our petition literally exploded," says Asha. "When we went on holiday there were maybe 15,000 signatures. And then when we came back it was like 200,000!"

Soon the media started to get interested in their story. The sisters were interviewed by newspapers and even invited onto a radio show. With the number of signatures on the petition constantly growing, Kellogg's finally decided they had to react. So they invited Asha and Jia to come to a meeting.

Together with their mom, the sisters travelled to the company's headquarters in Manchester. It was a bit nerve-wracking to meet all of the company's executives in their impressive, 12-story glass tower, Asha remembers. At the Kellogg's headquarters there is free cereal for all employees -- and visitors. But Asha and Jia weren't impressed by the fancy building, or the free cornflakes they were given.

"The first thing they said to us was 'What do you know about Kellogg's?'" Asha remembers. She kept a cool head as she calmly replied, "I know that you use 23 of the 26 worse palm oil suppliers." With that, the atmosphere of the meeting changed immediately: the executives had hoped to talk about their brand, their company's growth, and their social service activities, but Asha had instantly, and deftly, changed the conversation.

"As soon as we got home from that first meeting, we had two interviews," Jia says. News stations wanted to cover any upcoming meetings, but Kellogg's wouldn't allow it, explaining that they weren't a very public company.

It was the same reason they gave for not publicly supporting Wilmar, an important purchaser of palm oil that had come under pressure from Greenpeace, and as a result had recently announced more sustainable business practices. A public statement by Kellogg's in support of more sustainable practices would have sent an important message. But at their second meeting with Asha and Jia, it became clear that Kellogg's wasn't willing to take a stand.

"It must have been embarrassing for them," says Asha. "We travelled all the way to meet with them, and it was for nothing, just for them to tell us that they hadn't done anything," Jia says.

In the meantime, the number of signatures on the petition kept rising; at the time of this writing the number had climbed to over 900,000. Eventually, the bosses at Kellogg's had no choice: they had to do something.

So they called a third meeting with the young changemakers, and this time they delivered -- at least on paper. They pledged that until 2025 they would switch entirely to using segregated palm oil, which is a more sustainable product. They also launched a Global Deforestation policy that will help to mitigate deforestation. And they promised to enlist the help of nongovernmental organizations like Greenpeace to ensure that their policy is being implemented on the ground.

"But they need to actually *do* it!" Jia emphasizes. And she says that she and her sister will stick to their guns. They plan to meet with the executives at Kellogg's regularly, to make sure that the company is fulfilling their promises. "We need to make sure that they are doing what they said they were going to do," says Asha. "So, it's not just us coming by and them saying 'Oh we haven't done anything,' and then extending the deadline even more."

Besides holding Kellogg's to account, Asha and Jia have other big plans. After all, there are a lot of other companies that use palm oil in their products, without regard to the impact on the environment and on local populations.

"We are thinking about who we are going to contact next," says Jia. "We were considering Nestle or Pepsi."

Until these companies change their harmful practices, there are things that everyone can do to help, Asha says. Learning about the ingredients used in the products we consume is important, and wherever possible one should try not to buy products that use palm oil.

Since the sisters have discovered the horrible effects of palm oil production, buying gifts for their parents has become a lot more difficult. But as Asha points out, it is their parents' generation that has caused much of the damage to our planet, so they do own some responsibility for the problem. "They destroy the world, and now they've left it to us to fix it," she says. "And that's going to affect the way we live when we're older."

Asha and Jia have recently welcomed a new member to their family -- Benni, a furry, friendly-looking teddy orangutan. When they grow up they want to travel to Borneo, to see where the real orangutans live, and maybe even visit the Orangutan Jungle School.

Until then, they will keep on fighting to protect the orangutans, so there still will be something to visit once they get there. "If you think something is wrong, you can change it," says Asha. "But you have to put the effort into it." They have received several letters from David Attenborough congratulating them on their progress.

Thank you for what you are doing to help tackle the problems caused by palm oil. I am glad that young people like yourselves care so passionately about the planet – it gives me great hope for the future.

Sir David Attenborough

Call to Action: When you next go to the supermarket, check the ingredients list on the products in your shopping cart. If they include palm oil, try to find alternatives! If you can't, it's okay: the most important step is the first one. If you become aware of the problem you can always let the product producer know your concerns. You can also follow Asha and Jia's progress on www.petitiongirls.com and sign their petition on http://change.org/KelloggsPalmOil

STANDING ALONE, TOGETHER
Arshak Makichyan
Russia

In the largest country in the world, Russia, Arshak Makichyan stood for the climate -- for a long time -- all alone.

Starting in March 2019, every Friday the 24-year-old stood for two hours in the center of Moscow's Pushkin Square holding a simple sign: "Strike for Climate." Every week, for over a year he led his solo strike, braving the cold, the snow, the sun, and the police.

He wasn't striking all alone because he wanted to. He'd seen the youth-led movement around the world growing, with people marching by the hundreds, thousands, and even millions. But in Russia, striking *en masse*, unlike in other countries, is against the law. If there is more than one person, they must be approved by the government.

So he stood for the climate alone because he had to.

Arshak hadn't always been solo in his stand. In fact, his introduction to climate activism had been just a few days earlier, on March 15. Inspired by Greta Thunberg's global FridaysforFuture movement, a small group of activists had gathered in "Hyde Park," a small section of Sokolniki Park, far from the center of Moscow. Since not very many people go there, that was the place the government had assigned to them on their permit.

There, about 50-70 activists -- mostly young people -- gathered to send out a call to Russia's leaders, asking them to do more to protect the environment. After all, Russia is the world's fourth biggest emitter of carbon dioxide. And the activists were painfully aware of the myriad ways climate change is affecting Russia. There are forest fires in Siberia; there is flooding in the Irkutsk region that is melting the Arctic permafrost. That in turn destabilizes biodiversity, and creates a feedback loop that leads to further global warming.

Standing in an out-of-the way park just wasn't enough for Arshak. He knew that protesting in a preapproved place, far away from those who most needed to hear their message, wasn't going to attract enough attention. So he decided to venture out on his own and take the message to the public in a bold new way.

"What can I do to support FridaysforFuture in Moscow?" he wondered. He thought about it, and researched the laws about single-person strikes. "It seemed like that was the only way," he says. Then he chose to stage his solo protests in Pushkin Square because it is one of the most frequented plazas not just in Russia, but in the world.

"After that, I started to strike by myself in Moscow's city center, where lots of people could see my protest," he says. "I thought maybe they would be inspired if they saw me there with my sign every week," he explains. And he adds, "As fellow Russians, they knew that I was risking a lot by striking openly, and talking about it openly."

Next, in solidarity with other global youth climate activists, and in order to share his message with other Russian youth, Arshak started posting photos on social media. He was fully aware of the risk he was taking; everything from being arrested, to doing jail time or getting a heavy fine, or even being subjected to physical violence.

Soon people around the world began to notice his protests. One of them was Greta Thunberg, who began to follow him on Twitter and retweet his messages.

His solo protests began to morph into a shared experience, as the internet and young activists across Russia and around the world took notice. Then other young Russians began to mirror his actions, and the community of climate activists in Russia began to grow. "People started to think that maybe it's okay to do it," he says. "And that it's not so scary – they started thinking they can do something too."

In a way, Arshak's story of solitary activism didn't really start in Russia. It started in the mid-1990s, in Yerevan, Armenia, where he was born. Arshak's parents had fled to Russia from their Armenian homeland when he was just a year old. They were escaping a 10-year-long armed conflict that had devastated their country, reduced neighborhoods to shambles, and destroyed the economy.

Growing up in Moscow, Arshak had felt a profound sense of isolation. School was difficult for him, and other kids picked on him because he was a foreigner. "It's quite complicated to tell what it is like to live in Moscow," he says. "When I was a kid, I faced lots of challenges because I was Armenian." But instead of letting the bullying get him down, Arshak dove headlong into learning music. He picked up the violin at an early age and began to practice incessantly, learning ballads and other tunes. He developed a special affinity for the music of Chopin. At the age of nine, he was accepted to an academy for aspiring musicians, where he began his classical training.

And so, throughout his life, Arshak had spent a lot of time alone. Perhaps that's what gave him the determination and the stamina to go through with his solo strikes, despite the cold and wind of a Moscow winter, and his fears about breaking the law.

Even when he was still in the Russian school system, Arshak had realized the environment wasn't being studied. In fact, environmental issues weren't being taken seriously at all. Yet Russians have good reason to be concerned about the havoc climate change could wreak on their country and its economy. Scientists have warned that Russia's carbon dioxide emissions are warming at a rate twice that of the global average. As a world leader in international organizations, and with a seat on the United Nations Security Council, Russia has an important voice in deciding what the climate's future will look like.

"Other countries can say, if Russia doesn't act, then why should we?" Arshak says. "So, it's very important that every country should start acting as if this is a crisis, and reduce their emissions dramatically. Now!"

Arshak began to gain international renown for his activism. He was invited to join Greta Thunberg on stage at the 2019 COP 25 conference in Madrid. He realized that he might have to spend time in jail when he returned to Russia. But from the stage he told the people gathered, "I am not afraid to be arrested. I am afraid not to do enough."

Upon his return from the conference, Arshak returned to Pushkin Square for his strike. This time, he was arrested by the Russian police for staging an unlawful "mass protest" -- of three people -- and sent to prison for six days. As everyone knows, Russian prisons are infamous for their treatment of dissidents. People were worried about him and his future. Across the country and around the world, a wave of support swelled up from his peers.

Though his prison sentence was intended to slow down the climate movement in Russia, it had the opposite effect. During each day of his prison sentence, crowds gathered outside of Russian embassies in cities around the world to protest. Thousands more tweeted and posted messages of support. And after his release, the movement came through even stronger than before.

Arshak was touched by everyone standing up for him. "It's even helped our movement a little bit," he says. He pauses, then adds, "It's not so scary to be in jail for six days. It's more scary not to have a normal future, I think."

The more involved he's become with climate activism, the less lonely Arshak feels. The sense of solidarity he feels with other climate activists has even had an effect on his everyday life. "Before, I was playing violin, reading books, sitting at home and studying, but I was really quite lonely," he says of his life before joining Fridays for Future. "After I became a climate activist, I found a lot of friends, other activists who were supporting me, or striking with me. I was so much more lonely when I was just a person studying, and living my life."

Thanks to Arshak's efforts the climate movement in Russia is slowly growing, in spite of the restrictions on public protesting. They've found creative ways to get around the limitations imposed by Russia's authoritarian system. For example, during the global climate march in September of 2019, Arshak was joined by about 70 other "solo" protesters, who took turns staging their own personal protests one by one in Pushkin Square. They organized queues, and as each protestor took his or her turn, they would exchange posters, while other protestors stood nearby "so we didn't feel alone." About 700 people in more than 25 other Russian cities joined the climate march.

Then Arshak organized an online "flash mob" with the hashtag #LetRussiaStrikeForClimate. People who are afraid to strike can share pictures calling for climate action, and others from around the world can support them. Through his activism, Arshak has expanded the FridaysforFuture movement beyond Moscow to seven other cities across Russia. He attributes the success of the growing movement to a constant process of education and advocacy.

"We are not just striking," he says. "We are organizing lectures; we are communicating with all the movements that are trying to build a new society, and to find some ways to do it. So, I'm not alone anymore."

But he also knows that for every step forward, there are many more to take. "People are suffering from the climate crisis now in a lot of places," he says. "We cannot prevent everything from happening; but we can try to do something beautiful and good for our future."

The future depends on what you do today.

Mahatma Gandhi

Call to Action: Support Arshak by using the hashtag #LetRussiaStrikeForClimate on social media platforms. Join with Arshak and those organizing climate action strikes on the Fridays for Future website: https://www.fridaysforfuture.org.

THE ART OF SAVING THE PLANET
Alejandro Martinez
Juventud x Clima
Spain

Alejandro Martinez is fighting to preserve his country's natural beauty. "It's really about having an appreciation for beauty," he says. Alejandro is one of the founders of Juventud x Clima, Spain's branch of the Fridays for Future movement. "What we've been doing with Fridays for Future is not so much fighting *against* something, but rather fighting to protect what we love."

It's no wonder that Spain is the country that produced Pablo Picasso, Salvador Dali, and Antoni Gaudí. The vibrant palettes that make their work so stunning were inspired from the country's diverse natural landscapes: from the dense, green forests of the north to the red-soiled fields of olive trees in the south, the white-topped mountain ranges of the southern Pyrenees all the way down to the blue ocean vistas along the Mediterranean coast.

But over the next 20 years, this beauty -- these colors -- might fade away, due to climate change. Scientists have estimated that two-thirds of Spain could be covered by deserts by 2050. In terms of climate, Madrid would more closely resemble Marrakech than Paris. Much of the middle of the country would be unrecognizable: a flat canvas of yellow.

In Spain, saving the climate is also about saving art and beauty, and the country's colorful history. Through their movement, Alejandro and other young people in Spain are trying to ensure that future generations will be able to appreciate that beauty for centuries to come.

For Alejandro it's important to frame the fight this way -- fighting *for* something positive, instead of *against* something negative. Throughout his life, he's had to do this. Ever since he was a kid, he's seen things in a bit of a different light from the rest of his family, and from the rest of his *compañeros,* at school and elsewhere.

Alejandro's first big fight wasn't for the climate; actually, it was a fight to convince his parents to allow him to study art in Madrid.

Growing up, he had a creative mind. He loved science -- whenever he had the chance to do a class presentation, he would try to make it about the climate, or biodiversity -- but he also loved art. When he saw a documentary about Pixar, the California-based production house that brought together amazing technology and wildly creative artists, he knew immediately that he wanted to become an animator.

But when he told his parents, they quickly shut him down. They didn't see a career for him in the arts. They wanted him to prepare for a career that had more stable job prospects; and eventually they won that first battle. At the end of high school, Alejandro enrolled in law school. The first year of school was the most difficult of his life. He felt crushed by the studies, like his life was being lived in two dimensions instead of three.

"Of all the curiosity I feel for so many things, the law just isn't one of them," he says. "I was killing myself, going to class every day to study something I didn't love."

In his second year of law school, he decided to confront his parents. He told them that even if they didn't want to pay for his studies, he was going to find a way to go to school for fine arts.

Happily, when they realized how serious and passionate he was about his desire to study art, they let him pursue his dreams.

He didn't let the opportunity slip by.

Alejandro enrolled at the Universidad Complutense de Madrid's School of Fine Arts. Here, his art and his activism began to come together.

Climate change had always been important to Alejandro, and he strove to set an example for his family. As a kid, it was Alejandro, not his parents, who educated the rest of the family about how to be more environmentally responsible. From the simple things like recycling, to the more challenging ones, like eating less red meat, Alejandro instilled in them a greater environmental consciousness.

In art school, in a more multicultural and youthful setting, he joined the Spanish Fridays for Future movement, spearheaded by Greta Thunberg, and worked his way up to the role of the movement's spokesperson. He learned not just from people like Greta but also from environmental and human rights defenders like Berta Caceres, an Indigenous activist who had founded the Council of Popular and Indigenous Organizations of Honduras, and who was killed in 2016, for protecting the land.

He learned how to recite statistics about climate change off the top of his head, and he learned about the different degrees of global warming and what they could mean for humanity. As one of the older leaders of the group, Alejandro has been an important voice. At 25, he's already a veteran climate activist.

Juventud x Clima now has 60 members, and what they've accomplished is already quite impressive. In March 2019, they stormed the European Parliament in Brussels and called on leaders to set more ambitious climate goals. They succeeded at bringing Greta Thunberg to Madrid for a rally during the COP 25 climate conference. They've made their plea to the political left and right alike. In the next 10 years, they hope to push the Spanish government to set goals to reduce country-wide greenhouse gas emissions; their goal is 55 percent by 2030, and 100 percent by 2050.

Even this might not be enough to stave off a 2-degree warming scenario that could set off a number of tipping points, if natural processes create a positive feedback loop of warming that can't be stopped. In Spain, the effects of global warming have already begun to be felt in full force, Alejandro says. "The summers last for a month longer than they used to. The winters are warmer than before," he says. "Right now, as we speak, it's winter and it feels like spring."

But he still has hope -- and for months he saw that hope expressed by young people across Spain every Friday in the streets of not only Madrid, but other cities, too: Valencia, Barcelona, Bilbao. He heard it in their chants to the tune of the song *Bella Ciao*, a revolutionary Italian anti-fascist hymn that was repurposed for the climate movement:

> *We need to rise up*
> *We need to wise up*
> *We need to open our eyes*
> *and do it now, now, now.*
> *We need to build a better future.*
> *And we need to start right now!*

Giovanna Daffini

Even as he prepares to enter graduate school for animation, Alejandro has continued to work tirelessly for Juventud x Clima. For the past year, he has been putting together a personal art project that takes viewers inside the Fridays for Future movement.

Each month he makes a short video showing climate activists mobilizing, around the world. They gather in conference rooms and outside of government buildings. They take to the streets and ride together in buses. They go to museums, and also do the things that normal kids do: goof around and play games, be silly. Often the videos are sped up to a hyper-lapse speed. It's an apt image in a world of accelerating warming.

Alejandro calls this project "Document Your Life," and he has been sharing it on YouTube, to serve as a resource for future generations of young people to be inspired by.

"Document Your Life" is about creating momentum, but it's also about slowing things down and learning how to appreciate the moments of youth that can lead to great change. This is how Alejandro feels when he's making art. He feels like he's able to capture a powerful moment in time -- a feeling, a rush of motion -- just like Picasso and other great Spanish artists have done before him.

"When I decide to sit down to draw or to paint, it's because I don't want to forget things -- I don't want to lose these precious moments that will last forever," he says.

The role of the artist is that of the soldier of the revolution.

Diego Rivera

Call to Action: Join Alejandro in calling for Climate Action Now! Follow #FridaysForFuture Espana on Twitter https://twitter. com/JuventudXClima?s=20 and bring #FridaysForFuture to your community: https://fridaysforfuture.org/

THIRSTY FOR CHANGE
Alaa Salah
Sudan

The young woman's pose is defiant. She stares straight ahead, eyes wide open, a look of fierce determination on her face. One arm is raised to the sky, her finger pointing upward toward the heavens, as she stands on a car in the midst of a crowd in Khartoum, Sudan. She joins in on the chorus of voices of the peaceful protesters calling for the government to fall. Around her, the crowd swarms, cheers, chants *"Thawra!"* - "Revolution!" They turn their cameras to snap a photo of Alaa, whose all-white garb and golden, moon-shaped earrings make her stand out all the more amidst the falling dusk, the smog of the city.

It was this moment -- and one of these snapshots -- that changed Alaa Salah's life.

Taken by a local photographer, Lana Haroun, the photo quickly went viral when Lana posted it online. Alaa's powerful pose inspired more protesters to join the fight to peacefully topple President Omar al-Bashir, whose reign had become more and more authoritarian, and was leading to a number of horrifying consequences: bread and fuel shortages, the oppression of women, imprisonment of political dissidents.

Alaa became known as Sudan's "Lady Liberty" and the "Woman in White" -- and the photo brought international attention to their cause.

The photo was published on April 8, 2019. Three days later, al-Bashir's regime came tumbling down.

But the work of toppling the regime didn't take place over just three days.

Alaa remembers the first day young people took the streets to call for the end of the repressive dictatorship: December 19, 2018. She was a 22-year-old student at the time. She had lived a relatively normal childhood, growing up in Khartoum, the capital, and attending private schools. When she graduated from high school, she went to university to study architecture and engineering.

Despite her relatively privileged upbringing, she still felt the harsh effects of the regime at times. One night, she remembers, she was out on a stroll with her brother, coming back from an event. The police approached them and asked them what they were doing. They made her prove that her brother was related to her -- because at that time, in Sudan you could get harassed, or even thrown in jail, for being out in public with someone of the opposite gender. "It was really terrifying," she says.

Everyday life was hard in Sudan. Many young people were not allowed to get an education. Lines for bread snaked out of bakeries; people queued at the bank to take out money, but came away empty-handed. The police set up checkpoints where they checked for IDs without giving a valid reason why.

Alaa, and many others in her generation, grew up thirsty for change. They watched as other Arab countries were rising up against the dictators who had monopolized power for so many years: in Tunisia, Libya, Egypt. But throughout this period, Sudan's dictator, al-Bashir, somehow managed to hang on. He ruled over a massacre in the Darfur region that had killed more than 600,000 people. And he turned a blind eye to the widespread violence: against women, against the press, against defenders of human rights.

"There was a lot of energy piling up inside of me, because that regime was full of corruption," Alaa says, her anger still palpable. "They were killing people! There was a lot of hunger, and pain, and rape, and violence. For 30 years! And that was when the revolution started."

As is often the case in countries that experience conflict and unrest, there was a reason for the conflict that no one was talking about: and that "elephant in the room" was climate change.

To many observers and analysts, even some in positions as high up as at the United Nations, the war in Sudan's Darfur region was one of the first modern conflicts fought over climate. The Sahel region, where Darfur is located, used to be called the breadbasket of Africa, and was known for its lush agricultural lands. The Nile River runs through that part of the country, nourishing the region.

But as climate change has accelerated, the region is drying up: this has led to tensions between farmers of different ethnicities who produce crops, and raise cattle there. The Sahara Desert has expanded -- moving about 60 miles south in just 40 years. Rainfall during that time has decreased by 15 to 20 percent. By as soon as 2030, just 10 years from now, the main crop produced in the area, sorghum, could decrease by 70 percent due to climate change.

It was the food shortages Alaa experienced growing up that eventually led her generation to rise up. People were hungry. And these food shortages weren't just a result of corruption -- although that played a role -- it was also because of climate change.

Alaa saw firsthand how changes in the climate had had an impact on populations outside of Khartoum, where she grew up. "Usually the rain would come in August, but more recently it would be in June. These changes in the climate have affected certain regions," she says.

Farmers had to begin to bring their cattle further and further from home in order to feed them. Others would have to sell their cattle in exchange for seeds so they could grow other crops.

"There have always been problems, but the previous regime was not willing to put forward sustainable solutions," she says.

The moments during and just after the Sudanese revolution were filled with hope for the future. After the military staged the coup that overthrew al-Bachir, they eventually settled on a power-sharing agreement with civil society organizations and protest groups: a major step toward democracy. Al-Bachir went on trial, and was convicted of corruption and sentenced to two years in prison.

Not all of the promises of peace and stability from the new regime were kept, though. In June, security forces shot dead 87 protesters. There were still outbursts of violence; but it was nothing compared to what the people had suffered before and during the revolution.

The promises to include more women in politics also fell through, and many of the women who had led the movement felt that their voices were once again being left out. So in the fall of 2019, Alaa and a group of women activists from Sudan traveled to the United Nations in New York City, where they called on world leaders to ensure equal gender representation in Sudan's newly formed parliament.

They've received the support of some notable figures, like the actor George Clooney and his wife Amal, who denounced the corrupt regime.

Alaa knows that the fight for justice doesn't end when the dictator falls; it ends when everyone has an equal chance at success. She's made it her life mission to ensure that all Sudanese youth can get an education; and she is working with local nonprofits to expand educational opportunities across the country.

"In developed countries they have paid a lot of attention to education, and that's why they're improving," she says. "In developing countries, on the other hand, education has been marginalized and it hasn't been taken care of."

For many children in Sudan, even getting to school can be life-threatening. When Alaa heard that 22 children had drowned crossing a river to try to get to school, she was heartbroken. *No child should have to risk their life to get an education,* she thought.

For Sudan, education and climate change adaptation can go hand in hand. The country's next generation of children, growing up for the first time not under a dictatorship, could become the scientists who are coming up with creative solutions to address desertification, waste management, pollution of the Nile River, and many of the other problems the country is facing.

Alaa wants Sudanese children to know that they are the country's future; and that by staring down their challenges and being committed to solving them peacefully, as she and her fellow activists did in the spring of 2019, they can make their country a better, more just place to live.

"Every dream can be a reality, and every imagination can also be a reality," she says. "Between the dream and the reality, there are so many challenges, and the challenges could be big, they could be frustrating. If there's hope, you can get to that reality, but you need to work really hard, and you have to believe in your cause. And you have to stand up for it!"

Young people should be at the forefront of global change and innovation.
Empowered, they can be key agents for development and peace.
If, however, they are left on society's margins, all of us will be impoverished.
Let us ensure that all young people have every opportunity to participate fully in the lives of their societies.

Kofi Annan, former Secretary General of the United Nations

Call to Action: Learn how you can support Sudanese women and children in their fight for a more just society and a better life for all. Follow Alaa on Instagram https://www.instagram.com/lwolia_salah/

TO THE ENDS OF THE EARTH... AND BACK
Parker Liautaud
California & Antarctica

When he reached the North Pole, climate change activist Parker Liautaud realized a daring, Arctic dream -- at the age of 16. He isn't your ordinary Arctic explorer. Of course, there aren't really any *ordinary* Arctic explorers. But Parker doesn't cut a particularly imposing figure, nor does he fit the archetype one might assume when trying to conjure up the image of a heroic figure standing at the top of the world. On looks alone, Parker could even be considered unassuming. He's slight of build. Soft-spoken. He has said about himself that he's "the least athletically impressive person ever to visit the poles," which gives you a glimpse into his quirky, light-hearted nature. Parker is humorous, humble, and whenever he addresses a crowd, which he often does, he's always measured in his speech and clear in his singular message: it's his generation's responsibility to take up the reigns in the fight against climate change.

By the age of 17, Parker had already made three separate expeditions to the Arctic. His first visit was with the renowned Arctic explorer Robert Swan, who was the first person to walk both the North and South Poles. On this expedition, they stayed at a base ran entirely on renewable energy sources, which fascinated Parker. His initial foray to the Arctic had been in a scientific capacity. Here, his interaction with green technology, coupled with seeing the dire situation for himself firsthand, lit a fire in Parker that compelled him to get involved in the fight against climate change in a much more permanent and impactful way.

Climate change is affecting the entire planet, but it affects certain areas, like the Arctic, disproportionately. According to the Intergovernmental Panel on Climate Change (IPCC), "Antarctica has experienced air temperature increases of 3°C in the Antarctic Peninsula. Although that might not seem very much, it is 5 times the mean rate of global warming." Understanding the precariousness of the situation at hand, the expedition Parker was on set various scientific goals for their visit. Parker himself was involved in gathering the rarest of rare commodities: Arctic snow samples. These would ultimately act as a Rosetta Stone of sorts for scientists the world over, when Parker successfully brought them back to the research station. This is because the Tritium in the snow samples acts as a relatively reliable oceanic tracer of sorts, and can reveal hidden—and changing -- patterns of ocean circulation and ventilation that can't be observed with the naked eye.

These might seem like larger-than-life responsibilities for someone so young, and in a way they are. But that doesn't change the fact that in most every other way, Parker was just the same as any other ordinary teenager.

As an American student at Eton, an illustrious British boarding school for boys, Parker always "felt like an outsider," which he credits as a driving, if not painful force in his development as a socially and environmentally conscious citizen. His inability to fit in was no secret at Eton. He stood out as an obvious foreigner, a culture-shocked teenager trying to adjust to a very different way of life. During this period, he laments his "bad social skills" as being the reason he made no friends, and subsequently spent a lot of time with his nose to the grindstone, intently focused on his studies.

When Parker returned to school in England, he committed himself to serving a greater purpose than his own. He spent his days spreading the word about the desperate situation at the poles to anybody he could. It didn't take long for him to realize that not everybody shared his passion for protecting the earth. He wrote article after article on global warming, climate change, and stewardship of the polar regions, but got little reaction. No one seemed to care about a 15-year old's point of view on these harrowing topics, even with the factual evidence and scientific data at hand, backing his stance. So, what was it that was causing his message to fall on deaf ears? Did he lack credibility because of his youth? Was it political? Perhaps he needed to find someone more dynamic to help him spread the message?

It proved to be a very confusing and disheartening period for Parker, who had a quick, curious mind, and rarely struggled to achieve what he wanted to in an intellectual sense. He had a message, and it was an important message, but it wasn't getting through. Perhaps idealistically, he thought that the climate situation at the poles was so urgent, and indisputable from an evidentiary standpoint, that any rational person would share his passion equally. On a personal level, he was also struggling to fit in at school during this time, and it seemed to make his efforts, which weren't being received with any enthusiasm, feel all the more isolating and meaningless.

Over a century earlier, at the age of 22, Sir Ernest Shackleton had his

Eureka moment, saying, "I had a dream that someday I would go to the region of ice and snow, and go on and on until I came to one of the poles of the earth." At the age of 27 his dream had been realized, when he joined Captain Robert Falcon Scott on the now renowned *Discovery* expedition to Antarctica.

Ernest Shackleton is noted to have famously said, in the most understated fashion, "Difficulties are just things to overcome." And it would take an individual with the cunning and resolve of Parker Liautaud, to come up with a new plan in the face of this adversity, to truly make an impact in the expansive world beyond the walls of Eton.

Whether it was on the news or at school, Parker always heard people talking about global warming, and how climate change will disproportionately affect the next generation. That's why something has to be done – and now. "We have to think about the children," he recalls hearing someone say, and when he did, his natural curiosity took over. *If it's going to affect us, why are we waiting for someone else to address the problem?* he thought. And that's when Parker Liautaud, like his forbearer Sir Ernest Shackleton before him, had *his Eureka* moment. He knew that the global situation was dire, and that time was running out. More importantly, he'd knew that he needed to find a creative way to engage his peers, so as to involve his generation in the fight and get them invested in the larger cause. Besides, he didn't see anyone else doing anything but talking about the problem at hand.

After all, he'd had a rare experience that even the brightest Etonians hadn't–he'd actually seen the perilous Arctic firsthand. He had braved hostile territory. He had stayed at a base run on renewables, living in the spirit of the cause he was trying to marshal. He had learned about the Arctic's fragile ecosystem, and its unique role in moderating global temperature. He personally had done research in service of the region's protection and felt a kinship to it, even an ownership of it, in a sense. So why not take it a step further? If he intended to ask as much of his peers, surely he should have the wherewithal to stand up and lead them. Calling on his past experiences, and with some careful calculation, he felt it was his responsibility to do something more daring to increase his reach, that at once would fulfill his duty of spreading the message about fighting climate change, while getting the attention of his peers. Desperate times call for desperate measures, they say.

So that very day, Parker Liautaud decided he'd become the youngest person in the history of the world to set foot on the geographic North Pole.

To achieve this goal, Parker enlisted the partnership and guidance of environmental campaigner Doug Stoup, with whom he raised all the necessary funding for their trip. This independent fundraising was important to Parker, as he didn't want the tenor of his trip, which was to get a message out to the young people of the world about climate change and global warming, to be confused with some thrill-seeker's PR stunt. It would surely be a thrilling expedition, but as anyone who has been to polar regions knows, the reality of a trip to the Arctic can't be undertaken with anything but complete and utter reverence for the innumerable dangers that are sure to arise, even for the most seasoned adventurer.

This is the part of the story where Parker Liautaud found himself at odds with his forbearer, Sir Ernest Shackleton, who said, "Superhuman effort isn't worth a damn, unless it achieves results."

On Parker and Doug's attempt to reach the North Pole, their journey was cut short just 15 miles short of their destination. The geographic North Pole is simply a GPS location in the Arctic Ocean, and in the window of time they approached it, shifting polar ice sheets didn't allow them the opportunity to make landfall. For 14 days they waited for a break, but it never came. At last, with supplies dwindling, and being no closer to their destination, they decided with heavy hearts to abort the mission.

It pained Parker immensely to fail this way, and to fail so publicly. What wore on him the most was not fulfilling his promise to their sponsors, the scientific community, and above all, his peers, who he was asking so much of. But ultimately, the situation was what it was, and both men had to acknowledge that as far as their journey went, the Arctic environment "held complete control over us... and we'd have to respect that." Their superhuman effort wouldn't yield the desired result. To consider, as Shackleton said, that such efforts, that *their* efforts weren't worth a damn. Or worse, if they were in vain...

In 2010, Parker Liautaud failed to be the youngest person in the history of the world to reach the geographic North Pole. But it was in that moment of failure, 1,000 miles from home and freezing in a torn-up tent in the Arctic, that Parker remembered why he was out there – to serve a greater purpose than his own. And in that sense, Parker succeeded. News of the 15-year-old explorer's attempt gained a bit of traction, and each time a new set of eyes were trained on his story, there was a new opportunity to spread his message about fighting climate change.

It didn't take long for Parker's passion to grab hold of him again. A year later, in 2011, Parker did in fact reach the geographic North Pole (though this time, there was no record at stake, as he had been beaten by a younger adventurer). Shortly thereafter, having conquered what they set out to, he and Doug Stoup began to organize what would become The Willis Resilience Expedition, setting their sights on reaching the other pole. On this expedition, they set a record for making the fastest human-powered trek from the coast of Antarctica to the South Pole (a 397-mile journey in just 22 days, while trailing a 200-pound pulk). In the process, Parker became the youngest man in history to complete the journey to the South Pole.

If it weren't for the endless stream of videos showcasing Parker addressing enthralled audiences at the United Nations Foundation, TED talks, or the Clinton Global Initiative, to name a few, it'd be difficult to imagine he's a leading authority on modern polar exploration. But as it turns out, Parker is unassuming in appearance alone, and his credentials speak for themselves.

At the World Economic Forum in 2014, in Davos, he commanded a room of influential global leaders with his tales from the ends of the earth. Wearing a blue blazer and tie, and standing behind the heavy, wooden podium, he looked no different from any of the businessmen and women in the audience who were eagerly taking his story in -- but anybody who knows Parker Liautaud will tell you that what you see isn't always what you get. Parker is extraordinary in many ways, whether he looks the part or not. And perhaps his many, selfless efforts living the environmental advocacy he preaches around the world will prove, over the long haul, to be his most extraordinary achievement yet.

So, what's left for the man who has literally been to the ends of the earth? Well, a lot can happen in a short period of time, especially for someone with the drive and determination of Parker.

If you go to Parker's Flickr account, there is an album with images of a skinny, 15-year-old Parker pulling 25-pound tires through the grass, trying to simulate dragging the weight of the pulk across the Arctic. Those images are a long way off from the Parker of today, who is a gristled veteran of four polar expeditions. But what has remained the same is his dedication to the cause. All this just goes to show you that youthful energy, with proper guidance, and pointed in the right direction, can accomplish amazing things.

While his personal achievements are impressive, Parker finds a greater satisfaction in knowing that his generation is more informed about global warming and climate change, thanks to his efforts. That said, he remains as active as ever, trying to inspire involvement from the youth around the world. Climate advocacy needs young, passionate people to step up and be the leaders of tomorrow. After all, climate change isn't an ordinary problem that can be solved by any one person. It will take the teamwork, dedication, and passion of a lot of people -- a lot of *extraordinary* people who, like Parker, aspire toward a similarly daring dream: to save the globe.

When making your choice in life, do not neglect to live.

Samuel Johnson

Call to Action: Learn more about Parker's advocacy work as an environmental campaigner: One Young World. https://www.oneyoungworld.com/

TURNING TRASH INTO TREES
Vihaan Agarwal
One Step Greener
India

Vihaan and his little brother Nav were sitting in the back seat of the car, on their way to school. The traffic was dense, as usual, and the air outside was smoggy with exhaust fumes. The polluted air in Delhi had been a problem for Vihaan for a long time. Because he had asthma, he often wasn't allowed to go outside and play with his friends. So that day when he opened up the newspaper, one article in particular caught his eye.

"I read an article about how India's largest landfill, the Ghazipur landfill, had collapsed and caught fire," he remembers. "It released really dangerous fumes into the atmosphere, as you can imagine." That day, for the first time, Vihaan made a connection between two problems that had always bothered him: Delhi's dismal air quality, and the huge amounts of trash generated each and every day in the city.

Delhi's 19 million people produce around 9,000 tons of solid waste every day. Most of the trash ends up in landfills, where it is neither recycled nor disposed of correctly. But since many landfills are already overflowing, a lot of trash is simply burned in the street. These trash fires release toxic fumes into the air -- as do the landfills, which also burn on a regular basis. And the gigantic mountains of waste also contaminate the groundwater.

"You think about trash being soil contamination, or visual pollution," Vihaan says. "But the connection to air pollution was never there for me -- until I found out that almost 20 percent of Delhi's air pollution is directly or indirectly caused by trash."

Vihaan and his brother Nav decided to first tackle the problem in their own home. They started by recording how much trash they were producing. Instead of having it collected and brought to one of the landfills, they kept it in their yard for one month. "It was a staggering amount," Vihaan says. "No one would think that in just one month you would produce that much waste."

Vihaan decided that, at the very least, he didn't want his own waste to end up in the landfill and continue to feed the fires that ultimately were making it hard for him -- and everyone else -- to breathe. He started by segregating it into dry and wet waste, which made it much easier to recycle later on. But then, when the trash was picked up, Vihaan saw that the workers were simply mixing all of the trash together -- so his separating work had been in vain.

But he didn't give up: instead, he contacted a company that would pick up the segregated waste and make sure that it was recycled. However, once again they discovered that the company they hired to do the recycling wasn't doing it properly. So they decided to start their own organization, One Step Greener.

At first, he and his brother did the trash sorting and recycling for just their own home -- but soon 20 other households were doing it too. "From 20 households, it grew to a hundred, in a matter of just two months," Vihaan says. "We had so much waste that we had to hire a truck that went around and took the trash to a recycling facility."

The next step for One Step Greener was to hire workers to segregate the collected trash, which was then sold to companies that use the recycled materials to produce new ones. This gives the workers the chance to have a steady income, bank accounts, and health insurance.

"Initially our goal was just to survive, and to grow the project as much as possible," Vihaan says. But today, One Step Greener serves more than 1400 households in 14 different neighborhoods, as well as in a few schools and offices all over Delhi, and is operating in Gurugram. They have a one-of-a-kind center, where people can come and drop off their trash to be recycled. It is also their office. They recycle 99 percent of the trash they collect: this saves resources, and is much better for the environment than trash that ends up in overflowing landfills.

But from the very beginning, their work was not only about picking up trash and making sure that it is recycled. "What we've been able to do is not only to provide an essential service, but also set up a zero-cost process," Vihaan explains. "We charge for the monthly pick up; and the whole rationale is that if you see the amount of trash you're producing in a month, you will automatically reduce that waste."

Vihaan has observed this over and over again -- especially when it comes to plastic waste. When families see the mountains of plastic trash they are producing in just one month, they work hard to make sure they produce less of it in the following month.

Their model worked so well that soon their nonprofit organization was actually turning a profit. So Vihaan and Nav immediately invested the funds into a second project to help improve air quality in Delhi: planting trees. "Right in the heart of Delhi, we've planted an urban forest," Vihaan says. "Our vision was to create an urban forest, a biodiversity hotspot. We've been maintaining it for three years now."

Their forest covers a very small area, but it is home to a large number of species: butterflies flutter through the air, and a dozen species of birds are nesting in the trees. The biggest reward, Vihaan says, is the reaction of people who come to see the project. "I am very grateful for people's reactions to everything we have done," he says. "I see that people are genuinely worried about where the world is heading, and they want to do something to change it."

There certainly is a growing environmental movement in India. At first Vihaan didn't believe in advocacy work; but then he started attending the Fridays For Future protests in Delhi. This experience changed his mind. "It was an infectious feeling," he says. "I felt like we were making a change -- that if two or three hundred people could come together, the whole country could come together."

As a young environmental activist, Vihaan was invited to meet the Honorable President of India, along with the First Lady, and visiting dignitaries, the King and Queen of Sweden, at the president's house. While he knew that his visit might not change any policies, he was glad that at least the president listened to him. They discussed climate change, recycling, waste management, and how young children from around the world are stepping into this domain. This visit was a testimony to Vihaan and Nav that age is not a bar. Despite the common feeling of disconnection between politicians and ordinary citizens, Vihaan feels it is possible to bridge this gap.

But first, waste needs to become a political issue -- and for that to happen, people need to understand what is at stake. That is why Vihaan and Nav are using their organization's social media channels to educate people about the importance of segregating and recycling trash.

"I think it's really important, because we are going to grow up and live in this world," says Nav. "Seeing the climate in this state, it's important to fix our mistakes -- and right now waste in India is not taken seriously."

Vihaan and Nav have big plans for the future of One Step Greener. Before Vihaan heads off to college and leaves the organization in his younger brother's hands, he wants to reach 2,000 households, and expand beyond Delhi. He also wants to plant at least another 10 urban forests.

"At the end of the day, when you do something that actually creates a difference, everyone will notice you, everyone will know you, and want to do something that is as inspiring as the things you do," he says. And he adds, "What you're doing might not make a difference directly, but the domino effect it creates will create huge change -- even something as small as planting a tree in your backyard."

If you really want something, and really work hard,
and take advantage of opportunities, and never give up, you will find a way.
Follow your Dreams.

Jane Goodall

Call to Action: Segregate your trash. Produce less trash in the first place. Buy fewer packaged products. Learn more about Vihaan's and Nav's work at https://www.onestepgreener.org. Follow them on Instagram @onestep_greener or Twitter @stepgreener or LinkedIn @ vihaanagarwal

TRAVELING WITH A PURPOSE
Jessa Garibay-Yayen
Center for Sustainability PH
The Philippines

As a teenager, every third Saturday of June, at the start of the rainy season, Jessa and her schoolmates would wake up at 4 a.m. for the Pista y Cagueban (Feast of the Forest). "It's a massive community event, with students, government offficials, civic groups, individuals, families from our city," she explains. "We are all hauled in gigantic garbage trucks -- 100 people per trip -- and taken up to the mountains to the watershed areas to plant trees." It was exciting for her, that her whole community would wake up so early on a weekend. "It felt like such a special moment, to get my hands dirty."

Palawan's capitol city of Puerto Princesa is called "City in the Forest" for the lush green surrounding it. Only 3 percent of the pristine forests in the Philippines are left, and most of that 3 percent is in Jessa's hometown. It's known as the "last ecological frontier."

Jessa and the families in Palawan feel super-rich living in such a paradise. People come from around the world to see Palawan's natural wonders. With its wonderful coral reefs, ecosystems, and biodiversity of special plants, animals, and habitats, it's one of 17 mega-diverse environments in the world. It's extremely beautiful and extremely pristine -- and it is also a very challenged and threatened ecosystem, because over the years, it's become a hotspot for unsustainable tourism. "There's nothing like seeing your hometown being degraded at such a fast rate to inspire you to take really bold actions towards conserving this wonderful place we live in," says Jessa, adding "And where you want to raise your own children."

At an early age, Jessa dedicated her life to caring for her island's precious land. At 14, she was chosen as a youth speaker for local schools, speaking about what youth can do to help safeguard clean air for everyone. Since then, she's had lots of empowering experiences.

And she has lots of visual metaphors to share her story -- for one of them, she carries a childhood photo of an avocado. "In the Philippines, we eat avocados as something that's sweet, like as a dessert," she explains, adding, "We put milk and sugar on it. In the Western world I was surprised to learn that people eat avocadoes differently -- on toast, or in a sandwich or a salad. Everyone has different ideas." Jessa's "avocado moment" inspired her to travel, and explore new ways of doing things.

When she was 18, she first went to Manado, Indonesia, as a foreign student on an internship program, and stayed with a local family. "I was very curious about the world, especially about the environmental field. I was curious about how others discover solutions to their problems, and about how people are creatively solving their environmental problems in other communities."

Thus began Jessa's "traveling with a purpose."

Then, when she was 21, she traveled to the United States, to Seattle, to work with EarthCorps, where she met other emerging youth environmental leaders from different countries. There, building and restoring trails and salmon habitats, she learned about native plants, invasive species -- and herself.

In 2016, when she was 26, Jessa was invited to be part of the International Union for Conservation of Nature (IUCN)) in Honolulu, to speak alongside then-US Department of Interior Secretary Sally Jewell. There she encouraged other youth to pursue environmental-related careers. "It was such a big audience!" she says. "I met a lot of like-minded individuals my age. It keeps you inspired and motivated in the work you're doing. It really was such an amazing experience to get my voice to be on that kind of platform."

Invigorated by her travels, Jessa returned home to create the Centre for Sustainability PH in the Philippines (CSPH), a women-led youth environmental conservation NGO. It's a team of six young folks. "We all have had the same childhood, we grew up swimming in the sea with turtles and exploring the wild forests as our backyard," she says.

CSPH has found its niche as a conservation lobbying organization. The tourist boom in Palawan has led foreigners to buy land and build lodging and restaurants. Without zoning laws and permits to help govern them, a lot of the land is near critical areas. Much of the land is undocumented, so having legal documents to claim people's land rights is essential. "Unless we lobby for some control over local peoples' lands, the situation is going to continue to degrade at a fast pace...this is the only way to really ensure that we will be able to enjoy the land in perpetuity."

"At CSPH, we believe the best way to ensure the sustainability of our island is by legally protecting our natural resources -- fish stocks, forests, and our watersheds -- creating protected areas, led by Indigenous and local communities," Jessa says. "Our work comes *from* communities, *for* communities, *to* communities, for many years to come."

"As a young person, it's really easy to be disregarded by a lot of the old politicians and leaders who think youth are inadequate, just not capable of doing something." To strengthen their position, Jessa says, "We put everything on paper. When we write to politicians, we make sure everything is in black and white, everything is well reported and well published. We have good records, so people can see that we're actually doing the work."

Jessa works with local people to help them understand how their lands are being ravaged by illegal logging, mining, monocropping, poaching, and wildlife trade "Conservation work is stronger when it's backed up by strong science," she adds. "Thanks to our research, two amphibians that were lost track of for about four or five decades were rediscovered." Strong scientific rediscoveries like this have enabled Jessa to lobby more effectively to various stakeholders and government agencies.

Now at age 29, the heart of Jessa's work is focusing on conserving the forests, building on her success with the Cleopatra's Needle Critical Habitat Project. "Five years ago when I started this project, I said to myself that protecting Cleopatra's Needle conserve, 41,350 hectares of land, is enough of a legacy for me to my hometown." She knew this is her island's best protection against climate change. "To be honest, it's really addicting," Jessa admits. "You just want to go out and declare more areas for conservation." Their new goal is 300,000 hectares, more than three quarters of a million acres.

"It's very easy for people with initiatives and vision to just barge into a community and say, 'Hey, this is what we think you should do. One thing we've learned is to be really good at drinking coffee," Jessa says, with a smile. "We spend a lot of time sitting down with community members, especially with Indigenous people in their communities, and just drinking coffee with them. We hang out with them at their homes, and really try to listen to them, and build connections."

Jessa credits CSPH's success partly with being a small organization. "We've spent a lot of time really getting to know the people, showing them how sincere we are in the work we're doing. We've invested so much in doing community organizing work, really being out there. Our flagship project, saving the Almaciga tree, was conceived because of the time we had spent in the communities. It's very important to the Indigenous communities. And it's the first ever seed-based propagation of the Almaciga tree species."

As a nation of 7,000 islands, the Philippines is one of the most vulnerable to climate change. "We're seeing a lot of devastation happening in our communities due to climate change," Jessa says. Entire islands have been wiped out by typhoons, earthquakes, and tsunamis. Until now, Palawan has remained safe, but the rain patterns are unpredictable, and this affects farmers and food supplies. Jessa works with the vanishing Batak tribe. With just 200 people left, they live near river systems. As the rains become stronger year by year, the rivers flow higher, houses are devastated, forests are destroyed. Since the Batak are hunter- gatherers who still live by those traditions, if the forests are destroyed, there's no food for them. "The Batak people I work with, they're actually hungry; they don't have enough food to gather."

One of Jessa's biggest lessons learned is to be reflective. "When you do a lot of work in the environment, it's not easy," she admits. "A lot of people don't like to hear about what went wrong," she explains. "There's actually very little published about the failures in conservation work. And while it's great to see success stories, it's also important to reflect on what the failures are. To reflect on the past so we can actually take that on into something more, something bigger, something smarter. So we strive to account for all the things that went wrong for us."

In 2019 Jessa was invited to Geneva, Switzerland by the Conservation of International Trade in Endangered Species (CITES). As part of the technical advisory group for the Philippine delegation, voting on the Endemic Species Trade, Jessa lobbied for the Asian small-clawed otters, who are found only in Palawan. "We won, and got it listed in the CITES Appendix I," she says. "It was a big success for me as a young person, in such a very big and really old audience. It was such an empowering experience, to be able to influence other countries to do something about conserving animals that are present in your own hometown."

Each year Jessa joins in the Feast of the Forests, to reconnect with her community, and with nature, to get her hands dirty, and plant trees. "I look up to a lot of the women leaders in my community; they are my heroines," she says.

Jessa is also aligned with Greta Thunberg's 30 by 30 Campaign, to take immediate actions by 2030. "That's the path we're on; we want to conserve as much forest as possible in the next 10 years. We're lobbying our partners, our stakeholders, our donors, telling them that we have to conserve 30 percent of the Earth's surface to ensure good sources of clean water, fresh air for our habitats, and for biodiversity. We must act now, and act fast!"

"It is about time that the younger generation take the spotlight in conservation," she adds. "In my country alone 30 percent of voters today are young people. Together, we can stand strong and demand the change we need. It's time for the older generations to listen to us." She sighs, and adds, "So now that youth are standing up, and their voice is getting louder, it's time for them to give us the opportunity."

"If we as youth all act together, support each other, and help each other rise up, the impact we can have is unimaginable."

Ang Kabataan Pag-Asa Ng Bayan
The youth are the hope of the future.

Jose Rizal

Call to Action: Empower local people to protect your lands. Know your rights. Get it on paper. Learn about Jessa's work here: http://www.centreforsustainabilityPH.org/

WE ARE THE LEADERS OF TODAY
Kevin J. Patel
One Up Action
Los Angeles, California

Kevin J. Patel was sitting in class one day, listening to his teacher, when suddenly he realized that something was wrong. At first his teacher didn't believe him -- and he remembered that that morning he *had* drunk a lot of coffee, so maybe that was why he felt so strange. But it felt more serious than that; his heart was racing, and he could barely breathe. Finally, he went to see the school nurse, who immediately called an ambulance, and Kevin's parents. When he got to the hospital, his heart was beating at 200-300 beats per minute.

"I will remember that day for the rest of my life," Kevin says. "That one moment changed my life forever."

Kevin started researching. He was wondering why a healthy boy like himself, who was physically active, had regular check-ups, and had never had any prior health problems, would suddenly get such serious heart palpitations.

His health scare had serious consequences. For two years, he was in and out of the hospital. When they saw him, his schoolmates would ask him in a surprised tone if he had changed schools. "I knew that I was being affected by air pollution and smog, because my neighborhood is so heavily polluted," Kevin says. "What else would cause a heart issue like this?" And he adds, "A lot of other members of my community were getting heart issues as well."

Kevin lives in South Los Angeles, a community that he himself describes as marginalized. There are many issues in his neighborhood he says -- homelessness, no access to healthy foods, and of course, air pollution. Already in middle school he had been advocating on the issue of food inequality. "Our community is essentially a food prison," he says. "We don't have access to good food, organic foods, like more affluent communities have."

As an Indian-Asian-American in a mostly African-American and Latin-X community, Kevin had always felt marginalized, within a marginalized population. In school, there were clubs and resources for other members of his community, but he was often the odd one out. So in ninth grade, when he returned to school after the incident with his heart, Kevin decided to start his own club, to deal with the issue that had affected him on such a personal level: he started an Environmental Club.

To his surprise, and delight, the club was a huge success. For the first meeting, more than 100 students showed up; they couldn't all fit into one classroom. Over the next four years, Kevin's Environmental Club tackled issues like reducing food waste, often combining their environmental work with other societal problems, to create synergies. For example, they installed bins at the school to collect dry food items from students who would have otherwise thrown them into the trash, and donated the collected items to organizations working with the homeless.

They also got everyone to help with recycling: whenever someone on campus would find a bottle, they could throw them into the recycling bins put up by the Environmental Club. The club then used the money generated from recycling the bottles to donate to food banks.

"It was astonishing to see how much of a success we were," Kevin remembers. "It was a real change within our school. They're still continuing this project today."

Both as a student who had been interested in food issues from an early age, and then as an environmental justice activist after his heart problems began, Kevin feels he didn't have much of a choice.

"My activism is literally a survival tool," he says. "It's something I have to do, in order to make sure that my community has a voice."

Kevin had known about the facts of climate change for a long time: as a child he wanted to become a botanist, so he knew about the effect of global warming on plants. But because he is from a low-income neighborhood, he argues that his community is particularly affected by climate change.

"We are given little to no resources to combat these issues," he says. "We also have deadly fossil fuel infrastructure in our communities. Many affluent communities are not as affected by the climate crisis as much as marginalized communities like mine are."

Over the years, Kevin became a well-known activist. He has introduced motions in Los Angeles County, and for some time he also worked with a number of nonprofit organizations, like Zero Hour, Ignition Green, and the Student Climate Emergency Coalition. He has also given a lot of talks at protests and other climate action events. For some time he joined the Fridays For Future movement, and was trying to convince as many people as possible that it's high time to act.

"We really need to start taking action; this is not a time to wait around for change to happen through our government officials," he says. "It's really up to us to take up the mantle, and start taking action."

Kevin is also one of the UN ambassadors for the Together Band Initiative, which is fighting for implementation of the UN's 17 Sustainable Development Goals. And it was right before the 2019 UN Climate Summit, during the worldwide Strike for the Climate, that a vague idea that Kevin had had before began to take concrete shape. He started One Up Action, an organization that provides climate activists from marginalized communities with support and resources, to help them uplift their ideas to address the climate crisis and make them a reality.

"I started working on One Up Action because I saw that young changemakers and activists don't have the resources they need to make their ideas become a reality," Kevin explains. "I really wanted to create an organization that can give funds to young changemakers, or help them by providing them with connections and opportunities, or just help them with individual actions."

His organization started working in four different areas: they successfully set up a Youth Climate Commission in L.A. County; they started a Community Science Program, which supports local changemakers; they have started chapters of their organization in 32 countries around the world; and they introduced their action chapter program, to support activists on the ground in their initiatives.

"Young people are very, very smart," Kevin says. "We are not only the leaders of tomorrow. We are the leaders of today."

And, for him, that is what the first-ever Youth Climate Commission in the world is all about. It will connect 25 young changemakers in Los Angeles who act in the capacity of commissioners, and give their feedback and input on climate initiatives to the L.A County administration.

"Their feedback is key," Kevin says. "Whatever feedback the local government receives, they have to take it into account; they have to make the changes in order for their communities to be impacted in the right way."

For Kevin, this model is an efficient way for young people to have a voice in climate governance. One Up Action wants to introduce even more such commissions in the United States, and in cities across the world. That's why they are working closely with the C40 Cities Climate Leadership Group -- an association of 97 cities around the world that are dedicated to taking decisive climate action.

In Los Angeles, One Up Action has already been successful with their model of youth participation. "When it was time for all the supervisors to vote on this, they all voted yes. No one voted no on it," Kevin remembers. "Then they announced that the Youth Climate Commission had passed unanimously, and the room just erupted. There was so much excitement!"

Kevin feels that his prior work as an activist was an important factor in his efforts to get the Youth Climate Commission started in L.A. The connections he had built, and having an already elevated status that gave his voice weight helped him organize the community and exert pressure. But it was never easy -- and one of the most important lessons he learned, he says, is that you can never give up in the face of an obstacle. "It's an uphill battle," he says. "But in the face of adversity, people need to step up. You should never be deterred from doing the work you love, or the work that you want to do."

There's never been a ticking time bomb hanging over our heads.
You know, this isn't one war or one issue in one place.
This is the future of the entire planet.

Jane Fonda

Call to Action: Make yourself heard about climate initiatives in your hometown. Join the discussion about what is being done on the issues that directly affect you. Get the support you need from One Up Action: http://oneupaction.org

WE WILL ROCK THIS!
Linus Dolder
Switzerland

Linus Dolder has been an environmentalist from an early age. It all began with a letter that arrived at his house one day: it wasn't meant for him. It was actually addressed to his mother, but Linus saw it first. This was before he knew how to read, but his interest was piqued by the picture on the envelope: it was of a dead turtle, tangled up in a fishnet.

Linus asked his big brother to open the letter and read it out loud to him. What he heard shocked him: it was a report about how big industries were emitting chemicals and toxic waste, and using the planet as a garbage dump. "I just really wanted to do something about it," Linus says. "I wanted to know why these companies were doing something so destructive; something that would cause so much damage."

Now 17, that feeling of outrage, he says, has remained with him to this day.

Linus sprang into action. He got together with a couple of friends and started baking. Their idea was simple: they would bake delicious cookies, sell them, and donate their earnings to environmental organizations, for projects that were fighting against climate change. His parents supported him, not only by allowing him to take over the kitchen for his baking projects, but also by challenging him in his convictions.

"They're supportive, they often say, it's great what you're doing," he says. "But they also question me, and help me to reflect on what I'm doing." The animated debates over many family meals helped Linus strengthen his ability to justify the positions he takes. They would talk about activism and civil disobedience, or discuss the roots of the climate crisis in our economic system. Once, Linus wanted to discuss Obama's foreign policy at 7 a.m., before his mother had had her coffee. "She was a bit overwhelmed, although she is normally an early riser," he says. "I think these discussions were kind of a nice training for activism."

One day Linus started to realize how the environment right in his own back yard was rapidly changing. Since he was a small child, he'd loved looking out his bedroom window at the snowy peaks of the Bernese mountains, rising majestically above the clear blue water of Lake Thun, a layer of snow and ice covering the mountaintops. But he began to notice a change in the picturesque landscape. He could see that the snow and ice, which had appeared so ageless and so immovable to him all of his life, was slowly starting to disappear.

Linus knows these mountains well: he is a good skier, and he often hikes in the mountains with his family. He cherishes a memory from one family trek to the Aletsch glacier, the largest glacier in the Alps, near his home. His parents had taken a picture of him and his brother there, with the mighty glacier in the background, when they were young children. Ten years later, they took another picture of them, standing in the same place. This photo would prove to Linus that the climate crisis had arrived at his doorstep. Something had changed.

"There was no glacier in the background anymore," he says, sadly. "It was just gone."

Once he realized that the snowcaps on the summits of the Bernese mountains really *were* slowly disappearing, baking alone no longer seemed a sufficient response. So, in December 2018, right before the Christmas break, Linus once more got together with a couple of his friends: and this time they decided they would call for a climate strike in Thun.

It was a Wednesday night when Linus asked around in his school who would join in a climate strike the next day. Sixty people said they would join. But that wasn't enough for Linus and his friends; they wanted to have an even bigger event. So they printed flyers, sent a press release to the local newspaper, asked everyone to tell their friends and family, and to help them spread the word in their sports clubs and music groups.

For the next event, 800 people turned up.

"We all felt so empowered, because we just put tons of effort in," Linus says. "We got young people to take to the streets all over Switzerland. We got them to raise their voices. It felt so great!"

Although Linus got the climate strikes started in his hometown, he feels that much more needs to be done. As a youth movement, he and others have managed to spread the word and get their message out: *Climate Action Now*! "That should have been the point where the government takes action," he says. "But I feel like we are the ones who have to do it, because we are the ones that will be left with the pieces if nothing happens."

With its 40,000 inhabitants, the small city of Thun isn't exactly the most likely epicenter of climate activism in the country. "Switzerland has the second largest GDP per capita in the world," Linus says. "To me, that means it has a special responsibility in the fight against climate change. It's just so frustrating that they seem to not care." He adds, "We now *know* that this can be different: the climate strikes have moved online because of COVID-19. This has led governments around the world to take unprecedented action."

For Linus, this goes to show that if governments want to act, they can. He points out that industrialized countries, including Switzerland, have contributed the most to the situation we're in. So they are the ones who should be leading the effort to fight climate change. But at the moment, they are failing to fulfill even their meager commitments to help less developed countries with the loss and damages caused by the climate crisis. In 2015, at COP 21 in Paris, a hundred billion dollars were pledged to support the countries that are most vulnerable to climate change. But the money has never arrived.

"One hundred billion dollars is actually the budget that's spent on nuclear weapons every year," said Linus. "That's just kind of killing me, how they set priorities."

Luckily, Linus is not alone in his outrage. In an article for the German newspaper *taz*, Linus described his experience participating in the events surrounding the COP 25 negotiations in Madrid in 2019. There, climate strikers from all continents came together to share their experiences and perspectives on the climate crisis. They got up at 7:00 in the morning for working sessions on strategy and communications, and met with activists and politicians. They even met with Svenja Schulze, the German Minister of the Environment, to plead their case and demand urgent action.

"Campaigning is interesting for me," Linus says. "Thinking of which groups of society you want to address, what the message is, what the key points are if we want them to come to the strikes."

In March 2020 Linus went to Brussels with Fridays for Future representatives from all across Europe, to demand urgent climate action from the European Union. "It was amazing to see people out on the streets for climate justice; we will fight until we win," he says. Since many of the events had been cancelled because of the COVID-19 pandemic, members of the European parliament instead came to meet with these youth, to discuss the European Green Deal. "The Green Deal carbon emissions reduction targets are too low; 55 percent by 2050 is

NOT enough," Linus says. "Governments must increase their ambition for 2030 targets if we are to keep global temperatures under 1.5 degrees."

Of course campaigning and activism take time. That is why Linus's high school agreed to give him academic leave for one semester. He is now a full-time activist and plans to spend some of his time in France to work on his language skills. He knows that this will be time well spent. "With good campaigning and smart strategic moves, we're actually able to change some things," he says. And he adds, "There is nothing, at the moment, that makes me happier."

Linus's dedication to activism means that he has less time for his hobbies, like photography, basketball, and skiing. But he knows that it is a race against time to save the snowy peaks he loves. He also knows that he is not alone in this fight. "To all the amazing activists and trailblazers out there: we will rock this," he says. "We will keep fighting until we win!"

And to everyone else, he adds, "You do have a voice; and of course you want a future. So use the former to protect the latter!"

In the Andes and the Alps I have seen melting glaciers.
At both the Earth's poles, I have seen open seas where ice once dominated the horizon.

Ban Ki-Moon, Former Secretary General of the United Nations

Call to Action: Speak up. You will find people who are willing to stand with you in the fight against climate change. www.fridaysforfuture.org. You can follow Linus on Twitter: https://twitter.com/linusdolder and @ linusdolder

YOUTH UNSTOPPABLE
Slater Jewell-Kemker
Canada

"I am passing the baton to you," said Jean-Michel Cousteau, as he handed 12-year-old Slater the delicate skeleton of a sea urchin.

Slater had been invited to visit the island where the famous marine biologist and documentary filmmaker had started a children's camp, where youth could learn about ocean sustainability.

It all started when, the year before, Slater had written an essay for the MY HERO project. The assignment was to write about someone who inspired her. For Slater, the choice was clear. She had reached out to Jean-Michel Cousteau because she admired his work as an environmentalist, and his friendly and open way of talking to people.

Not only did the famous oceanographic explorer answer her questions: he invited Slater to come visit the camp. "That was the first time I felt like someone who was very important took me seriously, and wanted to listen to what I had to say," she says. "He was a big influence for me."

When she met him in person, she recorded a video interview with him. At the time she was working as a youth journalist with the My Hero project, a website that shared inspiring stories on the internet. With a father who was a writer, and a mother who was a film producer, Slater had always been in love with telling stories. She made her first film when she was only six years old. "It was a musical, and I wrote all the lyrics and the music. And I made my parents act and sing it," she says. The same week she also shot another film, which she starred in herself, along with her dog. It was entitled *The Girl and the Talking Dog*.

Slater also loved watching movies. When she 14 years old, she sat in her parents' living room and watched *An Inconvenient Truth*, a documentary made by Davis Guggenheim, about global warming. It was eye-opening for her. "I remember about halfway into the film, I started crying and I didn't really stop for about four or five hours," she says. "It scared the hell out of me. It wasn't something that I understood or knew how to fix, and the people who ***could*** fix it were not doing anything."

Slater felt betrayed. All of her life she had been told that she had

105

opportunities in her life, things that she could do and dreams she could realize if she wanted to. Suddenly, she started to question this. "None of it felt like it was real anymore, because there was this big thing called climate change rising up in the middle of my life, that made everything uncertain and unstable," she says. "And I wanted to *do* something. I wanted to be the person who had tried to do everything they could."

Slater was born in Los Angeles. Her house had a tiny backyard and it wasn't really safe for her to walk around the neighborhood. She constantly heard the blaring of sirens, and her school would have lockdowns semi-regularly, every time someone tried to rob the bank down the street. But when she was nine, she and her parents moved to a farm outside of Toronto.

"I think it really shaped the kind of person that I am, being able to spend days and days out in the woods, learning different bird calls," she says. "And just feeling like I was one small organism in this greater ecosystem."

Spending so much of her life in nature taught Slater an appreciation and awareness for the changing seasons, and the constant circle of life and death all around her. She also learned more about climate change, and the more she learned, the more she began to question political leaders and authority figures. If the people who were in a position to do something about climate change had decided not to do anything, then who would? *If they aren't willing to act, they should step aside,* she thought.

In May 2008, when she was 15, Slater went to the Youth Environmental G8 Summit in Japan. For the first time, she got to meet young people from all over the world whose lives were being impacted by climate change. And they had *all* had enough.

Slater brought her camera to the summit. There she made lifelong friends, and it was also there that she started what would become a 12-year documentary film project. She decided she would tell the story of the environmental youth movement from within. The result was a documentary entitled *Youth Unstoppable.*

"It was literally just me with a backpack and a camera, but I was lucky to have the support of two producers, my mom and Daniel Bekerman, who trusted me enough to follow my intuition. My mom went with me to most of the countries, and organized on the ground to get the footage we needed."

After the summit in Japan, Slater went on to travel to a number of other climate conferences, (COPs), in Copenhagen, Cancun, Paris, Poland, and Madrid, and she always brought her camera.

In Mexico, she would get up at 6:00 in the morning, take a bus to the conference venue, and go through strict security controls. Then she would talk to young environmentalists and try to find good people to interview.

"You go in, and there are just hundreds and hundreds of people surrounding you, everyone going seemingly in opposite directions," she says. "I was by myself, working 14 hours a day and then going back at the end of the day, downloading all of the SD cards onto my hard drive." Then she would sleep for five hours and do the same thing again the next day.

At the conferences, she would simply walk up to people and ask them questions. "At the beginning, I would have to say that a lot of it was adrenaline fueled by terror," she says, laughing. But soon she realized that she was actually in a position of power: she had the ability to share these people's stories, and they needed their stories to be heard.

But it was also exhausting. "It was too overwhelming," she says. "Climate activism forces you to deal with worst-case scenarios, to ask difficult questions. It makes you question a lot of the things that make up your life." She pauses, then adds, "And you do that alongside the frustration of seeing that year after year people are not taking it seriously, people are not doing what they need to do, governments aren't taking it seriously."

One thing that kept Slater going is the friendships she made along the way with other young climate activists. "It was a lot of fun," she says. "You're going up against something, and you feel like what you're doing is right. You feel this sense of camaraderie, being part of this community that has a purpose."

Besides, giving up the fight against climate change had never been an option for Slater. "I think we all share this feeling that this is the most important thing we've ever come across," she says. "It's a mixture of perseverance and stubbornness, but it's also the feeling that I am doing something that might actually matter. That it might affect other people, and create positive change."

In December 2015, after filming for eight years, Slater thought that she had found an ending for her movie. She was in Paris; and after having been disappointed so many times before, it seemed like finally there would be a global agreement to act on climate change.

"I was a bit wary of the excitement that was building about the Paris Climate Agreement, because I had seen that same thing happen before," Slater says. "But it also felt like it really was an opportunity, that this could potentially finally happen."

After a particularly long day of filming, Slater was on the way to a youth art space outside of the French capital, when suddenly her phone began to ring. The Paris Agreement had passed! Emails and texts started coming in like mad; some of her friends were celebrating the Accord; others were disappointed that the deal wouldn't be legally binding.

"I was very confused about how to feel," Slater says. "Because it felt like a victory; at the same time, it felt like it wasn't enough."

But, overall, Slater decided to look on the bright side: the way she saw it, this deal was an opportunity to finally stop bickering and get to work on the problem. That's why she thought she finally had the ending for her film.

But it still didn't feel quite right, and she still had lingering doubts. "It was like, oh, is that it?" Slater says. "*Is* this the end of the film? Did we really win?"

Then in 2016, when Donald Trump was elected President of the United States, it felt like a backlash to the successful environmental movement that had made the Paris Agreement possible. So Slater kept on filming: and within a couple of years, the environmental movement had come back in full force, led by a young Swedish activist who caught the world's imagination, and who helped bring together the energy of other dynamic and devoted youth leaders from around the world.

"To see Greta, Luisa, Jamie, and Xiuhtezcatl, and all the climate strikes, it's incredibly beautiful and inspiring and exciting, after trying for so long to have young people's voices be heard," she says. "The school strike movement has become such a worldwide phenomenon! Seeing millions and millions of people out in the streets, it's incredible. It's amazing!"

In the end Slater worked on *Youth Unstoppable* for 12 years. She shot over 500 hours of footage, and spent 19 months editing. It was finally released in 2018, and has played in over 100 film festivals worldwide, and has garnered 13 awards to date.

This film paints a clear picture of the roots of the youth climate action movement. "I've had young people come up to me and say that, for the first time, they felt like they were actually spoken to as human beings and not just spoken down to," she says. "And I've had older people come up to me and say that they had lost all hope. And that they feel re-inspired; that our generation actually cares and is doing something."

Slater still has the little sea urchin that Jean-Michel Cousteau gave to her all those years ago, after listening closely to what she had to say. "We're all in this together," she says. "I think we need to truly listen to each other, and allow ourselves to be inspired; and to re-inspire each other with our stories. Because the only way we're going to fix all of these problems is together."

To be truly radical is to make hope possible, rather than despair convincing.

Raymond Williams

Call to Action: VOTE. And if you're too young to vote, make sure the people around you are educated, and vote for representatives who care about the future of our planet. It will take all of us, but we can adapt if we work together. You can follow Slater's work at www.youthunstoppable.com, @slaterfilms and on YU socials https://linktr.ee/YouthUnstoppable

MOCK COP26 LETTER TO WORLD LEADERS

Date: 01 December 2020
From: MockCOP26Delegates
To: The Heads of State of all countries, and the Secretary General of the UN

Dear Leaders

Re: Our treaty for urgent climate action this side of COP26

We are writing to inform you that **we, the young people of 140 countries, ran our own inclusive online climate conference, Mock COP26**, which we concluded today. In light of the Covid-19 pandemic, many of you presumably thought it was a lesser priority to take climate action through the UNFCCC COP this year, and hence the UN postponed it. We remind you that we are still in a climate emergency as well as an ecological crisis and every moment of inaction makes things worse for our generation. We felt strongly that you should not further delay action, so we decided to run our own youth-led COP this year. We are tired of empty climate promises and are purely motivated by a desire to see real action.

With just three months of planning, we delivered a full two-week global conference, from 19 November to 01 December 2020, comprising 330 delegates, ages 11 to 30, representing 140 countries. **We set out to improve upon the structures of the real COP to reflect the mandate of young people to build inclusive, equitable and fair systems.** We made the following improvements:

- Our conference amplified the voices of marginalised and underrepresented communities. We made time to hear the uncomfortable truths about the Global North's neglect for the most vulnerable people in our world, and we recognised the valiant efforts of the leaders of nations who have contributed least to climate change but whose people are suffering first and worst;

- We actively sought the advice and experience of Indigenous elders, whose innate knowledge of, and respect for, our dependence on the natural world has mostly been ignored;

- We did not allow any corporate lobbyists into our Mock COP26 and were free to think outside growth-based economic narratives. We were not shackled by political short-termism or national self-interest. We gave science, optimism and ambition the centre-stage and were not held back by the pace of the slowest;

- 72% of our delegates were from the Global South; 63% were female or non-binary; delegates' average age was 22. The student staff team of eighteen young people was a 50% Global North / Global South split, with 73% of student staff female or non-binary.

- Our conference was run entirely online, resulting in just c14 tonnes of CO_2 emissions, compared to c40,000 tonnes from the real COP.

Through the process of high-level statements made by delegates and policy caucuses, and a voting process on amendments, **we formed our legal treaty, which is attached** to this letter.

We ask that each and every one of you reads our treaty and considers, with an open mind, what you can do to implement our policy asks in your country, whilst also building consensus for high ambition at COP26. Prior to Covid-19 we were of the view that governments were both unwilling and unable to take urgent joined-up action in response to an emergency. However, in the past few months, you have delivered dramatic unilateral and multilateral measures to mitigate the threat of the virus. We now ask you to take equally dramatic and urgent action to stop the threats we face from the climate emergency and ecological crisis.

Please act with urgency to enact all, or part, of our treaty in your own country in the run-up to COP26. You can register your intention to implement our treaty by contacting us at treaty@mockcop. org and treaty@sos-uk.org. Your national delegates, or our international student staff team, are available to meet with you, at your convenience, to brief you on Mock COP26 and discuss how we can support you in implementing our treaty.

Yours very sincerely,

Youth of the World

Mock COP26 Delegates

II
—
RESPECT
Environmental Justice
Changemakers

RESPECT:
Environmental Justice Changemakers

As we closed the Stone Soup Leadership Institute's event honoring the 35th Anniversary of Dr. Martin Luther King Jr.'s "I Have a Dream" speech, I leaned over to tell U.S. Congressman John Lewis, "We're going to sing *We Shall Overcome.*" He stood straight up, crossed his arms in front of him, and declared, "This is how Martin taught us to sing it." It was such an honor to stand alongside this legendary man, singing this Civil Rights anthem, and feeling the power flowing from his hand to mine. His speech at that event still resonates: "Don't give up," he said. "Don't become bitter. Don't get lost in a sea of despair. Keep the faith. Keep your eyes on the prize. Hold onto your dreams. Walk with the wind. Let the spirit of history be your guide."

I'd only recently learned that in 1965 my father, as a lay leader of our Catholic Church, had responded to Dr. King's call for religious leaders to join him for the Civil Rights March from Selma to Montgomery, Alabama. Upon his return, he was a changed man. To share the essence of this powerful experience with his family, he bought a guitar and taught his children to sing "We Shall Overcome." And to honor Dr. King and his legacy, the Stone Soup Leadership Institute now closes all of our events by singing that same song.

A few years later, when Congressman Lewis and I met again at a book signing, I told him about my new book. I asked for his permission to feature his story as a young man, when he marched with Dr. King in Selma, and had helped to create SNCC (the Student Nonviolent Organizing Committee), which played a key role in the Civil Rights movement. He gave me his blessing, so we could inspire young people to carry on his legacy. His passing last year was a great loss for our country.

It has been so rewarding to be able to feature stories in this book about young people who are carrying on Congressman Lewis's spirit; people like Jerome Foster II, who served as one of his interns. Jerome was inspired to found OneMillionOfUS, a nonprofit voting advocacy organization that galvanized the resources needed to facilitate an active voter turnout among youth for the 2020 election. And like Ilai Kenney, who lived in Congressman Lewis's district of Clayton County, and was outraged that her generation's right to a healthy, sustainable future was being ruined by bad decisions being made by older people. Ilai at age 14 won the Broward Award, for creating Georgia Kids Against Pollution. Raised in Alabama, Destiny Hughes was painfully aware there weren't many young Black environmental activists at Howard University, so she founded Generation Green, a network to help them share resources, and connect them with other activists in the U.S. and around the world.

These young Black leaders know that climate change and global warming impact women, minorities, marginalized peoples, and Indigenous communities disproportionately compared to the rest of the country. In the African American community alone, 71 percent of the people live in areas where the air quality is unsafe because of their proximity to industrial manufacturing, and other factors. "I can't breathe" has become a rallying cry against both police brutality and institutionalized systemic racism. The intolerable inequities of having their neighborhoods used as toxic waste dumps, along with the lack of funding for schools, jobs, and economic insecurity, create a vicious cycle of poverty and crime, which is at the intersectionality of climate change. After learning about the contaminated water in Flint, Michigan, Jaden Smith used his star power to get companies to bring clean water to this devastated community. And when Ferguson, Missouri erupted in the wake of the death of Michael Brown, Carmen Perez worked alongside the actor and activist Harry Belafonte and other Black Lives Matter leaders to create The Gathering for Justice. Belafonte, a friend of Dr. King, is also legendary in the Civil Rights movement. "Whenever we got into trouble or when tragedy struck, Harry has always come to our aid, his generous heart wide open," said Coretta Scott King.

Indigenous peoples are even more adversely affected. Their spirits have been robbed by centuries of broken promises, and their loss of tribal lands to corporate greed adds insult to injury. At age 15, Standing Rock Sioux youth leader Tokata Iron Eyes inspired Greta Thunberg with her fearless resistance to the Dakota Access Pipeline. In this book, I'm honored to shine the light on Indigenous leaders like Evon Peters, who was the youngest chief of the Alaskan Gwich'in Nation; water rights champion Autumn Peltier of the Anishinabek Nation in Canada; Lucia Ixchíu, of Guatemala's K'iche' Maya people; Mitzi Jonelle Ton from the Philippines, who is working with Indigenous fisherfolk; and Xiye Bastida, an Indigenous rights leader from the Otemi-Toltec people in Mexico, who now lives in New York City, and is leading Re-Earth to support the Escazu peoples.

Over the years, I've been on a quest to deepen my awareness and appreciation for my own Indigenous roots. My father's mother was from the Abenaki Nation in Peru, New York. I first learned about sustainability from her; she reused everything at least once. When I was 25 years old, living on the land as an herbalist and health educator in Clarksburg, California, I was invited to be on the medicine team for the Lakota Sundance at the D-Q University in Davis, California. Dennis Banks, from the Pine Ridge Reservation in South Dakota, was famously known for his use of hot sweats, which he believed strengthened one's prayers, for our ancestors and for the world. We were taught to ask permission before entering the lodge, and to say *Mitakuye Oyasin* ("All My Relations"). It was there that I met the Hopi elder, Thomas Banyacya, who was chosen to reveal the Hopi prophecies for the future. A few years later I was invited to the Indigenous Peoples Sunrise Ceremonies on Alcatraz Island, called the "Unthanksgiving." There I met Bedeaux Wesaw, who was also from Pine Ridge, and who led sweat lodges in Sebastopol.

My Indigenous friends have been my greatest teachers. It has been an honor to work alongside my lifelong friend Nane Alejandrez from Barrios Unidos, who serves as the Institute's medicine man. On Vieques Nane led a feather ceremony at El Hombre de Puerto Ferro, where the skeleton of a 4,000-year-old medicine man was discovered, to initiate one of our youth leaders. We then worked with a local artisan who, as the last of the Taino blood line, showed our young people how to create Indigenous designs and handicrafts using local seeds and calabash.

In Hawaii, Nane and I paid our respects to my Hawaiian *kupuna*, Keala Ching, and my dear friend Kaiulani Pono and her students at the Kanu o ka 'Aina Learning 'Ohana. There I developed a deep respect for the Hawaiian values, traditions, and sustainable practices that are the foundation for their intensive immersion program, which teaches the Hawaiian concept of *mālama* -- caring for the *'aina*, the land. Later our Hawaiian youth leader and I were invited to the Asian Pacific Economic (APEC) Summit, where Nainoa Thompson announced the three-year journey around the world with the Polynesian Voyaging Society's *Hōkūle'a*. Two years later, when this traditional Hawaiian voyaging canoe arrived on Martha's Vineyard during our Sustainability Summit, our Hawaii youth leader, Elijah Anakalea-Buckley, and our Wampanoag youth leader, Skyler Cameron, were the first to welcome them with their handmade leis. By honoring Indigenous youth leaders we can show our respect and help them preserve their culture, their way of life.

It is an honor to shine the light on these brave youth leaders, who are carrying on the legacies of their elders, working hard to undo the damage that has been done to our planet -- and to build a better future for their people.

AN INDIGENOUS LEADER
Evon Peter
Alaska

Evon Peter lived in a one-room cabin with his uncle and grandfather, in Vashraįį K'ǫǫ (Arctic Village), an Alaskan village located in the Gwazhal (Brooks) mountain range, about 1900 miles above the Arctic Circle. In this community of around 100 people there was no electricity or running water, but you could walk for nearly 100 miles in any direction and be surrounded by nature. The Gwich'in nation villages, some located in Alaska, and some in Canada, are along the migratory route of the porcupine caribou herd, a primary food source for the Gwich'in people. Whitefish, grayling, pike, and salmon migrate through the river systems, and ducks and geese migrate in the spring and fall. As a child, Evon's job was to haul water from the river, where they kept a hole in the ice throughout the winter. He carried five-gallon buckets of water on a wooden yoke over his shoulders. His family kept a fire going day and night.

Despite what seems like a storied childhood steeped in natural beauty, Evon faced challenges early in his life. The public education offered in his village was sub-par, with just one teacher for grades 6-12. Evon's mother moved them to Fairbanks for junior high school so he could receive a better education. It was during this time that Evon remembers being brought into a room with 14 other Alaska Native boys, where a counselor told them that they were more likely to end up dead or in jail by the time they were 25 than they were to graduate high school. Sadly, his words proved true. Of the 14 boys, one committed suicide and only one or two finished high school.

When he was 16 years old, Evon had an epiphany about the profound inequities between the Native and non-Native peoples in Alaska. "We are not taught in our schools about the history of colonization and the assimilation of Indigenous peoples; and the trauma and social challenges that persist in many Indigenous communities as a reflection of those experiences," he says. "And there is a continued colonization of Indigenous peoples that persists to this day as well."

He had learned about the boarding schools his mother had been sent to, where they were not allowed to speak their language, and told that

118

their spiritual practices and traditions were wrong, and that they must be forgotten if they wanted to fit into society. This deeply affected his mother, who demonstrated symptoms of a "heart wound," Evon says. When Evon was growing up, his mother would sometimes lock herself in her room and cry.

Evon had dropped out of high school, but later he argued for admission into the University of Alaska Fairbanks (UAF), where he received his BA in Alaska Native Studies, with a minor in Political Science. As a college student, he became active in student government, where he organized and co-led a Native student organization. These experiences launched him on his lifelong quest to learn about the history and laws that have contributed to the suffering of Alaskan Indigenous communities. "I learned that my grandparents weren't citizens of the United States when they were young," says Evon. "They didn't have the right to own land or own a business. They were explicitly discriminated against in our own homelands." So it was with great pride, and deeply personal, that Evon testified in February 2020 in a state legislative hearing on behalf of his people, for the passing of HB 221, a bill which formally recognizes the tribal sovereignty of 229 Alaska Native tribes.

In his early 20's Evon became the youngest chief in the Alaskan interior. He attributes this honor to being raised with strong roots in his Gwich'in identity, and a drive to acquire Western education as well. "I spent the next three years struggling to lead my people and learning the realities of being an Indigenous leader, subject to the powers of the state and federal governments," he says.

Because to a great extent Alaskan people live off the land, Evon is greatly concerned about how his people will survive. "When I was younger, it was not uncommon to face 65 degree below zero weather for a week at a time," he says. Over the years, there has been a shift upward of approximately 13 degrees in winter, and the change has had an undeniable impact on the people living in the Arctic. Lakes are either drying up or are flooded, depending upon where they are, and on how the thawing permafrost is affecting local geography. This leads to increased erosion, especially in coastal areas, and also in the river systems.

"We're seeing a shift in the types of animals and species that are showing up, or no longer showing up, in our lands," Evon says. "We had a major die-off in the Koyukuk River just this last summer. They're speculating that the thousands of salmon that died in that river died because the water was too warm. They overheated and couldn't make it up to their spawning grounds." Evon also believes that agricultural pollutants used in other parts of the world are migrating into the Arctic. "It's impacting the health and well-being of our people," he says.

In 2014 Evon was appointed Vice Chancellor for Rural, Community, and Native Education at UAF, which is the largest producer of Arctic research worldwide. The chancellor of UAF is committed to strengthening global leadership in Indigenous programs, including the preservation and documenting of Native languages that are at risk of disappearing. "I never in my wildest dreams imagined I would ever be a vice chancellor at a university," says Evon, who quickly realized the position gave him the opportunity to reshape education in Alaska, by modifying both the curriculum and the teaching methods. He was responsible for managing six community campuses across the state, serving students with 14 different Indigenous languages, coming from 140 tribal governments, and 160 communities. "I've been able to engage with so many young people," he says, a note of gratitude in his voice.

Central to the career path that led him to his role as vice chancellor was Evon's work as executive director of Native Movement, a nonprofit organization he and his wife, Enei Begaye, cofounded in 2004. "Native Movement is a collective of around 15 organizers. We work on a range of projects that focus on youth leadership development, sustainability, protection of sacred sites, and social, political, economic, and environmental justice," he says. They have hosted a variety of events, including vigils, marches, youth summits, concerts, and workshops. The organization was created while Evon was chief of his village and was encountering limitations even within his own tribal governance system. Today they have offices in Fairbanks and Anchorage; and they have expanded into the area of missing and murdered Indigenous women.

Evon focuses on issues related to healing and trauma, and the integration of Indigenous cultural practices with behavioral health interventions. "Our major goal is to prevent suicide, which is at epidemic levels in some of our communities," he says. (It is a leading cause of death for Alaska Natives between the ages of 15 and 24.) *We Breathe Again*, a documentary film that explores the impact of suicide on the lives of four Alaskans, premiered in 2017 on the PBS World Channel's America ReFramed; and being one of the film's producers offered Evon the opportunity to cast a wider net.

Native comedian and traditional Yup'ik teacher Keggulluk Earl Polk is featured in the film. "Sing. Go back to your roots. Dig deep," he urges. "Hit your knees, become humble. Realize that you're stronger than what is trying to take you away. And the only reason you're strong is because you're humble enough to ask for help." Evon hopes that the film will continue to be a useful tool to help build bridges of communication and healing for healthcare workers and patients alike.

Evon will be stepping down from his role as vice chancellor in June 2021 to deepen his work at the community level, as well as in international global advocacy. He plans to continue his work with suicide prevention and immerse himself in his passion for the preservation of Indigenous languages. "We have 20 Alaska Native languages, and one of them has already lost its last speaker," he says. "I want to be part of helping to revitalize my language, the Gwich'in language. We're down to less than 800 speakers worldwide. Now is the moment for us to work with our elders to document the language as best we can, and create a curriculum, and lesson plans." His dream is to create a Gwich'in language immersion school, or "nest," where, starting at three years old, children would speak only in Gwich'in.

"I know some people in higher education expect me to go on to be a chancellor, or president of a university. But my path has never been about career advancement," Evon says. "It's been about finding the place where my heart and my passion are calling me to make a difference. I feel like language intersects with so many of the themes that are reflected in my human rights work: the healing, self-determination, and leadership development of Alaska Native and other Indigenous peoples."

Treat the earth well: it was not given to you by
your parents,
it was loaned to you by your children.
We do not inherit the Earth from our Ancestors,
we borrow it from our Children.
We are more than the sum of our knowledge,
we are the products of our imagination.

Ancient Proverb

Call to Action: Support Gwich'in language revitalization; visit www. tananchatoh.com Follow Evon https://twitter.com/evonpeter?s=20 and visit https://www.nativemovement.org/

AN INDIGENOUS REBEL WITH A CAUSE
Lucia Ixchíu
Guatemala

There's a special feeling of harmony and balance that permeates the small city of Totonicapán, Guatemala. Nestled into a green valley below the Cuxniquel, Campanabaj, and Cerro de Coxóm mountains, Totonicapán is home to one of the most important populations of the K'iche' Maya people in the country. It's a place that for centuries has shown that humans and the natural world can coexist, in harmony with one another.

It's here that Lucia Ixchíu grew up. She's Indigenous -- as are her parents, and their parents before them -- and she is proud of her heritage. But she didn't always feel like she fit into the common stereotypes about Indigenous people, especially Indigenous women. In fact, growing up Lucia was a bit of a rebel.

Her first act of rebellion came when she was just four years old. When it came to after-school activities, the gender roles in her small community school were quite strict. Boys took karate classes, while the girls would learn to play instruments, dance, and cook. No one questioned this until Lucia came along and decided to flip the gender roles upside down. When she was told that she couldn't attend karate lessons, she went up to her music teacher after class and told him, simply and directly, that she wanted to do karate as well. He respected her choice. Looking back, she sees that this was the moment she became an activist. "From that age, from that moment, I discovered that my opinion mattered, that my opinion had value, and that it should be respected," she says.

Not only was Lucia the only girl in her school to participate in a boys' sport that year, she was the first girl to ever do so. She remembers walking proudly along with the boys, all of them decked out in karate suits and belts, in the community parade that same year. It was her first act of rebellion, and a sign of things to come for Lucia.

Lucia thanks her mother and father for teaching her how to think outside of the box and fight for what she believes in from an early age. They supported her creativity, gave her an education, and instilled in her a lifelong passion for art and sports. But she also thanks something else for her political awakening -- rock music.

Rock came into her life when she was 11. She liked the traditional music of her Indigenous community, but she loved rock 'n roll even more. She could hear it on the radio from time to time when the signal from larger cities flitted onto her radio at home. She listened to the Beatles, Rage Against the Machine, and the Spanish folk metal group Mägo de Oz. She was especially inspired by Mägo de Oz. In 2003, these Madrid rockers released the first album of a trilogy, "Gaïa." The album, which is named after the Latin name for planet earth, became like a handbook for Lucia.

"In my own personal development, I always talk about music, and especially rock music, because that was the first thing in my life that politicized me," she says. "These groups spoke to me about the importance of protecting mother earth; about sexual diversity, about the importance of loving everyone equally; and about a whole heap of things that impacted me at that age."

For Lucia, music provided a way to break down the stereotypes about Indigenous Mayan women. She says it helped her to "decolonize" her mind from Western thinking and begin to understand that being an Indigenous woman itself required an act of rebellion against a system inherently structured against her. She gained a newfound appreciation for the land, as well -- a land that her community had owned and protected against invasion from other countries for centuries.

Music would continue to be important to Lucia as she grew older, but now it took on political importance. She finished high school and went to college to study architecture. During her studies she became involved with student activist groups and Indigenous land protectors. And on October 4, 2012, she and a number of other students joined a national protest against a rise in electricity prices, which was adversely affecting poor, Indigenous Mayans, like the ones in her community. They took to the streets peacefully and called on the private energy monopoly to lower the prices, but the movement was broken up by armed police. Six people were killed, and many others arrested.

Less than three weeks later, the people protested the violent repression they had suffered, by spraying the presidential palace in Guatemala City with red paint. The government cracked down again and this time five more student activists were arrested.

Among the students arrested were friends of Lucia's, fellow activists like herself. It was another moment that marked her young life and inspired her to take action. She knew that if she wanted to see her friends freed, she would have to create awareness of what was happening -- and make it a loud statement. And what better way than music?

She'd already organized a number of cultural events in her community, around issues involving the marginalization and criminalization of Indigenous communities, and she knew a number of musicians from her time at school. After the October 4 massacre, she began to make her cultural activities more politically focused, and to tell both her story and the stories of others through art and music. She reached out to her musician friends, and one by one, they began to volunteer their voices, and their instruments, to the campaign to free the student activists.

Along with two friends, Lucia started Festivales Solidarios (Solidarity Festivals) as a way to counteract the repression they felt, as well as some of the broader challenges facing Guatemala's Indigenous communities. Through music, spoken word, poetry, and art they managed to build up the momentum to free their friends.

But Festivales Solidarios wasn't just a one-time event. Every time an activist or a student or a journalist faces prison simply for speaking out, Lucia, her sister Andrea, and the rest of the team at Festivales Solidarios bring together artists and musicians to amplify everyone's voices together.

And their action soon morphed into something even bigger -- a movement that uses art and music to create change and is bringing awareness to a variety of forms of repression and inequality that persist across the country. In 2019, the group created The Panal Project, which focuses on finding new ways to tell human rights stories, and strategic use of various media and digital platforms to address issues of territory, historical memory, and political imprisonment. In particular, this project promotes the use of public spaces to encourage and engage in dialogue on human rights among people gathered in parks, streets, and other public spaces.

Increasingly, the group is also speaking up and rebelling for mother earth–Gaia. "In our Indigenous language we call her 'Heart of the Land,'" Lucia says. "That's how we, as Indigenous peoples, see the earth. She is our heart, and we are part of her."

Guatemala used to be known for its "eternal spring," but now the climate is becoming more unpredictable. International corporations are desecrating their communal lands, bringing in extractive industries that pollute the water and the air, disrupting the precious balance of the ecosystem and threatening plant and insect species to the point of extinction.

Despite having received threats to her personal safety, Lucia continues to host the festivals. The government, she says, has never been supportive of the festivals, or of the Indigenous community, but she's not afraid. She believes in the causes they champion: protection of the land, civil liberties, and fundamental human rights. And that gives her courage. "I don't have any fear, because I know that what I am fighting for is the right thing," she says. "The only thing I fear is intolerance."

Today Lucia is 29, working as both an architect and a journalist. "So far, the government has turned a blind eye to the massive loss of biodiversity in Guatemala's forests, brought on by rising temperatures, pollution, and human activities like mining,' she says. In her lifetime alone, temperatures in the forests surrounding Totonicapán have increased by 2 degrees Celsius. The nights have gotten colder and the days warmer. Now people have to ration their precious water, with strict regulations on its use.

For Lucia, the best way to resist these environmental changes is through music and art that brings forth a new and hopeful message -- one that puts the needs of the community and the natural environment above those of people with greed and power. "We are supporting a future in which people can live better, where kids have the right to breathe clean air and drink clean water, where they can know clean rivers and mountains full of trees," she says. "Everything we are doing is for nature, and for our collective future."

> *What I treasure most in life is being able to dream. During my most difficult moments and complex situations, I have been able to dream of a more beautiful future.*
>
> **Rigoberta Menchu**

Call to Action: Join with others in your community to fight for a cleaner, safer, sustainable environment. Inspire others to join you through the use of art and music. Support Festivales Solidarios in the work they are doing: https://twitter.com/festivalesgt?s=20

BLUEPRINT FOR CLIMATE REVOLUTION
Srdja Popovic
CANVAS
Serbia

Like many young men, Srdja Popovic had a quite singular mind in his early twenties. He didn't see himself as a revolutionary. Quite the contrary -- what he most wanted to do was go to parties and play punk music. "At that age I was more into dating girls and playing in a rock band," he says. "I was thinking that basically activism is for old ladies who were fighting for dogs' rights."

Srdja played bass in the goth punk band BAAL, which was an up-and-coming name in the Eastern European music scene. He studied biology at the University of Belgrade, and -- as mentioned -- liked to chase after girls from time to time. He was, in many senses, a pretty typical youth. But as fate would have it, he would not be able to live this life for long.

In the early 1990s, in his native Serbia, the political situation began to deteriorate. The country's president, Slobodan Milošević, was ruling with an increasingly iron fist. Milošević, who became known as the "Butcher of the Balkans," repressed student protesters, detained and jailed activists, and stole elections. He left little room for dissent; the result was a culture of fear spread far and wide across the country.

Seeing Milošević's power grow, Srdja and thousands of other young people were confronted with a harsh political reality -- and a tough choice. Suddenly it didn't seem to Srdja that punk rock was the best use of his energy; nonviolent organizing to overthrow the regime was more important.

"Most of my generation had two options: One was to fight, and the other was to flee. I was stubborn, so I decided to fight," he says. Srdja set off on a path that eventually led him to be called "the architect of the revolution" in Serbia -- which led later to nonviolent revolution around the world.

Through the innovative practices they developed, Srdja and other student activists opened the world's eyes to Milošević's repression. In

1996, they marched peacefully through the streets of Belgrade every day for four months -- braving bad weather and police brutality. Two years later, Srdja founded Otpor! (which means "resistance" in Serbian) with 10 other student leaders, following in the footsteps of student groups who had protested Milošević's regime in 1992, 1996, and 1997.

Otpor! aimed to non-violently overthrow Milošević -- by voting him out of office -- and even to have a little bit of fun doing so. They made promotional T-shirts, mugs, and posters. The iconic clenched fist that appeared on their merchandise, like Shepard Fairey's Andre the Giant OBEY image Years later, it became a symbol of their resistance. Thousands were arrested, but the movement pushed forward nonetheless. "Being wicked, cool, brave, ready to outrun the police -- and well branded -- you can bring down the dictator," he says.

And in 2000 they succeeded. In the elections that year, nearly 90 percent of voters under the age of 29 cast their votes -- almost all of them against Milošević. He didn't even receive enough votes to make it to the second round of voting. Like many dictators, he refused to step down from power. So the students organized a nationwide strike. That was the final gasp for Milošević. On October 5, 2000, he conceded power amidst unrelenting public pressure.

Seeing Milošević fall was a great feeling, but Srjda's work wasn't done. In fact, it was just beginning. He kept working to grow Otpor! and to spread their message of nonviolent resistance across the region and around the world. In fewer than 10 years, Otpor! became one of the most well-known youth movements of all time. In the mid-2000s, it had more than 20,000 members. The group would even inspire -- in part -- the Arab Spring, which rocked the Middle East more than a decade later, and overthrew a number of dictators. "It turned my life into a long-lasting passion for activism," Srdja says.

Today, Srdja spends more time on planes than at home. In Los Angeles at the premiere of PBS's *Bringing Down the Dictator*, was honored to be among other great leaders who had taken a stand for their people and their country. Srjda has turned his student activism in Serbia into a lifelong commitment to helping to support nonviolent resistance in more than 40 countries. He says this type of work keeps him feeling young. "I am still figuring out what I want to be when I grow up," Srdja says with a smile. "Basically my life is helping people figure out how to build movements for social change."

After the fall of Milošević and the success of Otpor!, Srdja founded the Center for Applied Nonviolent Action and Strategies (CANVAS), which has worked with activists in 46 countries, including Venezuela, Iran, and Syria. Their list of successes is growing: the "Orange Revolution" in Georgia (2003); the "Revolution of Roses" in Ukraine (2004); and of course the "April 6 Movement" in Egypt (2011), which became an important part of the Arab Spring.

Climate change, he says, has always been a key issue for him -- and is increasingly the key issue of our time. After the success of Otpor!, Srdja founded the activist organization Green Fist to take the same fight he waged over democracy to the realm of climate change and the environment. He now leads the nonprofit Ecotopia, which pushes for green policies in his native Serbia.

In his travels, Srdja sees how climate change is at the root of most global conflicts. He's pleased that the environmental movement Extinction Rebellion uses his book, "Blueprint for Revolution" to galvanize people into action. It's been translated into 11 languages. Srjda teaches courses on political protest at some of the best American universities, including Harvard University and New York University.

Srdja knows that movement building is not easy -- especially when the enemy is something as overwhelming as climate change. But he wants to write a new blueprint to help tackle it. In fact, his many years of practice have given him a pretty good idea of what that blueprint will look like. It starts with four steps:

1. **Vision**. "You can never win by being *against* something," he says. Instead, climate activists around the world need to present a new way forward. A Green New Deal? Maybe. "You need to find the visionary document, or idea, and explain how the world will be different if you win."

2. **Unity**. In order for the movement to succeed, it has to stay together. "How do you unite different players?" Srdja asks. The ideologies behind climate change action can differ, but if nobody is on the same page about what steps to take, the fight will quickly unravel.

3. **Strategy**. What's the three-year plan, the five-year plan, for the climate revolution? "I think young people have always wished to change the world, but they very often lack the tools and skills to exercise their passion," he says. It's important to take the time to develop a plan that can succeed.

4. **Numbers**. There's one thing that's more important than anything

else, and we're seeing it displayed in cities and countries around the world -- as young people take to the streets *en masse*. "The most important thing to know is the importance to of having big numbers," Srdja says.

Becoming an activist -- whether for climate action or other issues -- is a lifelong job, Srdja emphasizes. And it can be difficult; but he assures youth that it's worth it. "It comes with a promise that you will never be bored; that you will be surrounded by very interesting people; that you may be misunderstood by your parents, who want you to work in a bank or have a law degree. But don't get discouraged by this," he says.

Now 46, Srdja is just as passionate about activism as he was in the days when he and his punk rock friends tried -- and succeeded -- in overthrowing a ruthless dictator. Today he has two children, and he knows how important it will be for them to carry on the work he's been doing for his whole life.

"Providing your kids with the skill sets they need to mobilize and work for social change can dramatically impact the world," he says. "If there is one thing I see that can bring dramatic change to my kids' generation, it may be enabling them to learn more about *how* to change the world; then they can decide *what* is the most pressing topic for them to work on."

Nonviolent struggle is the most powerful means available to those struggling for freedom.

Gene Sharp

Call to Action: Learn how you can build a movement or support those transitioning to democracy: https://canvasopedia.org/ Follow CANVAS on Twitter https://twitter.com/CANVASNVS Facebook: @ PeoplePowerCANVAS

CHANGEMAKING FROM THE NATION'S CAPITAL
Jerome Foster II
OneMillionOfUS
Washington, DC

As an African-American child growing up near the nation's capital, Jerome Foster explored the forests surrounding his home in the D.C. suburbs. "I was the type of kid who could just be outdoors all day. I loved it," he says. "I couldn't wait to finish my schoolwork and chores so I could go out into the forest and explore the creeks and plains; and watch the animals with my parents and grandfather." Little did he know that one day he would become one of the youth leaders passionately helping to bridge the gaps between environmentalism and social issues in the national political landscape.

When Jerome first heard about climate change and global warming, he did what he did with any academic subject – he read everything he could. Once he had a strong base in the science, he dug deep into how these issues were impacting the cultural conversation. "Watching *An Inconvenient Truth*, I was blown away by the scale of the crisis," he says. "Then when I saw how many people *Avatar* drew to the theatres, I realized how people really cared about social justice. It was a huge number! However, they weren't being spoken up for in my circles."

So when he was in middle school, Jerome started his first Facebook page: he wanted his peers to understand what climate change, global warming, and sustainability is all about. His habit of posting 4-5 times a day gained him a lot of followers. Seeing that he could raise such awareness by himself, he decided it was time he joined with others. "When I was in 8th grade, I jumped right in with The People's Climate March in D.C., as an intern," he says. "I helped organize climate marches, and made an immediate impact. It was so exciting; I even gave presentations at my school."

By the time Jerome was in high school, his bright, technical mind was fully engaged. He was fascinated to learn about how tech could be used to revolutionize education and get young people more involved in social justice movements. "I always understood what BLM (Black Lives Matter), women's rights, and other mainstream social justice movements were about," he says. "But I never realized that these had

130

anything to do with climate change. And when I did, I decided to do something about it."

Climate change and global warming impact women, minorities, marginalized peoples, and Indigenous communities disproportionately compared to the rest of the population. In the African American community alone, 71 percent of the people live in areas where the air quality is unsafe, because of their proximity to industrial manufacturing, and other factors. One day, Jerome's teachers challenged him to use his technical abilities to highlight these issues by creating his own little business. And they told him that the World Series of Entrepreneurship (TWSOE) was only five days away.

And so, at 14, Jerome founded TAU VR, a civics-based virtual reality company that promotes empathy and compassion. In TAU VR's 3D virtual space, people have a simulated experience of another person's experience. Jerome's model simulated the experience of a 5-year-old migrant child from Guatemala making the dramatic and difficult journey to Texas. "Parts of Central and South America are becoming uninhabitable due to climate change," Jerome says. "By vicariously experiencing a journey like this, it can give people a more sympathetic view of those who are suffering from our global environmental crisis. It can help the average person understand the many obstacles that my character is dealing with."

While TAU VR was a success, Jerome felt that he had much, much more to offer. Shortly thereafter, he had another jolt of inspiration. "I saw Leonardo DiCaprio's documentary *Before the Flood*. The whole film was amazing," he says. "At the end, he had a message that there aren't enough people covering climate change in a way that it should be covered -- especially young people. I realized that not only was he right, but I could actually be the one to try to remedy this problem." And so, in 2017 he created his next entrepreneurial venture in digital media: *The Climate Reporter*.

The Climate Reporter is a collection of international youth writing about climate change, global warming, environmental justice, and other sustainability issues around the world. The site has a wide range of journalistic products, including op-eds, films, videos, podcasts, interviews, breaking news, stories from frontline communities, and an impressive range of cutting-edge digital content. The environmental news site receives roughly 600,000 views a month, and is among the top up and coming publications in the youth sustainability space.

The Climate Reporter's excellent reporting got the attention of notable climate change youth leaders, like Greta Thunberg and her team. Then in 2019, Jerome organized the D.C. chapter of the worldwide youth School Strikes for Climate. To lend her star power and show her support for the Global Climate Strikes, Greta traveled for the very first time by sailboat from Europe to New York, and then went on to Washington D.C. Her presence at these strikes raised an enormous amount of awareness, and garnered overwhelming support for the movement. Other notable activists, celebrities, and entrepreneurs began joining in, inspired by Jerome's infectious spirit, among them lifelong activist Jane Fonda, who stood beside him.

Inspired by these courageous young leaders, Ms. Fonda launched her Fire Drill Fridays. Every Friday, from November through February, hundreds of people, including Jerome, have joined with this famous actress and lifelong activist to raise awareness about the climate emergency by protesting at the nation's capital. Other celebrities have joined her too, using their star power to get media attention for the cause. As they increasingly engaged in very visible and strategic acts of civil disobedience, some of them, including Ms. Fonda, were arrested.

After each climate strike, Jerome met with congressional staff at the U.S. Capital to talk about what they could be doing for climate justice. His diligence led to a life-changing opportunity for Jerome when he was invited to serve as an intern and be mentored by U.S. Representative John Lewis. Jerome was aware of how this legendary congressman had, as a 25-year-old, marched with Dr. Martin Luther King Jr. in Selma, Alabama, and had helped to create SNCC (the Student Nonviolent Organizing Committee), which played a key role in the Civil Rights movement. "To be able to learn from this true civil rights icon was amazing," Jerome says. "It really made me rethink a lot of my prior assumptions about what is important -- especially about giving back."

With service and social responsibility in mind, Jerome founded OneMillionOfUS, a nonprofit voting advocacy organization that galvanizes the resources needed to facilitate an active voter turnout among youth. To help make the voting process easier and more affordable for youth, Jerome created partnerships with companies like Lyft, which provides discounted rides for youth to help them get to voting stations. Then, before the 2020 elections, Jerome had a lofty goal–to get 1,000,000 youth voters registered in time to vote. It was an intense, exciting, and ultimately successful endeavor. It is estimated that 52-55 percent of the country's youth voted in that election, and their impact was huge -- especially among young people of color, who overwhelming supported President Joe Biden. It was an especially powerful time for

Jerome, who joined forces with other organizations to successfully fight for U.S. Congressman Lewis's former Congressional seat in Clayton County, Georgia. And in the spring of 2021, Jerome was honored to be invited to join President Biden's Inaugural Environmental Justice Advisory Council at the White House to help plan a strategy to combat the global climate crisis.

For youth who want to be involved in social justice, advocacy, and other cause-related work, Jerome's message is simple: "Start with empathy and understanding," he says, advice that applies to many diverse pathways. He believes that starting by educating oneself on the issues you are passionate about is the key. "Read an article about it. Then read five more. Watch documentaries. Reach out to the people involved with the issues you are passionate about. Learn from them. And join the organizations that serve and support these causes."

When it comes to solving problems, Jerome never has, and never intends to stick to one single issue – which is the exact kind of broad thinking we need more of this day and age. In our ever more connected world, more and more issues of social and environmental justice will continue to be interconnected. So, whether you are in Jerome's backyard in Washington DC, or a world away, take a step toward progress – toward a more just and equitable world for all.

There may be some difficulties, some interruptions, but as a nation and as a people, we are going to build a truly multiracial, democratic society that maybe can emerge as a model for the rest of the world.

U.S. Congressman John Lewis

Call to Action: Check out OneMillionOfUs for activism and civic engagement: https://www.onemillionof.us/

Get informed on the latest global news on climate and sustainability, at The Climate Reporter - https://medium.com/the-climate-reporter .

DIVESTMENT FOR A SUSTAINABLE FUTURE
Alyssa Lee
DivestEd
Medford, Massachusetts

As a freshman at the University of California-Los Angeles, Alyssa Lee had an eye-opening experience. "What really woke me up was a speech by Van Jones on plastic pollution as a social justice issue. It was the first time I had ever heard the term environmental justice. It was the first time I had heard of environmental issues related to issues of class and race."

Alyssa was eager to discover where plastic pollution comes from, how it's disposed of, and where it's shipped and processed. What she learned was devastating. "It's all about the hidden costs, and the 'sacrifice zones' of living the way we live; and who has to bear the brunt of that."

Alyssa began changing her habits. She started small by using less plastic; then, one thing led to another. She and a few students started a food cooperative that focused on environmentally friendly products, as well as issues of labor justice. The more she came to understand American society's dominant institutions, the bigger the issues she began to focus on. "And what bigger issue does the environmental community face than fossil fuels?"

Digging down into the research, Alyssa was shocked to discover that many universities across the country were investing in and profiting off of the very fossil fuel companies that were causing environmental catastrophes. She just couldn't stand to see the negative impact of an influential institution such as hers on the next generation of young leaders. So in 2013 she started the Fossil Free UCLA Divestment Campaign -- and by 2020 it was announced that the investment portfolio for the entire University of California system, not just UCLA, was fossil free.

Initially the divestment movement targeted universities, demanding that they change their investment strategies away from fossil fuel companies, and redirect and reinvest their funds in renewable energies, and programs that build community wealth, well-being, and regeneration; and that is where it all began. "There's a tradition going back a long ways," Alyssa says. "I'm just carrying the banner of so many great environmentalists before me. Recognizing the great work of pioneers from the past is essential to creating lasting change."

In 2015, Alyssa expanded the divestment movement by joining forces with the Better Future Project, where she started working as a divestment organizer. There she provided coaching and mentorships to hundreds of students in New England who were working to get their colleges to divest. But by 2018, the Better Future Project was at a crossroads: organizations like 350.org and the Divestment Student Network were no longer actively working on fossil fuel divestment. The Better Future Project was fighting the fight alone. So they decided to form Divest Ed to fill this crucial gap, and Alyssa moved into a new role as its director.

Divest Ed is now the national training and strategy hub for student fossil fuel divestment campaigns. It works specifically on training, coordinating, organizing, and refining the skills students need to engage in effective activism both on campuses and in their communities. Divest Ed tasks students with taking on the roles of civic leaders. It also helps create alliances between colleges to help them take a stand against environmentally irresponsible corporations. "It feels great to be reinvigorating the movement when it was in a lull," Alyssa says. "It's great to be able to be the voice of the people and the communities that are so disproportionately impacted by fossil fuel consumption."

In 2020, Alyssa and her team organized a national day of action, with students at more than 50 academic institutions across the country who are participating in divestment campaigns. And on February 13, Alyssa's actions culminated in a radio appearance on NPR. "We have an enormous opportunity as students to really shape our institutions to make a very powerful political statement about not just climate change, but specifically the fossil fuels industry," she said. "And divestment is one of the most powerful statements they can make."

The divestiture movement spread: worldwide, as of 2020, hundreds of institutions, 1200 institutions possessing 14 trillion dollars divested from the fossil fuel industry -- including 60 colleges and universities, religious institutions like the Catholic Church in Greece; municipalities, like the City of Denver; state pension funds, like New York City's; foundations, for example, the Rockefeller Foundation; and entire countries, like Norway, have taken a stand for the environment and against fossil fuels by divesting.

Currently Alyssa is working with Future Coalition, a national network and community for youth-led organizations and youth leaders supporting the youth vote and climate movements. "One way or another, I've been fighting the fossil fuel industry directly for about a decade," she says. "Now we are taking the next step by fighting the *financers* of the fossil fuel industries - not just the institutions themselves. We are making sure that banks, asset managers, and insurance companies understand the harm they are contributing to when they fund these efforts. We work with great partners like the Stop the Money Pipeline Coalition. And where ancestral lands are being invaded, we are making sure the testimony of Indigenous peoples is paramount in all that we do."

Alyssa now lives in Medford, Massachusetts, where she supports social justice initiatives that strengthen the health of the most vulnerable populations in her community. She is passionate about remedying environmental and social injustice in vulnerable populations, especially in Massachusetts prisons. DeeperThanWater (DTW) is a coalition of organizations dedicated to exposing the rampant human rights abuses that prisoners in the U.S. are subjected to.

On January 27, 2021, some of the goals Alyssa has been working for years began to be realized when President Biden signed an executive order, announcing that it would harness the purchasing power of the federal government to buy clean, zero-emission vehicles manufactured in the United States, and that he would be asking Congress to eliminate subsidies to big oil companies -- a massive investment "to the tune of $40 billion." His multicultural administration is committed to environmental justice by addressing the disproportionate health, economic, and environmental impacts on communities of color.

"How we decide to live is a lifelong process," Alyssa says. "It is a constant, iterative, dynamic experience. It is never too early or too late to decide you want to fight for justice. At the center of this decision is the choice to make a connection against all odds. Connecting to those whose circumstances are completely different from yours; connecting to the earth's history, and to its wisdoms and pains; and connecting to yourself. Making these connections is hard, emotional work. It requires rigor, self-interrogation, and living with constant uncertainty. But if you accept all this, fighting for justice, at its core, is about the capacity to build radical joy for yourself and for others."

Alyssa has a message of resilience especially for youth who want to get involved remedying social justice, sustainability, and other environmental issues. "Being a good person and fighting against injustice is a constant battle. It's not always easy. But when you make a difference, it is all worth it. I wish I had learned earlier how to be okay with being uncomfortable and being uncertain, because some of the greatest personal gains I've made are when I've come out the other side of a difficult situation."

She also believes in the importance of an intergenerational approach to community building. "When we create these imaginary dividing millennials, Gen X, Boomers, and so on, we separate our problems from one another. We become weaker this way. And we lose out on so much mentorship and wisdom with divides like this. There are tons of people who were involved in movements before us who have been through it. We need to invest in learning from them and from each other." But she adds, "Don't stop believing in yourself. If there's anything that working with students these last ten years has showed me, it's that there's good reason to have hope in the future generation."

Fire made us human, fossil fuels made us modern, but now we need a new fire that makes us safe, secure, healthy, and durable.

Amory Lovins, Rocky Mountain Institute

Call to Action: To get involved with one of the many educational institutes, nonprofit organizations, and community programs taking on fossil fuel consumption through divestment campaigns, please visit - https://divested.betterfutureproject.org.

FIGHTING ALONGSIDE THE MOST VULNERABLE AMONG US
Mitzi Jonelle Tan
Youth Advocates for Climate Action Philippines
The Philippines

Mitzi Jonelle Tan will never forget the first typhoon she experienced, growing up in Manila. "I have vivid memories of the thunderous sounds and the panic in the streets. I remember being scared of the huge trees being uprooted that could fall on our house at any time -- and the strong winds outside that were howling. It can be very scary for a child. For me, it was just a part of growing up in the Philippines."

The Philippines is a nation of 7,000 islands - and the second most vulnerable country in the world when it comes to the ravages of the climate crisis. This is due to a combination of factors, including its political history and lack of leadership as well as its geographic location and its proximity to naturally occurring tropical weather events, which have increased in both frequency and strength as a result of climate change. This uptick in major climate events has caused the region to experience a rate of sea-level rise nearly three times the global average; this in turn threatens coastal habitats and the Indigenous people who are occupying the at-risk land.

Human activity has hastened this loss of habitat and the related pollution. Roughly 30,000 hectares of land have been preapproved for reclamation projects that are destroying the surrounding ecosystems. What's worse is that this is happening in the coastal mangroves that act as barriers to erosion to the country's islands. More are being preapproved every day. The country also burns coal, among the dirtiest sources of energy, as 43 percent of its national energy mix. All this adds up to being the most typhoon-prone region on the planet, which is why the Philippines has among the highest rates of displaced persons in the world.

During typhoon season, electricity in the city of Manila routinely gets knocked out. Like most everyone in the aftermath of a typhoon, it became a common occurrence for Mitzi and her family to have candlelit dinners. These quiet evenings gave her time to reflect on and appreciate the power of nature, which she came to revere from quite an early age.

138

She always felt very affected by these forces, and was always trying to figure out a way to live a life that was in harmony with them.

In 2017, Mitzi went on a goodwill trip that would prompt her environmental journey to move precisely in that direction. She went with her college's student council on an integration project with the Lumad Indigenous people from the southern Mindanao region of the Philippines. One of the leaders told her about his people being displaced, harassed, and even killed, just for protecting their lands and the environment from extractive mining companies. Mitzi remembers that he then shrugged, and said, "This is why we have no choice but to fight back." "The simplicity of how he said something so powerful, in passing, about how we have to keep fighting no matter what. It just made me feel that we as students had no choice but to join their fight and become activists. It made me put things into perspective for the first time. I realized that individual lifestyle change is not enough when our lives are at stake. We have to join the struggle of our environmental defenders – our farmers, fisherfolk, and Indigenous peoples. The struggle for justice."

Since then, Mitzi has been passionate about demanding climate justice for the Global South MAPA (the Most Affected People and Areas), particularly in the context of places like the Philippines, which is disproportionately impacted by the climate crisis, and is always one of the top three most dangerous countries in the world for environmental defenders like the Lumad. This led her to partner with the international youth climate movement Fridays For Future founded by Greta Thunberg, and to form the regional Youth Advocates for Climate Action Philippines (YACAP).

With the formation of YACAP, Mitzi has taken a prominent leadership position fighting with MAPA in her region and beyond. "With this planetary emergency, common sense would dictate that climate should be at the top of the agenda, and that those who are already protecting the environment should be listened to. Instead, we have no concrete climate plans from our leaders, and our environmental activists and defenders are being harassed, displaced, even killed. This is why YACAP has laid out five simple Points of Unity, which spells out what actions we demand from our leaders."

YACAP's Five Points of Unity are centered around achieving climate justice; highlighting the urgency of climate action; defending environmental defenders who risk their lives to keep the natural habitat safe; driving youth-led collective action; and affecting systemic change.

Mitzi and YACAP are also intent on getting their government officials to declare a climate emergency, which should include a moratorium on building any new coal-fired plants, as well as building projects in vulnerable habitats and regions. With such victories, local jurisdictions would be forced to consider ways to implement green energy sources and to address habitat destruction, both of which would benefit the environmental defenders who are most affected by these policies.

On September 25, 2020, YACAP made headlines when they held a Global Day of Climate Action. This campaign aimed to amplify the voices of MAPA, who are often thought of as voiceless. "MAPA are often unheard – but we are not voiceless," Mitzi says. "We are battling the climate crisis today, and so we are fighting, not just for our future, but also our present. We will not let the most impacted among us be prisoners of injustice."

Their digital campaign (#FightClimateInjustice) consisted of "Twitter storms" during which youth activists posted pictures of themselves making the MAPA symbol of solidarity, with their hands chained. Forming fists with both hands, and holding them together, with thumbs up, is the sign for "solidarity" in sign language. It also has a dual symbolic importance, since this is the gesture one makes when being handcuffed. This symbol is meant to show that the environmental community will not be taken prisoner by the world at large.

This Global Day of Climate Action garnered so much support that it continued on in digital form for many days after the event took place in order to accommodate youth around the world who wanted to continue to show support and solidarity for MAPA.

On September 20, 2019, during YACAP's Global Climate Strike with Fridays For Future, Mitzi and YACAP met with Secretary Emmanuel M. De Guzman of the Climate Change Commission, who led the Philippines' climate diplomacy on the Paris Agreement at COP21. Recognized as a global leader, he hosted the first Climate Reality Leadership Corps Training Program in 2016. He was pleased to receive Mitzi and YACAP's Five Points of Unity and encouraged them to stay strong and keep fighting for the people.

Since she began her work with YACAP, aspiring youth leaders from around the world frequently contact Mitzi, and ask her for advice – and she's glad they do. "Getting involved can be intimidating, so don't be afraid to ask questions," she says. "Sometimes, it feels like we are expected to know the ins and outs of every issue. But no one person knows everything. My best advice is to find a mentor, ask questions, read everything you can, and be willing to learn." Mitzi is inspired by trailblazing youth leaders across the world like Greta Thunberg from Sweden, Disha Ravi from India, Nicki Becker from Argentina, and Laura Muñoz from Colombia, with whom she fights side by side as a youth climate activist. But she wants the spotlight to be on environmental defenders first and foremost. "It's the Indigenous forest defenders, the farmers and land defenders, the fisherfolk and sea defenders who really keep me going on this journey. What I do is easy."

Going forward, Mitzi plans to keep talking about the climate. "In the near term, there is still so much we have to do in order to avoid the irreversible effects of climate change. Which is why I plan to be vocal. But don't forget - the goal of climate activists should be to *not* be climate activists anymore." While she knows that's the eventual goal, she believes she has her work cut out for the next decade or so. Looking ahead, Mitzi plans to transition to working with a grassroots nongovernmental organization (an NGO), both to amplify her reach, and to find a network that will support her dream of mentoring youth environmental leaders. "I feel the need to fulfill my purpose of fighting for what is right. The way others guided and empowered me on my journey – I just want to be able to do the same thing for other youth. I want to help those who want to get involved be able to see their role in the movement."

One might wonder, how does such an active youth leader like Mitzi not get burned out? Well, she's figured that out too. "This work in service of climate justice doesn't come from a place of anger for me. It comes from a place of love. It comes from my love for the MAPA in the Philippines – for the most vulnerable among us." Surely, the power of love is the most sustainable form of power -- and it will drive a more united and effective front of youth leaders into environmental activism.

"Once upon a time, I conquered," said the
climate catastrophe.
"Once upon a time, we changed the story," the
climate activists replied.

Vanessa Nakate

Call to Action: Get involved with Mitzi's chapter of the Youth Advocates for Climate Action Philippines at https://yacap.org. If you're not from the Philippines, connect with the global youth climate movement at fridaysforfuture.org

GET INTO GOOD TROUBLE!
U.S. Representative John Lewis
Atlanta, Georgia

It was a Sunday morning in 1955 when 15-year-old John Lewis turned on the radio. The voice he heard was of a man who would change his life forever. It was the voice of a young minister, Dr. Martin Luther King, Jr., who was giving a sermon. The words he preached that day inspired John to write a letter to Dr. King, and ask for his support.

As a sophomore in high school in Troy, Alabama, John aspired to get a good education, go to college, maybe even be the first Black youth to attend Troy State College. He knew that college was the best way for him to build a better life for himself. He'd seen how hard his parents worked every day as sharecroppers. Growing up racism and bigotry were part of his everyday life. He knew deep in his soul that something needed to change. So when he heard Dr. King on the radio that day, his powerful words resonated with what John had already been feeling all his life.

John felt fortified in his understanding that there are causes that one needs to stand up for, even if it means getting into trouble: what he called "good trouble, necessary trouble." His first formal act of protest was a petition arguing that the City Library of Troy should be open to all Black people. But what seems self-evident today didn't even get a response back then.

That fall, when he hadn't heard back from Dr. King, he decided to go to a small Black college in Nashville, Tennessee. It was then that Dr. King invited him to come for a visit, during his spring break. John vividly remembers the day he met the legendary civil rights leader for the first time. "Are you the boy from Troy? Are you John Lewis?" Dr. King said. And John answered, "I am John Robert Lewis," giving his full name. From that moment, he knew then that he wanted to follow in Dr. King's footsteps, and become active in the movement.

While in college, John became an active member of the Nashville Student Movement (NSM) and joined them in their fight for desegregating the city, as a step toward racial equality and voting rights for the Black community. Voting rights was an issue close to his heart: his great-

great-grandfather was the first person in his family to vote, in 1867, just as soon as he had been freed, as part of the Reconstruction Act of 1867. It was more than a hundred years later that John Lewis was the next person in his family to exercise his right to vote.

But before they could tackle such underlying questions of power, John and his fellow activists had to turn to much more basic forms of discrimination. So, along with other NSM members, he organized sit-ins at segregated diners and department stores in Nashville. Every day at lunchtime, John and his fellow activists would gather to simply be visible in public spaces. "We *wanted* them to see us," he said. "We wanted white people, everyday citizens, everyday customers to be exposed to us, to see us as we were, not as something in their minds, in their imaginations."

As his activism made him an increasingly well-known figure in Nashville, he was invited to study nonviolent action with Rev. James Lawson at the Clark Memorial United Methodist Church. It was there that he became a dedicated believer in its fundamental principles. He then applied to be one of the first Freedom Riders -- seven white and six Black activists who planned to travel together, on the same bus, from Washington DC to New Orleans. They knew that this strategic act of protest could lead to their being attacked, and that they couldn't count on local police to protect them. These brave young men and women risked their lives by just taking a bus ride to stand up against racial segregation, and in fact three of them were abducted and murdered by members of the Ku Klux Klan. John knew two of them personally. Despite this horrific violence and sustained resistance to their campaign, they were ultimately successful. In 1963, President Kennedy announced that his administration would introduce the most expansive civil rights bill the U.S. had ever seen. And John Lewis's participation in the Freedom Rides, and his being arrested 24 times for his involvement in nonviolent activism had made him a celebrity, and a beacon of hope for the Black community, especially among college students.

Buoyed by his experience, and his desire to engage many more Black youth, John Lewis became a founding member of the Student Nonviolent Coordinating Committee (SNCC). He rallied them to join with Dr. King, Ralph Abernathy, A. Philip Randolf, and Bayard Rustin to help organize the Civil Rights March on Washington on August 28, 1963. Hundreds of thousands of people marched that day to demand their civil and economic rights. And it was on that historic day that Dr. King's iconic "I Have A Dream" speech fed their souls.

John Lewis was the youngest speaker that day. "We are tired," he said. "We are tired of being beaten by policemen. We are tired of seeing our people locked up in jail over and over again. And then you holler, 'Be patient.' How long can we be patient? We want our freedom, and we want it now!"

As chairman of SNCC, John Lewis zeroed in on the fight to register Black people to vote. The next year, he launched the "Mississippi: Freedom Summer" campaign of 1964, to register as many Black voters as possible in order to change the balance of power. He travelled across the country, cajoling college students to get everyone they knew to register to vote so they could make their voices heard, and fight for equal rights.

Then in 1965, when Dr. King invited him to lead the march from Montgomery to Selma, Alabama, he proudly accepted this life-changing offer. Together with his fellow activists, he fearlessly crossed the Edmund Pettus Bridge in Selma. Police in riot gear were waiting for them. When the marchers stopped in front of the police to pray, the police attacked. John Lewis was badly injured by a strike on the head, the scars of which he bore for the rest of his life.

But he and his fellow activists continued protesting the pervasive racism throughout American society. Eventually, as a politician he gained the power needed to develop laws to strengthen the voting rights he'd fought for as a young activist. He worked tirelessly on the bill that enshrined important protections against racial biases that were part of the 1965 Voting Rights Act. But the bill was never passed, due to opposition in the Senate. "It makes me sad," he said. "It makes me feel like crying when people are denied their right to vote."

Until the end of his life, John Lewis continued to fight for the right to vote for all Americans. Even in his 80s, he was sought after to speak at rallies across the country. "You have been called to do something," he would tell the crowds. "The vote is the most powerful nonviolent tool we have for our democracy."

As the representative for Georgia's 5th District, he used his platform to challenge and mentor a younger generation to take over and carry on his legacy. From their work on voter suppression to issues of prison reform and police brutality, as well as the disproportionate effect of climate change on Black communities, he was proud of the young activists who are speaking up today.

Until his death in July 2020, John Lewis had lived by a simple philosophy. "When you see something that is not right, not fair, not just -- say something, do something! Get in trouble, good trouble, necessary trouble!"

One of John Lewis's greatest joys was seeing Barack Obama become America's first Black president. At his funeral President Obama said of him that he "brought this country a little bit closer to our highest ideals. You want to honor John? Let's honor him by revitalizing the law that he was willing to die for. And naming it the John Lewis Voting Rights Act." Then he added, "But John wouldn't want us to stop there. Once we pass the John Lewis Voting Rights Act, we should keep marching to make it even better."

Our lives begin to end the day we become silent about things that matter.

Dr. Martin Luther King Jr.

Call to Action: VOTE: Racial inequality continues to this day, and, sadly, racism is all around us. We each have a responsibility to change this: to inform ourselves to speak up. Go out and get into good trouble! Watch the movie *Good Trouble*. Be inspired!

GENERATION GREEN
Destiny Hodges
Washington DC

Not too far down the street from where Destiny Hodges's grandmother lives in Demopolis, Alabama, there is a paper mill. As a child, Destiny would see the smoke rising from the factory towers in long white columns. It gave the air around her a funny smell. She would cover her nose, hold her breath, and wonder where that stench was coming from.

"I looked into it, and I found out that there's all kinds of carbon monoxide and stuff in there that everyone in the community is breathing," she says. "I think about the health of the people who live around there. It's just terrible." This left a lasting impression on her, that would one day lead her to a life-changing career decision.

Destiny Hodges has been a writer for as long as she can remember. She started by writing poetry, but when she went to middle school, she found a new passion: journalism. Every Friday in her last class period, her peers led a live broadcast. Destiny would watch the small monitor molded to the wall of the school's studio, and watch the video stream. "And I was like -- I want to do that!" Destiny said. "So I became the producer, and then an anchor, and reporter on the show. I loved it all."

It was an exciting beginning for Destiny's career in journalism. Then, when she was ready for high school, her family moved to Tuscaloosa, Alabama. Destiny joined the school's newspaper, the *Northridge Reporter*, and was quickly promoted to news editor. She wrote about issues of identity and race, as well as her high school's sports teams and musicals. Then one day in May of 2016 she was forced to leave her high school -- and her beloved newspaper. She pleaded with the administration to let her stay; she was happy there, and she was an integral member of the news team. "They just pushed the black kids, for the most part, back to the other side of the river," Destiny says. "What's happening in Tuscaloosa is, they are resegregating schools. And they're redlining."

Destiny was assigned to Brown High School, a predominantly black school. Although she was promised that her new school would start a journalism program, Destiny soon found out what that really meant.

146

"The teacher who was supposed to teach it was informed that I would handle the newspaper. She never had any journalism experience, never taught journalism," Destiny said. "That's the day I found out I was going to really have to start from scratch."

In order to get the newspaper going, Destiny invited students from her old school's newspaper to give talks to students at her new school who wanted to be involved. And she captured what she had learned in writing for the *Northridge Reporter* in Power Point presentations and worksheets so she could share it with students at her new school. It was hard work, but it paid off: there were some good writers, and some students had a good feeling for design. But most of all, the students appreciated having the chance to see their own stories featured in their own newspaper.

"I've always said that everybody has a story to tell," Destiny says. "I'm a giver. I'm an empath. This wasn't about me; it was about providing people with the opportunity to explore a new career path."

Many students in her high school came from difficult backgrounds, and there was no real outlet for them, no one to tell their stories to. "The education system in general is not meant for black students," Destiny says. "It's not designed for us, or by us."

Destiny had also realized there was a lack of reporting on environmental stories, like the stench emanating from the paper mill by her grandmother's house. She had always been fascinated by environmental stories, and she watched National Geographic's *Animal Planet* show almost every day. She knew a little bit about climate change, but now she started to wonder who were the people that were being the most affected. And where were their voices? "They don't even talk about people like me," she says. "Usually, we're impacted first and most by everything."

It was then that she discovered her passion for covering issues of environmental justice. She wanted to tell the stories of those communities that were impacted first, and worst, by climate change. "I made it my mission to do whatever I could to use media as a form of narrative organizing," she says. "To share the stories of people from marginalized communities who were being impacted by environmental inequity."

Environmental issues are often reported on as a matter of protecting the natural environment. For Destiny, that is short sighted, and incomplete. "We need to broaden our awareness and look at how our health is being impacted by environmental factors like clean air and water," she says. "When we talk about natural disasters, like Hurricane Katrina, we need to think about who lives in those regions, and who is being impacted the worst; it is primarily people of color."

The even greater injustice is that although people of color are disproportionately affected by climate change, they have historically been excluded from the environmental movement, Destiny says. So when she entered Howard University, a historically black institution in Washington D.C., to study journalism and environmental studies, she was on a mission.

Right then, all around the world, climate strikes were happening. People everywhere were expressing their concerns. Destiny closely followed the fires in the Amazon on social media, and she felt so bad for the Indigenous people of color who were on the front lines of this disaster, breathing toxic fumes, while also losing their homes and their loved ones.

"I could see that at Howard, people weren't necessarily connecting the dots to the larger picture," she says. "And I was like, you know what? We need a climate strike here."

She started by designing a flyer. Then she set up a social media site, shared it in a couple of groups, and urged people to sign up. "People responded, and they were actually really curious about it," she says.

On the Howard campus, there were a lot of misgivings about the school's sustainability policies. There was an Office for Sustainability for a while, but no one ever heard anything coming out of there. "Of course, protesting at the national level or at your local government is important," Destiny says. "But we wanted to do it on campus because that's where we knew we could make an impact firsthand."

The protest didn't go quite as planned: one week before students took to the streets, the administration invited Destiny and her fellow students to a meeting. They had developed an impressive 50-page document detailing their demands. The University's administration sat down with them and listened to what they had to say. It became clear that it wasn't a lack of will; it was actually a lack of resources, and not enough communication that had caused the students to have a negative perception of their university's commitment to sustainability.

But realizing solutions for more sustainability on campus isn't always easy.

"There's a lot of things that are considered the norm in sustainability for other campuses," Destiny says. "However, with the financial burdens placed on historically black colleges and universities, it's not easy to do."

With two other students that Destiny met at the protests on campus, she founded the Howard University Student Sustainability Committee. They were able to facilitate conversations about sustainability on campus, and came up with a number of proposals. "We came up with ideas for improved recycling in residence halls, and ways of enriching the entire university curriculum with environmentalism and sustainability," she said. They got in touch with different departments in the university to discuss and plan environmentally friendly projects. They also created a database of scholarships and internships focused on environmental and sustainability issues, gave presentations about climate justice, and organized community cleanups. "We got to where we are by speaking up for what we believe in and standing together."

As she continued to engage with her community on the issues of sustainability and climate change, Destiny realized that there weren't many young black environmental activists, and those who were out there hardly knew each other. That is why she decided to start her own nongovernmental organization, Generation Green.

"The purpose is to build a network to uplift us so that people can share resources with each other, and help each other out." Generation Green is planning urban gardening projects, designing sustainable fashion, and planning an international exchange program to give students the opportunity to connect with activists in other parts of the world.

"If our students are mostly low-income students, and our communities are impacted first, and the worst, by environmental inequity, then why aren't we encouraging them to go into this field and create innovative solutions to help our communities?" she says. "Engaging and implementing effective solutions can't happen without the knowledge, wisdom, understanding, and expertise of those who have experienced it, or who are going through it."

From time to time Destiny remembers how she used to ask her mom what caused that horrible smell when they would drive by the paper mill close to her grandmother's house. "I don't know," her mom would say. "Whatever byproduct of the paper that they're making."

Soon, with journalists like Destiny reporting to their communities on the frontlines of climate change, everyone will know the answers to these questions. Then, Destiny's Generation Green will *do* something about it!

> *It really boils down to this: that all life is interrelated. We are all caught in an inescapable network of mutuality, tied into a single garment of destiny.*
> *Whatever affects one directly, affects all indirectly.*

Dr. Martin Luther King Jr.

Call to Action: Approach climate change issues as multifaceted social, economic, and generational, and search for holistic solutions. Learn more about Destiny's ventures: www.gen-green.org

INDIGENOUS LEADER INVITES
YOUTH TO SHARE THEIR GIFTS
Xiye Bastida
New York City

As a child, Xiye Bastida had learned from her father's Indigenous Otomi-Toltec culture to respect the Earth. From her mother's historical studies on Maya culture and society, she learned to respect Mesoamerican knowledge systems. Her family lived a simple life in San Pedro Tultepec, a wetland community in Toluca Valley home to migratory geese and ducks from Canada where families still fish and weave baskets from bulrushes. "Everything about my upbringing taught me to be that voice of unity and balance," she says.

Then, in 2015, when Xiye was 12 years old, after a long drought, her hometown was devastated with massive floods. She and her parents, who had been offered a job to teach about Indigenous value systems and philosophy, left for New York City without knowing how the town would recover from the flood. "At the time, I didn't really understand about climate change and its role in these increasingly volatile weather emergencies," Xiye says. "I never even considered that there were people and businesses who didn't care about Mother Earth the same way my family and I do."

Thinking back on what happened in San Pedro Tultepec, Xiye realizes that the climate crisis was already there, and affecting frontline communities like hers. What was an island in the middle of a wetland in the 1970s was severely impacted by a modernization program that included the elimination of the 8,000-hectare lake, the exploitation of the underground aquifer to supply Mexico City, and the stigmatization of the traditional way of living. Half of the island lost its wetland and, little by little, urban sprawl invaded the wetland bed. Just to make a living villagers had to adapt to wood furniture making, and as demand grew, shops were built beneath the original water level.

"The people who don't have the resources to deal with flooding by going somewhere else, or who don't have the infrastructure to tolerate it when it comes, are left to bear the brunt of the crisis," Xiye says. "In the wealthy sections of Mexico City, people were given aid, and repairs from the flooding were swiftly made."

Now a 19-year-old college student majoring in environmental studies with a concentration in international relations, Xiye says, "This was the first time that I realized just what climate injustice really was. That's when I set my sights on fighting climate change for the most vulnerable among us, who are being so disproportionately impacted."

Inspired by Greta Thunberg's Fridays for Future movement in Europe, Xiye responded by cofounding the Fridays for Future chapter in New York City. At the Beacon School, she created an Environmental Club and rallied her classmates to join her in the upcoming climate strike on March 15. "I did everything I could. I organized. I did graphic designing. I put up flyers; they'd get taken down every day. I'd put up more," she says. "I even got my teachers to understand what we were protesting. They understood. But nobody was really imagining how big of an impact a few kids could make. Myself included."

A month later, when the day finally arrived, Xiye thought it was going to just be her and few friends striking. As it turned out, 600 fellow students from her school participated in the walkout. Empowered by this show of solidarity, Xiye next set her sights on the Global Climate Strike scheduled for September 20. She, and a core team of only 10 teenagers and 50 others, worked together with 10 adults from climate organizations, and rallied 300,000 to strike for climate action. They marched from Foley Square to Battery Park, carrying signs that read, "There is No Plan(et) B," and chanting "Green New Deal, make it real," and "The sea is rising, so must we." It's estimated that more than 4 million young people and adults joined together that day to make their voices heard. When Greta Thunberg arrived by sailboat in New York Harbor to attend the United Nations Climate Summit with world leaders, Xiye officially welcomed Greta. "Fridays for Future NYC really showed our leaders the power that young people have to impact climate change, and there's no looking back," she says.

Now, as a leading voice for Indigenous and immigrant visibility in climate activism, Xiye has gone on to work with The People's Climate Movement. Then, when the Covid-19 pandemic hit, with the lockdown Xiye shifted from rallying people in the streets to educating people online. Her new venture, Re-Earth Initiative, focuses on radical inclusivity, diversity, and accountability through workshops, toolkits, and webinars. She is especially passionate about increasing awareness of the importance of reciprocity and intersectionality in the global youth climate movement.

A powerful public speaker, Xiye has gained a reputation for her ability to inspire climate action. At the Global Citizens Festival in 2019, she spoke about the intersection of climate change with human rights issues, which many people outside of activist circles don't yet understand. "We haven't thought too much about the effect the climate crisis is having on refugees." Xiye says. "But the displacement of people is an inevitable consequence of the climate crisis. And it's not just that the climate crisis *will* create climate refugees; it's already happening!" Reflecting back to her own personal story, she educates people about how extended periods of drought result in instability of crops, and force people away from their ancestral lands. And when there are irregular flooding patterns, people must seek shelter elsewhere. "We need not only to mitigate these issues, but to adapt, with well-structured systems and policy to deal with climate refugees."

For Xiye, UN Sustainable Development Goal #17 is the most important goal: *Strengthen the means of implementation and revitalize the global partnership for sustainable development,* since it has the capacity to link people, goals, and places of all kinds in service of a broader, sustainable world. "Partnerships are a necessity. Cooperation is the key," she says. "We need for people to not focus just on one goal without thinking about all the others. Having all kinds of people from all types of background is what will make this possible."

Xiye also speaks out on educational platforms like TED Talks to inform people about the climate crisis. "TED has become a great advocate for climate education with its Countdown," she explains. "A lot of businesses are shifting their whole way of thinking to be more sustainable. And when educational networks partake in community building around these issues, it creates a really cohesive coalition going forward."

Xiye gave a memorable TED Talk, which was framed as a letter to her *abuela*, her grandmother. "The world is so big, and it has so many bad habits," she said. "I didn't know how a 15-year-old was supposed to change anything, but I had to try." Reflecting back on her speech she says, "It was a way to share my story, my frustration, my hopes and dreams for the future in a new way that I hoped would influence people, because what we need is more people supporting this movement. We especially need more youth to be involved as climate activists. If there were more of us, none of us would have to be full-time activists."

Wherever Xiye goes, she finds youth eager to get involved but they don't know how or where to start. For them, she has some guidance. "It doesn't matter what your gift or passion is in life. We need youth from all walks, because diversity of thinking and skills is what is going to make solutions possible. Any skill that you have can be used to address the climate crisis; whether you are an architect, photographer, educator, scientist, or activist, we could use your skills because we need all the skills to face up to this emergency."

That said, she cautions youth to avoid the pressure to change who they are to fit into a particular role. "Be who you are, know yourself, and ask yourself what you can add," she says. "If you don't find anything that fits you, just Google a cause that you are interested in supporting and get involved. If there's nothing, come up with it yourself. It's true that a lot of times there are no spaces for us at the table to share our voices and opinions. And if you can't find a seat at the table, just build your own table! You will make an impact, because youth always do. We have more influence than we think we do, and we need to take advantage of that."

For adults, Xiye doesn't necessarily want support for the youth as much as she wants support for the overall climate movement. "The youth grow really fast. I started out at 15, and in a snap of my fingers, I'm 19. And I've left my youth behind. I had a lot of great things to say as a youth, and I was heard by plenty of adults. But what it boils down to is that the youth can't vote. So when adults work to amplify the demands of youth, to be heard in their circles of influence, that's great, and we are grateful for that. But when you vote for what we want, that *really* makes an impact. Beyond that, if you have the means, support us. And if you don't, get out there and organize–that doesn't cost anything. Both are important. We are going to need all the help we can get to face up to this crisis of our age."

To her family, and her ever-supportive grandmother, the words she spoke under the bright lights at TED still ring true. "Thank you for inviting me to love the world since the moment I was born." With this love, she will devote her life to making this earth a better place for everyone. And she hopes for many more allies to join her on the journey.

The meaning of life is to find your gift.
The purpose of life is to give it away.

Pablo Picasso

Call to Action: Learn more about Re-Earth Initiative: www.reearthin.org

JOVENES POR EL CLIMA
Nicki Becker
Argentina

"When I was younger, I thought the climate crisis was just about Antarctica and the polar bears," says Nicki Becker. "It's all we ever saw in the media. Now I understand how far that message was from the reality of the climate situation."

Argentina has had a long history of organizing strikes to galvanize support for social change. Growing up, Nicki had seen how her people had rallied against the multinational mega-mining operations in oil-rich province of Chubut that were irreparably polluting the waterways, air, and farmland, and devastating the local economies of these rural regions. That was ten years ago - and Argentinians are still trying to slow the exploitation of the people's lands.

When she was 15, Nicki joined her first strike, for International Women's Day. "Through this work, I began to be more aware of other issues -- mainly, how there is no climate justice without justice for women and social justice," she says, and adds, "It's all intertwined."

Then in 2019, she saw online how young people in Europe were banding together through the climate movement Fridays for Future. Ever curious, she started researching the environmental issues that were facing her country, and those she'd heard about at the strikes. She quickly realized the scale and severity of the environmental problems Argentina was facing. She learned about the role of climate change in creating more severe heat waves and longer, more devastating droughts -- which were responsible for the fires that in 2020 burned over 1 million acres of land, and nearly another 100,000 acres in 2021 in Argentina. She also learned about the brewing humanitarian situations occurring at mega-mining sites all over the country. "I knew right then that my work had to be focused on climate action. But clearly, fighting for the environment is not just about demanding a reduction in greenhouse gases. It's also about demanding climate justice for the most vulnerable among us."

The more Nicki learned how pressing the crisis was for Argentinians, the more she couldn't understand why people in her country weren't talking about it. In fact, she wondered why young people in other parts of the world had information she didn't have. Why don't schools, universities, and media outlets in Argentina talk about the climate crisis if it's so important? "At the beginning of my journey I got really motivated to find answers," she says. "Seeing all these white Europeans, I was very aware of the lack of a Latin American perspective in the movement. Greta Thunberg got me thinking that we should try to create a movement in Argentina."

So she formed Jovenes Por El Clima–Youth for Climate Argentina (YFCA) -- to engage young Argentinians who were concerned about climate change to join with Greta and young activists around the world who were bringing the spotlight to the youth movement. In September 2019, for the first Global Climate Strike, YFCA organized climate rallies of 5,000, 10,000, and 45,000 people, across Argentina. "It wasn't easy to pull it off. But it was worth it in the end. With this kind of turnout, we showed our government officials that we the people care about remedying the climate situation. And we sent a message: the people have the power to change anything we want."

Empowered by this momentum, Nicki and her YFCA team finally got Argentinian leaders to listen to their demands and declare the country to be in a state of climate emergency. It was the first nation in Latin America to do so, and it set the stage for wide-sweeping reforms in the country. Later that year, the government signed a bill to create a committee of scientists, experts, youth leaders, and businesses to help guide the country to a more green and sustainable future.

For her pioneering work, Nicki was invited to travel to Madrid in December 2019 to be a representative at COP25, the Conference of Parties to the United Nations Framework Convention on Climate Change (UNFCCC). One of the highlights for her was the opportunity to meet with the first woman president of Chile, Michelle Bachelet, who now serves as the United Nations Commissioner for Human Rights. "It was an opportunity for the media in Argentina to see a youth leader from their country on TV speaking about these issues," she says, and adds, "I thought perhaps I could get them talking about the climate crisis back home."

Nicki's voice continues to be heard both in her country and around the world. In March 2020, she was selected as one of just five young people chosen by the United Nations Economic Commission for Latin America and the Caribbean as a champion of Escazu, a regional agreement that concerns the right for people to have access to information on environmental issues, and protects environmental defenders.

The resulting media attention from Nicki's work has opened a lot of people's eyes about the climate crisis. But she knows that activism must be combined with legislation, both in Argentina and internationally. Without legislation, Nicki doesn't see a sustainable future. "We need our activism to lead to legislative change in the energy sector," she says. "A just transition takes time, and it's time that we don't have."

Nicki firmly believes we need specific legislative priorities on cleaner energy, plastic pollution, and multinational mining operations. "Even if every individual in Argentina does all of the things we are demanding, we are not going to change the climate crisis. We need legislation, cooperation from the global north, and we need corporations to join us in making these changes and having conversations about these issues in a more nuanced way. For example, we all want electric vehicles. But where is the mining being done? Who is being affected by the operation? And who is profiting? Without forward-thinking dialogue about *how* we go green, we don't have a chance at redeeming the whole environmental situation."

While Nicki has galvanized youth throughout her country, she knows that it will truly take an intergenerational approach to solve the climate crisis. "We need the adults in the room to hear us. Because sometimes, we just get 'yes'd' and receive nothing but empty promises. When we say we are afraid of what future we are going to live in, we are very sincere. We aren't asking for a lot. We are asking for collective action to combat an emergency. We understand that the world is complex and that change takes time. But the change needs to start today, not tomorrow. And we need to get the adults on board to help enact the systemic change the world needs *now*."

While the climate emergency young people have inherited is of epic proportions, Nicki believes it is precisely such situations that can give rise to the great potential within us. "We are burning bright in a precarious moment where we can change history," she says. "We didn't decide to be here. We were given the climate crisis and we can't do anything but face up to it. In 50 years, we won't have that opportunity. We *must* build a more fair and just future to persevere. And going forward, we will need everybody on board."

Hope is what sustains Nicki through the ups and downs of her struggle for a more just future -- and she wants to see more of it. "Hope is a great motivator, because it's not born in a president or a company; it's in the people. Hope is in your friends and in your family. It's in you. Together, with hope, we can change the world."

"Ecology without class struggle is just gardening."

Chico Mendes

Call to Action: To learn more about Jovenes Por El Clima - Youth for Climate Argentina: www.jovenesporelclima.com Instagram @ jovenesporelclimarg Twitter @jovenesclimarg Follow Nicki on Instagram @nickibecker or Twitter @nickibeckerok

RAISING OUR VOICES FOR CHANGE
Carmen Perez
Justice League NYC
New York, New York

Today she's one of the faces, and the founders, of the largest protest movement in U.S. history -- the 2017 Women's March on Washington -- but getting there wasn't easy for Carmen Perez.

Carmen grew up in the small farming community of Oxnard, California -- a town that was plagued by inequity and injustice. People in her Latinx community are twice as likely to live below the poverty line as those in white communities. As a result, they are more likely to suffer from health problems, and also less likely to graduate from high school and go on to escape poverty: a vicious cycle.

The deep-seated poverty in Oxnard created challenges for Carmen. She was introduced to violence at an early age. There was domestic violence in her family; gang violence in her community; police violence in the streets that often targeted her family members, specifically her older brothers, because of the way they looked. Drug and alcohol abuse negatively impacted families, and racism often showed up in their contact with police, and in high school.

Then, right before her 17th birthday, Carmen's older sister was killed in a one vehicular car accident. Her sister and Carmen were one day and two years apart, and she was killed right before her 19th birthday, and buried on Carmen's 17th birthday.

Carmen's relationship with her sister had been challenging. While Carmen focused on sports and schoolwork, her sister got involved in hanging out with the wrong crowd, which led to tension at home. Often having to chaperone her sister, Carmen would stick to the sidelines, dribbling her basketball and not saying much. But they were close in age, shared a room and a very special bond that was unbreakable.

Her sister's death put everything into perspective for Carmen. "She went out with her friends one night and never came back home," she says. "That became the catalyst that changed my life, and is what made me want to change the world. Losing her made me realize that life was too short and you couldn't wait for tomorrow to do what you could today. So I made a decision to live life to the fullest from that moment on."

As Carmen and her siblings suffered in the wake of her sister's death, their parents had to support them unconditionally, to love them and help them through their pain. And her parents stayed strong. They found it in themselves to perform an act of astonishing forgiveness: they decided not to press charges against the person who had taken their daughter's life. "At the time, I didn't understand my parents' decision, but looking back, that was my first exposure to restorative justice," she says.

Carmen embarked on her journey by enrolling at the local community college and playing basketball, and she went on from there to the University of California, Santa Cruz. There, she suddenly found herself exposed to a different sort of crowd -- one where both privilege and resistance came together in different ways. She enrolled in a class on Chicana feminism, and studied with some of the great activists and scholars of the protest and feminist movements: Aida Hurtado, Angela Davis, Craig Haney, and others.

Unlike many of her peers, Carmen had to pay her own way through college by working multiple jobs. But this opened up unexpected opportunities. She began to work at the Youth Community Restoration Project, where she helped mentor young people coming out of the justice system by getting them jobs and creating leadership opportunities for them. She also cofounded Girlzpace, which provided gender-responsive services for girls in the community. Ultimately she went on to work at the Santa Cruz County Probation Department to serve girls within the system, and do system accountability. Like Carmen, some of the girls had a vision of a different sort of future for themselves -- one not defined by violence, but by resistance to it.

Through this work Carmen came into contact with the organization Barrios Unidos, and its founder, Nane Alejandrez. Nane had founded the organization in 1977, and he had a radical idea: instead of isolating and locking up young people who had committed crimes, he said, we should listen to them and support them with the tools to succeed. Returning from Vietnam, where he had seen the injustice and cruelty of war firsthand, he saw injustice echoed at home through mass incarceration. Thirty-five members of his family had been behind bars -- an entire generation locked up and forgotten.

Nane saw a spark in Carmen; he brought her on board, and became something of a father figure and mentor for her. He was a humble and fair person, and expected a lot from her, but he also supported her and knew she was destined for greatness. "I was able to really learn from him," she says. "He didn't have to tell me what his ideology was or what his theory of change was; you could see it in his mannerisms, in the way in which he lived, and led."

For example, when Nane would be invited to be a keynote speaker somewhere, he wouldn't be on stage waiting for the guests to come in, but in the aisles welcoming them, as an usher would. Nane embodied servant leadership, and Carmen saw how people responded to this kind of warmth, which led her to bring it to her own work later on.

During the 1990s the need for organizing around criminal justice issues was increasing in the United States. The War on Drugs saw the prison population skyrocket across the country, and communities like Carmen's were the most affected. She made it her mission to right these wrongs, and fight against the injustice she saw.

One day Nane introduced Carmen to one of his mentors, Harry Belafonte, who was partnering with him on prison reform for black and brown youth. The beloved Jamaican singer and actor, a friend of Dr. Martin Luther King Jr., was a legend in the Civil Rights movement. He had raised millions of dollars by engaging other celebrities to perform at his fundraisers. His generosity was so pure, and so unwavering, that Coretta Scott King, an activist in her own right, said, "Whenever we got into trouble, or when tragedy struck, Harry has always come to our aid, his generous heart wide open."

When Harry and Carmen met, they immediately hit it off. Soon after, Harry asked Carmen to join his organization, The Gathering for Justice, as a founding member, and move to New York City. The Gathering for Justice grounded communities in the ideology of Dr. King -- Kingian Nonviolence -- and was embarking on building a national movement to end child incarceration.

The introduction to Mr. Belafonte brought Carmen's activism to a whole new level, and gave her the opportunity to fight for real, structural change in communities across the country that had long suffered from inequity, discrimination, and the legacies of racism and slavery. But she never lost sight of the lessons she had learned from Nane. "The movement is not about one individual, it's about building collective power," she says. "There are times when even though *you've* not done something, it is your responsibility as a moral leader to repair the harm that's been done."

Carmen's star as an activist was on the rise after she founded Justice League NYC, a manifestation of The Gathering for Justice, when in 2014 another tragedy struck, and moved her activism into another arena. That summer, she went to Ferguson, Missouri, where a week earlier, an unarmed black man, Michael Brown Jr., had been shot by police, sparking protests that would eventually spread across the city, and the nation. When she landed in Ferguson, the August heat was oppressive, ominous. That day, her phone rang: it was a call from back home. Her nephew, just 22 years old, had cancer. "That became the second catalyst for me," she says. "It gave me this sense of urgency, and again the feeling that life was too short."

In Oxnard, which is one of the country's top strawberry-picking regions, pesticides sprayed by large-scale fruit farms waft across the countryside and into the respiratory systems of the people who live, work, and go to school there. Although it is not known how her nephew got cancer, the school that he attended is right across the road from one of these farms. Breathing those toxic fumes was not healthy for anyone who lived nearby.

Latinx farmworkers in California have long fought for the state to recognize the harm inflicted upon them by agricultural practices. They took their case to court, suing the California Department of Pesticide Regulation for discrimination, because the chemicals that are sprayed disproportionately affect Latinx communities. After a decade-long battle, they won; and the Environmental Protection Agency was forced to restrict its chemical use.

Carmen's nephew's illness, and his daily fight to live forced Carmen to realize that invisible, insidious attacks on the environment can play just as big a role in perpetuating inequity as overt violence and discrimination. "When I got the news about my nephew, I realized that this movement was not just about criminal justice reform, or police brutality," she says. "It's about environmental justice. It's about immigration reform. It's about all these other things that impact us all."

"One of the teachings from Barrios Unidos that we talk about is honoring Mother Earth, and also honoring our spirit," she says. "It's all interconnected. It's all valuable. It's all important. And it needs to also all be recognized." When people see Carmen's image today on posters and banners; or when they hear her on stage at the Women's March in front of a roaring crowd of 2 million people in Washington, DC, and 5 million people around the world, they may not know the story of the little girl who was passionate about basketball and hip hop, and who sought to escape her small farming community after her sister's death. But her message to potential activists from across the country is simple: that little girl could be you.

She sees a new generation of activists coming of age and bringing their own passion to causes across the board. "Whether it's climate justice, immigration reform, criminal justice reform, violence prevention, Black Lives Matter, whatever it may be, there's a lane for them," she says. "Young people should always remember that their voice is powerful, and they have always been at the forefront of every movement in America. Our youth are powerful, sacred, and are the leaders we've been waiting for. We are ready to mentor them and for them to lead us, and build together with. If I can share anything with them is that they should never ever take for granted the opportunity that is presented to them. Don't be afraid to take a leap!"

These days, Carmen has a small child of her own: a vocal baby boy who is already clamoring for change -- though at this stage, it's more likely for a change of diapers than for political change. The world she wants for her son, and for his generation, she says, doesn't start in the future, however. It starts now.

"I often remind young people that although we believe that they are our future, they are actually our present, and are the greatest gift that we have," she says. Still, she recognizes that it can be hard to take the leap into the life of an activist. "And if they're not ready, it's okay, because those of us that are out here are going to be ready to receive them whenever they are."

Thinking back to her younger years, she is grateful to Nane Alejandrez, who first saw her spark; and to Harry Belafonte, for giving her a platform to raise her voice; and to everyone else who has taken Carmen under their wing. "It is not only our responsibility to create pathways of leadership for our youth," she says. "But also to cultivate them."

You can cage the singer but not the song.

Harry Belafonte

Call to Action: The Gathering for Justice League NYC | Justice League CA: https://www.gatheringforjustice.org/justiceleaguenyc Barrios Unidos: http://www.barriosunidos.net/

RISE UP FOR AFRICA!
Vanessa Nakate
Uganda

It was meant to be a celebration -- an opportunity for young peoples' voices to be heard. World leaders, philanthropists, and celebrities at the Davos World Economic Forum were all impressed with the bravery of these young climate activists, as well as by their bold statements.

They'd been planning for months. More than 20 of them had worked hard to develop a statement, challenging their leaders to take specific actions. Some of them had traveled to Davos from all over the world. They spoke on panels, attended VIP events, and were invited to prestigious photo ops with Prince Charles and other dignitaries. They were prominently featured by the media. And on the final day, #FridaysforFuture held a press conference to repeat their demands for concrete actions from the world community.

An Associated Press photographer captured the moment, showing climate activists Greta Thunberg, Luisa Neubauer, Isabelle Axelsson, and Loukina Tille standing next to one another, looking very serious. But, for whatever reason, the photo cropped out the only young *black* woman: Vanessa Nakate, #FridaysforFutureUganda's champion. In response, Vanessa posted a powerful message on Twitter: *"You didn't just erase a photo. You erased a continent. But I am stronger than ever."*

Many times in her young life as an activist Vanessa has experienced Africans being left out of the picture -- both literally and figuratively. "At some point it feels like the world just doesn't care," she says. "But Africans have been fighting for climate action for many years now."

That one photo lit up a firestorm. Vanessa received messages from people all over the world voicing their outrage. African activists reached out to her, sharing how they had experienced discrimination, and even overt racism. Their complaints became a global refrain. Eventually the AP took down the cropped photo and released a new one. In that one, Vanessa stands in the middle of her fellow activists -- front and center.

It was a small victory, but it provided a broader metaphor for the climate movement. Vanessa quickly seized the moment and leveraged the attention to get the media to focus on the profound role of Africans in the fight against climate change.

To Vanessa, fighting for the climate *must* include Africans -- who are contributing the fewest greenhouse gas emissions and yet paying the highest price for climate change. In Uganda, in Madrid at the COP25 climate conference, at Davos, and indeed, around the world, she has made it her mission to make sure African voices are being heard in the global movement. "I personally want to amplify the voices of other climate activists in Africa, because we've always been underrepresented in climate change conversations," she says. And she adds, "I really want to change that."

For Vanessa, finding her own voice as an activist didn't happen overnight, however. Growing up, she tended to keep to herself. As a shy person, she didn't like to be the center of attention. "I really don't open up to people very easily, so it was quite hard for me to walk through the streets and strike for the climate," she says.

Complicating things was the fact that in Uganda, Vanessa didn't have much access to a climate change education. While her teachers would mention climate change as a theoretical problem, the reality of it never really hit home until she was older.

But what she didn't get from her school, she got from her father. As a member of the Kampala Rotary Club, he often went on tree-planting missions to communities across Uganda. This inspired Vanessa as she grew older and became more independent. Curious to learn more, she started watching the news and doing her own research. She was shocked to see the devastation that climate change had already wrought on Uganda and neighboring countries like the Democratic Republic of the Congo.

In the Congolese rainforests, trees were already losing their ability to capture carbon because of higher temperatures and long-term drought. In the next 15 years, according to scientists, the trees will be unable to capture any CO_2, which could irreversibly impact biodiversity, and the environment generally. Then in 2019, when the Congo basin -- the second largest rainforest in the world, after the Amazon -- caught fire, Vanessa saw just how dangerous climate change could be, not just for African countries, but for the entire world.

Vanessa soon began to understand how climate change was affecting her on a personal level. In her own country, which is still largely agricultural, she learned about how droughts have already affected farmers, and how that in turn has impacted her own family's consumption habits. With higher temperatures, farmers can't produce as much grain and other staple foods; what they do produce, they are forced to sell at higher prices to make up for the loss.

"I may not be affected directly, because my parents are the ones who buy the food at home, but there are nearby communities where the less privileged don't even have the ability to get food or access to clean water when these disasters strike," she says.

Vanessa decided that despite her natural shyness, she just had to take a stand. So, inspired by the brave activism of Swedish student Greta Thunberg, she stood outside, in front of the Ugandan parliament building to call for more climate action. It wasn't until she stepped out of her house that she realized just how easy it was to make a difference. "The moment you step out, I don't even know where the fear goes, but it actually goes away," she says. "The only way to overcome your fears is to confront them."

For months, Vanessa's protest was a solitary one. She carried a simple sign with four lines printed on it:

"Green love, green peace."

"Beat Plastic, Polythene, Pollution."

"Thanks for the global warming."

"Climate Strike Now."

At first, she dealt with a lot of hostility. People would yell things at her from their cars, saying that she was wasting her time. After a while, however, others began to join her cause. In Uganda, activists joined her climate protests in front of the parliament building. In all, Vanessa has now participated in more than 60 Fridays for Future marches, mostly in Uganda, but also at the United Nations Youth Climate Summit, at COP25 in Madrid, and at Davos, where she was invited to join other climate activists from around the world.

She also joined with other activists to form a movement called Youth for Future Africa. As the group grew, and activists and concerned citizens of all ages and nationalities got involved, they changed their name to the Rise Up Africa Movement. Vanessa hopes that through their activism, people will not just take action for the environment, but they will begin to see other African issues as an equally important part of the puzzle.

For Earth Day's 50th Anniversary in 2020, Rise Up Africa participated in the digital strike for the climate. They filled their Twitter feed with videos of young Africans speaking out about the importance of protecting the environment. And they launched a podcast called "Why Climate Activism," where the hosts speak with climate activists around the world and share tips about how to get involved.

At first, I thought I was fighting to save a tree.

Then I thought I was fighting to save a rainforest.

Now I realize I am fighting for HUMANITY

#Earthdaywerise #Riseupmovement #EarthDay2020

Vanessa has increasingly become one of the most well-known African youth climate activists. She's now an official influencer, with 208,000 Twitter followers. She was honored to be the first to be featured on the new TV series, *People of the Planet*. And Jane Fonda featured her on Fire Drill Fridays.

Now, despite not being allowed to gather in large groups due to the coronavirus pandemic, Vanessa has continued her activism. In fact, the pandemic has shown her even more clearly the importance of people not waiting to step up, step out, and make a difference. "Everything about climate change greatly affects our lives," she says. "It's a matter of life and death. When people say we have 10 years to save the planet, I say no: we have *no* time!"

Sometimes, it falls upon a generation to be great.

Nelson Mandela

Call to Action: Join Vanessa and other youth climate activists around the world in fighting for climate action *now*. Follow the Rise Up Africa Movement on Twitter and listen to the "Why Climate Activism?" podcast to learn what you can do to get involved. https://twitter.com/vanessa_vash https://twitter.com/TheRiseUpMovem1?s=20

SUSTAINABILITY FOR BLACK COMMUNITIES
Illai Kenney
HBCU Green Fund
Georgia/Washington DC

From a very young age Illai Kenney understood the connection between sustainability and her identity as a Black woman. Her mother, Felicia Davis, was working in the sustainability field: she would often bring home magazines from work with articles about global warming and climate change. Illai was intrigued, and she was always curious to learn more -- and find ways she could get involved to help remedy the situation. But at school, when she read her science textbooks, she didn't find much about these issues.

Illai was troubled. She knew that Black communities like hers are the most negatively impacted by global warming and climate change. And as a young person, she was outraged that the planet, and her right to a healthy, sustainable future, was being ruined by decisions made by an older generation disconnected from her reality. "We are the ones who are going to be the most impacted by the decisions being made today," she said. "But what recourse do we children have? We can't vote. We can't run for office." Thinking back on it now, years later, she says, "It was a daunting realization to come to."

So, at age 12, Illai and her friends created the nonprofit organization, Georgia Kids Against Pollution (KAP), to do something about it. She wanted to be a bridge between her friends and those who were engaged with more visible social issues, like gun violence and voting rights, than with environmental activism.

Illai had grown up around community organizing, and had seen how protesting can help people get their voices heard. "I had a knack for finding common ground. And I did a lot of organizing," she says. Still, she needed a little guidance. "So we went to the adults in our lives, who helped us flesh out our ideas, and prepare us for some of the challenges we would meet with KAP. The environment was affecting us, giving young kids in our neighborhood asthma. These things were affecting us, but we really didn't understand," she says. "Things like carbon dioxide, sulfur dioxide, and mercury, were being put out into the air by power plants and major pollutants. They cause smog; they cause global warming; they cause acid rain, which in turn affects us. These power plants dump pollutants into low-income areas." And she added, "Somebody needs to let the people who live there know that yes, you do have a choice; you aren't forced to live with this stuff. And you can make a difference if you want to."

In 2003, when she was just 13 years old, Illai led the first KAP protest, held outside of the Southern Company, a gas and utility corporation based in Georgia. "Our demonstration actually made it into the shareholders report," she says proudly. "This gigantic corporation actually heard our concerns about alternative energy. At the time, I didn't realize it was such an effective action." She smiles, and adds, "I started small. And I still haven't let up in the fight."

That same year, Illai received the prestigious Brower Youth Award, which is given each year to six youth environmental leaders across the country. "Despite the struggles of organizing, that really gave me validation," she says. The following year, Illai joined her mother at the U.N. Conference on Sustainable Development in Johannesburg, South Africa. She was eager to learn about how people around the world were being affected by environmental issues, and what they were doing to find solutions. "At the conference, I saw firsthand how communities of color face the same issues wherever we are on the planet; economic issues, social justice issues, environmental issues." She adds, "Environmental issues are often the last ones to be talked about."

The visibility from the Brower Youth Award led to a nonprofit organization, Corporate Accountability International, reaching out to Illai when she was 16. They wanted to partner with her on some advocacy work at a Coca Cola international shareholder's meeting. Illai spoke on behalf of farmers in India who were having their local groundwater supplies devastated by the company. She asked a roomful of shareholders what they planned to do when young people refused to buy Coca-Cola due to their abusive water practices in India. Shortly thereafter organizers succeeded in getting Coca Cola to shut down two of the most predatory plants in India, which were impoverishing local communities. "Getting involved with shareholder advocacy opened up a new world of ways to engage civically," she says. "Today it's a common tactic, but back then, there wasn't much conversation around this sort of engagement."

When it was time for college, Illai chose Howard University, her mother's alma mater, in Washington D.C. as the place she wanted to further her studies in communications. While at Howard, she interned with the university's Office of Sustainability. That's when she discovered the gaping holes in support for sustainable development among Historically Black Colleges and Universities (HBCUs), especially around tech, solar energy, and green education issues. "The expertise that a lot of universities take for granted -- HBCUs just don't have access to that," she says. So she set about changing that too, step by step, as she always had.

As a project manager in the Office of Sustainability Illai helped support projects like the installation of solar panels on buildings at Howard; green energy retrofits around the campus; the formation of a full-scale recycling program; and an organic garden with a composting program. Each of these projects was a huge step toward creating a more sustainable university. However, each project was also a standalone project. This awareness challenged Illai to think about bigger questions concerning the nature of longer-term sustainable growth.

In partnership with her mother, Illai cofounded the HBCU Green Fund, to create a capital infrastructure for long-term sustainable growth projects to generate money for HBCUs. Their strategy is to support projects that reduce energy and water usage on HBCU campuses – which creates financial savings, which are then reinvested into more sustainable projects and infrastructure. Illai hopes that it will also inspire a whole new generation of African American students to appreciate the value of green living.

In all of her successes, Illai is always quick to recognize the tremendous legacy she inherited from her family, who were among the most forward-thinking environmentalists, at a time when such thinking was in its infancy. "My great-grandmother was the greatest conservationist and communicator," she says. "She mastered so many of the strategies that are just now becoming common -- recycling, urban agriculture, living simply, investing wisely -- and also, the power of proactive community engagement."

Illai's mother, Felicia Davis, continues to be a leading voice for advancing sustainability in the HBCU community and beyond. At the United Negro College Fund, she has created impactful projects like the Building Green Initiative, which has helped Black, Hispanic-serving, and tribal colleges move toward a more sustainable future. In the early 2000s, Felicia carried on her family's legacy when she started a network of eco-cyber centers in rural Ghana, South Africa, and Senegal. She has also used technology to create powerful cultural exchanges and environmental stewardship programs, through projects like beach and village cleanups.

This dynamic mother and daughter duo are frequent spokespersons who represent communities of color at predominantly white conferences like Project Drawdown. They also ensure that they are not the only Black voices in white spaces by securing funding for other Black leaders to join them. "While there's a legacy that runs down from my great-grandmother, to my mother, to me, that sense of stewardship is not only for my family, or my community alone. It should extend out globally in our actions, far beyond ourselves and our own communities."

For youth who want to pursue a path in sustainability, Illai has some practical advice. "What I tend to tell young people is that every day, we all make choices. And the worlds we create are a reflection of the choices we make." Responsible choices create responsible individuals – and ultimately, this creates responsible communities.

Illai wants young people to understand how their actions can reach far beyond wherever they started. In her eyes, it's important to be informed about what you want to pursue as a youth, because knowledge leads to better choices, and better choices lead to empowerment. By educating yourself as much as possible, you are also creating a person that is resilient. This is important, especially for Black youth and communities of color, in a time when we are constantly surrounded by overwhelming amounts of conflicting information, and we face the constant existential threats from police brutality and structural racism. In these trying times, we need more youth and adult leaders to make space for those who are most impacted by these issues.

Illai, ever the practical leader, says that she could give us a long story, or a big lesson, to try to get the legacy of sustainability that her family has embodied across to others. But to put it quite simply, for those of us who want to make the world a better place, she says, "When you know better you are obligated to do better."

As you enter positions of trust and power, dream a little before you think.

Toni Morrison

Call to Action: Support Illai's work to create an equitable, environmental infrastructure, with green endowments for Historically Black Colleges and Universities. https://hbcugreenfund.org/

WALKING BETWEEN WORLDS
Shilpa Jain
YES!
Berkeley, California

From a young age, Shilpa Jain learned how to "walk between worlds." Born and raised in a multicultural community in suburban Chicago, Shilpa didn't realize how unusual it was to coexist with people from the Philippines, Haiti, India, Taiwan, Korea, Pakistan, Thailand, and Syria. "I had no idea at the time what a privilege it was to grow up with that kind of diversity; I just thought it was normal."

At the same time, she was blessed with belonging to a strong Rajasthani community. She would spend her weekends with her parents and their friends speaking Hindustani and Marwari, celebrating traditional festivals, and sharing traditional food. Multiple childhood trips to India cemented her connection to her family's homeland. "So, I felt myself simultaneously rooted in a community and comfortably building bridges across differences with others."

Shilpa was raised Jain, which is a small minority faith in India. She has been empowered by several of the core principles of the faith. The first is *anekantavaad*, which means "There are many paths to truth." Everyone has a part of the answer, and therefore, there is no need to judge anyone. The second is *ahimsa*, which focuses on creating a culture of love, compassion, and understanding. It's about doing as little harm or violence as possible. For Shilpa, this manifests powerfully not only with people, but with "how I feel toward the trees, the birds, the small insects... that sense that we are all connected." The third principle is *aparigraha,* which is living with a sense of enough. This principle focuses on sharing and completeness, as a means to restore balance and achieve justice and fairness.

Shilpa has integrated all of these principles into her practice of activism – from awareness, to service, to advocacy, to teaching, to the creation of development policy, to cocreating learning communities. This journey has taken her from Chicago to the East Coast of the U.S., to India, Lebanon, Jordan, Egypt, Iran, Pakistan, Senegal, Malaysia, Thailand, Bolivia, Mexico -- and back to the United States, where she now roots herself in Berkeley, California.

For the last nine years, Shilpa has been the executive director of the nonprofit YES! Founded in 1990 by Ocean Robbins and Ryan Eliason, YES!'s mission is to connect, inspire, and collaborate with changemakers to build thriving, just, and regenerative paths of life for all. For Shilpa, the military-industrial-institutional model has stranded many people, keeping them from "the lifeboat of living in community." This disconnection isolates and socializes us in ways that can lead to violence and dehumanization. Instead, Shilpa has embraced a core YES! value: that personal, interpersonal, and systemic change are all interconnected. "We welcome different sectors of communities that have been disaffected...and try to move the needle in a positive direction. Together we recognize that our cultures and identities can transform as we transform ourselves."

Shilpa began her journey by serving the elderly and poor. Soon, she realized that charity and service work did not address the larger systemic issues that are generated by failed political and economic institutions. She tried advocacy and activism through petitions and protests and struggled with asking those who were causing the problems to fix them, when they didn't seem to have an incentive to change. She experienced a similar revelation while teaching peace-making and creative self-expression programs for at-risk youth. "These activities could only serve as a band-aid for the attack on young peoples' souls from the violence and intensity of the school system and the larger world," she says.

At the height of her frustration with trying to fix a broken world, in 1999, Shilpa attended a conference on Gandhian education in New Delhi. There, she met a Tibetan monk, Samdhong Rimpoche, who later became the prime minister of the Tibetan government-in-exile, and asked him, "Don't you think we need to just destroy this system?" she explained. "It's so violent, oppressive, and exploitative. I can't see a way forward without breaking it all down." He responded, "Shilpa, instead of thinking about destruction, think about renunciation. If you let go of the system, if you organize around freedom and possibility and building the world we want, the system will lose its power and you will regain yours."

This revelation shifted Shilpa's work as a "learning activist" at Shikshantar: The Peoples' Institute for Rethinking Education and Development, based in Udaipur, India. She worked with Shikshantar's cofounder and Shilpa's elder brother, Manish, and they were a powerful team for more than 10 years. It was at Shikshantar that Shilpa was first able to see her way toward an integrated life, *where living is learning, and learning is living.*" Through the work of Rabindranath

Tagore, known as "the Bard of India," she studied creativity as a core aspect of self, and collective, liberation. Shilpa integrated this learning by leading workshops for children using theatre, art, and cooperative games as forms of self-expression, collective communication, and vision development.

"I had the chance to investigate and understand real-world crises and conflicts, from struggles against the building of big dams to the death of the small farmer," Shilpa explains. "I also was blessed to meet extraordinary people who, maybe by others' standards, might be called just ordinary. But in them, from them, I saw wisdom, dedication, and firm belief in the true and good."

Then, in 2002, Shilpa attended her first YES! Jam. She was drawn into the World Youth Leadership Jam because its core principles aligned with her ideas of co-learning - where everyone would be learning together during this week-long intensive experience. Inspired by the way that musicians gather, the Jam is the heart and soul of YES!'s work. By design, the Jams offer an improvisational, fluid, creative, and collaborative paradigm of human community. Over the last 20 years, over 150+ YES! Jams have been held with changemakers on six continents. Each of them touches on different issues and creates a shared place for an integrated learning community.

"The Jam community is an ever-expanding network with a worldwide reach, a cauldron of human potential," Shilpa explains. "People bring their unique tools and talents to share and grow together. Jam leaders and attendees reflect a kaleidoscope of diversity in origin, religion, vocation, and culture. There are Sufis, Christians, Buddhists, Muslims, Jains, Jews, those without a specific faith, and more. Jams bring together artists, activists, educators, lawyers, dreamers, visionaries, healers, academics, data analysts, and small business owners, and so many more people who are part of other movements and organizations. We come together to learn from each other, to face our fears and challenges, to uncover solutions and ways forward, to dream of a more truthful, loving, whole world – and to practice ways to get there."

Shilpa recalls one of the most memorable moments she had, at the second-ever Jam in Turkey: "At the end of an incredible night of gifts and offerings from the community – dances, songs, poems, 'angel walks' – a transcendent feeling, something beyond me, entered the space. The group formed a circle and started singing beautiful songs of friendship and love, and, all of a sudden the sky was full of shooting stars. Then Aysegul, one of the cofounders of the Jam said, with tears streaming down her face, 'It's possible. The world that we dream of. It's possible. It's here.' I felt that Rumi had entered the circle, and I truly felt what it is to accept each other with all of our struggles, imperfections, beauty, and grace."

Shilpa remembers this moment often. It inspires her to continue expanding this powerful community, especially during these times. She knows that the more we can listen to our inner truths and to each other, the more we can slow down and work through our conflicts, the more we can uncover and manifest all the solutions we need -- which are already here. She hopes the next Jam will transform more people's lives, giving them the courage to join in cocreating a world that works for all.

Develop enough courage so that you can stand
up for yourself
and then stand up for somebody else.

Maya Angelou

Call to Action: Support YES! or sign up for a JAM. Visit www. yesworld.org. Follow YES! FB - yescommunity and YES! Twitter – yeschangemakers

WATER WALKER
Autumn Peltier
Anishinabek Nation • Canada

Autumn Peltier remembers her first-ever Water Walk. It was the spring of 2017 and she was just 12 years old. The weather that day was pretty stormy. As she and a group of Indigenous activists crossed a treacherous bridge, the wind blew so hard that Autumn could barely move forward. The rain swirled down around her. Nevertheless, she pushed on.

Autumn's great aunt Josephine Mandamin was leading the small group, which was walking all the way from Duluth, Minnesota to Matane, Quebec -- more than 3,000 miles. It was Autumn's first Water Walk, and for Josephine, at 75 years old, it was her last: an important moment in both of their lives.

This walk was their shared legacy, passed down from their ancestors, for future generations of water warriors. "When you think about how strong Indigenous women are, you're never supposed to let anything stop you," Autumn says.

Activism runs through Autumn's blood. Her great aunt Josephine started the Water Walk movement in 2003, before Autumn was even born. A respected Anishinaabe elder, Josephine wanted to bring attention to a problem that affects First Nations peoples across Canada: a lack of access to safe drinking water. She decided she would walk around the Great Lakes and pray for them, and then she would keep on walking.

Josephine's first walk was around the entire perimeter of Lake Superior, a 2,500-mile journey. She then walked around the rest of the Great Lakes: Michigan, Huron, Erie, and Ontario. And she kept walking, even as she grew older and older. Eventually she had completed 13 journeys, and walked tens of thousands of miles.

Why fight to save the water? For the people of the Wiikwemkoong First Nation, water is the most sacred of the elements, but for Indigenous people across Canada and around the world it is also one of the scarcest. And with climate change this precious resource is becoming even harder to find, as temperatures rise and desertification accelerates.

"It's really important to us because when we're in the womb, we live in water for nine months," Autumn says. "We learn how to love our mothers and how to love the water."

Josephine always reminded Autumn of how important this element was in sustaining life, and also in their Indigenous culture. When Josephine passed away in February of 2019, at 77 years old, Autumn knew it was her turn to be a leader and to make sure that her people's water was protected.

"I had to think to myself, 'Who is going to carry on her work?' she says. "And if I don't do it, then who is going to protect the waters?"

Autumn didn't just walk the walk; she also talked the talk. Over the last few years, she has become a global voice for water rights -- speaking at major international conferences, starting trends on social media, and calling for action from world leaders, including her own -- Prime Minister Justin Trudeau.

"I am very unhappy with the choices you made," Autumn told the prime minister at a First Nations water conference in 2016. Her simple honesty caught the attention of many worldwide. During his election campaign, Trudeau had painted himself as a champion of Indigenous rights, saying that he wanted all water advisories for First Nations peoples in Canada to be eliminated by 2021. This would mean that instead of having to boil their drinking water to avoid infections and illness, they could just turn on the tap like all other Canadians.

While Trudeau has made progress in reducing the number of water advisories -- from 105 when he took office, to 56 in September of 2019 -- it just hasn't been enough. "You see people talking about what they have done and what they're saying they're gonna do," Autumn says. "You never really see people talking about the other side of that: what they're not doing."

Autumn has also called on Trudeau to stop the construction of oil pipelines that cut through First Nations lands and seep into their water resources.

Autumn has never been afraid to raise her voice and speak up. She began to learn public speaking at an early age, just eight years old. It has become a way for her to honor her Indigenous heritage, and to share her own voice as an activist.

Still, she says, sometimes she gets nervous. She gave her first big speech when she was 10, to a conference of First Nations people. Staring out at the more than 500 leaders gathered there, she worried that she couldn't do it. But then she reminded herself of why she was there and what she wanted to accomplish.

"Everybody here just wants to listen to me. They're not gonna judge me. They just want to listen," she thought.

As she has grown up, Autumn has continued to speak up for her people, traveling from Canada to the U.S. and Europe. She spoke at the Children's Climate Conference in Sweden; the United Nation Secretary-General's Climate Action Summit in New York; and the World Economic Forum in Davos, Switzerland. Each time, she proudly wore her traditional water dress, which her mother made for her.

At a conference in New York she told world leaders, "We can't eat money or drink oil," a quote that sent shockwaves around the globe.

Autumn's environmental leadership and activism have been recognized around the world. She was named one of the 30 under 30 climate leaders by the North American Association for Environmental Education; she received the 2019 "Planet in Focus" Rob Stewart Youth Eco-Hero award; and she has been featured on the BBC as one of the 100 most influential women in the world.

Maybe most importantly, on a personal level, she was named the chief water commissioner by the Anishinabek Nation -- carrying on her family's legacy, and the position once held by her dear great aunt Josephine.

For Autumn, the global spotlight is not what is important. Rather, it's the message behind her activism that she wants to see resonate, to have a ripple effect around the world.

"Anybody can do this work, and everybody can make a change," she says. "It's not only young people that are already making change, it's everybody."

For Autumn, who is now 16, the immediate goals are clear. More than 100 First Nations tribes in Canada are still on short-term water advisories at any given time. As some of her people gain access to clean water resources, others lose it. She is committed to doing whatever she can so that this number is decreased to zero.

Her mission, in addition to carrying on the work of her great aunt Josephine, is a deeply personal one. The first time she ever encountered a community with a water boil notice, she was shocked to learn that many kids from communities much like her own had grown up their entire lives not knowing what it was like to simply be able to use water from the tap.

"And I was just like, 'Why, for 20 years, has nothing been done about this?'" she asks.

The Canadian government has begun to take the problem more seriously. Its 2016 budget provided nearly $2 billion for clean water projects across the country. But there's still a long way to go -- not only in Canada but around the world.

Nearly 850 million people worldwide lack access to clean drinking water. Many of them are located in Sub-Saharan Africa, but that's not the only place where this is a problem. Even American cities like Flint, Michigan, and developing countries like South Africa experience water shortages that have lasting negative side effects. A lack of access to clean drinking water can lead to water-borne illnesses, difficulties in school, and even mental health issues later in life.

This is why Autumn marched alongside her great aunt Josephine around the lakes, and this is why she has continued to hold truth to power through her activism.

"When I speak to decision makers, I tell them that their decision is going to impact not only their grandchildren; it's going to impact our future, and our children's future, and our great grandchildren's future," she says. "So, I feel like the decisions they make today need to be more thought-through."

As women, we are carriers of the water. We carry life for the people.

Josephine Mandamin

Call to Action: Respect water. Take a stand for the water rights of Indigenous peoples. Follow and repost: Autumn https://www.instagram.com/autumn.peltier/.

YOUTH ORGANIZATIONS DEMAND THE ENTRY INTO FORCE OF THE ESCAZÚ AGREEMENT

As young people, we understand the immense health crisis of the COVID-19 pandemic, which has exacerbated injustices and disproportionately harmed vulnerable communities across the world. Because of this, young people from South America, Central America, the Caribbean and North America have come together to urge the entry into force of the Regional Agreement on Access to Information, Public Participation and Access to Justice in Environmental Matters in Latin America and the Caribbean also known as the Escazú Agreement.

The Agreement was adopted in Escazú, Costa Rica on March 4, 2018 after six years of negotiation, becoming the first Regional Treaty of the Economic Commission for Latin America and the Caribbean (ECLAC). Of the thirty-three States in Latin America and the Caribbean, twenty-two States have signed it. As for the eleven remaining States, it is imperative that they sign the Agreement by September 26, 2020, so that they can participate in the decision-making process. Additionally, the Agreement has achieved nine ratifications out of the eleven ratifications needed for its official entry into force. However, it is necessary to clarify that September 26 only represents the deadline for signature, not future ratifications or accessions. As September 2020 marks two years since the Agreement was open for signing, the prompt ratification and implementation is paramount to the success of the Agreement to benefit the public.

Originating from "Principle 10" of the Rio Declaration on Environment and Development, the Escazú Agreement is the first legally binding environmental Human Rights treaty in Latin America and the Caribbean. The citizens of the region are the main beneficiaries -- in particular, the frontline communities most vulnerable to the climate crisis who are often environmental defenders who face Human Rights violations. The Agreement secures the right of all people to have free access to environmental information, participate meaningfully in decisions that affect their lives and their environment, and be protected by the law if these rights are violated.

Additionally, the Agreement provides essential legal provisions to protect the rights of defenders of the environment who face persecutions and murder. It also seeks to avoid conflicts that have increasingly affected the States of the region because of extractive projects, such as the fracking projects in Colombia, the planned oil exploration and extraction in Costa Rica, the development of the Mayan Train in Mexico, the illegal deforestation in Argentina, the violation of Indigenous rights in Peru, pollution of waterways in from increased development Grenada, and the increase of illegal sand mining in Saint Lucia, among many others. Latin America and the Caribbean is one of the most vulnerable regions to the Climate Crisis. The increase in temperature of just 1.1° C has resulted in increasingly intense hydrometeorological effects, including sea level rise, ocean acidification, and many others directly concerned with Human Rights and Food, Health and the Right to Life. If the temperature increases further, these effects will be magnified, especially affecting frontline communities. Latin America and the Caribbean only contributed to less than 10% of the overall total of greenhouse gas emissions in 2014. Nevertheless, according to an ECLAC report in 2018, its land use change and agriculture contributed to 42% of the greenhouse gas emissions in 2014, compared to the global average of 18%.

This region has the characteristic of having a large number of defenders, who are mostly Native, dedicated to protecting the biodiversity and ecosystems that are necessary to prevent damage to the environment, even if this means putting their own lives at risk. According to the Global Witness, by 2019, 212 murders were committed against defenders worldwide, of which 148 were from Latin America.

Protecting environmental defenders and improving democratic participation in environmental decisions is crucial to halting the destruction of the environment and solidifying the commitment to action on the Climate Crisis.

We have an urgent responsibility to fight for a sustainable future, with prosperity and respect for all forms of life and their rights in present and future generations. Therefore, we demand the signature of the remaining States and the necessary ratifications for the prompt entry into force of the Escazu Agreement, which would signify a historical milestone in the protection and progression of Human Rights and Environmental Justice.

III

INSPIRE!
Education Champions

INSPIRE!
Education Champions

As a young person, I responded to President Kennedy's Call to Action -- and decided to become a teacher. I pursued a socially progressive humanistic education led by Dwight Allen, who was Dean of the School of Education at the University of Massachusetts-Amherst. When I was 19, during my junior year of college, I began a quest in search of a more humane education, especially for children with special needs. Fortunately I discovered the Rudolf Steiner International Training Center in Aberdeen, Scotland, and became immersed in their "whole child" teaching model. As a "special needs" teacher, I've treasured being with children who have these "superpowers." So when I met Greta, I sensed the importance of her message and her timing. I've dedicated my life to working with young people, and to finding better ways to build a more humanistic, sustainable, just, and equitable world. At the heart of the Institute's books, curriculums, trainings, youth leadership initiatives and Sustainability Summits is Steiner's whole child teaching model with the Socratic questioning method. Given our mission of inclusivity and equity, we emphasize multicultural education though our bilingual tools so we can inspire, educate and empower all children to build a more sustainable world.

It's estimated that there are 10 million new blue-green jobs. Imagine if we educated the millions of young inspired by Greta to rebuild the planet!

The young and emerging leaders in this chapter know that education is at the heart of all social change: from Adenike Oladosu in Nigeria to Shreya K.C in Nepal, from Jett Zhang at FridaysforFuture Digital, to Angelique Pouponneau in the Seychelles, from Aadya Joshi in India to Benita Davis in Guyana, Jasper Ralph on Martha's Vineyard, and Joshua Gorman of Generation Waking Up!

After graduating from Harvard University Shilpa Jain spent 10 years as a "learning activist" at Shikshantar: The Peoples' Institute for Rethinking Education and Development in India. There she was able to create an integrated life, "where living is learning and learning is living." Later she learned about The Jam, which she describes as "an ever-expanding network; a melting pot of human potential." Now at YESWorld.org Shilpa offers Jams for artists, activists, educators, dreamers, and visionaries. She hopes her Jams will transform people's lives, and give them the courage to join others in building a new world.

As the son of a U.S. diplomat, Scott Warren grew up in countries where democracy is less taken for granted than it is in the U.S. One of the most important lessons he learned growing up abroad is that democracy is fragile. When he returned to the U.S. for college, he became concerned that young Americans weren't more involved in making change in their own communities. He decided that a new, action-oriented approach was needed to bring youth into the political process by engaging them in issues they care about, and he founded Generation Citizen.

In Mohamad Al Jounde's home, activism was a part of daily life; both of his parents were involved in the Syrian revolution, and as a result the family had to flee to Lebanon. There, at the age of 12, Mohamad had the idea to start a school for refugee children. "Revolution isn't only about protesting what is wrong," he says. "It's also about building community."

On her first day as a Peace Corps volunteer in Malawi, Jill Bhowmik was welcomed by one of her students, who told her, right off the bat, "I'll be a great student!" But as the student showed her how to plant seed potatoes in her yard, Jill quickly realized that she would be learning at least as much from her students as they would be learning from her. "I'll never forget what was important to that community," she says. Jill is now a journalism teacher at Granite High School in San Diego. What she learned in Malawi is relevant today, since some of the answers to creating a sustainable world can be found in the agricultural practices of traditional cultures.

The heroes featured in this chapter have created and discovered a myriad of ways to make education fun, effective, and above all meaningful. Their stories can inspire all of us to find ways to both learn and share knowledge that can help us expand our thinking about education and find a way to make a better world for tomorrow's children.

A CALL TO CIVIC ACTION
SCOTT WARREN
Generation Citizen
Providence, Rhode Island

When Scott Warren was in 10th grade, he witnessed Kenya's first truly democratic election. "It completely changed my way of thinking," admits Scott. "It was in Kenya, for the first time, that I understood the power of democracy. I got to see how excited people were to cast their vote. For many of them it was the first vote they had ever cast in their lives that really mattered." For over 30 years, Kenya had been ruled by the Kenya African National Union (KANU), in a one party system. Until that fateful day, the people of Kenya had no say in their future.

When Scott was 8 years old his father joined the State Department. His family left their home in San Diego to experience the world. Frequent travel was part and parcel of growing up for Scott. He was constantly moving about, experiencing different people, languages, cultures, and most importantly, systems of government. By the time he was 16, he had been all around the United States and Latin America. It's been said that travel helps create a charitable mind. He credits his most formative experiences to living on the African continent.

"When you are living in a place without a democracy, things can be scary. People see that the democratic effort is towards good. But they doubt that a democracy could actually thrive, since it never had."

Scott would hold these lessons close to his heart; the main one being, democracy is fragile. This is something he wasn't taught in school when he was young, and it troubled him. Considering how important a concept this was. From that point forward, he made it his mission in life to ensure more young people in the United States were civically educated and engaged.

When Scott returned to the U.S., he attended Brown University. Here, he immediately got interested in learning all that he could about international politics on campus. By the end of his Senior year, he felt like he had the tools to start a civic movement of his own.

"A lot of young people want to make a difference, but don't necessarily see politics and local government as the best way to do so. There are a whole host of reasons for this. And people can be cynical about politics. But I think the main reason is that young people don't understand how these systems work – because we don't teach civics in schools anymore. And when we do, it's boring. It's like - how a bill becomes a law, that kind of approach."

So it made Scott wonder, how do we bring civics back to the classroom? How do we get young people excited about participating in a democracy? We need a new approach, and it needs to be action-oriented. It needs to bring young people to politics by engaging them in issues they care about. From here, while still a senior at Brown, he co-founded with Anna Ninan Generation Citizen (GC) to ensure that every student in the United States receives an effective action-oriented civics education.

In September 2008, they had their first success in Rhode Island schools, serving 300 students. In a year, they had offices in the Greater Boston area. By 2010, they had won a prestigious Echoing Green Fellowship for their work.

"We work with high schools to ensure that students take action civics, just like they would science or math. In our curriculum, they learn about local issues, and then take real plans of action to local government. It's getting at the root cause of a problem, and addressing it through the process from start to finish," Scott adds, "But it isn't always easy."

"I organized my first event when I was 23. We were working with the Providence Public School District, and all seemed well. That is, until I realized I messed up the bus registration process – and I did. It wasn't a small error. I was reprimanded. I felt incompetent. And more than anything, I felt so bad that an action of mine would take away any of the spotlight from these amazing youth leaders. It took me a lot of time to rebuild that relationship. But it was important that I recognized it was on me, and to get better. There was a bigger cause to serve out there."

"GC is a great organization, but I've made many mistakes along the way. Going through the ups and downs is what got me where I am today." Scott recalls another struggle he had. It occurred when he was lobbying at the state house of Rhode Island for divestment from Sudan, which was suffering from the genocide in Darfur. "While I was lobbying on the floor, a treasurer came by and said "this is a cute student project," – they didn't take me seriously at all. It made me feel like I was too young. Like I wasn't going to succeed. It can be hard to push forward without support. But I learned from this experience, and applied it to

GC. When you start a nonprofit, there are countless obstacles. You are always worried about having enough funds to support your cause, so you are always trying to raise funds. Because of this, you are living in a world of rejection, and you have to be able to deal with that. It's hard too, when it seems like more people should care about the issue that you care about. Having a greater cause in mind helps."

Scott describes the culmination of Generation Citizen's curriculum, where students really have the chance to shine. "We have a Civics Day that takes place at the end of the Fall and Spring semesters in each of our program sites. It's kind of like a science fair for civics, where our students present their action civics projects to the community, local officials, and community leaders who bridge the gap between them. It's a great place to see young people taking civic action."

Scott is especially eager to lower the voting age to 16. GC has a policy and advocacy component. It tries to ensure that action civics is a need-to-have in curriculums across the nation. A major advocacy issue of GC is their push for legislation to lower the voting age to 16. Scott believes that if younger people were going to be voting, schools would be much more motivated to properly provide civics education. "Our country has dismal voter participation, especially recently," says Scott adding, "Lowering the voting age is a necessary reform that's needed for spurring higher voter participation, more education, and more civic engagement."

This year alone, 30,000 students across the country have been engaged in action civics with GC. With offices in New York, Oakland, Massachusetts, Rhode Island, California, Oklahoma, and Texas, it might be easy to think Scott was an instant success. But this isn't the case.

Scott wants young people to know one thing about themselves – they hold a great amount of power. "Every time we have seen a positive change in this country, youth have been at the forefront. Whether it was the Civil Rights Movement, or Climate Change Advocacy, the youth have led the way where others wouldn't. So I believe it's up to young people to build a better democracy than the one we have today."

And he has all the faith in the world that they will. Especially when they are supported by strong adult leadership. "For too long, we've heard it said that young people have to wait their turn. We've heard that they don't have anything valuable to add to a conversation. We've heard that young people should wait until they are older, when they can really understand the way things work. To this sort of thinking? Well, I would just say that we need more of the unique knowledge that young people have out there. We need to hear more of their points of view. More of their abilities to unify people. And we need to support them now, more than ever."

In all of his work, Scott has demonstrated an amazing capacity to unify people through civic education. GC has acted as a bridge between organizations, and has brought many differing causes together. With its Community Change Fellowship, GC has funded students to partner with causes around the country. Those include YouthUprising (Bay Area), Make The Road New York, and the Boston Education Justice Alliance.

GC has countless alumni still making an impact by carrying on the tenets of civic education. In San Francisco, Democracy Coach Alumni Carmen Sobczak is educating on homelessness. In Boston, Community Change Fellow Giancarlo Castenda is informing students on injustice. And it's probably safe to say that Scott will continue leading young people for a long time to come through his educational programs.

Soon enough, these young people will have the tools to be civic leaders themselves. And that's really what Scott's work and messaging is about. The youth will lead us into a brighter future, and thanks to Scott, they will be the most prepared generation yet to take on the many challenges to come.

The philosophy of the school room in one generation will be the philosophy of government in the next.

Abraham Lincoln

Call to Action: Learn more about Scott's work in helping educate young people in basic civics: Generation Citizen at https://generationcitizen. org. Check out his book, *Generation Citizen: The Power of Youth in Our Politics* at https://www.amazon.com/Generation-Citizen-Power-Youth-Politics/dp/1640091270 .

ACTING LOCALLY & IN SOLIDARITY WITH OTHERS
Shreya K.C.
Nepalese Youth for Climate Action
Nepal

When Shreya K.C. went to her first class at Tribhuvan University in Lalitpur, Nepal, she was in for a surprise. Since she was a new student, she first met with her advisor to choose her academic track: her options were "E," "C," and "B." "That's easy," Shreya thought. "I'll pick E, for English."

However, when she arrived in class, she discovered that her professor didn't talk about William Shakespeare, or Charles Dickens. Instead, he started talking about the effects of global warming. He talked about environmental problems, and the serious effects the climate crisis was having on people all around the globe. And he challenged the students to think about their responsibility as environmentalists.

As it turns out, "E" actually stood for the environmental science track of her program.

"When I got back home that night, I was eager to learn more," Shreya says. "I wanted to learn about the people who are being forced to migrate from Nepal's higher mountain regions due to climate change: that really frightened me."

Before Shreya had come to university, she'd heard about global warming, and about issues like greenhouse gases and acid rain. But she had never really understood how serious the situation really was; or how it was affecting people in her own country.

"At first, I just felt like there was nothing I could do," Shreya says. "And I was just afraid: I thought, we only have a few years left to live on this planet."

But she decided that instead of giving in to her fear, she would dig down and educate herself about the negative impacts of climate change.

For Shreya, the fight against global warming is a fight for the survival of her own community. In Nepal, climate change has led to erratic and often drastic fluctuations in weather patterns. Scientists have warned that one third of the Himalayan glaciers could melt by the end of the century, filling glacier lakes below the mountains. These lakes would then overflow, causing more flash floods and mudslides, which have already displaced thousands of people. "None of the communities in Nepal are safe," says Shreya. "All of them are vulnerable to the impacts of climate change."

The poverty level is comparatively high in Nepal. And while most people have noticed a change in the weather patterns, few know about the underlying causes. "Most of the people here don't know about these things," Shreya says. "They don't know about the climate crisis, and they don't know what we should be doing to protect the environment."

Shreya started searching for solutions, and stories about people who were standing up and fighting for the future of our planet. "I studied what we can do as individuals, and especially how we, as young people, can lead," she says. "This really inspired me."

Then she learned about the 6th National Youth Conference on Climate Change, organized by Nepalese Youth for Climate Action (NYCA), together with the United Nation Development Program (UNDP). She promptly filled out the application form and sent it in. The following week she heard that she'd been rejected. But Shreya isn't one to give up easily. "Not a problem," she thought, and she gave the conference organizers a call. She let them know that if someone dropped out, she would love to attend. Much to her delight, on the very same day, another participant decided not to come, and Shreya was officially invited to attend the conference.

"I met all sorts of people there. It gave me hope that yes, we *can* do something, even though climate change is a global problem," she says. "If we act locally, and if we act in solidarity with others in our own communities, then of course we can do something!"

Inspired by the young people at the conference, Shreya started volunteering with NYCA. At the same time, she found a position teaching environmental science in a local school. For her, this was a perfect opportunity to engage young people in the issues that were close to her heart. "I helped the children develop a better appreciation for nature, how to understand the importance of preserving a balance," she says. "We talked about caring for our resources -- water, air, and life; and of course we talked about global warming and the climate crisis."

For Shreya, the best way to learn is by doing. So she set up a club at her school, where children could engage in all kinds of hands-on activities.

They planted trees, and learned how to properly separate waste. "We discovered together that each of our actions matters, whether it is small or large, whether it has a big impact or not," Shreya says. "It was truly inspiring."

For the first project she organized with NYCA, Shreya wanted to help the environment while educating her fellow citizens about the importance of environmental protection. She brought together 60 people, and they traveled together down a road that was particularly littered. For the next three weeks, they picked up trash and talked with the people who lived along the street. They also reached out to the local shop owners and talked with them about environmentally harmful practices, like burning trash out in the open. "We just connected with the people and explained how a clean community is the foundation for good health -- and a good economy," she says. "That was our big first event; that's how it all started."

For Shreya, it was a very rewarding experience. Some days after the clean-up campaign, she and two friends were walking through that same area. One of her friends, who hadn't participated in the event, was surprised. "This place was so dirty before! Now it's so nice!" her friend said. "The city must have done something here."

"I was so happy inside," Shreya says. "Because it wasn't the city; it was us!" Her friend was impressed. "If there is another event in the next weeks, make sure to invite me as well!" she said.

Shreya continued her work with the NYCA, organizing events, educational talks, and mobilizing students for climate strikes. They even wrote a letter to the Nepalese prime minister, asking him to rethink his energy policy.

"We organize awareness campaigns and conferences, and we advocate for environmental policies," she says. "We meet with those who are responsible, and we try to push them to take climate-friendly decisions."

Then, in September 2019, Shreya was very interested to learn about Youth Climate Scholarships. This organization funds young climate leaders from around the world to be representatives at climate conferences. They want young people to be able to provide their input into discussions about the National Determined Contributions (NDCs), the commitments that countries agreed to under the 2015 Paris Climate Agreement. Shreya was eager to go to the COP25 conference in Madrid, where this would be discussed. Unfortunately, there was a problem.

"The deadline had already passed," Shreya says. But again, she wasn't going to give up easily. "I just filled out the form anyway and sent it off."

Two weeks later she got an email: she had been selected, along with a handful of other young climate activists, from more than 20,000 applicants! She was so excited that she would be able to travel to Madrid to represent Nepalese youth there.

"When I arrived there, it was amazing," she says. "But it was also very complicated at first. Since we had been sponsored, we had a specific schedule to follow, with all the important meetings we were to attend."

But Shreya hadn't traveled all the way to Madrid to just sit in conferences and listen to others speak. "One of my friends from Poland and I were asked to give the youth statement at the final plenary session," she says. "At first I was so nervous, because there were leaders there from all over the world, and also from my country."

The closing session of COP25 had been postponed again and again, and Shreya had been sitting there waiting for her turn, all through the night. But there was no going back now. "It was clear to us that this was the platform where global leaders would finally hear us, the youth," she says.

And what did she say when her time to speak finally came? "We want more ambitious actions," she, and the other youth leaders demanded. "There's more we can do at our homes, at local levels through awareness campaigns and inspiring people for change."

"We wanted them to really hear that the COP25 outcomes were just not satisfactory to us," she says now, remembering.

After her speech, Shreya gave interviews and talked to other COP25 representatives. "They came up to us and told us that they appreciated us speaking up and telling the truth," she says. "Many of the people who work for governments and NGOs know that something is wrong, but they cannot speak out because they are scared that they might lose their jobs, or their funding."

For Shreya, this just goes to show why youth need to be on the frontlines of the fight against climate change. "As young people today, we are the most important generation that will ever live on earth," she says. "But we need to recognize our responsibility, and we need to acknowledge our power to *do something*."

As people alive today, we must consider future generations: a clean environment is a human right like any other. It is therefore part of our responsibility toward others to ensure that the world we pass on is as healthy, if not healthier, than we found it.

His Holiness the Dalai Lama

Call to Action: Invite your friends to join you in organizing a clean-up campaign in your community! Visit NYCA: https://www.nyca.net.np/ Follow Shreya on Twitter https://twitter.com/KCShreya1?s=20 and read her blog https://kcshreya.wordpress.com/

A VOICE FOR YOUTH & OCEANS
Angelique Pouponneau
SYAH-Seychelles
Seychelles, East Africa

Angelique Pouponneau grew up on Mahé, the largest of the 115 islands in Seychelles. Growing up in a little village, her childhood was "typical for an islander," with the beach only a five-minute walk away from her house.

She liked to play a game all children growing up near the ocean know well. You stand in the water, up to your hips, and when a wave comes at you, you try to jump over it. One day when she was three years old, her father was standing in the water, holding little Angelique tight in his arms. When he saw a really big wave coming at him, he realized he couldn't jump over it -- and he couldn't dive under it either. "When he landed on his feet, I wasn't in his arms anymore," Angelique says.

Her father looked for her frantically, everywhere in the water, but she was nowhere to be found. In a panic, he turned around and scanned the beach -- and there she was, lying under a tree and enjoying the sun! The wave had swept her onto the beach. "The wave had kept me safe," Angelique says. "So, I now see the ocean as a friend; and at the same time, I know it can be threatening."

By the time she was five, there was a muddy path she liked to walk along. It was called Barracuda Lane, and it ran alongside a marsh that was teeming with life, with all kinds of little animals crawling around, and insects buzzing through the air. She would step out onto the beach, listen to the waves crashing on the sand, and breathe in the smell of the ocean breeze.

When she was 19, Angelique left Seychelles to study law at the University of London. It was a very different kind of life there, and soon she realized that there were many things that she had always taken for granted. "People used to ask me what it was that I missed the most," she remembers. "I would always say the sea breeze."

She missed other things, too. In a city like London, where most of the time you can't see further than the next block of housing, she would

195

daydream about the infinite view she had known back home, spanning the horizon over the Indian Ocean.

But when Angelique returned to Seychelles after finishing her degree, it wasn't the same anymore. Barracuda Lane was no longer the muddy little path that she used to walk down to get to the ocean: it had been turned into a boardwalk. And there was no longer a marsh full of mudskippers and other insects. In its place was a fancy new hotel. What was left of the marsh was full of discarded plastic bags and bottles.

"I saw a Seychelles that I hadn't ever seen in my life," Angelique says. "It's a very beautiful country – but it's also one that's had many challenges with development as well as climate change."

In fact, small island nations like Seychelles are among the most vulnerable to the effects of the climate crisis. Sea-level rise and land degradation threaten the very existence of these nations. With coral reefs dying, one of the last natural barriers against more extreme flooding is disappearing. And changes in the water temperature are a threat to the livelihoods of many islanders, who depend on the sea for their income.

Angelique decided to take action. She joined the Small Island Developing States Youth AIMS-Hub (SYAH), an organization that had advanced youth-led initiatives on sustainable development. She travelled to Mauritius to help set up the organization's regional chapter. And when she returned home, she started the organization's Seychelles office.

Soon she became an accomplished speaker for the Seychelles National Youth Assembly. She found a network of other young activists like herself to help recruit volunteers for her efforts. "When you are a young person, you have these great ideas and you want to make a difference," she says. "But it's important to first identify, and map what already exists."

Building on the existing infrastructure, and drawing from her own network, Angelique and her fellow SYAH activists were able to make remarkable changes in a very short period of time. Within three months of the official founding of the national SYAH organization, they managed to push the Seychelles government to pledge that they would outlaw the use of single-use plastic bags -- a major victory for the youth activists, *and* for the environment.

The campaign against plastic bags had originally been a much more modest idea. Angelique and her colleagues had planned to organize a celebration of July 3rd, the international day for the banning of plastic bags. But they quickly realized that they didn't just want to protest for one day, and then return to their normal lives. Instead, they started a long-term campaign that was built on two pillars: education and action.

"There was the need for education, which we did through community engagement -- going to schools, and targeting different audiences," Angelique explains. "And then there was action -- every month we would dedicate one day to cleaning up an area that had a lot of plastic bags lying around."

They shared before-and-after pictures of their clean-ups on social media, reached out to politicians and decision makers, and invited them join them in their actions. Eventually, even the Minister for the Environment showed up. "You know, it was a great photo op for him," Angelique says, with a smile.

But it was more than good publicity -- by inviting decision makers to join them, and reaching out to other youth, Angelique and her fellow activists from SYAH managed to turn single-use plastic bags into a political issue. This was in 2015 -- and 2015 was an election year in the Seychelles. "We managed to make the environment, and plastic pollution, a political issue that mattered," Angelique says. "This became a determining factor of who the young people would vote for."

When the ban on plastic bags was passed, Angelique and her colleagues learned about it from newspapers and the radio. It was a very exciting moment for them: they exchanged high-fives and big smiles, and everyone cheered. "It was a feeling of pride and appreciation of our work," Angelique remembers.

Buoyed by their success, SYAH expanded their environmental work. They set up the Blue Economy Internship Program, to organize work experiences in sustainable jobs for young people. And to encourage unemployed youth to become entrepreneurs, they launched a project to produce canvas bags to sell to tourists in the hotels. Next they set up a collaborative project with a prison. "The female inmates had a lot of great skills with designing bags," Angelique explains. She was proud that the women were learning new skills, and that once they returned home, it would be to a cleaner, healthier environment.

With all of these initiatives, SYAH was able to increase the prominence of their voice in their country's environmental decision making. "We were always asked to give our views about young people," Angelique says. "Whether we thought that this or that was a sustainable path."

Over the years, Angelique has leveraged her wealth of knowledge and experience in environmentalism as an important asset. Now, as CEO of the Seychelles' Conservation and Climate Adaptation Trust Fund, she is "Investing in the Country's Blue Future," dispersing $700,000 dollars each year to research and conservation programs. "Business has a significant role in driving the climate change agenda, and then bringing about the change," she explains. "So, helping them do that has been very fruitful."

For Angelique, financing ocean and environmental projects means fighting for sustainable development. It brings her back to her childhood, when the marshes and beaches weren't plastered with fancy hotels and polluted with plastic waste.

Looking back at her career in activism, Angelique has one important piece of advice to share. "If you want to see something change, start somewhere," she says. "It can be as easy as a little change in your everyday life, all the way to bringing others with you. But start somewhere -- don't just sit back."

The greatest danger to our planet is the belief that someone else will save it.

Robert Swan

Call to Action: Learn more about best practices in the Blue Economy: https://seyccat.org/ Angelique's work with young people: http://syah-seychelles.weebly.com/

AWARENESS CAMPAIGNS
Iqbal Badruddin
Fridays for Future Pakistan
Pakistan

When he was five years old Iqbal Badruddin's family moved from their home in Karachi to Pakistan's capital, Islamabad, so he could get a good education in the country's best schools. Many Pakistanis aren't as lucky as he was. Iqbal was determined to use his education to help his others learn about climate change, to protect the earth for future generations.

In 2016 he graduated from Iqra University with a degree in international relations. And in 2017 he heard His Highness, Prince Kareem Aga Kahn say, "Climate change is a major threat to much of the developing world, and it needs to be looked at with great care." Iqbal was determined to not only look closely but see what he could do about it.

For a few years he worked for environmental organizations like Water Aid Pakistan, where as a research associate, he learned how badly inadequate sanitation facilities were impacting the city's groundwater. There, when he worked with the local government to spread awareness about water-saving habits, Iqbal enjoyed talking directly with the people. He then worked at LEAD Pakistan as Young Professional Officer Climate Change Inspiring Leaders for a Sustainable World. In 2017 he joined forces with some like-minded friends and designed a plan for how to educate his people to be more aware of climate change. They called it the Awareness Campaigns. "Instead of working in an air-conditioned office, I resigned," Iqbal says, so he could dedicate himself 100%.

The activism that he practices now, as founder of Fridays For Future Pakistan, is aimed at the roots of his country's primary climate-change problems -- educating the people and protecting their water. To some, the odds seem overwhelming. But Iqbal has accepted the challenge, and like a modern-day Pied Piper he's convinced more than 1,000 college students to join him. His goal is to reach 10 million people. "I'm a nature lover," he explains, and adds "Without water we cannot survive."

In terms of the effects of climate change, Pakistan is one of the world's most vulnerable countries. It is also the most dramatically inclined country, with the second highest peak in the world -- K2 in the Himalayas -- down to the lowest point of elevation. At the Gwadar seaport, toxic waste from Pakistan's neighbors, India and China -- the two largest polluters in the world -- is collected. This is especially unfair, since Pakistan emits less than 1 percent of the total GHG emissions. Waste goes untreated into Pakistan's rivers, flowing into the Arabian Sea polluting its marine life.

Iqbal is determined to do something to correct this situation; and to protect his people and equip them to respond to the effects of climate change.

With Pakistan's high poverty rate, and poor education it's a tough job. "Uneducated, illiterate people are more vulnerable," Iqbal says. "More vulnerable to climate change, to the 'religious card,' to corruption, and to wars." The effect of wars has had a profound effect on his country. "Starting from the Afghan War 1979 the 'religious card' has been used to gain the people's support," he explains. Then, as a result of the U.S. response to the 9/11 attacks, "Our economy lost $127 billion, and 70,000 lives," Iqbal says. shaking his head sadly. Furthermore, Pakistan's defense budget has had to increase to address India's threat of stopping Kashmir's flow of water, the life blood of the country's economy. "Had this money been invested in education, things would be very different in my country," he says.

Since 2018 Iqbal has roamed around Islamabad talking with ordinary people. Islamabad is a planned city, and a very green one. Tourists come to visit its lush Margalla Park. According to his own research, Iqbal says, "70 percent of the people don't understand what's going on. Changing weather patterns are affecting our water reservoirs and our food. It's already happening." But some of the people he talked to remembered that in 2014-2016, they had to ration water.

New developments are also threatening Islamabad's future. "They are cutting down our trees to expand - horizontally," Iqbal says. "The impact is devasting: the land's ability to absorb water is gone." But he has an idea for how to save the trees. "Why don't we expand vertically?" he asks. "Why shouldn't we build tall buildings instead of single-story homes?" His idea is well aligned with the government's campaign of planting 10 billion trees in five years. "They are even asking people living in the slums, trying to get them to plant trees too," he says.

Pakistan's agrarian economy depends on its high mountain glaciers. With increasingly unpredictable and unprecedented rains, floods often devastate local farms. "We need to build dams so we can more effectively manage our water," Iqbal says, and adds, "It's going to cost billions of dollars. And with the high cost of IMF loans, our people are defenseless to prepare themselves for these increasing threats."

Reflecting on what he'd learned from his studies, his jobs, and most importantly what he'd learned from ordinary people. Iqbal prepared a presentation to share with college students at his alma mater and invited everyone to join him in the fight. He was touched by the positive response he got – everyone wanted to help. "It's so hot now!" they said. "In the summer it's really hard to even go outside. It didn't used to be like this."

Iqbal asked them to be ambassadors and help spread awareness of climate change to young people. "We're focusing on 12-14-year-olds," he says. For him it seems a very natural thing to do. "Environmental stewardship is something that is imbued in every human being when we are born," he says.

In just one year Iqbal's Awareness Campaign had spread to 17 universities across Islamabad. Now, every Friday, more than 1,000 students join the Awareness sessions with #FridaysForOurFuture. Iqbal's software engineer friends told him, "We don't know much about climate change, but we want to do something to help." They offered to use their skills to build a website and use social media to help spread awareness of the problem -- and urge people to join in doing something about it.

Emboldened by the energy of their fellow ambassadors, Iqbal and his friends next reached out to remote areas, where they created Awareness Camps. Some are for just a few hours, some last a few days. They organize "eco-activities" and talk directly with youth about the importance of nature in our lives. "We give them a chance to come up and talk to us about issues they see happening in their communities," he explains.

Slowly they build awareness, while exploring some key questions with participants: How can we adjust to this new climate reality? How can we prepare ourselves? How can we use our scarce water resources more efficiently? What kinds of irrigation systems will help farmers? How can we all reduce food waste, to reduce the demand on farmers? And how can we create early warning, and disaster risk reduction systems?

Then they work with the youth to organize small projects to help their communities. "Take one issue, learn a skill, develop it; then start working on making things better," Iqbal tells them. At the end of each Awareness Camp, he asks them to report back biweekly on their progress, so they won't give up or get discouraged.

Iqbal remembers one long trip they took, a 24-hour journey along the dangerous mountainous road to northern Gilgit-Baltistan. When they arrived, he was thrilled to see how many people were there, full of energy and eager to learn. In the Yasin Valley, kids asked him why the weather in their communities was changing. "We helped them to see that they are sitting on a 'hot tipping point'" he says.

That trip was in stark contrast to the one they took to the remote Sindh province in southern Pakistan. "There they are more inclined towards religion and less willing to listen to scientific facts," he says. He pauses for a moment, then adds, "I believe that God knows everything, yes. But this global warming, this climate change is man-made." When he talks with people who are very religious, he quotes the Koran and finds clever ways to subtly challenge the traditional orthodox mindset of 'Inshallah, everything will be fine.' "When we come into this world, we are taught that we have a responsibility to leave the environment in a better condition," he reminds them.

It's an uphill battle. The climate change clock is ticking. It can be a discouraging effort. "The team is my backbone," Iqbal says. "They are the linchpin of the Awareness Campaign." He is eager to get everyone involved, from social scientists to electrical engineers, and entrepreneurs with ideas for green businesses. "We are trying to encourage those who actually can come up with ideas for ways that we can have clean and cheap energy," he explains. "If enough people were encouraged to become entrepreneurs, we could create solutions to the enormous issues we are facing today."

Wherever he goes, Iqbal promotes sustainable solutions that enable communities to take responsibility for their own future development. Technology has opened up so much information. "We know everything," Iqbal says. "And the youth *really* know everything!"

He impresses upon them the UN's Sustainable Development Goals, like SDG 12, which focuses on responsible consumption and production. "In our cities, the consumption and waste are really alarming. People have so much stuff, like 3-4 cars: that emits a lot of greenhouse gas." He challenges people to be more environmentally responsible by using bikes, or public transport. "Stop relying on the government," he tells them. "Take responsibility for yourselves and make a long-term commitment to where you are living. We need to strengthen our civil society."

"The elder generations have had pretty good lives; they haven't had to deal with these issues we have now," he says. "It's our collective responsibility to do something. It's time to work with our youth. Build trust. Find common ground. Help them build communities. We need to work together for our future. Youth are the ones who will have to live with the consequences of what we do -- or don't do -- today."

For the Global Strike Day in 2019, there were climate marches in 34 cities in Pakistan. "I was expecting hundreds...but thousands came to the march and I'm so excited at the response," he said. "Now we have to reach out to rural areas and make our movement bigger." It was great to have Zartaj Gul, The Minister of State for Climate Change march with us and promise to take their demands to the Government."

In 2020, Iqbal was honored that Fridays For Future Pakistan was invited to co-host a Special Talk on Sustainable Development and Climate Change sponsored by the UN. And he was touched when UN Secretary General Antonio Guterres said, *"Everyone who is fighting against climate change is Greta."*

Iqbal challenges us all: "We all have to pitch in. It's the only way to secure our future."

The world will not be destroyed by those who do evil, but by those who watch them without doing anything.

Albert Einstein

Call to Action: Create awareness of climate change in your community. Take Action. Support Iqbal's Awareness Campaign: Fridaysforfuture Pakistan Fridaysforfuturepk@gmail.com

BUILDING COMMUNITY FOR CLIMATE REFUGEES
Mohamad Al Jounde
Gharsah Sweden
Syria/Sweden

In December of 2017, 16-year-old Mohamad Al Jounde found himself standing at a microphone at the International Children's Peace Prize award ceremony in the Hall of Knights in the Hague, with a roomful of people applauding him. Looking into the audience, he could see his mother clapping along with everyone else, wiping tears from her face as he accepted the award. Sitting right in front of her was Malala Yousafzai, the young Nobel Peace Prize winner, who had just introduced him. It was an emotional high point for Mohamad, part of his long journey away from his home in Syria to his new life in Sweden.

The road that brought Mohamad to this moment had actually begun in Lebanon, where he and his family had fled for safety in 2013. Mohamed was 12 at the time, and the adjustment was difficult for him. When he, his mother and uncle had arrived in Lebanon, they had a house and a roof over their heads, but it didn't feel like home to him. His father had had to stay back in Syria, so Mohamad's family was torn apart. In Syria, Mohamad's world had been built around his school, his family, and his friends. In Aley, the city where his family now settled, he didn't know anyone his age.

There was no school for Mohamad in Aley because government regulations did not permit Syrian children to attend Lebanese schools. So, without school or friends, Mohamad's social life disappeared. As any young person would, Mohamad struggled and felt very alone.

Climate change had forced thousands of Syrians to leave their homes and become refugees in Lebanon. Since farmers in Syria use only the rain -- not irrigation -- to water their crops, they are especially vulnerable to climate change. And since droughts are increasing -- from once every 55 years, to once every seven years -- it's hard for them to survive. Most of the farmers and unskilled laborers who fled Syria to go to Lebanon ended up in the Beqaa Valley. And even if the conflict in Syria ends, many can't go back there, since climate change has ravaged their lands.

While Mohamad was home, without school, he discovered photography.

His father had introduced him to a well-known photographer, Ramzi Haidar, who mentored Mohamad like his own son. It was the first time Mohamad had ever touched a camera. He loved photography because it helped him to see and appreciate the details of his new environment, as well as the wide range of human emotions in a new light. Over the years, Mohamad's photography has evolved: he's now produced three documentaries as well.

One day, he went with his mother and uncle to volunteer at a nearby refugee camp. They brought food, clothing and materials to build tents. Mohamad was too young to help the volunteers distribute everything, so he played with the children who were living in the camp. After visiting several times, Mohamad made new friends with children there. He soon realized that his volunteer work was a two-way street. While he was helping them, doing something positive also made him feel happy again: he liked being able to do something useful and productive. He encouraged the children to take photos, and showed them how to do it so they could share their stories. "These kids are too shy to talk, but they can take photos," Mohamad says. "They can create images of home, pictures of happiness."

Mohamad started thinking about how he could do something more meaningful, something that would help the children in the camp in a more significant way. So, he decided to start his own school. At first, the "school" was very basic. There were not many resources to work with. The school consisted of tents that volunteers put up with their own hands. To begin, his family pooled their knowledge to teach classes at the school. His mother taught math; his uncle taught Arabic. And even though he was only 12, Mohamad taught the English classes.

On the very first day, Mohamad was thrilled to see that 100 children showed up! To make room for everyone they had to hold different classes throughout the day. They taught classes from 8:00 in the morning until 8:00 at night, so everyone who wanted to could have a chance to learn.

With the school project, Mohamad finally felt like he had a new home. And he had discovered his own form of activism as well.

From a young age, activism and revolution been part of his family's life. His mother was an active political organizer, and both of his parents had protested in the Syrian revolution. Their living room was a hub of activity: there were always activists coming and going from their home. Mohamad didn't fully understand what was happening at the time, but he understood that this was important work. "From watching my parents, I started envisioning what it means to be an activist; how you socialize with other people, how you build social networks," he says.

He also came to understand that it was dangerous work: his mother was arrested twice for her organizing activities. After her second arrest, she was told she had a week to leave the country, or she would be arrested and killed. That's when Mohamad fled Syria with his family.

But for Mohamad, revolution is not just about protesting what is wrong. "Revolution is also about building a community," he says. And it is about fighting for positive ideas and values.

So, to expand the school they had started, Mohamad reached out to family friends from Syria who now lived in Germany and asked them for help. Soon schools all around Germany were sending school supplies and monetary donations. He named this initiative Kids for Kids. After a while, this new partnership started to get media attention, and with the additional exposure came more resources.

Unfortunately, the school didn't last long. After only six months the Lebanese government destroyed the school and the four surrounding refugee camps. This was a devastating loss for Mohamad: he felt like he had lost the underpinning of his new life. To him it felt like a second displacement.

However, undeterred by this blow, Mohamad and his family found a creative way to reopen the school. They rented a big house and turned it into a school. The Lebanese owner was very sympathetic, and offered them legal protection so they were safe to reopen.

Today Mohamad's activism has expanded to an international stage. In 2017, he and his mother and uncle moved to Sweden, where he started an NGO (non-governmental organization) called Gharsah Sweden, to support the refugee school in Lebanon. And he is continuing to work tirelessly to preserve the educational values most important to him.

After winning the International Children's Peace Prize, he now has more money and resources to help the school. But Mohamad stresses the fact that money isn't all that is needed. "Activism can't be focused only on raising money," he says. "It has to be a fight to end systemic issues. Even global issues are best addressed when smaller communities are empowered. With enough support and resources, local people and organizations can create the solutions that will work in their own communities and situations."

By building the school in a refugee camp, Mohamad and his family challenged the system that creates refugees. "No one can expect refugees to start building schools out of nowhere and then just start teaching," he says.

When Mohamad meets other young people on the frontlines of activism, he feels encouraged and energized by their work. He also likes knowing he's not alone. "I realized you can be an activist, and also be normal," he says. He considers himself lucky because he has mentors like his mother and father who taught him about the values needed to create this global revolution. "Most young activists don't have someone telling them that," he says.

Despite everything, Mohamad sees himself as an optimist, though not in the traditional sense. His version of optimism is not based on the belief that the future is bright and beautiful. Instead, he believes in maximizing happiness each day. And he strongly believes that providing refugee children with the chance to continue learning, even in very difficult circumstances, is not just a way of keeping them on track educationally: perhaps even more important, it is a way of helping them to be happy and hopeful about their future.

Refugees are mothers, fathers, sisters, brothers, children, with the same hopes and ambitions as us – except that a twist of fate has bound their lives to a global refugee crisis on an unprecedented scale.

Khaled Hosseini

Call to Action: Support the school Mohamed created for Syrian children in Lebanon: donate through Gharsah Sweden. https://gharsahsweden. org/the-school/

DIGITAL TOOLKITS FOR INCLUSIVE
CLIMATE JUSTICE MOVEMENTS
Jett Zhang
Fridays for Future Digital
Florida

As a youth, Jett Zhang had difficulty finding a community that shared his interests. Born in Atlanta, Georgia to immigrant parents from China, he had a hard time finding people who shared his interest in entrepreneurship. At times, growing up in the American South was quite difficult for him. Some days his mental health suffered, and most days he felt very alone.

One day, after meeting an entrepreneurial high schooler, he realized there must be others who felt the same sort of isolation that he did. So he decided to use his experience, as well as his entrepreneurial and technical skills, to create communities intent on bringing all kinds of people together. "In high school I tried social entrepreneurship," he says. "I designed several apps, which won me a few pitch competitions, but they didn't end up going anywhere. I loved the concept of connecting changemakers to each other, but I wasn't even sure yet what issues I cared about myself."

While researching an essay he was writing on the Paris climate agreement, Jett reached out to 350 Pensacola, a local climate action network, for some expertise, and they invited him to come to a meeting. This network was an amazing source of information for Jett, and it set him on a path working toward climate justice. But he noticed that very few youth environmentalists belonged to the network. "So naturally, I began looking for a network of young people who were also getting involved."

Jett used Instagram to send direct messages to climate activists about getting involved with youth movements. Eventually, Iris Zhan, a Chinese-American activist from Maryland, replied to him with a show of support. "This showed me that there were people like me out there willing to help, and it really inspired me to get involved in this movement in a bigger way."

At 17, Jett took up the mantle as director of the 350 Pensacola Youth

Climate Coalition. Shortly thereafter, on September 20, 2019, using his social media savvy he organized a climate strike, and he got more than 150 people to attend. His digital organizing experience brought him to Fridays For Future Digital (FFFD), and he began collaborating with them on a much larger scale.

At FFFD, Jett found a niche, creating and developing digital protests. Through various social media platforms, youth activists were urged to send photos and messages, and to create digital collages showing the extensive support network of youth around the world. "Activism is similar to entrepreneurship, only the end goal is impact, not money," Jett says. And considering the near-global lockdowns from COVID-19, his impact has been all the more extraordinary. When the quarantine started in March 2020, people couldn't physically protest. "But you can still keep these important environmental issues on the top of your mind and that sense of community strong, with digital activism."

Jett's efforts have helped FFFD empower thousands of activists, many of whom are new to the movement. He hopes that getting more youth involved in these campaigns can further help those in isolation feel some sense of community. "I ended up creating some of the strongest relationships of my life during a time of isolation; which goes to show us the beauty that the technology can have if it's used in a positive way," he says.

Jett often leverages the FFFD platform to assist environmental groups that have less reach and visibility, and that normally wouldn't have access to the resources or networks to help them get meaningful exposure and community support. One story that was particularly important to Jett came to light via the work of a partner group called Defend Defenders. Defend Defenders stands up for the human rights of environmental defenders and Indigenous people in the East and Horn of Africa subregions. Through this group, Jett learned about Friends of Zoka, and he decided to get FFFD virtually involved with them.

Friends of Zoka is a group of northern Ugandans who are trying to stop illegal logging in the rainforests, which has destroyed roughly 60 percent of the standing rainforest of the country in the last 20 years. "I reached out to the Whatsapp on their website and was able to speak with William Amanzuru, who was cataloguing evidence of the devastation," Jett says. At the time, William was hiding from the local commissioner in the Moyo District. The Whatsapp technology not only allowed Jett to communicate with him, but helped them work together to coordinate a digital campaign to put pressure on the Ugandan government through tweets and emails sent from around the world. "It just goes to show you that even a social messaging app can impact change," Jett says. "This wasn't something that was possible for wildlife defenders like William 20 years ago, when the illegal foresting began."

Jett has also played an integral role in connecting FFFD with the Re-Earth Initiative, and combining their expertise as leading digital activist networks to influence legislation for vulnerable groups worldwide. The focus of their most recent joint effort is to raise awareness and support from Caribbean and Latin American governments for the Regional Agreement on Access to Information, Public Participation, and Justice in Environmental Matters. This is a groundbreaking piece of legislation for persecuted Indigenous peoples, which is better known as the #EscazúAgreement because it was first adopted in Escazú, Costa Rica.

The #EscazúAgreement is the first binding treaty in Latin America and the Caribbean to deal with environmental democracy and environmental human rights. In many places in these regions, the Indigenous populations are horribly abused by powerful corporations and the rogue government officials that allow the corporations free reign, simply for standing up for and protecting their land. Currently, there is little legal recourse for a defender of the environment who is being persecuted, strong-armed, bribed, physically harmed and intimidated, or even murdered by outside interests. Ratifying this agreement would provide the Indigenous populations who are being exploited proper access to data about ongoing projects, and the chance to participate in the planning and conversations around what projects will be allowed. Perhaps most importantly, it provides legal protections for those who are persecuted while defending the natural habitats they call home. "I'm honored to spend my time defending the most vulnerable people in the most vulnerable places," Jett says. "This sort of community building is something I will always be involved in."

Jett wants young people to understand that whatever the scope of the cause they are interested in, or whatever your personality is, you *can* get involved in a way that suits you as an individual. Many types of people coming together is what makes the climate movement so impactful. "For example, I like to design systems behind the scenes," Jett says. "I like to engage in digital community building. I play many roles for FFFD that aren't obvious or glamorous, but they make just as significant an impact on the cause as the outward-facing figures of the movement. I like to say to other activists who are reserved, like me, you can't make a movie without the camera man, can you?"

With up and coming leaders like Jett, who are so effective at digitally organizing youth communities, the climate justice movement has significantly expanded its reach to a network of tech-savvy, motivated activists across the virtual world. This virtual approach by FFFD and youth leaders like Jett shows that no matter what logistical problems may arise from something like a pandemic, innovative activists will always have opportunities to use their intelligence and their creativity to keep the momentum of their work rolling forward.

While incorporating the guidance of environmental activists before him, Jett has set an example of digital resilience in the face of myriad obstacles, through his efforts at organizing online protests and shining a light on stories that will no longer go untold. The climate justice movement will surely need more of this type of innovation and resilience in the future, as the challenges will be more varied and complicated. Jett hopes we will all learn from this digital triumph, small as it may seem, and take an intergenerational approach to solving the next hurdle, which is sure to come.

The Earth is a fine place and worth fighting for.

Ernest Hemingway

Call to Action: Don't let the lockdowns stop you from supporting a cause that's important to you - get out in virtual space and support digital climate protests with Jett at Fridays for Future Digital - https://fffdigital.carrd.co

ECO-FEMINISM FOR CLIMATE ACTION

Adenike Oladosu
iLeadClimate
Nigeria

Adenike Oladosu grew up in Abuja, Nigeria, and is from Ogbomosho, where delicious cashews and mangos are grown on nearby plantations. From a young age, Adenike could see that unfair agricultural practices were harming rural communities, especially for Indigenous people. So when it was time for her to go to college, she moved to north central Nigeria to study agricultural economics at the University of Agriculture in Makurdi.

Thus began Adenike's journey into the environmental movement. Her university, Benue State, was in "the food basket of Nigeria," near Lake Chad. While there, she was a firsthand witness to the destruction that climate change was having on this vulnerable region of her country. Water scarcity was turning farmland into desert. Communities that had never known floods before were watching their lands and livelihoods disappear under torrents of water. Powerful heat waves blasted the arid pastures, leaving nothing left to farm. As the land grew arid and pastures disappeared, farmers and herdsmen were fighting for their survival. Their conflict became so widespread that her classes were disrupted, and it took her an extra year to finish her studies.

Nigeria prides itself on its natural wildlife reserves, waterfalls, dense rainforest, savannas, and rare primate habitats. However climate change is ravaging this nation. Nigeria is not alone: many African nations are desperately facing water scarity. Without water, crops can't grow, which leads to millions of people at risk of malnutrition. The U.N. Food and Agriculture Organization has estimated that more than 815 million people are malnourished around the world. Most are in Africa, and climate change is making this dire situation worse.

The implications are far-reaching. When conflicts arise, food becomes even more scarce. When farmers and herdsmen lose their livelihoods, they are more vulnerable to being recruited by terrorist groups like Boko Haram. The increasing severity of climate change escalates violence, and in turn, strengthens the powerful grip of such groups. In 2014, when Boko Haram militants kidnapped 276 Nigerian girls from the Chibok High School, the world finally took notice.

The rise in gender-based violence is deeply troubling to Adenike. "Wherever there are security issues arising from the environment, the women are always the default victims," she says. "This deters us from ever achieving gender equality." The kidnapping of these girls made Adenike realize that girls and women's rights must be at the center of the climate movement.

Adenike knew that something had to be done. And the 2018 U.N. Intergovernmental Panel on Climate Change (IPCC) report has confirmed her worst fears: that report says that the world has only twelve years to take drastic measures, or it will be too late to stop climate change. "These issues have a timeline," she says. "We are heading toward a point of no return. We need to deal with climate change *now*, so that we can overcome it and be victorious."

In 2018 Adenike joined the worldwide Fridays for Future movement started by Greta Thunberg, the young Swedish activist. Now 25, Adenike serves as Nigeria's Fridays for Future ambassador. And working with Nigeria Earth Uprising and African Youth Climate Hub, she focuses on women's rights, security, and peacebuilding across Africa, especially in the Lake Chad region.

Adenike calls her own personal brand of activism "Eco-Feminism," and stresses that climate change solutions must prioritize the safety and well-being of women and girls. She travels around the country, going to schools to educate students about the effects of climate change. She works with Indigenous communities, to learn how traditional knowledge can contribute to climate resilience. She shows people how new technologies can improve their well-being and livelihood. She teaches them about renewable resources, and about how they can use better sources of energy in their own communities. And she shows them how to advocate for renewable energy on a larger scale. Through education, she hopes the movement will spread. "When people know how to use alternative energy, they can replicate these actions, and other people will learn how to use them," she explains. "With that, changing habits becomes more rapid, and naturally people will switch from fossil fuels without being forced."

For International Women's Day in 2021, Adenike believes that environmental issues should be the core theme, so that women's issues can be brought to the forefront of the climate justice movement. As she has grown into her role as an international leader in the climate movement, she's concerned that there is too little focus on communities in the Global South. In 2019, when she attended COP 25 in Madrid, she expected that the regeneration of Lake Chad, and its innovative climate finance programs, which are helping communities adapt to and reduce the effects of climate change, would be spotlighted. But to her dismay, climate change in the Lake Chad region was hardly even mentioned. "If international representatives don't recognize the current dangers of climate change in African countries, there will be global repercussions," she says. For example, the people who are being displaced by climate change are increasingly migrating to countries in the Global North. Many have already been forced to leave their homes and live in refugee camps. "If Africa loses the race of climate action, it's going to affect all of our countries," Adenike says, and she emphasizes, "We really need to support Africa *now*."

In Nigeria, Adenike is fighting to re-subsidize renewable energy, and find sources of energy that have low carbon emissions. "Every nation everywhere needs to prioritize renewable energy," she says. She also wants to see more unified government action, so that climate change is treated as the crisis that it is. She was disappointed that representatives at COP 25 failed to ratify Article 6 of the Paris Agreement, which promotes international cooperation among nations in order to reach their carbon emission targets. "Article 6 is essential if we are to reduce the effects of climate change," she says. "There *must* be more unified action in order for the Paris Agreement to succeed."

Currently Adenike's climate activism focuses on two major fronts. First, she is trying to engage the world's youth, especially in African countries, and get them to really care about climate change. "Many youth have yet to pay attention to these issues that will define our future," she says. Through her education outreach, she helps the children of today to understand what is at stake. "I believe education is a powerful weapon that we can use to conquer climate change," she says. Planting trees is now an important part of Fridays for Future in Nigeria. As a form of positive protest, school communities plant trees, while some of the children hold signs that say things like "Keep It In The Ground." And they talk about how if they take care of the trees, they will grow into a forest for their own children.

Adenike is also the founder of "ILeadClimate," a panAfrican movement that is advocating for the restoration of Lake Chad for sustainable development and disarmament. The lake, which borders Nigeria, Niger, Cameroon, and Chad, and supports about 40 million people, has shrunk by 90 percent. "Climate change is disproportionately affecting this region," Adenike says. "It is estimated that about 10.7 million people have been displaced, and 2.7 million are food insecure." She adds, "The strongest weapon against peace and security is the loss of livelihoods, because it affects food security, which leads to poverty and hunger." In 2020, IleadClimate was recognized by UNICEF Nigeria as a changemaker for their work in the environmental movement, along with other global recognition.

According to Adenike, climate change should be the top priority for everyone, everywhere; and the media should be amplifying climate issues and helping to promote climate action. She wants more youth everywhere to join the climate movement, and to participate in initiatives like Fridays for Future. To connect with more young people, she does a lot of social media outreach. "As more youth join this movement, it will make our leaders wake up to the reality of what is happening," she says. "We need both individual and collective action to combat climate change. Everyone has to take responsibility. We don't have to wait for government action." She adds, "The only way to solve climate change is to keep going, and keep demanding action. We are on the winning side. We can't lose this race. We need *everyone* to join this movement for climate justice."

> *The seeds of success in every nation on Earth are best planted in women and children.*

Joyce Banda, former President of Malawi

Call to Action: Join Adenike Oladosu and others around the world in demanding climate action now. You can visit her website http://womenandcrisis.blogspot.com/ or follow her on Twitter @the_ecofeminist. And visit Fridays for Future to find out about climate action in countries around the world. https://www.fridaysforfuture.org/

FROM INVISIBLE TO VISIBLE
Michelle Dilhara
Sri Lanka

In 2017, when Michelle Dilhara heard Leonardo DiCaprio speak to the United Nations General Assembly, she was deeply moved. As an aspiring actress, she'd enjoyed his films -- but to see how he was using his influence to make a change was truly inspiring.

Addressing world leaders from around the globe, DiCaprio spoke about the climate crisis and the urgent need for action. It was an issue that Michelle cares deeply about. "As an actor I pretend for a living. I play fictitious characters, often solving fictitious problems," DiCaprio said. "Mankind has looked at climate change in that same way: as if it were fiction. Ignoring the crisis won't make it go away."

These words struck a chord with Michelle. She realized that as an actress, she too was now in a position to speak truth to power. After finishing high school, she had joined an acting school and studied with famous Sri Lankan actors like Anoja Weerasinghe and Damayanthi Fonseka. When she was 20, she got her first big role in a television series called *Salsapuna* -- and it was a big hit.

"I get a lot of media attention, from TV channels to national newspapers," Michelle says. "So, I try to use all these platforms to educate, and create awareness on all these issues that I care about."

Michelle grew up with a passion for speaking up for those whose voices were too often ignored in society. When she was 15 years old, she visited her uncle in the hospital and witnessed some of the inequalities between those had less means and who were visible in society and those who were not. It made the difference between being surrounded by family and cared for by the system, and being lonely and left behind.

Michelle wanted to do something to help -- but as a teenager, she didn't have the money or influence needed to support anyone. However, she did study English, and she knew the language well.

"So, I thought maybe I could help children with learning English," she says. "I volunteered at several children's homes, as an English and meditation teacher."

216

When she saw the overwhelming need among the children she was helping, she mobilized others to join her. She formed a committee with other young leaders to coordinate and strengthen their efforts. This was the beginning of her "Invisible to Visible" movement, a campaign founded to address the social exclusion of those who are marginalized. She also wrote a book about her experiences, and what she had learned from her research into social issues, entitled *Social Invisibility Is Not a Fiction It Exists*.

Michelle had often heard her elders talk about changing weather patterns in Sri Lanka. She learned that farmers and those with low incomes -- exactly the "invisible" people she had been fighting for -- were increasingly being affected by climate change.

Farmers struggle with frequent and intense floods and droughts, leading to decreased crop yield. The lack of available drinking water poses a risk to all Sri Lankans, especially the poor. And climate change is a grave threat to the country's rich biodiversity. With one of the highest rates of endemic species worldwide, the negative effects of climate change threaten to irreversibly destroy many plants, animals, and marine ecosystems. "In the past few years, the rainfall has been heavy," Michelle says. "I witnessed all of these problems and I knew that something was very wrong."

After doing some research, she knew what her first action would be. The beaches in Negombo are beautiful -- palm trees sway gently in the wind, as the waves slowly roll onto the beach. But mixed in with the sand was all kinds of plastic bottles and bags, all of the trash left behind by visitors.

"The trash just mixes with the sand, and it is not going to decompose," Michelle says. "That also causes many problems with water pollution."

Michelle took to social media and called on her followers to gather on the beach. For three consecutive days, they roamed the beaches of Negombo, collecting mountains of plastic trash. Each day, the youth who were there would tell their friends about what they were doing; and the next day even more people would show up.

"The best thing was that all these young people joined together and started this project," Michelle says. "And to our surprise a lot of the people who were at the beaches actually joined us -- so I think somehow they must have gotten the message."

Michelle has continued to use her steadily growing social media channels, and the airtime she gets on TV, to talk about the issues that are close to her heart. She also organizes awareness campaigns in schools and universities.

And her popularity continues to grow. In 2018, she received the Asian Inspiration Award; in 2019 she won the National Youth Icon Award; and in 2020 she was nominated as both the Best Upcoming Actress and Most Popular Actress of the Year. She uses these platforms to let people know about good causes to support -- and she has pledged 60 percent of her income to pay for computer labs in rural schools, beds for children's and retirement homes, and to give out scholarships for language classes to 1,000 children.

Thinking of the new generation that is being born into this world every day, she feels the need to live sustainably. "We have a responsibility for the future of these children," she says. To engage others, Michelle decided to use her platform as a well-known actress to mobilize young people for climate action. "What I always tell everybody is that one small contribution from each of us can make a huge change," she says.

And her climate activism has grown exponentially. Since she had mobilized so many fans to help with the beach clean-up, she decided to reach out to her followers for help with another project. Together, she and the volunteers she gathered planted 1,000 trees in Katana, in western Sri Lanka.

In 2020, after three years of climate activism, Michelle was named as the Earth Day Network Ambassador in Sri Lanka. Every year on April 22, Earth Day highlights both the value and the vulnerability of our natural environment. In 2020, the initiative celebrated its 50th birthday, with social media campaigns, educational events, and broad mobilization -- and it is now working with more than 75,000 partners in over 190 countries.

For Michelle, this honor is an added responsibility, and an opportunity to push her climate activism even further. She was featured in the My Future, My Voice campaign, which presented the work of 50 young environmentalists from 16 different countries. To maximize their outreach, these young activists recorded videos and used their social media platforms to educate others about the problems that need to be addressed, and explain what they are doing to help.

With her appointment as ambassador, Michelle has also gotten one step closer to the person who inspired her climate activism in the first place: Leonardo DiCaprio acted as the cochair of the 50th anniversary global committee. "I am really grateful that I was appointed Earth Day Ambassador," Michelle says. "With this honor, I think I will be able to address even more people on these issues."

And indeed, she already has: together with the Sri Lankan Government Nursing Officers' Association, which has about 33,000 members, Michelle championed another tree planting campaign. "I organized this campaign in the Negombo district, to highlight the value of planting a tree to fight the climate crisis," she says.

Michelle has come a long way as both an actress and an activist. For her, it is important to always follow your instincts. "If your intention is to do the right thing, the universe will remove all the obstacles in your path," she says. "You just have to believe in yourself, and work until you reach your goal."

Clean air and a livable climate are inalienable human rights. And solving this crisis is not a question of politics, it is a question of our own survival. This is the most urgent of times, and the most urgent of messages.

Leonardo DiCaprio

Call to Action: The Earth Day Network's global map of climate activists in 17 countries is ever-expanding: https://www.earthday.org/ Follow Michelle on Facebook (@mishdilhara), and on Instagram (@ michelledilhara).

GENERATION WAKING UP!
Joshua Gorman
Berkeley, California

Joshua grew up in suburbs of Washington DC. His was a world wholly influenced by the dominant aspects of American culture. From a young age, nothing felt like enough. By his mid-teens, he started to become conscious of the troubled world he was born into. "I was a really sensitive young person," he says. "And I was really troubled by the state of the world. I had a broken family, which caused internal struggles. I was from a broken community. I was aware of the climate crisis we were in. It was overwhelming. I was lost. Alone. Most of my peers were in the mainstream flow of things, and I was just sitting there alone, with these big questions. And wondering, how do we do something about it?"

He didn't know what to do. But he'd read authors like Hermann Hesse, Jack Kerouac, and Joseph Campbell, whose work awoke in him the call to adventure. "I felt like that archetypal character who had the same big questions, longing for answers. So I dropped out of high school, left my family and friends, and went to the West Coast. It was a time of deep existential crisis. I was very depressed. I felt no hope or meaning. I felt like I was born to watch the world fall apart."

At 21, Joshua went to visit a friend on the Big Island in Hawai'i. He planned to stay two weeks but it would be three full years before he boarded a flight back home to D.C.

"In Hawai'i, I found myself having a back-to-nature experience. I was taken in by a local farmer. I lived on his farm, worked the land, and learned how to grow things. Mainly, I got out of my head. I had all these negative thought patterns my whole life that I couldn't escape. Working on the land helped me to drop out of my head and into my body. To connect with the natural world, which is so majestic. The Big Island feels like it's from a fantasy book. You're on an island, sitting on top of a volcano in the middle of the Pacific Ocean. I could feel the world was alive, healing, and restorative. It was a deep and embodied ecological awakening. So much of what my soul was longing for, I found in Hawai'i."

With this grounding in nature, Joshua began to explore other spiritual paths and traditions. He started to meditate and do yoga, and spent long stretches of time in solitude and in nature. Slowly, through his own organic process of spiritual awakening, he started to experience simple yet profound moments of happiness and inner peace. "I didn't know those things were possible, coming from a culture of so much darkness. It was a whole different side of life. It was also a time when I was reading lots of books and beginning to understand the larger historical process at play. It helped me realize that our world is not just falling apart, but that we're at a turning point. An old paradigm is dying, and a new world is being born."

One day Joshua was walking and he had his epiphany. "I realized the young people of our generation have a purpose like no generation before. To be a bridge from the old to the new. On one hand, it's one of the hardest times for young people to be alive. But we can also look at these times in a different light. What a gift and a privilege it is to be the ones that get to make the leap! Young people today have the opportunity to lead social movements and make sweeping changes on our planet like we've never seen before. In that moment, I really believed, in the depth of my soul, that we are going to make it. That was when the vision of Generation Waking Up came into my life."

Joshua returned home and enrolled in George Mason University, knowing that he had to further hone his leadership skills. He had a vision, but he knew he needed the training and education in order to fulfill it. But what he wanted to learn was hard to find, so he created his own major – Global Youth and Social Change. He began working, learning, volunteering, and mentoring with all types of nonprofits, youth programs, and social justice organizations.

As he engaged in social change movements, he approached it in a holistic way. "We don't need environmental, political, or economic change. We needed a *systems* change. A complete cultural shift in our values and structure," he says.

In trying to answer the question of how to bring about this larger, systemic change came Joshua's vision for Generation Waking Up. Its mission: to ignite a generation of young people to bring forth a "thriving, just, and sustainable world." Its flagship workshop is called "The WakeUp Experience," a 2-3 hour multimedia experience that explores four specific questions: Who are we? Where are we? What has to change? and What do we do now?

"It's a framework and curriculum for these times," Joshua explains. "We are training spiritual activists and systemic change makers. There's a lot of personal and interpersonal leadership training involved, which is so often lacking in workshops and training programs. It really helps, to connect the dots between the inner work and the outer work. This connection is essential for any individual and group to be effective."

Addressing these complicated social issues can be daunting. This holistic worldview is important to Joshua because it's precisely this understanding that he himself lacked as a youth. "There's this notion around urgency that I think is incomplete. Yes, we need to be out there taking action against these big problems. Mobilizing and spreading awareness. Because it's true, our times are urgent times. But sometimes we also need to take a step back. Retreat. Take some time alone in nature. Meditate. And listen. Just listen. To the wisdom that comes from that deeper place when we're alone in nature. Or to a spiritual advisor or mentor. We need to tap into that deeper well of meaning and inspiration that is necessary in order to sustain our social change work. Without that grounding, it's so easy to get overwhelmed, or to burn out. And of course, without that grounding, it's impossible to come from a place of our full power and potential."

It is here that Joshua's message of oneness and cooperation can guide the way to a healthy path forward for youth who are seeking to be changemakers. "It's a delicate dance, lifting young people up as protagonists while understanding that the scale of the change required demands the participation of us all. Even as young people are uniquely gifted to create social change, there needs to be collaboration and connection. Especially with elders. Young people have amazing energy. But it's important to remember that our elders have another kind of energy in wisdom, which is complementary. We have to make this journey together. Synergy and new possibilities emerge from cross-generational connections. Let's not think that today's young, heroic generation is going to swoop in and save us all by themselves. We all have to come together in service to the just and flourishing world we know is possible."

If the world is to be healed through human efforts, I am convinced it will be by ordinary people, people whose love for this life is even greater than their fear.

Joanna Macy

Call to Action: Connect with Joshua: https://www.joshuagorman.com Support Generation Waking Up: www.generationwakingup.com

LIKE KIDS EVERYWHERE
Samantha Smith
Maine

Samantha Smith was just a normal ten-year old-girl from Manchester, Maine. She liked to put off her homework, ride bikes, and have sleepovers with friends. But lying in bed at night, she had nightmares about nuclear war.

Stories she heard on television, and discussions in her fifth-grade classroom about nuclear war made Samantha nervous, and scared. It upset her that two countries could really start a war that could actually destroy the world, so that the children would never have a chance to grow up. Like most children she believed that people should learn to get along. She believed the United States and the USSR had to make peace, for the sake of kids all over the world.

One cold November afternoon in 1982, Samantha thought of what she could do. She picked up a pencil and began to write a letter to Yuri Andropov, the leader of the Soviet Union. She put stamps on the envelope, and asked her Dad to mail it on his way to work.

My name is Samantha Smith. I am 10 years old. Congratulations on your new job. I have been worrying about Russia and the United States getting into a nuclear war. Are you going to vote to have a war or not? If you aren't please tell me how you are going to help to not have a war. This question you do not have to answer but I would like it if you would. Why do you want to conquer the world or least our country? God made the world for us to share and take care of. Not to fight over or have one group of people own it all. Please let's do what he wanted and have everybody be happy too.

Samantha Smith

P.S. Please write back.

Months went by, but in April Samantha finally received a letter from the Soviet Embassy in Washington D.C. The letter was from Yuri Andropov. He called Samantha "a brave and honest girl," and praised her initiative. "We want peace," he wrote. "We have a lot to do: grow grain, build, invent, write books, and make space flights. We want peace for ourselves, and for all people of the planet, for our kids and for you." He added, "I invite you to come to our country and see for yourself. In the Soviet Union, everyone is for peace and friendship among peoples." He closed by saying, "The best time to come is in the summer."

Samantha accepted his invitation. When she traveled to the Soviet Union that summer, it attracted attention around the world. Journalists filmed, photographed, and wrote about her journey. Adults saw pictures of Samantha laughing in Moscow, swimming at a children's camp on the Black Sea, and riding bicycles in Leningrad. The Russian children in the photos with Samantha didn't look like enemies, or like monsters; they just looked like kids everywhere.

During her two-week visit, Samantha made deep friendships with some of those children. None of them hated the United States, and no one wanted war. "Sometimes at night we talked about peace," she said when she was back home. "It seemed so strange to talk about war when we all got along so well together." She returned home with a single question, "Why can't grown-ups get along, like kids?"

Over time Samantha became a symbol of peace to both countries. Her high spirits, warm smile, and love for others were an inspiration to people around the world. She inspired hope for resolving conflicts, and a new beginning for the US and USSR.

In 1985 a new beginning seemed like an impossible dream. But Samantha's dream came true. That year, the President of the United States, Ronald Reagan, and the President of the USSR, Mikhail Gorbachev, signed a nuclear disarmament pledge.

Children were no longer haunted by nightmares of nuclear war. Kids in both countries can now grow up thinking of each other as friends. However, Samantha never experienced the future she longed for so desperately for all children. Tragically, a plane crash took the lives of Samantha and her father just before the nuclear disarmament agreement was signed. She was just 13 years old.

But as America's youngest ambassador of peace, Samantha's courageous spirit lives on. In honor of her, her mother created the Samantha Smith Foundation to facilitate cultural exchanges between American and Soviet citizens. In 1986 twenty of Samantha's classmates from Maine traveled to the Soviet Union. They visited the same children's camp on the Black Sea that Samantha had visited, and met some of the Soviet teens who had made friends with her. To this day, Samantha is remembered as a folk heroine in Russia. All fifth graders now read about her in a chapter of their history books that is dedicated to her life, and her dream of peace. And so the hope and courage she demonstrated is constantly reborn in the minds of children.

In 1993, the Samantha Smith Summit was launched by 160 fifth graders from 71 schools in Florida's Pinellas County, to discuss why people are hurting each other, and what can be done to stop it. As each student entered the auditorium, they paused, one by one, to read Samantha's letter to Yuri Andropov. More than 15 groups from around the world were represented at the Summit -- Egyptians, Bulgarians, Iranians, African Americans, and Vietnamese students, among others. They came from all different economic backgrounds. Normally they would have felt they had little in common. But at the Summit, they put their differences aside and worked together.

They talked in small groups, brainstormed solutions, and presented their best ideas about how to make a more peaceful world. "Talk to your parents to let off steam." "Form neighborhood patrols." "Involve all people in solutions to community problems." "Assign people community duties so they learn to care about one another." "Help stand up for criminals so they can get jobs." We can't ignore anyone!" Cheers broke out after each solution was read aloud. The kids clapped high fives, and smiled at their new friends all around the room, laughing at how easy it was to "think positive."

"We found out that we have more in common than we thought," ten-year-old Aubrey Angelillis said, speaking for the group. "We all want to stop violence and crime, and try to show that kids -- not just adults -- can make a difference in the world. "

When the fifth graders left the auditorium that day, they were convinced that they had the power to make their communities better and safer. They believed that anyone, large or small -- whether the president of a huge, powerful country, or a fifth grader who dared to ask a president some big questions -- could create change.

A letter on the door of the school, signed "Samantha Smith" proved it.

*God made the world for us to live together in
peace and not fight.*

Samantha Smith

ONE GOAL AT A TIME
Lesein Mutunkei
Trees4Goals
Kenya

As a young child, there was a story Lesein Mutunkei's mother read to him over and over again. He loved this story, and for him it has become a touchstone.

> *A big fire broke out in the forest, and all of the animals ran away - even the elephants and the lions. Only the hummingbird decided to stay. It picked up water from the river with its tiny beak, and began dropping it onto the raging fire below. All of the other animals asked, "What do you think you can do? You are too little!" But the hummingbird replied, "I will do my little bit to help stop the fire. I will do what I can." And it continued fighting the fire.*

Everyone in Lesein's country of Kenya respected the great Wangari Maathai, who shared this story with people to inspire them to join her Green Belt Movement, and plant trees to restore their country's degraded watersheds and save their livelihoods. In 2004, the year Lesein was born, she received the Nobel Peace Prize for her contributions to sustainable development, democracy, and peace. She is one of Lesein's biggest heroes.

One day, when he was 14 years old Lesein was on his way to school, sitting in his mom's car, when he realized something awful. He was reading about deforestation and air pollution in Kenya. Lesein loves going on hikes, cycling, and camping out in the nature. But he realized that unless something was done about these issues, soon all of this would no longer be possible.

"I decided to do further research," he says. He learned that Kenya's forests have suffered a lot in past decades. In 1963, when the country became independent, 12 percent of Kenya was covered in forests. By 2015, the forest cover was down to only 7.6 percent. "I calculated that in Kenya, we were losing ten football pitches [of forest] every hour."

Ten football pitches -- Lesein knows very well how much that is. Because above all, he is a passionate football player. He plays for Ligi Ndogo, a football club in his hometown of Nairobi, the capital of Kenya. And it was the combination of his passion for sports and his environmental awareness that gave him an ingenious idea: he decided that for every goal he would score, he would plant one tree. He would fight deforestation one tree, and one goal, at a time.

"No matter how big the problem is, I just needed to make a difference," he says. And so, in honor of his hero Wangari Maathai, who died in 2011, Lesein founded the organization, Trees4Goals.

Every week Lesein would go to football practice and train with his teammates. When he came home, he would note down how many goals he had scored in a little book. The next week, he would buy a little tree from a roadside store; then he would head out and plant it in a school, park, or forest.

"The problem is that people are not replanting," he explains. And the consequences of this are deforestation and air pollution. "Trees take in polluted air," he says. "Planting trees is really important to reverse climate change." That is why Lesein set himself a clear goal: he wants forests to grow back to cover more than 10 percent of Kenya.

For Lesein, fighting against climate change means fighting for the survival of his community. Last year, mudslides devastated Northwestern Kenya after a rainy season that was much heavier than usual. "There have also been droughts, and because of that, we have less food," he says. "So there are farmers who are in real trouble, who aren't able to grow their crops."

After a while, Lesein realized that he needed to do even more. "I decided to increase my commitment. So for every goal I score, I decided to plant *ten* trees." Soon, the people around him took note of his efforts. His teammates joined in planting the trees. Then his school's rugby team wanted to participate. And when one of his friends asked if he could do the same thing, only for basketball, "I told him of course he can!" Lesein says. So now, there is also a Hoops4Trees group, joining with Trees4Goals in planting trees.

When a high school in South Africa invited Lesein to join forces, he began extending his work to other African countries. "As we expand, I make sure people learn from the experience," he says. "And that they take home with them an appreciation for *why* we're they're doing this."

For Lesein, making sure that people understand what is at stake is an important aspect of his activism. "Many people in my generation don't know about what's happening to our planet," he says. "No one is teaching them; we're not taught this in school." Too often, he says, people feel that you need to be an activist or a scientist to understand what is driving climate change. With Trees4Goals, Lesein gets people involved and educates them at the same time. "For them to know what's behind deforestation and pollution, and how we can reduce it by planting trees, that really keeps them interested," he says.

Lesein is keen on getting as many people as possible to talk about the topic, and take action. Last year, together with his football club, he planted 600 trees in the Karura Forest, a park in Nairobi. In Ngong Forest he planted another 350 trees, together with his schoolmates. "We would finish one tree and move on to the next," he says. "When we really got the hang of it, it was fun."

Lesein feels that football, which is the most popular sport in the world, is a great way to educate people. "There are so many famous footballers who have a powerful influence on people," he said. "With their large stadium audiences, they can influence thousands of others to go out and learn more about the problems, and create a very, very big awareness." He has an ambitious goal to take his Trees4Goals campaign to the next level: he wants to get FIFA, the International Federation of Association Football, on board. "If this happens, there'll really be a big difference on the topic of climate change," he says. "There'll be a large number of people that will then know about environmental conservation. It would be amazing!"

Over the last few years, Lesein has become an emblem of environmental activism in Kenya. He uses his social media channels on Instagram and Facebook to advertise his tree-planting projects. And last year he was invited to participate in the United Nations Climate Summit. "That was an amazing experience," he says. It was the first time he had travelled outside of Kenya. He especially liked getting to know activists from all around the world at the conference. And he participated in a climate strike, where he heard Greta Thunberg address the crowd. Because he was wearing his Trees4Goals T-shirt, people came up to him and asked him about it.

"I was happy to be able to share my story, and tell why I was doing it with great confidence," he says.

When Lesein returned from his journey, he had a very special meeting on his schedule. President Uhuru Kenyatta had invited him to plant a tree at the State House, the official residence of the president of Kenya. "I was so excited," he says. "I'm becoming friends with the president!"

But, as the story of Lesein shows, you don't need to be the friend of a president to make a change. "I've learned that no action is too small," he says. "Everything counts, no matter how small it is."

Lesein says it is his generation that will have to pay for the poor choices of previous ones. He believes that young people need to be at the frontline of the discussions about climate change, in order to prevent previous mistakes from being repeated. "We have our voices, we have the numbers, we literally control social media," he says.

When times get tough, Lesein thinks back to his childhood. He remembers the story of the hummingbird, and the work of Wangari Maathai. "We must take any action that is possible, because every action counts," he says. "And we should just start. Even if it is something small; just like the hummingbird did."

It's the little things citizens do. That's what will make the difference.

Wangari Maathai

Call to Action: By planting trees we can fight against the effects of climate change. Are you in a football club? Basketball? Hockey? Plant a tree for every goal or point that you score. Follow Lesein on Instagram (@trees4goals) and Twitter (@Trees4Goals_Ke).

PLANTING THE RIGHT KIND OF GREEN
Aadya Joshi
The Right Green
India

Every day on her way to school, Aadya walked by the local police station in her neighborhood in Mumbai, India. In front of it there was a garbage dump that had been used by the police to store confiscated vehicles that were never reclaimed by their owners. Slowly, the locals had added their trash, creating a landfill right in the middle of Aadya's neighborhood. The cars were stacked on top of each other, some decades old, and the stench of the trash between the car wrecks would drift through the streets in the hot summer months.

"For a long time, my friends and I tried to figure out why no one was doing anything about it," says Aadya. "So in the end I went to the police commissioner and the inspector and I said okay, I can make a garden in this garbage dump if it's not being used productively."

It took another month of convincing, but ultimately the police agreed. Aadya got some friends and local residents together, and for a month they met every weekend, cleaned out the trash, removed the contaminated soil, replaced it, and moved the old cars. They even cut up some of the cars, turning them into pots for some of the plants. Then they spent another weekend planting the garden in the old garbage dump. "It turned into a community project," says Aadya. "This garbage dump had been an issue in our community for a while."

For Aadya, this urban gardening project was the spark that lit a fire. She saw the power of one community garden, so she wanted to create even more. Then, at a workshop on gardens she was inspired to become the environmental activist she is today. "Their philosophy was to plant a lot of native trees to create an urban forest," Aadya explains.

Aadya had learned about native and nonnative plants in biology class. However, she had never realized how important native plant species were to the planet's ecosystems, even in a big city like Mumbai. "What I learned in the workshop, I thought that's actually really smart," she says. "You plant things that are native because they provide more ecological stability."

230

Aadya embarked on a discovery process that led to the research of Dr. Doug Tallamy, a professor in the Department of Entomology and Wildlife Ecology at the University of Delaware. From him she learned how important native plants were for supporting local insects, which in turn were an important source of food for local bird species.

This reminded her of the stories her grandfather had told her about the Mumbai of his childhood. He had described trips with his family, where they would see leopards, and colorful birds in the trees. It was a very different Mumbai from the one that Aadya knows, polluted and smelly; the only birds she ever saw were pigeons and crows.

Suddenly Aadya understood why there were no more colorful birds in the trees of Mumbai: they were the wrong trees! The problem in India goes back to colonial times, Aadya explains. The British brought with them many types of trees that weren't native to the region, and they were slowly adopted by local people. But because these trees weren't from India, the local insect and bird populations couldn't feed off of them or adapt quickly enough.

"In India, but especially in Mumbai, you see a lot of these colonial, nonnative invasive plants," Aadya says. "For example, rain trees. People say they've been here for so long, they must be a vital part of our ecosystem."

But actually, rain trees are from Costa Rica, and so is the wildlife they support. Those species that can live on the rain tree simply don't exist in Mumbai.

"If you plant native plants, then the insects come back, the butterflies come back, you have caterpillars, and with them the birds come back," Aadya explains. When she read the work of Dr. Tallamy it was like a switch was turned inside her head.

"I realized that maybe planting gardens was not the right thing to do," she says. "But if I could teach people what we should be planting and why, that would be a much more valuable lesson."

So Aadya launched her new plan, and sprang into action. In a local nature park, she started offering workshops for children ages five to twelve. It was late 2019, and the beginning of her organization, The Right Green.

She tested out her workshop ideas on her little brother, and her aim was simple: teach children about the importance of native plants for local ecosystems, and make sure they have fun at the same time.

"The first part of the workshop gets them into nature, since we have a lack of open spaces here," she says. "And the second thing is that I try to teach them how native plants support insects and biodiversity, and how nonnative plants *don't* support it."

Aadya makes sure that her students have fun: she takes them around the park and lets them find trees based on different clues. When they find the trees, she asks, "What kind of tree is this? Did you notice more insects on this tree versus another? What differences do you see?"

"I get them thinking about why it is that this mango tree has so many insects, butterflies, and birds living in it, while something like a rain tree has maybe one bird resting on it, but not even nesting within it."

Aadya is happy that these workshops are having a positive impact: children are sharing their new awareness with their families while they plant their gardens at home. And adults are reaching out to her for advice about what plants they should put in their gardens.

This need for advice gave Aadya her next idea. She created a database of native plants and ranked them by the amount of biodiversity they supported. Dr. Tallamy had accumulated this kind data for the United States, so Aadya got in touch with him to learn more about his methods. What she learned from him she used to produce a dataset on native plants in India. "What I want to create is a resource that a lot of people can use so that when they plant their gardens, they will seed well," she says.

Aadya's innovation has brought praise and support. She was awarded funding by The Pollination Project, an international organization that funds projects aimed at social change. With the money she received, Aadya printed booklets to give people in her workshops. She also produced a short animated video for social media that explains the importance of planting not just any trees, but the right ones -- the "right green."

With climate change causing ever more extreme weather in India, the need for planting native trees only becomes more urgent, Aadya says. Native trees are more resilient and can adapt more easily to changing conditions than nonnative trees. And having a healthy population of plants is indispensable for the sustainability of ecosystems anywhere.

"The whole point about planting native is to reduce the damage that climate change has done," says Aadya. "There is this relationship between the plants, the insects, and the birds, and then the rest of the food chain, to help repair some of the damage."

With her workshop and her database, Aadya is educating both future generations and those making seemingly small decisions today, like what plants to put in their garden, that can have a big impact. "If we don't make a conscious effort to change, and to make the world someplace that we want to live in, then we're really not doing our duty as current and future leaders," she says.

"It's like my dad and my grandfather always told me, if you want something to happen, you have to do it yourself. You can't just wait for other people to have the same idea that you have."

Because life is fueled by the energy captured from the sun by plants, it will be the plants that we use in our gardens that determine what nature will be like in 10, 20, and 50 years from now.

Doug Tallamy

Call to Action: Plant a garden. Learn about native plants in your community. Keep local biodiversity in mind! Learn more about Aadya's project at www.therightgreen.org

SEEING THE OCEAN IN A NEW WAY
Cruz Erdmann
New Zealand

For Cruz, being underwater feels like being in space. He feels weightless. He can dive in any direction and gaze at his surroundings. "It's like a dream," he says. "Swimming through an ocean is like visiting another planet."

At first, the infinite seascape might seem empty. But it is really full of life. There is plankton flowing through the water. If you listen closely, sometimes you can hear dolphins clicking in the distance, or parrot fish crunching coral. And you can see reefs that are teeming with life: fish of all colors and shapes.

The ocean has been a part of Cruz's life since he was born. His parents met in South Sulawesi, Indonesia when his father, a marine biologist, was working on his PhD, and his mother was traveling through Asia. Later she became his father's field assistant, and then a marine conservationist working with local communities to help them protect their natural resources. "Living in Bali, there is always the ocean that you go to," Cruz says of his first eight years of life. "I just have been immersed in that since I was born."

Cruz's family would spend their holidays in nature, traveling around Asia and going on diving trips. Sometimes he would accompany his father on expeditions, searching for unknown species in the depth of the oceans. There he would be his father's field assistant, holding jars and syringes for him while he documented the underwater wildlife.

When Cruz was 10, his father decided that he would invest in a new underwater camera for his work. So, after a long lecture on the value of the equipment, Cruz got to try his hand at underwater photography for the first time, using his father's old camera. His father gave him a quick explanation of what the different dials on the camera would do, but from there on out it was all about experimenting with different perspectives, and trying to capture various species underwater. "It wasn't something I really thought of taking to a high level," he says. "It was just for fun."

Then one day, on a diving trip in the Lembeh Strait off North Sulawesi,

Indonesia, camera in hand, he had an unexpected encounter with a Bigfin Reef Squid. Cruz raised his camera and pressed the shutter. In the photo, the animal hovers in the pitch black, glowing in different shades of blue, green, brown, and red, its tentacles stretched out in front of it. It won Cruz the Young Wildlife Photographer of the Year Award, organized by London's Natural History Museum. "Winning that award was a real opportunity to get a footing," he says. "I've always wanted to do something that revolved around media, or art, or science, around the oceans."

Receiving the award opened up more doors for 14-year-old Cruz: he was invited to speak at the Davos Forum in Switzerland, the yearly meeting of leading economic decision makers, dignitaries, celebrities, and heads of state. He was thrilled to meet Dr. Sylvia Earle, a marine biologist he greatly admires, who spoke there, and said, "I wish you would use all means at your disposal -- films, expeditions, the web, new submarines -- to create a campaign to ignite public support for a global network of marine protected areas -- 'hope spots' large enough to save and restore the blue heart of the planet." And as he began *his* presentation, Cruz said, "We blink 15 to 20 times a minute. Why? We blink because our eyes haven't yet fully adapted to seeing outside of water."

"Life on our planet is shaped by the oceans," Cruz says. Ocean currents regulate the earth's temperature. Plankton and other ocean plant species produce more than 60 percent of all of the oxygen found in our atmosphere. But human activity is destroying biodiversity and the intricate ecosystems that support life underwater. "It's a great natural resource," Cruz says. "But it's become expendable, and we've been pushing it to the brink."

Growing up in Indonesia, Cruz was able to witness the importance of marine life and coral reefs for local communities. "Coral reefs are fish factories," Cruz said, on the stage at Davos. "They produce a large amount of fish mass that spills into the surrounding ecosystems, linking it with the food chain that extends into the open ocean."

Oceans provide a livelihood to people where crops simply can't grow, and other natural resources aren't available. Ecosystems like coral reefs support coastal populations as well as all the other life in the ocean. But climate change is causing them to bleach and die off more than in the past. "Most instances of bleaching occur during El Nino warming events," Cruz says. "And those are now more intense, and more common, with climate change." During diving trips in Indonesia and the Maldives, as well as in Papua New Guinea and the Solomon

Islands, Cruz has noticed that some coral reefs are more resilient to changing temperatures than others. But he adds, "Most of them are suffering badly around the world."

Cruz explains that the invention of trawl nets and large-scale fishing has led to a new level of consumerism that is simply not sustainable. "For a long time, there was an assumption that we could just fish as much as we wanted, without decimating populations. But we can't."

The main problem, as Cruz argued on the stage at Davos, is that we have become so disconnected from the oceans. We buy our food from the shelves of supermarkets, without thinking twice about where it came from. This means that most people are unaware of the negative effects their decisions as consumers have on the environment–effects that include overfishing, pollution, and habitat destruction. "We've basically grown used to it as consumers of the ocean," he says. "And it hasn't really stopped, even though we know that it is having a very negative impact."

Another threat caused by climate change is ocean acidification. This happens when the oceans have to absorb more carbon dioxide from the atmosphere than usual. That changes the chemical balance of sea water, and many organisms can no longer grow properly. Oysters, mussels, and plankton can even be dissolved if the water is too acidic.

"If the foundations of our ocean food chains are not able to grow their shells, the consequences will be disastrous," Cruz says. "It's a serious issue, with real consequences that affect every single one of us, no matter how far from the ocean we live."

Cruz wants to change the way we look at the ocean. By sharing powerful photographic images, he wants to give the creatures living underwater a face -- and help us to see that our current way of life is unsustainable.

As an underwater photographer, Cruz feels it is his responsibility to bridge the gap between humans and the ocean. "I want to captivate people's attention about a world they may never have seen before," he says. "And allow us to develop a better appreciation for our dependence on the ocean." He is particularly interested in macro photography, in which the objects photographed are very close to the lens. "It's like exploring a hidden world through much sharper eyes than my own," he says. Many people don't really think of fish as animals. It's hard to imagine that they can feel pain, and even harder to have an affinity for them. But fish -- especially the tiny fish that Cruz likes to take pictures of -- are the "rice of the reef." "Without them, the coral reef ecosystem would crumble and starve," he says. "They are the staple base food; they keep the coral reef ecosystems going."

On a recent dive in the Maldives, Cruz was overcome with a feeling of awe. He was surrounded by marine wildlife. Around him, the entire ocean was filled with sharks, and fish, and rays. Animals that he rarely saw in Indonesia were found by the dozens in a single dive.

"I've heard stories about how the ocean used to be so full and rich, and so thick with life," he says. "It didn't really hit home until I saw that dive site -- this what it is supposed to be! The clicking and crackling of creatures on the reef, and the sound of fishes rushing by, was deafening."

"If you genuinely love or believe in something and you want to do something about it, no matter how insignificant you may feel about it, you should do it," he says. "Because if you do what you love, and you fight for what you believe in, then ultimately, you're going to get there."

Protect the natural systems as if your life depends on it, because it does! Our lives do depend on making peace with nature.

Sylvia Earle

Call to Action: Natural beauty and life is all around us! Grab the camera. Inspire others to protect the environment. You can follow Cruz on Instagram: @cruzerdmann

THE LAND OF MANY WATERS
Benita Davis
Sandwatch Foundation
Guyana

Benita Davis grew up on the beautiful Caribbean coast. As a young child, all she had to do was walk out of her home in a middle-class neighborhood in Georgetown, Guyana, cross the Rupert Craig Highway, and she would be at the ocean, where the broad expanse of brown waters meets the horizon.

In Guyana, water and life are inextricably connected. From the majestic Kaieteur and Marshall waterfalls in the north of the country, to the Essequibo River, which snakes through more than 1,000 kilometers of this South American country, Guyana's waterways give the country its Indigenous name: "the land of many waters."

But Benita never truly understood the importance of water until she followed it away from the ocean, and into the interior of her tropical country, along the Essequibo. When she was in University, Benita and a group of researchers traveled to the center of the country to assess the water quality of the rivers while spending time with and learning from the Indigenous communityy who live there. It was for her final year thesis.

For several weeks, Benita slept in a hammock, fished in the rivers, and hunted in the forests. She spent time with Indigenous leaders whose families had lived in the country's interior for centuries. They taught her the basics of living off the grid, and emphasized the importance of being in tune with the sacred water of the river. There, without cellphone service, and temporarily free from the distractions of the screens and radio waves she was used to, she was able to fully connect with the rhythms of the earth.

"The leader's seven-year-old grandson was so shocked to know that even though I was an adult I didn't know how to hunt, or where I needed to go on the river to catch certain fish. Or even how to steer a canoe!" she says. "That's when it struck me that for the Indigenous people, the river is much more than a food source; it's also their cultural heritage, transportation, and recreation."

Having studied environmental science in college, she did know, however, that the waters of that sacred river were being polluted by mercury. And two weeks in the interior forced her to reckon with what might happen to Guyana's Indigenous population if the pollution of the river continues. "They have no other means of survival," she says.

As a child, Benita had always been drawn to the natural world. Growing up in a city and attending school in the capital, Georgetown, she didn't have many opportunities to learn about environmental issues. But she did what she could. She joined her school's environment club, went on "green walks," and participated in a scout's program that allowed her to go on several trips to the country's interior.

When she was first admitted to the University of Guyana, she had planned to study to become a nutritionist. But then she decided to follow her heart and study environmental science instead. She was shocked to learn what a devastating impact the mining companies were having on Guyana's environment. The two smallest countries in South America -- Guyana, and neighboring Suriname -- alone account for 10 to 15 percent of the entire nation's freshwater resources. However, the mining practices of the 40,000 artisanal gold miners who work along the rivers in Guyana are threatening the water quality. And the recent discovery of vast oil deposits in the country is making it easier for people to strike it rich; but it also poses an existential threat to the environment.

Benita realized that for many people in her country, the problem is basic: they simply don't understand the importance of protecting the water. "I decided that if I could help students, teachers, and youth groups develop an appreciation for the importance of protecting freshwater, it could filter down into their homes and communities. The problem needs to be tackled by all age groups and demographics," she says. "Many adults aren't aware of how their activities can affect this precious resource. We need to help everyone, regardless of their level of education or economic background, to understand that water is essential for life."

After she graduated from the University of Guyana, Benita began to volunteer with Policy Forum Guyana, where she learned about various educational tools to help inspire young people to take action for the environment. And she took an environmental workshop called Sandwatch, where she was connected and learned from global scientists and educators.

Sandwatch is an interdisciplinary educational process through which students, teachers, and local communities work together in the field to monitor coastal environments; identify and evaluate the threats, problems, and conflicts facing them; and develop sustainable approaches for addressing them. With the Sandwatch approach, involved groups not only learn to understand their environment; they also develop critical thinking skills, and learn how to apply them to conflict resolution. Sandwatch seeks to integrate the values inherent in sustainable development into all aspects of learning, through a practical hands-on approach, empowering citizens of all ages to become involved in positive environmental and social change.

Benita's exposure to Sandwatch impressed upon her the importance of getting young people to start thinking about the environment from an early age through hands-on activities, like going out into their communities to monitor water quality, observing how climate change is affecting beaches, and learning what must be done to offset the dire impacts of climate change and natural disasters. She also wanted to make environmental activism fun for kids. Inspired by the Sandwatch approach, which incorporates a range of disciplines, from biology to woodwork, from geography to art, and from poetry to mathematics -- and following her lifelong passion for cartoons and games, she set out to develop a game about preserving freshwater resources. The game she created, the River Guardian Freshwater board game, is now in the process of being distributed to students across the country.

Meanwhile, the environmental movement in Guyana has begun to steadily increase, and what was once a small trickle of activism has become a steady stream. On September 29, 2019 Benita, with the help of volunteers, organized a rally in solidarity with Greta Thunberg's global Fridays for Future movement, which brought more than 500 youth climate activists into the streets of Georgetown. Many of them carried signs and banners proclaiming their fight as river guardians. Others called for people to protect the ocean, which is steadily rising and threatening the homes and communities of coastal residents.

Guyana's government has taken notice of this growing, and increasingly vocal, movement. The Green State Development Strategy is now a key part of President David Granger's development plan for the country; and the country's Ministry of Communities recently launched a #GreenGenerationGy hashtag as a way to bring more youth into the movement.

"At first, no one really wanted to support teaching climate change in the schools," Benita says. "But then, literally after seeing what was happening globally, a lot of people became interested in being a part of this movement." It was called the River Guardian Project. The board game Benita invented has also turned heads around the world. The government of the Netherlands even reached out to her to see how they could get involved in producing more educational games for kids.

Benita realizes that it's not just young people who need to become sensitized to the importance of freshwater resources, but all of the people of Guyana. She sees her job as letting both young people and adults know that everyone can play a role in becoming a river guardian -- and everyone is needed in the effort.

Now that she's graduated from university, Benita is focusing all of her efforts on activism: she spends a lot of time meeting with representatives of NGOs and government officials. But she hasn't forgotten the people whose rights she's defending: the people of the Indigenous communities who taught her how to be one with the river. And she recognizes her privileged situation.

"If I didn't have the experience of being in the interior myself, without clean food and water, I wouldn't have truly understood how dependent the people who live there are on the rivers; and how urgent it is for us to fix this matter. Because they've been drinking this water, with mercury in it, all the time," she says. "I only had to drink it for two weeks." She pauses, then adds, "Hopefully by getting the message out to both young and old, it will lead to a change in the way we view this land of many waters."

Thousands have lived without love, not one without water.

W. H. Auden

Call to Action Clean water is essential to sustaining human life. Learn more about Sandwatch at http://www.unesco.org/new/en/natural-sciences/priority-areas/sids/sandwatch/

THE PEACE CORPS IN MALAWI
Jill Bhowmik
San Diego, California

On her first day in Malawi as a Peace Corps volunteer, Jill Bhowmik was warmly welcomed to the community by Gertrude, who vowed right off the bat, "I'll be a great student!" Which came true. But on that first day, Jill knew there was more to this greeting than just a playful ice-breaker, as Gertrude handed her a basket of seed potatoes. "They looked rotten to me," Jill says, remembering. "I'd never seen a seed potato before, let alone planted one. There I was, with this degree from a great American university, taking on the role of student my first day."

Before she knew it, Jill was doing the backbreaking work of digging and planting a small patch of land in her yard, while Gertrude taught her the subtleties of the process. Some months later, Jill would celebrate a successful harvest by eating the potatoes she'd planted. "I'll never forget what was important to that community," she says now. "And it's especially relevant today, during this pandemic." This is especially true since some of the answers to creating a sustainable world can be found in the agricultural practices of traditional cultures.

Planting seed potatoes was only the first of Gertrude's lessons for Jill. "When you decide to go halfway around the world with the Peace Corps, you think *you* are going there to teach." She laughs, then says, "It didn't take long for me to realize that these amazing people and places involved with the Peace Corps end up teaching *you*."

Since her days in the Peace Corps, Jill has joined the ranks of many other notable returned Peace Corps volunteers whose lives were changed by their experiences -- for example, Netflix CEO Reed Hastings, President Jimmy Carter's mother Lilian Carter, political news anchor Chris Matthews, writer Paul Theroux, Congresswoman Donna Shalala, television host Bob Vila, Senator Chris Dodd, and film director Taylor Hackford.

"When most people think of the Peace Corps, they tend to think we send over resources to help people in need," Jill says. "But there are actually three explicit goals of the Peace Corps. The first is to help the people of interested countries meet their need for training men and women,

242

and this always comes from the host country. For example, Malawi had expressed a need for more English teachers, so that's why I was sent there." The other two goals are about promoting better understanding among Americans toward the rest of the world, and of other people toward Americans.

Along with her fellow teachers, Jill lived in a row of houses made with bricks that were formed from the dirt and clay underfoot. She taught English classes in Malawi in their developing community day schools. These secondary schools were built by, for, and in the community, with locally sourced material -- and astounding ingenuity. "Early on I was told that I could farm the land in front of and behind my house, which I hadn't thought about doing. I was there to teach English, after all."

Soon other teachers noticed her empty plot, and asked Jill if they could use her untended land. She was happy to share what was allotted to her with her colleagues. Some had families who relied on these plots for their day-to-day food supply. Jill enjoyed watching them tend the land expertly; and she observed their intimate knowledge of the land, a knowledge she hoped to have one day.

According to the United Nations Development Programme's (UNDP) Vulnerability and Adaptation Assessment Report, Malawi is subject to a unique combination of climate change issues and extreme weather events like intense rainfall, regional floods, seasonal and multiyear droughts, dry and cold spells, strong winds, landslides, sustained thunderstorms, hailstorms, mudslides and heat waves.

When a nation's environment is suffering, its people suffer too. There are countless downstream effects from these climate events for the people of Malawi. Floods and droughts, which are becoming both more frequent and more erratic, disrupt supply chains and energy grids – and when these are disrupted, medical supplies, food, clean water and other necessary goods and services can't efficiently reach the people. The resulting food insecurity in turn leads to malnutrition. And malnutrition and lack of medical treatment makes a population more vulnerable to epidemics. This happened in Malawi in the 1990s, when HIV/AIDS surfaced, and today it is struggling with COVID-19. "It's heartbreaking that they have to bear the brunt of climate change and droughts, floods and famine, when their carbon footprint is nothing compared to ours," Jill says.

Jill found many novel ways to teach the young people of Malawi how to rise above their trying circumstances. As an English teacher in the making, Jill taught the standard curriculum. But she always felt that she could inspire them in a more profound way with a bit of creativity. "One thing I'd do is take their writing assignments, mail them back to America for my mom to type up, then bind these pages in spiral notebooks and send them back to Malawi, so I could show my kids what their words looked like 'published' in a book. It really gave them a lot of confidence."

Jill also inspired her community outside of the classroom. She created competitive clubs for games like Scrabble – which led to a natural exchange of cultures, when her friends taught *her* the traditional Malawian game of Bawo. "I definitely didn't get any favors or special treatment learning to play Bawo," she says with a laugh. She even started a girls' soccer team, hoping to further empower young women in the community. "I was nominated as a coach, and we ended up organizing a girls soccer game with a neighboring village." When one of the members of the local parliament showed up at the game and seemed to be scowling, Jill thought she might be upset because the girls were wearing pants instead of their usual dresses. Some girls were so concerned about this taboo that they had even worn skirts over their pants. "But when the MP finally spoke up, she wanted to know why the girls were wearing skirts. 'It's slowing them down!' she said. 'We're going to lose!'" Looking back on her time there, Jill says, "I felt great doing what I could to empower youth. I hope I did so successfully."

After her tour of duty in the Peace Corps, Jill returned to her home in San Diego, where she now teaches English and Journalism at her alma mater, Granite Hills High. For the last 19 years she's been advocating for and amplifying the voices of San Diego youth, just as she did in Malawi. She also runs the school newspaper and the literary magazine, where the bravery of her students' writing never ceases to inspire her.

At her high school, Jill uses the AVID program - (Achievement Via Individual Determination) to close the opportunity gap by preparing all of her students for college readiness and success in a global society. Many students in AVID are first-generation college students, and a lot of them are from underrepresented backgrounds. "The AVID framework helps them keep their eyes on the prize," Jill says. "I've seen the benefit of guiding students to the right classes, teaching them organizational skills, time management, leadership, how to be lifelong learners, how to be in control of and advocate for their own learning. If something is going wrong in class, they speak up. It's these skills that inspire confidence, and with confidence, we hope to inspire change."

Jill has been a pillar of the educational community the world over.

But what young people and her experiences in the Peace Corps have taught Jill is equally inspiring. "Whether in Malawi or San Diego, they've taught me to be more idealistic," she says. "Being around that youthful energy can really reinvigorate you. Mostly, the students see the offerings of the world as being so great. Over the course of nearly two decades in my teaching career, what I have seen is that they have hope. It's taught me to keep dreaming."

> *On your willingness to contribute part of your life to this country I think will depend the answer, whether a free society can continue. I think it can. And I think Americans are willing to contribute. But the effort must be far greater than we've ever made in the past.*

President John F. Kennedy, University of Michigan, October 14, 1960

'The Founding Moment of the Peace Corps' Speech

Call to Action: To get involved with one of the many good will Peace Corps Initiatives around the world please visit - https://www.peacecorps.gov .

WE CAN DO BETTER!
Jasper Ralph
Plastic Free MV
Martha's Vineyard

Jasper was sitting in a restaurant enjoying a cool drink on a hot summer day. As he played around with the plastic straw he'd been served, he wondered, "Why do they automatically give you straws, even if you don't ask for them? That's weird: if people don't really want a straw, it's just a waste."

Jasper had been aware of plastic pollution in the oceans, and how harmful it is to marine wildlife, for some time. "Plastics wash up on our beaches, and kill our seagulls, dolphins, and even whales," he says. It's been predicted that by 2050, the oceans will actually contain more plastic than fish. When he was in elementary school, Jasper organized beach cleanups, and posted pictures of himself on social media, to motivate others to join him.

Jasper's home community prides itself on its commitment to its many sustainability initiatives. A picturesque island off the southern coast of Massachusetts, Martha's Vineyard is known as a beautiful vacation spot. Celebrities appreciate its low-key lifestyle. Presidents and other dignitaries treasure its quiet respite from the pressures of world affairs. During the summer, the year-round island population of 20,000 swells to more than 100,000. And almost everyone there is concerned about the rising sea levels, and its effect on the island. In the winter, and at high tide, major roads are washed out. Waterfront homes have been moved back onto land; after one big storm one home even fell off a cliff. "Sea levels are rising faster here than in other places," Jasper says. "When climate change happens, islands are the most affected."

Jasper decided he wanted to do something about this problem. He knew that his local community was passionate about sustainability. Jasper hoped that if he shared his passion and vision with others, they would join him.

So, he joined his fellow students from the West Tisbury School to start the "Straw Free MV" initiative, and encourage people to stop using plastic straws. The students started by visiting restaurants and take-out counters around the island: they would boldly walk in and introduce themselves to the staff. "Hi, we are Straw Free MV. We're a group of kids on the island," they would say. "We are concerned about plastic straws. They're wasteful, and they're harmful to the environment. We'd like to ask you to give straws only to those customers who ask for them, or to not use them at all."

Jasper and his friends created "Straw Free MV" stickers to give to the restaurants that agreed to join in this effort. Restaurant owners proudly displayed them, and began giving out straws only to the customers who specifically asked for them. The students also created educational postcards that restaurant owners could place on their tables. And they suggested alternatives to plastic straws, like paper straws, or reusable straws that people could carry with them. Jasper carries his own stainless-steel straw in his backpack, and he keeps another one in his mom's car.

Sometimes the students' reputation would precede them. One day they visited the Black Dog Café, a popular restaurant located right next to the ferry in Vineyard Haven. "We assumed that since it was such a big restaurant, they wouldn't want to help us," Jasper says. But when they arrived there, the manager was excited to see them: "Oh, great, Straw Free MV, we've been waiting for you!" she said. She took all of their postcards, put them out on the tables; and asked for more.

While reducing the use of plastic straws was an important first step, Jasper knew there were other wasteful practices, like single-use plastic bottles of water and soda, that needed to be addressed. With such a large tourist population, these plastic bottles were everywhere on the island -- strewn along the beaches, and filling up the recycling bins and landfills. "Plastic doesn't just go away," Jasper says. "Almost everything else breaks down and decomposes. But if you have a plastic bottle that you use for just two seconds, it will be in the world for thousands of years."

So Jasper and his fellow youth activists set themselves a new goal. They developed a plan to introduce a bylaw that would forbid the selling of single-use plastic bottles that held less than 34 ounces. They called their new group Plastic Free MV, and they campaigned tirelessly for their cause.

To gain a broad base of support and build a strong grassroots movement, they organized educational forums at the local libraries. They would put up posters, set up chairs, and then share what they had learned through their research with the audience. In their PowerPoint presentations, they gave a brief overview of current climate science, and discussed how plastic production is accelerating the climate crisis. "We are producing more than 300 million tons of plastic each year, 50% of which is for single-use products," reads one slide. "We can do better!" says the next. After their presentations, they would open the forum up to debate. "We take time to answer people's questions," says Jasper. "It's important to listen to people's opinions," he adds. "The only way anything is achieved is by working together."

"Sometimes people who come to the forums yell at us. They want their single-use bottles! They want their convenience," Jasper says. "We explain that it's really not about just one person -- it's about the whole world, and we all need to help, because this is a major global issue."

The next step for Jasper and his young changemakers was to present to the selectmen and concerned citizens at the island's town meetings, urging them to adopt the new bylaw. So far three of the six towns have done so.

This work is not always easy, and not everyone is happy about the new rules. "Some businesses don't really like the bylaw," Jasper says. "If you are a store owner or a distributor you can't sell single-use plastic bottles under 34 oz. Some shops would like to keep the plastic bottles; it's been hard to get them on board."

As these youth activists have learned, in the political world, it's always important to be on high alert. For more than a year, they'd been speaking at selectmen meetings, carefully presenting their ideas, and respectively encouraging dialogue about this issue. But then, when the time came to create the warrant for the town meeting of Tisbury, the Board of Selectmen simply decided to take it off the agenda. "One of our parents saw on Twitter that this happened," says Jasper. "They ran right over to the meeting, and said, 'Stop! You can't do that!'" It took three days of bickering, but eventually the bylaw was put back on the agenda for the town meeting - to be held on June 13, 2020.

Jasper's activism has now grown beyond Martha's Vineyard. As a young environmentalist, he knows how important it is to strengthen one's network and get in touch with other activists. So in September 2019, inspired by Greta Thunberg's speech about the urgency of addressing climate change, he and a couple of friends went to New York City to join the climate strike.

For Jasper, seeing so many others marching together for the climate and taking steps -- even little ones -- to protect the environment is really important. "We made signs with a little polar bear on it, and then we marched along with everyone else," Jasper says. "It was really inspiring to see that everyone cared enough to come down there, just to march for climate action."

Jasper believes that children all over the world should be more aware of the power and influence they have. "We really do have the power to change what is happening," Jasper says. "Adults listen to us: if it was just a bunch of adults saying we should have this bylaw, it might not have been passed. But when they see that kids are standing up for something, it makes it look like it's really important."

Jasper is convinced that his activism, and that of his friends, can have a large impact. He hopes that the changes made on Martha's Vineyard will inspire tourists to introduce sustainable practices in their own communities. "Maybe if they see what we're doing, they'll go back to where they live, and they'll say, 'Hey, why don't we do something like that?'" Jasper says. "So, it can just spread."

> *Young people, when informed and empowered,*
> *when they realize that what they do truly*
> *makes a difference, can indeed change the world.*

Jane Goodall

Call to Action: Adopt sustainable practices in your life: bring your own straw. Bring shopping bags to the market. Every bit counts. **Check out:** www.plasticfreemv.com; https://www.instagram.com/plasticfreemv/ https://www.facebook.com/pg/plasticfreeonmv/about/?ref=page internal

IV

INNOVATE!
Green Entrepreneurs/ Inventors

INNOVATE!
Green Entrepreneurs and Inventors

Innovation is the key to building a more sustainable world. As 15-year-old *Time* magazine Kid of the Year, Gitanjali Rao says, "Many of my inventions have been inspired by just watching the news." Her first invention was in response to the public health water crisis in Flint, Michigan.

As a freshman in high school, Ana Sophia Mifsud took a class in solar energy, where she learned that innovative technologies could both help impoverished areas improve economically, and safeguard the environment. That was when she knew she had found her calling. After college, she began working at Amory Lovins's Rocky Mountain Institute, where she was introduced to the concept of Applied Hope–a mantra that she had unwittingly been living, and aspiring toward all her life. In 2017, after Hurricane Maria ravaged Puerto Rico, Ana Sophia helped install microgrids in 10 public schools, giving more than 4,000 students and faculty access to clean, resilient power.

Azza Faiad is an up-and-coming leader in Egypt's renewable energy industry. In high school, she discovered a way to convert plastics into biofuel, while significantly reducing the cost of the manufacturing process with a cheap, abundant catalyst not used before. Her work was supported by the Egyptian Petroleum Research institute in Cairo, who saw her incredible potential as a scientist and creative thinker. She was awarded the EIROforum prize, and was invited to participate in the European Union Contest for Young Scientists (EUCYS).

Vincent Kimura always remembered his grandfather's stories of working in the sugarcane fields in Hawaii. He decided early on that he was going to dedicate his life to protecting the environment, and the small farmers who've always known how to care for it. Vincent is now the CEO of Smart Yields, a globally recognized agricultural technology company revolutionizing the way small and medium-scale farms operate. He is involved in various green enterprises, including AgriGro and Inovi Green. A main focus of his work and life is on supporting struggling farmers around the world and repairing food systems using technology, data, and collaboration between the public, private, and nonprofit sectors.

Daniela Fernandez founded the Sustainable Ocean Alliance (SOA) when she was just 19 years old. SOA develops leaders, cultivates ideas, and accelerates solutions in the field of ocean health and sustainability–and is the world's largest network of young environmental leaders, with contributors from more than 150 countries worldwide. SOA's Ocean Solutions Accelerator supports brilliant start-ups that contribute to the health of the ocean. For her work, Daniela has been recognized by the likes of U.S. Secretary John Kerry and former President Bill Clinton. She is also a member of the World Economic Forum's Friends of Ocean Action, and has been recognized by Forbes's 30 Under 30 for her environmental achievements.

Gary White discovered his calling to civil and environmental engineering in college. "That was where I found an intersection of my greatest passion and the world's greatest needs," he says. "Engineering answers to the world's problems would be the path that I would take from there on." He'd read about Dr. Muhammad Yunus, who founded the Grameen Bank in 1983 to provide micro-credit loans to entrepreneurs, mostly women, in Bangladesh, and who had gone on to win the 2006 Nobel Peace Prize. In 2008, Gary met Matt Damon at the Clinton Global Initiative. At the time, Gary was running an organization called Water Partners that was helping people living in poverty get access to microloans for clean water and sanitation, and Matt was running an organization called H20 Africa, which helped to supply people with drinking water in rural Africa. They merged their organizations to form Water.org, which to date has mobilized $2.6 billion in capital to support safe water and sanitation projects around the world.

At the Institute we expose young people to opportunities to explore the exciting world of innovation in business with startups. Our strategic partner in Hawaii -- Design Thinking Hawaii -- uses an innovative approach to getting people to "think out of the box" which has led to numerous start-ups at the groundbreaking company Oceanit. And at the Institute's Job Shadow Day young people got a chance to meet them. 17-year-old Mickie Hirata was intrigued to learn about IBIS Intellisockets. "It was great to meet those who've developed the programming, designing, project planning, business, assembling, and even invented the Intellisockets!" she says. "I had no idea how new this company was, and how special I was to be their first experiment! It was incredible to see them upgrading their top-secret blueprints."

Young people are eager to learn how to innovate solutions for the myriad of climate change problems we are facing. We need to find ways to match their desire to innovate with the opportunities, and connect them with green entrepreneurs and inventors who are working on creating tomorrow's solutions. The stories in this chapter show how this combination is a win-win!

APPLIED HOPE: BUILDING RESILIENT COMMUNITIES
Ana Sophia Mifsud
New York, New York

Growing up, Ana Sophia Mifsud always felt split between two worlds, but what exactly those two worlds were wasn't quite so easy to figure out. As is the case in many modern families, Ana Sophia split her time between her parents' homes: her mother's home in Miami, and her father's in Guatemala. Her experiences in each place were very different: and often this led to inner turmoil.

Guatemala is rich in natural beauty and culture, and Ana Sophia spent her time there immersed in nature. On any given day, she could be found hiking active volcanoes, playing on black sand beaches, or splashing around in the many cascading tidal pools. There she developed a sense of wonder and adventure, as well as a love of being outside. But for all its natural splendor, Ana Sophia came to understand that Guatemala is a poor country. Poverty and economic inequity are persistent problems. And there are other challenges to consider - high rates of malnourishment, issues of Indigenous and women's rights.

Her life in metropolitan Miami was very different: there she went to well-funded public schools, received a great education, and could spend time hanging out with friends without worrying about her safety. "I was conflicted about all these differences between my two homes," she says. It made her sad to realize that not everybody had the opportunities she had. One day, she decided that it was her mission to help more children have access to the educational and socioeconomic experiences she had. But she was still just a high school student herself, and she didn't know yet how she could do that.

As a budding environmentalist, she knew that Miami and Guatemala are both uniquely vulnerable to climate change. Situated as it is between two coastlines, Guatemala is geographically vulnerable. And its economy is dependent on agriculture, so it's also vulnerable to droughts and rains. Miami is also on the front lines of climate change. At high tide in Miami Beach, the streets are flooded, even without hurricanes.

When Ana Sophia was a freshman in high school, she enrolled in a class taught by Dr. Wafa Khalil, which was the only solar energy course taught in public school in the United States at the time. Here, her passion for environmentalism was nurtured. She learned about climate change and green energy. And as an aspiring engineer she was overjoyed to learn that innovative technologies could help impoverished areas improve economically, while also safeguarding the environment. This is when Ana Sophia's two worlds became one. "Once I realized I can care about the environment, and address the economic health of communities in need at the same time, I had a renewed sense of hope. I knew I'd found my calling."

So she set about learning everything she could about renewable energy technology. She attended local workshops given by NGOs and climate change organizations, and she even took a course on solar energy installation. "I even learned how to install a solar array on a rooftop," she says with a laugh. Even more impressive, she achieved her B.S. in Environmental Systems Engineering from Stanford University. "I always wanted to be an engineer, because to me, an engineer is a problem solver. I wanted to be a part of implementing the technology that could help people solve their local issues related to climate change, and inject some life into local economies. I just wanted to make peoples' lives better."

Ana Sophia always knew she wanted to work at a mission-driven organization that had the same positive, hopeful outlook she had, and the same focus on developing technical solutions to climate change that would also lift up communities economically. After college, she began working at the Rocky Mountain Institute (RMI), where she was introduced to the concept of applied hope – a mantra which she had unwittingly been living, and aspiring toward all her life, well before she had heard of it. Amory Lovins, RMI's co-founder, describes the concept of applied hope this way:

> *We work to make the world better, not from some airy theoretical hope, but in the pragmatic and grounded conviction that starting with hope and acting out of hope can cultivate a different kind of world worth being hopeful about, reinforcing itself in a virtuous spiral. Applied hope is not about some vague, far-off future, but is expressed and created moment by moment through our choices.*

At RMI, Ana Sophia found her professional home, working on the front lines of climate change in the Island Energy Program. Her work was focused on the Caribbean Islands, including St. Lucia and Belize -- until Hurricane Maria tore through the region in 2017. In the immediate aftermath of the hurricane she went to work in Puerto Rico, building microgrids in remote areas that had been devastated. Microgrids are technologies that work with existing energy grids, but continue working when the energy grid goes down—a commonplace occurrence in the remote mountainous regions of Puerto Rico, which became the norm after Hurricane Maria.

It's estimated that Hurricane Maria caused Puerto Rico roughly $91 billion in damages. Keeping the concept of applied hope in mind, Ana Sophia decided to bring the microgrid technology to those who needed it most – the children. In such a difficult time for the island, she knew she'd need help taking on such a big challenge. So she partnered with several organizations such as Save The Children, to install renewable microgrid infrastructure in schools, including the schools in mountainous communities, which were experiencing the longest outages. More than anything, she hoped her efforts would help return these island communities to some semblance of normalcy. By the project's end, Ana Sophia had helped install microgrids in 10 public schools, giving more than 4,000 students and faculty access to clean, resilient power. "I can't tell you what it was like when the students could see firsthand what is possible. This is what applied hope fosters, in its purest form," she says, smiling.

As positive as she was, the situation was hard for Ana Sophia to handle at some points. "I went home and cried almost every night. I couldn't believe that citizens of the United States had to go to school in the conditions that I was seeing. But I never lost hope. And that's important to get across to the children." She stresses the importance of tone in communicating with communities that are suffering. "Doomsday messaging doesn't galvanize people. You can't show up to a disaster area and say the sky is falling. It's necessary to rally those in need to action, behind a message of positivity and hope—*applied* hope."

Ana Sophia wants youth to understand that there are many ways to get involved with the climate change movement and help communities in need. "There's not just one type of person that cares about tackling climate change. Everyone should." She believes tackling this issue will, and must, happen across economic sectors, political parties, countries, and disciplines. "It's going to impact every aspect of our lives. It's important we take a whole-systems approach. Activism is great. But having all sorts of people engaged in solving this issue will give us the best chance in the future."

She also believes in the importance of getting out into nature as the most effective way to help people gain reverence for the natural world. "To this day, I find a lot of joy and renewal when I get to spend time outdoors. So my advice to young people is simple: *Go outside!*"

Now, 25 years old, Ana Sophia's latest goal at RMI is to try to get the 70 million homes and businesses across the U.S. that burn gas, oil, or propane in their buildings to eliminate combustion. It's a project with huge emissions implications, and huge hurdles to overcome. Thankfully, Ana Sophia is the one who is tasked with achieving such a lofty goal. After all, she was able to deliver reliable electricity to 4,000 schoolchildren in the remote mountains of Puerto Rico.

As a problem solver at her core, there's no doubt Ana Sophia will figure out a way to lead on any climate issue that arises – which is why youth should feel confident looking to her as a source of knowledge, experience, and inspiration. And of course, as she continues to abide by the tenets of applied hope in all the work she does, she will continue to lift up the underserved communities that she has always so diligently served.

Infinite gratitude toward all things past;
infinite service to all things present;
infinite responsibility to all things future.

Gôtô-roshi

A favorite quote of RMI's founder, Amory Lovin

Call to Action: Learn more about green infrastructure, remote electrification, and green community education, and The Rocky Mountain Institute - https://rmi.org

A LIFE OF SERVICE: WATER.ORG
Gary White
Kansas City, Missouri

Gary White was raised to lead a life of service. "My parents, teachers, and faith really instilled this passion in me," he says. He discovered his calling to civil and environmental engineering in college, from what he had learned in high school from the Congregation of Christian Brothers -- to live a life of service. "That was where I found an intersection of my greatest passion and the world's greatest needs," he says. "Engineering answers to the world's problems would be the path that I would take from there on."

Gary first started on his path of helping people living in poverty get access to microloans for clean water and sanitation with Water Partners in 1990. He'd read about Dr. Muhammad Yunus, who founded the Grameen Bank in 1983 to provide micro-credit loans to entrepreneurs, mostly women, in Bangladesh, and who had gone on to win the 2006 Nobel Peace Prize. "Access to finance was the main barrier people always came up against," Gary says. "They understood the issues their communities were facing and what approach was needed to remedy their issues. They just didn't have any savings to do it. In rural areas, the issue is usually access to water and the tradeoff is time. A few hours' walk might get you water, but a six-hour walk will get you higher quality water. In either case, there's a lot of cost associated with all of that in lost time. Water Partners has worked to alleviate that with our microloan program."

In urban areas, the tradeoffs manifest a bit differently. "When there's no water available, people have to pay vendors 10-15 times the amount they'd pay if they had the money to get a direct connection to their local utility. The problem is that many people may have just $1 a day to buy water from the vendor, but not $300 to get the necessary connection. So they have to wait in long lines at public water faucets, which is another time sink. This is where loans can help in the long term."

Gary quickly realized that the biggest bottleneck was getting access to wholesale capital, which he would need in order to get help to all the people who needed it. The problem was just too big to be addressed through microloans.

As fate would have it, Gary met Matt Damon in 2008 at the Clinton Global Initiative. At that time, Matt had been running an organization called H20 Africa, which helped supply people with drinking water in rural Africa. After talking with Gary, Matt realized that Water Partners had a track record of doing what he was trying to do, and he had the name and brand that could help them gain access to new and greater levels of funding. They realized that working together they could change the future of water. And so, with equally lofty goals in mind, they merged their organizations to form Water.org and Water Equity, an investment capital project and a sister organization that they hope will be able to scale the work of Water.org through wholesale capital.

Water.org and Water Equity have grown to include a committed team of corporate philanthropy and engagement partners helping to provide microloans to those in need, including the World Bank, Caterpillar, Mastercard Foundation, Ikea, the Bank of America, Pepsi, and the UN General Assembly.

Gary and Matt are leaders in a new generation of social entrepreneurs who are viewing problems like urban and rural water resilience, water scarcity, and water-stressed communities through a progressive lens. "To me, social entrepreneurship is basically looking at some of society's biggest and most overlooked challenges and trying to apply more innovative and creative solutions to them," Gary says, pointing out that in hubs like Silicon Valley, it's of the utmost importance for entrepreneurs to fuel value creation. "When you apply that type of mindset and ingenuity to social problems, we can remake the world for the better. As a global community, we should agree to apply the same level of talent and ingenuity to social issues as we do to getting out the newest iPhone." Gary hopes that his work has raised awareness and inspired more people to get involved working on a solution to Sustainable Development Goal 6: clean water and sanitation for all.

In his travels to rural places, Gary noticed that accessing water has a variety of social ramifications he'd never really considered -- like girls' education, which is among the most concerning. Not having reliable access to water keeps girls out of school disproportionately. "In a lot of rural areas, if a family needs somebody to spend hours every day waiting in line fetching water, they usually end up sending a girl. So they don't get to spend as much time learning, and occasionally they stop going to school altogether." This is one of the most important reasons to get reliable water sources close to peoples' homes, so that girls can go to school.

Perhaps the most widespread and least discussed impact of climate change is in terms of water resources and water scarcity. Gary sees climate change as potentially preventing hundreds of millions of people getting and maintaining access to clean water. "We know that climate change is contributing to stronger and more frequent floods, which are occurring with greater irregularity. This puts the most vulnerable among us in a very precarious situation. And flooding also raises sea levels, which can contaminate wells and make them unusable." It can also interfere with infrastructure, making communities that have gained access to water less water resilient. "The way this problem manifests itself mostly is through water," Gary says. "We need to ensure that our communities are resilient enough to tolerate the negative effects of climate change in the future."

For young people interested in social entrepreneurship, Gary believes that education is the first responsibility of any venture that is trying to make a lasting impact on the world. "The first thing to do is to study up on sustainability issues and understand them inside and out. As you go through that process, you are going to see a lot of things that may stand in the way."

Gary believes the best way to get overcome these obstacles is by connecting with a like-minded community. "In any venture, it's important to look for people who are trying to work on the same problem, and get together with them to try and push your shared concept forward. That's where entrepreneurship comes in. Most people individually can see a current problem and how to solve it now. But it takes a lot of people working together and looking at what is going to be the best way to fix these problems two or three years from now to fully realize what's needed to make that happen."

Gary has an inspiring question he says young entrepreneurs should ask of themselves. "Once you have the data and the community, it's time to ask yourself, *Why not?* If there's a gap that corporations and organizations aren't able to fill, it's incumbent upon you to fill that gap." He adds, "I encourage the youth sustainability leaders and entrepreneurs to go out and try to implement creative solutions to the climate crisis. And I have a great amount of faith in the next generation to lead us through."

Just keep running those numbers up, keep running them up.

President Bill Clinton, on the success of Water Equity

Call to Action: To get involved with Gary and Matt's work helping communities gain access to clean water and sanitation, please visit https://water.org.

A SMART RESPONSE TO DISASTER RELIEF
BEN SMILOWITZ
Disaster Accountability Project
Rockville, Maryland

From an early age, Ben Smilowitz had a charitable ethic instilled in him by his grandparents. In his home, *Tzedakah* –the Hebrew word for charity -- inspires his family to serve social justice. Not surprisingly, in carrying out this tradition Ben Smilowitz has become a leading name in innovative disaster relief efforts.

By the time Ben was in elementary school, he was already on the path to becoming involved in his community and bringing about positive change. "In the first or second grade I knocked on my state senator's door, selling oranges and grapefruits for a school fundraiser," Ben says, recalling his youthful efforts. When the senator asked him to get involved in his campaign, Ben's lifelong foray into civic engagement had begun.

In no time, Ben was touring the state capitol with the senator, learning the ropes, and handing out flyers for causes he wanted to support. All the while he was asking questions about policies and agendas that he didn't yet understand. He quickly became versed in the workings of local politics thanks to mentoring from forward-looking campaigners and staff. And by the age of 8 he had started to develop a practical toolkit for impacting local change.

Next he aimed to get his peers involved. When he was 16 years old, "I read that someone had resigned on the state Board of Education," Ben recalls. "I wrote the governor a letter and asked him to appoint a young person." He wrote a press release announcing that he was launching a campaign to fill the vacant seat with a young person. Even though an adult was appointed to that seat, Ben didn't let it deter him.

He then launched a new campaign to add student seats to the board. This time around, he ramped up his efforts. He held public hearings, lobbied, and organized multiple press conferences with the media to get the word out. "We got about 50 students from across the state to write letters. We created a petition and got a few thousand signatures. And then we had about 20 students attend our rally, and another 15 students went to the state capitol to lobby... A year and a month after our first letter to the governor, we had a bill signing." Ben and a few other students were in the gallery watching the vote, which passed 145 to 0. The standing ovation, for a bill Ben had written, brought all of their combined efforts to heart. "It was a successful grassroots campaign in every sense, with passion and collaboration every step of the way," Ben says.

Ben went on to champion a variety of other issues. He founded the International Student Activism Alliance, which aimed to organize young people in communities across the country to serve as a student watchdog group, representing students' rights and public education issues. And in Missouri, he helped create the nation's first Youth Cabinet, in which all the cabinet positions were occupied by youth.

No matter what issue he gets involved in, Ben's message is always about getting youth and local communities to act in support of public service. When asked what youth need to do to make progress on causes important to them, he says, "They need the trust of others. They need validation that they are on the right track, that they have the power to do what they're doing, and that they should pursue their ideas." In 2005, when Ben was 24, Hurricane Katrina made landfall in the southeastern U.S., wreaking havoc anywhere it touched down. In the immediate aftermath of this national emergency Ben decided to volunteer for the American Red Cross in Gulfport, Mississippi. And at ground zero, he assisted in a very real, practical sense.

When he first arrived, he noticed from the start that something didn't seem right. Inexperienced, first-time volunteers were being assigned to entire sites with extremely difficult, expansive, tough tasks that they weren't equipped to manage. There was little to no accounting of what was being distributed, and to whom. This created massive queues: mothers with babies waited in long, hot lines, without attention. People with disabilities were suffering and too often neglected. Medical professionals were unlicensed to operate. Worst of all, in a multiethnic, multiracial area, hate groups showed up to intimidate those receiving aid. After experiencing all this suffering, Ben learned one of the hardest lessons of his life: sometimes there are great obstacles that lie in the way of doing good.

"Don't get me wrong," he explains, describing the bungled relief efforts. "People were extremely generous. Americans and people from other countries donated all they could to help. However, that aid just wasn't reaching the people that needed it most. I realized that a lot of things could be improved to help more people. We were there to help the people in Mississippi who had lost everything...So, I spoke up -- and broke policy, by allowing the media to see the mismanagement at hand. For the sake of the people who were suffering, I needed them to see what the actual needs were on the ground, compared with what we were providing...It was tough to point a critical eye at those trying to help those in need. However, if they weren't helping, and were even exacerbating the pain, I felt it just wasn't right for it to go on unchecked."

Recognizing the inherent flaws in a system that was trying to fundraise, execute, and coordinate a relief effort simultaneously in the immediate wake of a natural disaster like Katrina, Ben saw another way. He knew that with a little planning, and a lot of hard work, he could influence the system to work with much greater efficiency and help more people more effectively.

"My initial reaction when I got back home was to ask 'Who is accountable? And how do we prevent such mismanagement from happening again?'" He decided the best way was to start a nonpartisan watchdog organization focused on accountability in relief situations. Out of the ashes of his Katrina experience was born the Disaster Accountability Project (DAP).

The three primary issues DAP addresses are 1. Improve the effectiveness of disaster relief and humanitarian aid; 2. Make sure help reaches those that need it most; and 3. Make sure lessons are learned so we do not make the same mistakes, disaster after disaster. DAP has made assessments in the wakes of earthquakes in Haiti (2010), Japan (2011), and Nepal (2015).

In October-November 2012, Superstorm Sandy devastated the eastern United States, inflicting tremendous damage on the coastal regions. By the time the storm had passed, there were 233 fatalities, $68.7 billion of damage, and over 305,000 homes were lost in New York alone. DAP filed a successful complaint in New York against the American Red Cross for gross mismanagement, and won $4 million, to be released to survivors of Superstorm Sandy. Large victories like this, won by such a comparatively small organization, show just how significant a positive impact a few dedicated individuals can make for the people most in need.

DAP was the first organization of its kind in the industry, and Ben knew it was making a significant impact in the world of disaster relief. As a result of DAP's work, millions of misappropriated funds have been recouped, and that aid has been reappropriated to the individuals that it was promised to in the wake of emergency situations.

Ever the innovator, Ben knew there was still more he could do to make a bigger impact. He understood that having oversight was great, and the resulting accountability was necessary for improving processes and results. But what if there were an aspect of the disaster relief cycle that, if addressed, could significantly reduce the number of negative outcomes in the first place? With this question in mind, Ben created yet another answer, in the form of an online system: SmartResponse.org.

SmartResponse.org is an interactive data repository: through this platform, people can identify the local organizations responding to disasters and support them directly. "If we can preemptively curate a list of organizations operating locally, we can effectively direct donations to deserving local organizations at the most critical times. We really want to change how money moves after disasters and put the power into the hands of local groups."

SmartResponse.org helps to get much needed funds quickly to local food banks, community and cultural organizations, disability rights groups, and other entities that will be there after the smoke clears and the media's cameras leave. "They have the numbers on the ground to react to different situations. This type of response strengthens the local economies affected, creates and protects jobs, and ensures that money and efforts are also invested into future preparedness and mitigation efforts."

Given the increasing number of disasters in the world due to climate change, both DAP and SmartReponse.org have been well received by local communities. DAP is now in its thirteenth year of operation, and SmartResponse.org has aligned with more than 600 participating organizations from 58 countries.

While organizations like DAP and SmartResponse.org have made significant positive impacts in disaster response and relief efforts, they both started with a first step.

What can other young people do to help? "Think about what issues or causes you are passionate about, then get involved," Ben says. "Volunteer. It's great to go to the beach with a group to pick up plastic. But while you're there, think about how the plastic gets to the beach in the first place. Try to attack the root cause of the problem." He pauses, then adds, "Find a way to work in service of something greater than yourself."

It is a message that no doubt his grandparents would be proud of.

The charity that is a trifle to us can be precious to others.

Homer

Call to Action: Learn more about Disaster Accountability Project: http://disasteraccountability.org/ or SmartResponse.org; 1-202-556-3023 or email info@disasteraccountability.org

CLEANING RIVERS TO KEEP OUR OCEANS CLEAN
Gary Bencheghib
Make a Change World
Bali

Growing up in Bali, Gary Bencheghib loved walking on the beach with his younger brother Sam, and their older sister, Kelly. Bali beaches are famous among tourists for their beauty - clean, white sand beaches as far as the eye can see. However many of these gorgeous beaches are increasingly being covered with plastic litter -- from water bottles to straws, and single use products.

Each week they picked up the litter hoping they could help return it to their natural state of beauty. At first Gary thought that the beaches would stay that way. But the very next day, there was more trash — plastic waste everywhere. Week after week, more plastic kept appearing on the shores.

Gary soon realized the sheer volume of garbage on the beaches couldn't just be from tourists and local people littering. It was a much bigger problem. And as it turned out, he was right: it was an upstream issue. He soon discovered that Bali's rivers were actually the source of the plastic pollution. People living along Bali's rivers were using them as a garbage dump, since they was no waste management system, nor any green alternatives. So Gary and his brother Sam started rallying volunteers to clean up plastic pollution from the beaches. They formed Make A Change Bali to explore ways to help clean up the riverways.

Gary was curious to see if other countries had this problem too. They were shocked to learn that 150 million metric tons of plastic are in our oceans, and 8 million metric tons of plastic waste are added each year — and a sizeable percentage of this waste is from river sources. So Gary and Sam expanded their local organization to create Make A Change World to address this problem globally. What made their second venture different from their first is that they now decided it was equally important to focus on education — knowing that if people didn't understand the consequences of their habits, then they'd have no reason to change to greener lifestyle choices. And Gary felt that the best way to educate people about the environmental crisis is through film.

So Gary embarked on an adventure: first he moved to New York to attend film school at the New York Film Academy. In conversations with Americans, he noticed the same lack of awareness around plastic pollution that he had found in Bali – rivers were largely being ignored as a source of ocean pollution. So he decided to make his first film about the Mississippi River, the longest river in the United States, which runs right through the center of America's heartland.

He decided that linking his film with one of the most famous characters in American literature, Huckleberry Finn, would be a good way to get people's attention. So he sailed the 2,300 mile length of the Mississippi River on a raft constructed of 800 plastic bottles, and created a short documentary series to raise awareness of this problem.

Gary named his raft "Ioco" and he put together a team of skilled engineers, who took readings about the health of the river's water as they traveled. What they discovered was frightening. There were unsafe levels of microplastics, extremely tiny particles of plastics, in nearly every area they tested. This type of pollution is toxic to the fish and harmful to the humans who eat them. "My purpose in making the film was to show the problem visually," he says. "But since you can't see microplastics, you can only measure them, that wasn't successful in raising awareness."

Thankfully, this problem didn't stop Gary.

To get his message across, Gary knew he had to find a way to create a great visual. So, as he searched for a great visual image that would inspire action, he learned, much to his dismay, that the most polluted river in the world was in his very own backyard, in Indonesia.

The stretch of the Citarum River in West Java is the textile capital of the world. There the factories of the world's largest clothing companies are dumping dyes and other pollutants directly into the water, in alarming amounts. To raise awareness of this catastrophic issue, Gary and his brother Sam made another film as they sailed down the river on two boats made of recycled plastic.

Downstream from the factories, they saw the water tainted with artificial colors from the dyes, dead animals floating in the water, and piles of burning trash. What was most shocking to them was that the river was entirely covered in plastic. With every stroke of their paddles, their oars would hit another bottle. "It really hit me how far we've come in the destruction of our planet," Gary says. "I just wanted to do everything I possibly could, every day of my life, to clean the environment and save the planet."

Gary and Sam's first video went viral overnight. "Our little journey, traveling on a raft of plastic bottles, became international news," Gary says. "We were speechless! We were finally starting to get the attention that this movement needs."

People all over the world began messaging Gary and Sam online to find out ways they could help. Four months later, the brothers were invited to meet with Indonesian President Joko Widodo. They talked about the urgency of the Citarum's situation and he assured them that he would personally see to it that they receive help to address the problem. Gary and Sam were very pleased when he declared a "garbage emergency" a few months later. In February 2018, he mobilized 7,000 military troops for a cleanup campaign, with a seven-year commitment. Gary joined in, with check-ins every 2-4 months, to see the progress that was being made, and to learn from the cleanup effort what he could bring to the rest of the world.

One day while observing the workers, who were both troops and technical experts from the Ministry, Gary had an idea for a new kind of monitoring process. *What if we could measure the things we can see -- like plastic bottles-as well as the things we **can't** see -- like lead, uranium, and toxic chemicals in the water?* he asked himself. *Would that make a difference?* He envisioned this new system as a way to exchange knowledge and best practices from the global community, who'd been reaching out to him in droves, wanting to help.

Sungai Watch is an open-source online platform that uses geographic software like GIS and AI to track ocean cleanup in real time. It then provides data on what pollutants are in the water. This allows scientists to determine which cleanup methods – barriers, skimmers, or other technologies -- are most effective. This open sourcing of environmental solutions encourages the global community to share both data and technologies, so that effective solutions can benefit more communities, and can become refined through applying collective wisdom.

"It's exciting, exchanging ideas and methods from around the world," Gary says. "But to be most effective, we really need local communities to inform our work." The local communities he works with span from Jakarta to Singapore and beyond. And it's in these local communities that he's found valuable knowledge about things that he didn't know about prior. For example, they know the local irrigation channels, and how seasonal things, like monsoons, can impact places on the equator. "The monsoon effect causes cities on the equator to produce a disproportionate amount of plastic pollution, because when the rivers swell, it sends garbage into the oceans. These are the kinds of things we're now learning from people around the world." He adds, "Now more than ever, we need our global community to inform our decision making."

For young people looking to make an impact on the environment, Gary has two main messages. One is that positivity bridges all divides. "We learned early on to always take a positive approach," he says. "No pointing fingers. This isn't about blame, it's about finding solutions. We want to help, and we don't want anybody to feel as if they need to apologize."

Gary also believes that big, far-reaching ideas are what the movement needs most. "No idea is too crazy!" he says. "We need big ideas, and we need risk takers to go above and beyond to put these wild and crazy ideas into action. That's the only way for us make sure we sustain the planet for future generations."

As a filmmaker, Gary is always thinking of new ways to get his environmental message out to the world. One day, with his brother Sam, they had an idea for another way they could raise awareness – and that was to run across the United States. He realized that people living in middle America might not feel very connected to the problems of the ocean. And, as he had learned in Bali, an overwhelming amount of ocean pollution comes from upriver. That's why it is important that even people living far away from the ocean understand that they may be contributing to the problem. And also learn that they can also contribute to the solution.

And so, on July 26, 2019, Sam embarked on a 191-day, 3,055-mile journey from New York City to Los Angeles. He ran an average of 23 miles a day for 145 days–almost a marathon's length nearly every day, for more than five months. He ran in upcycled plastic shoes, made from the very plastic they'd collected on their cleanups. On the days he wasn't running, Sam was busy raising awareness, working with the media, with schools, and with local governments. He met face to face with more than 10,000 people. And through the six-part film series he and Gary made to promote the journey, they will connect with thousands more.

Through his filmmaking, his explorations, and his passion for positivity, Gary has vastly expanded environmental awareness about the health of our oceans. There's no telling what's in store for the future – but with youth leaders like 25-year-old Gary pushing the boundaries of what is possible, more youth than ever will be inspired to join the exciting journey toward remaking our world sustainable.

Indonesia's pledge is to have the Citarum become the Cleanest River in the World by 2025. With a clean river, comes clean beaches. And with a committed community behind the effort, Gary, Sam, and Kelly will be able to enjoy their favorite past time in Bali – once again taking walks along the pristine, white sand beaches of their beautiful home.

> *In rivers, the water that you touch is the last of*
> *what has passed*
> *and the first of that which comes; so, with*
> *present time.*

Leonardo da Vinci

Call to Action: Get involved with Gary and Sam's work of cleaning up our rivers and oceans. Learn how at Make A Change: https://makeachange.world/ .

CONNECTING ISLANDS VIRTUALLY FOR CLIMATE ACTION
James Ellsmoor
Island Innovation
United Kingdom

James Ellsmoor is a modest 28-year-old island-hopping, globe-trotting, serial entrepreneur and digital nomad. "I was born in a rural area in England," he says. "My parents were farmers, so growing up was my caring-about-the-environment intro." Shropshire, where James grew up, is a picturesque county bordering Wales. It has all the trappings of a fairytale scene – medieval castles, rolling green hills, and a town with quaint brick shops.

Growing up on a farm helped James see firsthand the challenges that rural and island communities share. But he had to travel halfway around the world and back before he fully realized how important his upbringing was in shaping him for environmental advocacy.

At 19, James left home for the University of North Carolina at Chapel Hill, with the esteemed Morehead-Cain Scholarship. "It changed the course of my life," James says. "Once I got here, I began living like a digital nomad, out of a suitcase. And I got involved with studying renewable energy in North America, Latin America, and the Caribbean."

At UNC James met his mentor, clean-tech entrepreneur and energy sector veteran Danny Kennedy, who helped him hone his environmental skills. "Danny gave me a lot of the tools I needed to grow and helped me understand how the industry works. If you don't understand that, you'll have a lot harder time making an impact."

At age 21, while a sophomore in college, James joined his first major endeavor, Solar Head of State, a nonprofit organization whose mission is "to help world leaders become green leaders." Its vision statement explains: "Working with governments, we install solar photovoltaic systems on iconic buildings, leveraging their visibility and social impact. We support world leaders to champion solar, acting as a catalyst for wider adoption of new solutions for renewable energy."

This small organization made waves with its campaign to install solar panels on the White House during Barack Obama's presidency, and

James was brought on board later as a cofounder. "I don't believe in starting up new organizations for the sake of it," he says. "I really believe that this was an opportunity to grow an existing campaign that had stalled and help take it to new heights."

Solar Head of State also made a big splash when they partnered with the President of The Maldives, Mohamed Nasheed. The Maldives, a small island developing state (SIDS), is a chain of islands in the Indian Ocean whose highest point is just 2 meters; they've been seriously impacted by coastal sea rising and even a tsunami. Nasheed, who was featured in the movie *The Island President*, dramatically showed the precarious situation of his country by holding a cabinet meeting underwater, fully dressed in scuba gear. He also made sure that the Maldives was the first country to install solar power at an executive residence.

Other island nations, from Jamaica to St. Lucia, have followed Nasheed's lead. Over the next two years, 12 new solar installations are lined up for Pacific Island nations. The Youth Solar Challenge, put on by Solar Head of State and the Caribbean Youth Environment Network, invites young people to create unique communications campaigns, to educate their communities about green energy. Successful campaigns in Jamaica and Guyana have already been implemented, with more to come. Time and again, James has seen that regardless of the innovation, it is local leaders who drive its adoption. He points to a recent Yale study that showed that community leaders who install solar in their homes convince 62 percent more residents to join them vs. those who didn't. According to James another problem is that too often scientists and techies miss the "soft skills" needed to get their message across. He uses his communication and collaboration skills to bridge this gap.

His experiences with Solar Head of State challenged James to delve deeply into finding solutions for the problems small island nations face. He discovered that they have similar challenges: building roads and schools; recovering from natural disasters; developing sustainable trade practices; and dealing with the isolation of their remote locations. Most significant is the challenge of creating reliable alternative energy resources. "Take, for example, the Caribbean," James explains. "On average, they pay 3-6 times more for electricity than Americans. This leads to "energy poverty" -- people who just can't afford it. And it's not reliable when it's frequently bombarded by tropical storms with high winds, rains, and flying debris." He adds, "Since islands are the most vulnerable to climate change, it's important to have alternative ways to provide energy, in case of a disaster."

When he was 24 James's journey led him back to the U.K. to attend the University of Highlands and Islands in Northern Scotland. "The conversations happening on Caribbean islands are also happening on Scottish islands," James says. "Issues of energy poverty, rural infrastructure, and communication were the same, halfway across the globe. That's when the lightbulb went off!"

From his travels, James had gained a unique vantage point on how things operate in different countries. He knew how to interact with governments and their communities, and how to get investors. He'd seen that solar technology means different things to different communities. In East Africa where the poor use solar, it has a lower-class stigma. This makes it hard to convince people that the technology is worthwhile. "If we want to expand renewable energy, we need to understand where the needs are different, and where they are the same," James says. "An island-networking community!" And that is how Island Innovation was born.

"Islands are particularly vulnerable to climate change," James explains. "A single event can knock out an island's economy. A hurricane won't affect 100 percent of the U.S., but it clobbered Puerto Rico. Island people need to work together and learn from each other. What works, what doesn't work. How can we get engineers and politicians to communicate effectively across their disciplines? Things like that."

Island Innovation brings together business, government, utilities, NGO's, universities, and citizens to explore innovations and share best practices in sustainability on island settings worldwide. In our modern, ever-connected world, it has taken a modern, tech-savvy approach, by a modern, tech-savvy individual, to leverage these new means of communication in the service of island nations. James's mission is to strengthen communities on island nations; strengthen the bonds between them; and build their knowledge base, to help them face their most pressing collective challenge -- climate change.

To bring disparate island communities together, James began by asking questions: "What has Fiji done that Hawaii can learn from? How can Scotland have a conversation about sustainability with Jamaica?" He developed the Virtual Island Summit, a free annual online event, connecting global island communities on a common digital platform. During the Summit, people from around the world come together virtually, to share ideas, innovations, and the best practices they've come up with to deal with the challenges of island communities.

When the inaugural Summit was held in October 2019, world-class experts shared their knowledge with more than 100 island communities from the Arctic to the Pacific Islands and beyond. Participants raved about the experience, which was focused on learning and cross-sector collaboration. "Amazing things happened that week," James says. "Someone in our Facebook group from Vanuatu posted about a solar project. A reply came from Jamaica. Then from Scotland. Then, in a single thread, people from all over the world were communicating. That's what the Virtual Island Summit is all about."

James believes this kind of remote collaboration will create great change going forward. "Virtual meetings are often seen as a last resort for professional collaboration, but when we're talking about rural island communities, they often don't have the money to travel from afar. This is a new approach to sharing information." The Virtual Island Summit is already gearing up for an even bigger 2020 event.

James encourages young people who want to get involved in the fight against climate change, and advocate for renewable energy. "Set up your own hubs in your communities. Start conversations. Create partnerships. Strengthen relationships. Every little bit of good helps the cause."

No other planet in the solar system is a suitable
home for human beings;
it's this world or nothing.
That's a very powerful perception.

Carl Sagan

Call to Action: Check out The Virtual Island Summit https://www. islandinnovation.co/summit/ .

ENGINEERING SOLUTIONS
TO CLIMATE CHANGE PROBLEMS
Alex Perkins
Nantucket/Vermont

Alex Perkins peered through his binoculars, carefully scanning the blue surface of the ocean around him. As first mate and "whale spotter" on his family's 47-foot catamaran, he and his dad had a little competition going, to see who could spot the first whale.

Alex grew up on the small island of Nantucket, off the coast of Cape Cod, Massachusetts. Starting at a young age, he helped his parents with their ecotourism company, Shearwater Excursions. Alex started navigating and steering the boat for whale watches and seal cruises when he was a teenager and first mate. Now as a captain himself, Alex guides ecotourism trips around the island.

"My passion for sustainability and renewable energy evolved from growing up on a small island," Alex says. "Each and every day you're aware of the beauty and fragility of your environment; and you're immediately more connected with all of nature."

Early on Alex had observed the dangers of pollution for the ocean's precious marine life. When they sailed out to visit the colonies of grey seals, he would frequently spot at least one seal tangled up in discarded fishing nets. "As the seals grow," Alex explains, "The fishing line doesn't, and it starts to strangle them."

When he was in high school Alex joined his school's Students for Sustainability Club. And when he learned about an exchange program with The Island School in the Bahamas, he immediately applied. He was always ready to explore island life in other places, and he was especially excited to leave the cold New England winter behind and head to warmer waters. At The Island School, 50 students from all around the world live together on a remote campus for a semester. And as they learned about sustainability, leadership, and marine biology issues, they would also strive to live as sustainably as possible. "It really checked a lot of boxes for the things I was interested in, and I was lucky enough to be accepted," he says.

Alex's time in the Bahamas was a wonderful learning experience. However, one thing that really bothered him was the way the country discarded plastic waste. At home, he grew up recycling everything -- especially plastics. He learned to be conscious of the importance of doing this, since islands have very limited space for landfills. He was shocked to see that plastic was simply being tossed into pits with the rest of the trash. Then, once the pits were full, they were lit on fire. The thick, nasty, terrible-smelling smoke would fill the air. "It was awful," he says.

An even greater source of pollution was the island's source of energy. Generators as big as houses burned diesel fuel around the clock to supply the islanders with energy. "The oil gets shipped in on huge barges and then they just burn it," Alex explains. "And they're old generators, they are not efficient."

The sight of these generators spewing ugly black smoke across the light blue Bahamian skies was sickening to Alex. He could see that something needed to be done; and he was determined to continue to learn whatever he could about sustainability, and was especially keen to see how emerging technologies could help solve these kinds of problems.

Upon his return to high school in Nantucket, Alex put his newly acquired knowledge about sustainability to use. He reconnected with the Students for Sustainability Club and collaborated on a proposal to install 100-kiloWatt wind turbine at their school. A turbine of this size would be able to satisfy fifteen-percent of the energy needs for the island's middle and high schools with a clean, renewable source of energy: wind power.

First, they would have to overcome many obstacles. Locals worried that a 131-foot turbine in the center of the island that was visible from almost anywhere on the island would be an eyesore. They were also concerned about how this would affect the island's main economic engine: summer tourism.

"One of the hardest issues was convincing the Nantucket Historic District Commission that this was good for the island," Alex says. "Getting them to approve a wind turbine and convincing them that it wasn't going to negatively impact the historical integrity of the island was a huge challenge."

Like most wind turbines, the turbine Alex and his schoolmates were planning was supposed to be white. But the Commission decided that they would have to repaint the turbine gray, so that it would blend in better with the sky. "Little things like this became very challenging,"

Alex says.

Working with school and town officials, the utility company, and the project's funder, ReMain Nantucket, they were successful in gaining permission to install the turbine. After all, wind turbines represent the future -- a sustainable future.

Alex is understandably very proud of his island community. "It's a huge testament to the commitment to renewable energy on the island that we were able to do this," he says. And awareness of the importance of renewable energy on Nantucket has only grown over the years -- from dialogues with business leaders and influential seasonal residents, to teachers who have incorporated wind power into their lesson plans. "It's a great tribute and a successful case study for our island," he says.

Alex's passion, commitment, and hard work was noticed: in 2011 he and his classmate Will Horyn were nominated to serve as youth delegates to the Stone Soup Leadership Institute's 7th annual Youth Leadership Summit for Sustainable Development. Held on the neighboring island of Martha's Vineyard, Alex joined with youth from islands like Vieques, Puerto Rico, Virgin Gorda, the British Virgin Islands, and Hawaii for an intensive, week-long real-world solutions-oriented training. "It was a fantastic experience," Alex says. "We shared our own stories and were exposed to inspiring stories from other youth leaders from around the world who were also striving to bring sustainable solutions to their islands."

Learning from other young island leaders, and finding ways to collaborate with them, was a huge benefit for Alex. When he went back home, he and Will organized a community forum with the local Chamber of Commerce, and presented their vision for a Sustainable Nantucket. Former U.S. Secretary of State John Kerry commented on their vision by writing, "Alex and Will's passion for the environment has empowered their peers and their entire community to make positive changes in their daily lives. I commend them on being inspiring young leaders who are willing to confront -- and to solve -- some of the most difficult and perplexing problems that our world faces."

When it comes to fighting the effects of climate change, there are various aspects that make up the struggle, Alex says. While activism and policy changes are needed, Alex was most interested in finding solutions through technology. "I always thought of myself as an engineer," Alex says. "The technology side has been my approach to solving these problems."

So, after high school, Alex pursued his education at the University of Vermont and studied mechanical engineering. As a senior, Alex created Books4Equity, to encourage upper classmen to donate their books. The free library with an online database for all UVM students to search, view and borrow donated textbooks now has over 2,000 textbooks, calculators and iClickers.

Then, with his freshly minted diploma in hand, Alex returned to his adopted island home in the Bahamas to work with the Center for Sustainable Development (CSD). This time, he hoped to be able to work with the local community to solve some of the problems he'd seen during the high school semester he had spent there.

The global warming potential from the emissions of burning plastic are significantly worse than CO2," Alex says. "It's pretty much the worst thing you can do. Not to mention the plastic contaminating the water through leaching or hurricanes.

Courageous enough to accept this challenge, and curious to see how mechanical engineering could address this issue, Alex and his new CSD team embarked on an ambitious venture. Their idea was simple: since plastic is a petroleum-based product, made from fossil fuels, what if there were a way to take the plastic and turn it back into petroleum?

"It turns out there is this process called pyrolysis, which is kind of a reverse process," he says. "It turns plastic back into its petroleum building blocks."

Alex and his team decided to use this discovery to build a small-scale reaction vessel. Using this vessel, at first they were able to convert a hundred grams of plastic at a time, and use the end product to run a diesel engine. "We were super excited about that," Alex remembers. "So we got some more funding, and we were able to scale up our machine so we could do about 10 to 15 kilos of plastic at a time. We were turning a zero-value product (waste plastic) into a value-added product (fuel)."

While the project was eventually discontinued due to costs, Alex learned a powerful lesson — and it is one that is fueling his own future.

"We need to find innovative solutions to the problems we're facing," he says. "A lot of times I've been working on cutting-edge projects that have not been commercially proven yet. But to me, that's where change happens, from a technological point of view."

Alex has moved back to Vermont, where he is now a sustainable manufacturing research & development engineer for the technology start-up Synticos. Alex and his team are building a system to reduce the cost and environmental impact of a manufacturing process.

Alex believes that it is up to everyone to ask themselves a few important questions: What issues or problems do I feel passionate about? What skill set can I bring to solving them? What do I need to learn in order to be able to *do* something about it?

"If you have an awesome skill, and you're trying to solve a problem, you'll need help from someone else," Alex says. "Then it's all about collaboration: talking about problems with friends, talking about ideas that you can build together."

The future will be green, or not at all.

Jonathon Porritt

Call to Action: Identify a problem you feel passionate about and figure out what skills you need to learn so you can *do* something about it. Find others who can work with you to create a solution. Learn more about Alex's work in technological solutions to climate change problems. https://www.roadpitch.co/pitcher/synticos-llc/

FARMING THE OCEAN
Perry Raso
Rhode Island

When Perry Raso was a boy, his father often spoke about his dream of being a fisherman. After he retired from the police force, he moved his family from the suburbs of New York City to Rhode Island so he could pursue that dream. It was an ambitious dream for someone who'd never worked in that field. Unfortunately, he soon realized that becoming successful fisherman in retirement was pretty tough. After many struggles and failures, he decided it'd be wiser to continue the life he knew, in police work. But that wasn't the end of the story…

In time, the Rasos would achieve this dream through Perry, who from an early age grew up clamming in the pristine waters of Point Judith Pond. "In many ways, my dad's vision inspired me," he says. "Luckily, I was able to pick up the dream where he left off."

Perry started out by digging shellfish when he was about 12 years old, with a commercial fisherman he knew. "I still remember the first time I went out digging for clams," he says. "When I pulled my rake out of the water, I couldn't believe it. I was thinking, that's 7 or 8 bucks worth of clams! I knew that the harder I pulled on the rake and the longer I did it, the more money I'd make. I liked being able to determine how much I made by how hard I worked."

And he would be working hard. Clamming is an extremely physically demanding job; clammers work in all seasons, including wading in icy New England waters in the middle of winter. It's not for the faint of heart.

When he first started clamming, the specialized rake Perry used to dredge the pond with must have been taller than he was. At his TedX talk, he brought one of the rakes onto the stage and showed the audience how you drag the rake through the mud to catch clams. "There I was, just a kid, standing in chest-deep water, pulling on the handle," he explained. "Every few minutes I'd pull the rake up, and shake the sediment out." And he'd repeat this action, over and over again throughout the day, rain or shine. But, as tough as the work was, it gave him the background he needed for commercial fishing.

Perry was off to a promising start. Still, he knew he needed a proper education if he was going to become the successful businessman, he knew he could be. So, he studied aquaculture and fisheries technology at the University of Rhode Island. Upon graduation in 2002, with the help of a Reed Aquaculture initiative grant, he had the tools and experience he needed to start his first sustainable venture - the one-acre Matunuck Oyster Farm. It was an instant success.

"When I first started selling oysters at local farmer's markets, the reaction was fantastic," he says. "I didn't expect everyone to say that the oysters I was offering tasted better than what they were used to. It made me feel great. But more importantly, I realized that there was a tremendous untapped market for local, sustainable seafood. Far bigger than my small operation was capable of supporting."

Before long, he was farming two acres to fill the gap. Then three acres; then seven. Locally, his organic product was such a hit that he eventually expanded his operations nationally. In fact, he was expanding so fast that he bought the only commercial property available in East Matunuck on the pond -- which was a rundown clam shack.

"When I started the Matunuck Oyster Bar 10 years ago, I didn't expect much from it," he says. "I bought the place because I needed the dock. But to my surprise, it worked really well as an oyster bar. And then I saw an opportunity to make my restaurant even more sustainable. So, I started organic vegetable farming to supplement the oysters. Before I knew it, I had a shellfish hatchery across the street. And at long last, I had a setup that was entirely sustainable."

A pioneer, Perry has become a legend -- in the world of sustainable aquaculture. His combined farm-to-table/ pond-to-table approach is a model of success. And this sort of diversity in food production is critical. It is a hedge against economic uncertainty. It's an alternative approach that can help save struggling farmers. And the data says the opportunity is there for entrepreneurs who want to make a mark.

According to the National Oceanic and Atmospheric Administration (NOAA), the United States is the leading importer of fish and fishery products in the world: 90 percent of the seafood consumed in the U.S. comes from abroad – and more than half of that is sourced from aquaculture. What this amount to is a $14 billion seafood trade deficit that can be addressed on the home front of New England's pristine waters.

However, the specter of climate change is raising concerns. Many of the shellfish raised -- like mussels, oysters, and clams -- are especially vulnerable to extreme weather conditions. "If the waters increase in temperature, the growing season increases," Perry explains. "That means the amount of time the oysters can be stressed increases, since most of the stress occurs during the summer. So more extreme weather increases the occurrences of the conditions that can lead to disease and ultimately, mortality. There are benefits to being a little inland on a pond, as opposed to on the coast. It's protected. But climate change poses great risks no matter where you are."

With his $200,000 a year business, Perry employs more than 200 people at his very popular restaurant, many of whom started out as shuckers. But he is much more than just an entrepreneur. On summer mornings, he takes local youth out on his boat so they can observe firsthand the life of an oysterman. In the fall, he serves as a mentor for the Coastal Fellows program at the University of Rhode Island. And for the last 11 years, every spring his oyster bar has held an annual Earth Day beach cleanup at East Matunuck State Beach.

"Since before the restaurant started, we've been taking volunteers to the beach, the salt marshes, and Succotash Salt Pond," he says. "We pick up all the trash lined up on our shore. The amount of debris we've cleaned up is just been amazing. Over the years, it's really added up. It's become a community staple. It's something we will always do."

Perry believes it's very important for young people with an interest in sustainability to get involved any way they can. "If you want to know how something works, ask questions," he says. "Track down people who are doing what you want to do and learn from them. Find a farm, and work or volunteer with them. Attend trade shows. Read up on things. And look for funded opportunities. There are always grants and internships, as a way in for young entrepreneurs. Aquaculture is not an easy field; it's farming. But it's very rewarding."

In regard to his own personal journey, Perry credits the many mentors who guided him toward being a leader in sustainable aquaculture. "At every stage, I myself asked a lot of questions," he says. "I went to a lot of conferences. I studied under and collaborated with a lot of great professors at the University of Rhode Island. Dr. Michael Rice. Dr. Dave Bengston. And of course, Dr. Marta Gomez-Chiarri, with whom I still work today. They've all done so much for me – but I was willing to humble myself and put in the work to learn. You can't have one without the other and expect to be an overnight success."

That said, Perry feels that it's important for people to become as familiar with aquaculture as they are with other type of farms. "We need to make more people aware that aquaculture is a good use of our water bodies. It's also a great use of the public trust. Our water bodies are owned by all Rhode Islanders. As of now, I think it's viewed as more of a niche industry. But I want to change this. Aquaculture should be viewed in the same way as sustainable agriculture. Then we can really make an impact."

If there's anybody capable of bringing aquaculture into the mainstream, surely, it's Perry. It's a big ask. But there's no reason to think he's done innovating yet. He's already done a great deal for the sustainability movement, and given back to his community more than he could possibly know.

That includes his father, who in Perry has surely seen his dream come true. And there's no telling what great dreams and people he will continue to inspire.

No Fishermen, no fish.

Lailah Gifty Akita

Call to Action: Visit Perry at the Matunuck Oyster Bar: https://www.rhodyoysters.com .

HUMAN NATURE PROJECTS
Elliot Connor
Australia

It was a clear night in northern Botswana. Ten-year-old Elliot and his family had set up camp for the night, with their tents grouped around a little campfire. There was nothing around, except the infinite expanse of the veld, the stars in the clear night sky, and the sounds of the bush. Elliot was trotting along behind his parents and his big brother, on the way back from the campground bathroom to their tents.

Suddenly, he sensed a movement behind him, and he froze -- they were in the wilderness after all. There were all sorts of animals around. He turned around slowly.

"There, about two meters behind me, was a young leopard, crouched quite low to the ground," Elliott remembers. "It was stalking me."

For three never-ending seconds, Elliot looked right into the leopard's eyes. Luckily, at that very moment, his older brother turned around, flashlight in hand. The beam of light scared the leopard away; but for the rest of the night Elliot and his family stayed in their tent while the leopard kept circling the camp site. His father stood guard by the fire, with a bottle of wine and a shovel in his hands.

Elliot would never forget this encounter with the leopard. From the time he was a small child, animals had been an important part of his life. His parents were passionate bird watchers and he often tagged along with them, using their old camera gear to take pictures. When his family moved from the U.K. to Australia when he was five, his passion for animals only continued to grow.

But as he grew older, he realized that animal species around the world face a lethal enemy. Human activities have decimated natural habitats and changed the climate, which causes many species to go extinct. According to UN estimates, about 200 plant, insect, bird, and mammal species are disappearing from our planet every day.

To fight this trend, conservationists around the world are trying to educate people about the need for saving endangered species. When he was 15, Elliott decided that he wanted to turn his passion for animals into doing something. So he started volunteering with the Birdlife Australia Discovery Center, which was just around the corner from a local park in Sydney. But soon he understood that there was a long way to go.

"It was quite a shock for me," he says. "All the volunteers were at least 70 years old. And there were almost no visitors coming through."

Elliott was appalled to see how isolated the field of conservationism was in Australia. So, six months later, he decided to start his own club for naturalists. It was the first of its kind in Sydney. The main purpose of it was just to try to inspire more people to go outside and experience nature. He also joined many other organizations, and volunteered wherever he could. In fact, he put in more than 300 hours of volunteering in just12 months -- but in all that time, he never met anyone his age.

His volunteer work also took him abroad. In January 2019, Elliot was working in a rescue center for raptors and hedgehogs in southern France. One night he was doing research into various conservationist organizations, when he realized that many of the websites he was looking at were decades old. A lot of the organizations had ceased operations, and even the well-established ones were struggling to incorporate young volunteers.

"It was very difficult for me as a minor, to work my way into these organizations so I could gain experience," he remembers. "That is sort of what triggered it for me."

Taking long winter walks through the beautiful landscape of southern France, he started wondering what could be done to get young people involved in conservationism. "That's where a lot of the philosophy for Human Nature Projects came about," he says. "It's designed as an entry point for volunteers. We're trying to promote it as a very accessible, engaging, community form of conservation."

For Elliot, it was the beginning of a very exciting project: in June 2019, he officially founded his organization, Human Nature Projects. It has quickly grown into a decentralized network of more than 1,400 activists in 110 countries. "We want to empower each of our volunteers as an individual, and help them create the impact that they want to make," Elliot explains. "But we also recognize the power of the collective."

The semi-independent country teams organize their own outreach and fundraising efforts, and projects, which ensures that their activities have the biggest possible impact on the local level. The teams organize a wide range of activities: the Australian team has just started a campaign on bush fires, while the team in the Congo is focusing on climate change, and volunteers in Uganda are fighting to rescue chimpanzees.

"I think it just goes to show the power of being able to link up such passionate youth leaders, and supporting and engaging them in this process," Elliot says.

For Elliot, who describes himself as an introvert, it was hard to take the initial step of presenting his ideas and his vision to a wider audience. "The biggest challenge was having the confidence in myself, being able to just put myself out there," he says. "In a sense, I just needed to have the ambition to aim for something so large."

But even during the very first meetings with other activists for Human Nature Projects, Elliot felt that he had created something that could inspire others, not just himself. "It was an amazing realization that I was able to speak with people all around the globe," he remembers. "That's something I never even dreamed of. I'm very introverted myself, I never took on leadership roles in school."

But Elliot is dedicated to the issue: when he first started his project, he would work on it after school, from 5 pm until 9 pm, trying to learn more about the underlying problems at night. It was tiring, and in the beginning, responses to his outreach work were slow to come in.

"You just have to have the perseverance to move on," Elliot says. "You have to find new routes, be creative about how you set about projects like this."

Elliot knew for sure that the issue of conservationism needed a new approach, and a new generation to take up the fight. Being a resource-poor field, conservation projects often struggle with a lack of funding. But there are also issues of duplicated efforts and miscommunication, he says.

"We need to redefine how we're measuring our impact," he says. "We need to work through the people first. We need a community-centric model of conservation. This means changing the perspective of communities -- which is obviously the root cause of these problems."

That is why Elliot came up with the four C's of conservation: Connection, Curiosity, Creativity, and Collaboration. For him, it is all about educating and engaging people in the fight for animals, and changing their perspective on nature.

"Increasingly, we're learning that animals are just as intelligent, just as complex as we are," he says. "My life goal is reframing our relationship with nature. I think if we can reevaluate what it means to be human, then that is the ideal way to be able to live alongside animals."

It is therefore a central part of Elliot's work to make people appreciate the nature around them and build a community around a positive message on conservation. "The positive side of things is often lost when we talk about conservation," he says. "In order to get people involved in the cause, you need a positive message about how we all can contribute our share to saving nature."

Elliot's Human Nature Projects is a successful example of this approach. He has an Excel spreadsheet on his computer, with the names and contact information of over 1,400 volunteers around the world, working to save endangered species.

"When I scroll through it, it feels amazing, I can't quite describe it," he says. "Seeing all of the volunteers conducting these amazing projects is definitely what drives me forward."

When Elliot finishes high school in November, he is planning to take the Human Nature Projects to the next level. He has been dreaming of going into wildlife filming for a long time. Together with an international wildlife movie production company, he and his organization are planning to set up a website where 200 volunteers from around the world will produce a 24-hour live stream of wildlife in their home countries. Elliot is going to take a gap year to travel around the world, meet his fellow volunteers in person, and start working on the film project.

"You need to get out there and do something," he says, and he adds, "Whatever you do, aim for the stars. If you miss, you will hit the moon."

The least I can do is speak out for those who cannot speak for themselves.

Jane Goodall

Call to Action: Join Elliot's Human Nature Projects: https://humannatureprojects.org/

INVENT SOMETHING TO HELP OTHERS
Gitanjali Rao
Colorado

Gitanjali Rao loves the news. In the evenings, she enjoys learning about new advances in the scientific communities around the world. They give her inspiration - and plants seeds for her ideas. Gitanjali has a knack for developing inventions of one kind or another. "Many of my inventions have been inspired by just watching the news."

Over time, she noticed disheartening stories running each day on climate change. She started thinking deeply about all the different crises that her country was facing. Thanks to her good education in STEM -- Science, Technology, Engineering and Math - she had a strong scientific base. She wondered what could she do - with her affinity for tinkering, and the joy she gets from problem solving -- to help people who are suffering.

Gitanjali's first venture was a response to the public health water crisis in Flint, Michigan. "When I saw the TV broadcast from Flint, I was appalled. I couldn't believe how many kids my age were drinking lead poison everyday. And this causes lifelong health problems. It was just so unfair. And no one was doing anything about it." The inadequate re-routing of the public water system resulted in highly toxic levels of lead in the water supply. Hundreds of thousands of people in the region were being affected since 2015. "The worst part is that by the time people realize a problem like this, one that oftentimes can't be physically seen, it's almost too late. They already have consumed it, and will suffer the negative effects for the rest of their lives."

At age 13, Gitanjali created Tethys to detect lead contamination in drinking water sources. With this invention, people can assess -- in real time -- if their drinking water has safe levels or not. The implications for places like Flint are enormous. Gitanjali's Tethys gained the attention of many national outlets - including by 3M, which awarded her a $25,000 prize for winning their Young Scientist Challenge in 2017. Now she is looking to partner with an incubator to raise funds and expand the reach and breadth of chemicals she can test for. "Finding partners to expand this idea is going to help me evolve into being an entrepreneur, not just an inventor. As an entrepreneur, hopefully I can reach a lot more people."

Another national health crisis Gitanjali learned a lot about on the news was the opioid epidemic. Over the last decade, the opioid crisis has wreaked havoc on communities in the United States. Since 2016, roughly 45,000 people a year have been killed by opioids, mainly by overdose – and what's especially tragic is that roughly 2,100 of these overdoses a year occur in youth ages 15-24. Aside from overdoses, there are many negative health-related consequences from the misuse of opioids. Prescription opioids -- from sports injuries - make up the majority of health emergencies nationally. The Centers for Disease Control and Prevention estimate that for every overdose a youth has related to opioids, there are 119 emergency room visits and 22 treatment admissions. In October of 2017, the opioid epidemic became so impactful, that it was declared a public health emergency.

Gitanjali knew she wanted to do something about the opioid epidemic, even though it on the opposite side of the scientific spectrum from her first invention. "I knew it wouldn't be easy. But I like to solve problems affecting those in my age group. I can relate more closely to problems that way." And so she began working out a biological solution to help with the prescription opioid addiction impacting youth everywhere. And so she created Epione.

Epione is an app connected to a testing device, that detects how addicted someone is or isn't to opioids. The test detects the protein produced by a specific gene when it comes into contact with prescription opioids. So the higher the protein level, the higher the indication is for opiates. "It's sort of like a litmus test for ph. An easy to read color strip shows on app, and you can see where a person is on the spectrum of addiction. The app also has corresponding maps to local counselors, physicians, doctors, and others where youth can get help." For this invention, she won the TCS Ignite Innovation Student Challenge.

Gitanjali saw horrified to see how many young people her age were struggling with was bullying. Bullying -- physical, verbal, and social. Direct, or passive. In person and online. As a technically minded student, she began focusing on a way to help prevent a modern form of bullying that has been on the rise in recent years – cyberbullying.

It's estimated that around 5 million students a year are bullied, either in person or online. This has serious mental health consequences for both the bully and the victim. From higher rates of anxiety, suicide, depression, substance use, as well as declining academic achievement. According to the HHS, over 60 percent of youth who experience cyberbullying are significantly challenged to learn and feel safe at school.

To help combat this epidemic, Gitanjali designed the app Kindly. Kindly is an extension that can be added on to web browsers, social media sites, and other mobile and desktop applications, that helps parents, educators, and students alike detect potential bullying incidents – and stop them before they happen. It highlights text that may be problematic, and blocks it, or allows it to be sent with adjustments, depending on the severity of the language. In the near future, Gitanjali hopes schools will adopt her app, and act as the first line of defense for protecting victims of bullying.

For the youth who want to explore a similar path to Gitanjali, she has a few words of wisdom surrounding fun, community, togetherness, and the hands on nature of a practical STEM education. "Whatever you are trying to learn, have fun with it. Create communities to support your ideas. Learning happens most productively when people can learn together. Don't be afraid to make it hands on. Lectures have their place. But hands on learning skills with real world experts is the quickest way to becoming proficient. This sort of STEM training needs to be in all of our classrooms."

Gitanjali believes that the support of adults is critical for those youths pursuing their educational goals. "If we're talking about parents, support whatever your child wants to learn. If you are a teacher, do the same for your students. We've all got a dream in mind, and it's hard to follow that dream when you don't have support. I couldn't imagine approaching such complex problems without that support structure."

Gitanjali also recommends that parents learn with their kids, and even try to learn new things themselves as inspiration. What's the same, is her advice to adults who approach learning themselves, "Have fun with it. There's never a limit to fun. I like to say, *Go after it like a teenager!*"

As a youth leader in STEM, who is vocal about advancing female involvement and leadership in tech, Gitanjali has a message to women and girls. "I had a mentor say to me, 'don't go into it thinking you're a girl or woman in tech'. You are going after big ideas. You are solving incredibly complicated problems. You are creating and inventing things. No matter who you are, these things are commendable. So don't qualify what you are and aren't. Just break the stereotypes that exist by being the best you can be. And do it while you are doing what you love, and what you want to do. Don't ever stop doing that."

Gitanjali's work has shown that traditional ideas of what STEM is and isn't, are outdated. Knowledge in STEM can lead to incredible advancements in a society, beyond our institutions. Tethys, Epione, and Kindly, are inventions in what are seemingly three very different spaces. But in reality, each of these technical creations play an important role in alleviating a specific contemporary public health issue that is harming people on a day to day basis. It's time to think of a STEM education as being a pathway to healing our communities. And with youth leaders like Gitanjali showing us the way – intellectually and socially – the possibility of having a bright, healthy, and sustainable future is certainly in reach.

If you can do it, do it. If you can achieve it, achieve it.

Bessie Blount Griffin, Inventor

Call to Action: Explore STEM learning and project-based opportunities. Invent something to help humanity. Gitanjali has partnered with UNICEF Voices of Youth to educate others on the importance of cyber-safety. Check out her blog https://www.voicesofyouth.org/campaign/your-world-reimagined

LIGHT AND HOPE FOR PUERTO RICO
Salvador Gabriel Gomez Colón
Puerto Rico

On the night of September 20, 2017, nobody slept well on the island of Puerto Rico. Winds gusting at over 150 miles per hour blew across the island, tearing up trees from their roots and whipping debris into the air. Over the course of 24 hours, more than 20 inches of water inundated streets and highways. The electricity went out across the entire island, and everyone, rich and poor, found themselves suddenly in darkness, facing an uncertain future.

That night, as he huddled with his mom and grandparents in the lobby of his apartment building in San Juan, worried about would happen next, Salvador Gabriel Gomez Colón hoped he would be one of the lucky ones. He could feel his building swaying in the wind. He hoped that the roof wouldn't be torn off, or that the building wouldn't come down completely. "It was definitely the night that I felt the most vulnerable and scared of my life," he says.

When he woke up, there was about six inches of water on the floor of his bedroom and water was seeping through the air conditioning vents. His room was completely waterlogged, and would eventually fill with mold, forcing a remodeling. But the building was intact, and his family was safe. That was what mattered most.

For many this was not the case.

Across Puerto Rico, the dawn of September 21 felt apocalyptic. Entire buildings had been destroyed, reduced to piles of rubble and mud. Knee-deep water flowed through residential streets, making it hard for emergency services to rescue the injured and displaced. Fallen power lines snaked along the roads.

In the northeastern part of the island, where many people had already been living in dire circumstances, ravaged by poverty and neglected by their government, the storm mercilessly pillaged thatched huts, rickety apartment complexes, and neglected homes for the elderly.

Salvador woke up that morning knowing that that day -- and the days that would follow -- would change his life and the lives of every one of the more than 3 million people who live in Puerto Rico. "There's always one person that's having a worse time than you," his mom told him. Salvador didn't wait a second to spring into action.

He was only 15 years old, an enterprising ninth grader at a private school in San Juan, when Hurricane Maria hit. He excelled in his classes. But Hurricane Maria was not a class exercise. All around him, people were really dying. It has been estimated that more than 4,000 people were killed during Hurricane Maria, but the actual number is likely much higher. We might never know exactly how many lives the hurricane took: what we do know is that in the days and weeks following the storm, people were hungry, unwashed, and plunged into darkness.

Salvador didn't have the power to turn "five loaves of bread and two fish" into enough nourishment to feed the multitudes, but he was determined to do what he could. Knowing that the storm had knocked out power across the island, he realized two things. Without electricity people would feel unsafe going into the streets after dark; and they would have trouble washing their clothes, which could lead to a number of preventable illnesses, not to mention a pervasive feeling of uncleanliness that would negatively affect their mental health over time.

Salvador knew that Puerto Rico's strong sun -- the same sun that gives elderly residents heat stroke, and forces Puerto Ricans to carry umbrellas during the day -- could provide the energy to power new equipment. Solar power could make it possible for people to cleanse themselves, protect their families, and feel safe during the night. It could also help usher in new modes of sustainable living that would last well after the power had come back on.

Salvador calculated that a donation of around $100 could provide a solar light, a mobile phone charger, and a hand-crank washing machine to a family in need. With the help of his mom and Neha Misrah, the cofounder of Solar Sister, a nonprofit that distributes solar panels to women entrepreneurs in Africa, he started a GoFundMe campaign and called it Light and Hope for Puerto Rico. "Neha was my guiding light and mentor from the beginning," Savador says.

His GoFundMe campaign was an immediate success. He reached out to his parents' friends and colleagues in the mainland U.S., and anyone else he could think of, and invited them to pitch in. In only four days they had raised $36,000. Within the first three weeks, the campaign had raised $65,000. Salvador shared his story online so people from around the world could help too. In the end, more than 1,200 people pledged more than $160,000 -- enough to provide 3,500 households with solar light, mobile phone chargers, and nonelectric portable washing machines.

But he didn't stop there: he began researching, and then reaching out to organizations that could help. He came across The Laundry Alternative, a company that sells sustainable, hand-operated washing machines. Soon other companies offered to pitch in: Gentlewasher, EasyGo, Mpowerd, Schneider Electric, and Omnivoltaic Energy Solutions. The crowdfunding campaign grew into a movement, defined by a simple, universal equation: C + Feel = Hope (See + Feel = Hope).

In the wake of the storm, good news in Puerto Rico was hard to come by. Perhaps that's why the media took notice of Salvador's campaign. He quickly found himself the subject of profiles in *CNN Money, Teen Vogue* and the online site Remezcla, and he became inundated with requests for interviews. He was even named a TIME Magazine Teen of the Year, alongside *Stranger Things* actor Millie Bobbie Brown and snowboarder Chloe Kim.

Thrust suddenly into the spotlight, Salvador remained humble. He remembered what his mom had told him, and kept his focus on helping others. And he didn't just talk the talk: he walked the walk. While some kids were spending their weekends playing video games, Salvador was out in the streets teaching people how to use the lanterns and set up the washing machines. His goal was simple: to hand out solar lanterns, phone chargers, and washing machines until the need was completely met; or until every single light came back on.

Salvador traversed the entire island, going door to door to deliver the supplies. He started by delivering supplies in the town of Loiza, which had been devastated by the eye of the storm. But soon community leaders from other towns learned about the project, and asked if he could help them out, too.

He ended up visiting 17 towns, as well as a pediatric hospital in San Juan. When he saw the desperation of people's situations, it inspired him to keep going. "I hadn't really seen, really experienced, what people were actually living," he says. "But when you're there, you're literally among piles of debris, piles of clothes, of belongings, that are just broken or wet or destroyed, or just gone. Ruins of houses. You see doors lying on the ground...that's when you realize: 'Wow!'"

It took almost 11 months for power to be restored to Puerto Rico, making it the largest and longest blackout in U.S. history. Months after the storm had receded, rural communities across Puerto Rico were still plagued by rolling blackouts. For the people who lived through this period of darkness, it was an excruciating exercise in holding out hope. For scientists, sociologists and decision-makers, it was also a lesson in how to deal with the pernicious, often invisible, effects of climate change.

Puerto Rico's energy grid was outdated, made more for the 20th century than the 21st. When the utility poles came crashing down in the storm, backup generators across the country weren't prepared to handle the enormous energy needs of hospitals, schools, and modern apartment complexes. And the darkness -- quite literally -- sent many people into a state of depression, leading to a record number of suicides.

Climate change will undoubtedly bring about more storms like this. Warmer seas will increase the wind speeds of tropical storms, and storm surges, where tidal waves crash onto coastal areas, are expected to grow in size as sea levels rise. It's places like Puerto Rico that will be hit the hardest: tiny islands that are already more likely to suffer from poverty and underdevelopment. But it's also in places like Puerto Rico that communities are gaining the tools to allow themselves to strike back. Time and again, Puerto Ricans have proved that they are resilient and resourceful people.

If there is more darkness in the future, it can only be counterbalanced with more light -- and like Salvador's campaign to bring light back to Puerto Rico, the tiny island is giving itself hope.

By 2050, Puerto Rico aspires to run on 100 percent renewable energy. All across the island, solar panels are appearing on rooftops, in gardens, on the tops of schools and hospitals. And they are decorating the landscape, reflecting the blue of the ocean. Puerto Rico wasn't ready for Hurricane Maria, but in the years to come it will be more prepared. Solar panels are more resilient than the old-fashioned energy systems, and switching to solar will make it easier for places like Puerto Rico to regain power in the wake of future storms. Out of tragedy comes change.

Salvador is still in high school, but he is already taking his message on the road. At the Davos World Economic Forum he spoke about his campaign to bring light and hope to Puerto Rico to the world's top political and business leaders. On a panel with other teen changemakers and environmental activist Greta Thunberg, they held the rich and powerful accountable. Offstage, Salvador also got to speak with inspiring activists like Jane Goodall. She told him that in order to create change, young people and older generations would have to work together. "We can't do things alone, we have to be able to communicate with each other," she said to him.

Salvador spoke proudly of his Puerto Rican roots, and the broken promises that have led us to where we are today, with a climate that is being destroyed and a political system that badly needs fixing."We're tired of too many people coming to Davos, and then going back and not doing anything," he said. "We're tired of empty promises, we're tired of too much talk." He added, "Our people need action. They need our support. Today."

Every individual matters.
Every individual has a role to play.
Every individual makes a difference.

Jane Goodall

Call to Action: Adopt renewable energy in your home. Learn about solar power. And follow Salvador on Twitter: https://twitter.com/sgomezcolon

NAVIGATING BY THE STARS
Nainoa Thompson
The Polynesian Voyaging Society
Hawaii

Nainoa Thompson was in awe when he first saw the Hōkūle'a, a traditional Polynesian voyaging canoe that navigates by the stars without using any Western implements. In 1976 the Polynesian Voyaging Society's now famous flagship project had set sail from Hawaii to Tahiti, retracing the original journey taken by Nainoa's ancestors, the first time such a vessel had completed this journey in over 600 years. "I was in Tahiti when it arrived," Nainoa says, reflecting back. "17,000 Tahitians flocked to the port -- so I climbed up a monkey-tail tree just to be able to watch it make landfall. I didn't know what the future held, but I sensed how historic this moment was. And I knew I was going to be a part of that future somehow."

Nainoa had grown up on a dairy farm in Niu Valley on the island of Oahu when it was still an agricultural community. Here, Nainoa's first teachers were close to the land -- and close to home. "My mother was a great inspiration for me. She would always make us go out into the bush, and encouraged us to spend our days in nature. She had the spirit of all the great naturalists, and it rubbed off on me." Another teacher that guided Nainoa was Yoshi Kawano, a family friend and worker who lived on the dairy farm. "Yoshi was my great teacher about the ocean," Nainoa says. "One day he gave me a four-foot bamboo fishing pole and took me to Maunalua Bay. With this gift, I found a place of wonderment where I could really be at peace with myself. As a kid, a lot of things didn't really make sense to me -- but the ocean did."

With modernization, industrialization, and an influx of people that the land couldn't support, Niu Valley changed. Nainoa saw two different ways of living, and realized that the effects of this modern approach couldn't be sustained. "Growing up, there was no question as to why the natural world would need to be protected," he says. "To watch the world change so rapidly without being able to do anything about it, and watch the things you value, and love, get destroyed; it was a helpless feeling."

Nainoa devoted himself to learning more about environmental issues, which wasn't easy. "When I was in high school, sustainability wasn't even a word. Climate change wasn't taught. We were really unprepared to deal with these issues in every way." Nainoa also struggled with his Hawaiian identity, since that wasn't taught in schools either. "I realized that people don't care to protect something they have no connection to," he says. "And so I realized why our Hawaiian identity and heritage, which is so deeply connected to this place, was being ignored. Reviving one's understanding would inevitably awaken both. I realized that as a culture going forward, we needed a new kind of teaching so that the next generation of Hawaiians would be better prepared than we were."

In the early 1970s, Nainoa found exactly the community of educators he was looking for with the Polynesian Voyaging Society (PVS). After witnessing the Hōkūle'a arrive in Tahiti, Nainoa was eager to learn from these great navigators. "I owe all that I am to the great navigators and educators who gave of themselves to build me up," he says. "Mau Piailug. Katharine Luomala. Ben Finney. And perhaps my greatest influence from a sustainability perspective, Lacy Veach."

Lacy Veach was Hawaii's second astronaut, and he made a great impact on Nainoa's crowning achievement with the PVS, the Worldwide Voyage. "He taught me about the Island Earth, which is how he saw it from outer space. And how fragile and interrelated everything is. It's also when he realized that down on earth, our solutions don't evade us because of an absence of technology, but an absence of culture. He planted the seed that we need millions of trained 'navigators,' both metaphorically and literally, to build a future of values and education. He saw the parallels between navigating space and the PVS. And he was the one who instructed me to sail Hōkūle'a around the world to continue to inspire these values."

"With the Hōkūle'a, I've witnessed the Hawaiian Renaissance in real time," he says. A government mandate to teach the Hawaiian language has had a profound impact on this island nation. "Before the Hōkūle'a, there were less than 100 native speakers left on the islands," Nainoa says. "Now there are more than 22,000 native Hawaiian speakers."

"The PVS and Hōkūle'a has given us hope. It's showed us that we need to change our relationship to the earth, and we need to educate ourselves about how to get back to more sustainable ways. And it's shown that in navigating by our shared values and navigating by the power of community, we can change anything. To put it simply, our relationship with Hawaii was renewed."

Nainoa has since devoted his life to reviving ancient Hawaiian traditions that were nearly lost. Whether he is working on cultural preservation, environmental advocacy, or championing sustainable education for Hawaiian youth, he credits everything he's achieved to the guidance of generous teachers. "I'm not a particularly smart or courageous person. If you read a headline about some of the things I've done, you might think that," he says. "But you'd be wrong. I owe everything I've done to the great teachers I've been fortunate to learn from in my journey of life."

Nainoa has been involved with all of the Hōkūle'a's voyages after the initial one, and has remained a central navigator for the PVS since the early 1970s. Over a period of 45 years, his voyages have totaled more than 250,000 nautical miles -- the equivalent of circumnavigating the earth 20 times. From 2014-2017, the Worldwide Voyage covered 41,000 miles, visited 322 ports, and heard stories from concerned communities all over the world who are suffering from climate change. "It's clear that if we don't do anything to combat climate change, there's going to be a lot of suffering," Nainoa says. But he adds that there's reason for hope. "We met extraordinary people doing work in environmental and cultural spaces. We learned from hundreds of Indigenous communities that have been sustained for thousands of years with the common understanding that Mother Earth will take care of it all, if we take care of her."

Nainoa is now planning the launch of the Moananuiākea Voyage in 2022. "We are planning to circumnavigate the Pacific, since the engine of environment is the Pacific. It regulates climate, food sovereignty, distribution of temperature -- all of the most important issues of sustainability for the 21st century." For this boundary-breaking voyage, Nainoa has advocated for youth involvement at all levels of the process. "We're mandating that at least a third of the 300-person crew has to be under the age of 25, so that these skills are passed on to the next generation."

Nainoa is hopeful about the future. "Within weeks of asking for youth volunteers for the Moananuiākea Voyage, we had to start turning people away -- which is a good thing. It shows us that the young people are ready to fight for cultural and environmental preservation." And Nainoa is glad that they are taking up the mantle. "My generation couldn't crack the code to build a sustainable world, but I think that these amazing young people can -- and will."

If I have courage, it is because I have faith in the
knowledge of my ancestors.

Mau Piailug

Call to Action: To learn more about the Polynesian Voyaging Society, please visit www.hokulea.com

NEVER APOLOGIZE FOR DREAMING BIG

Daniela Fernandez
Sustainable Ocean Alliance
San Francisco, California

From as early as she could remember, Daniela Fernandez was an animal lover. Growing up in the vibrant city of Quito, Ecuador, she was surrounded by marvels of nature on all sides. Ecuador is home to many rare and unique natural environments. This country on the equator contains everything from misty cloud forests to glowing, active volcanoes dotting the horizon.

Ecuador has the distinction of having the planet's greatest biodiversity per hectare. Among the rare animals found there is the spectacled bear, which exists only in a narrow ribbon of land in South America. There are also the many endangered species of the Galapagos Islands, such as the giant tortoise. Ecuador is also home to the world's largest flying bird, the Andean condor. All of these unique species drove Daniela to want to understand how to protect and preserve them and their environments, whether they be in the forests, grasslands, or the ocean.

"When I was young, my family used to take long trips from the city to the coastline. Growing up surrounded by nature really molded my life and my appreciation of the environment. I found that being around pristine nature in such a beautiful place is really necessary for happiness. I always had an innate feeling, even from the time I was very young, that these natural wonders had to be preserved."

When she was 7 years old, Daniela moved with her mother to Chicago, to an urban environment that couldn't have been more different from where she lived in Ecuador. "Landing in Chicago and looking out my window, it was flat land all around. As a kid, not seeing any mountains or nature around scared me. It made me appreciate what I had back home."

At age 12, she had a wake-up call. Walking home from school one day, she passed a shop window and saw something that would change her life. "I remember looking at this movie poster that had a penguin walking on sand – it turned out to be *An Inconvenient Truth*, Al Gore's documentary on climate change. So, I ran to the Blockbuster, because my favorite animal was a penguin and I wanted to understand why it was walking on sand. I got the movie, I was so excited... and the next thing you know, I'm in tears, learning about what could happen to our environment and to the penguins that I adore, the animals I love, and our entire climate. It was a catastrophe. But it opened my eyes to the reality."

After that Daniela dedicated her life to protecting our environment. She talked awareness, took environmental classes, and raised money to get solar panels for her high school. She even got involved with the debate team, with aspirations of running for office so she could influence environmental policy. And she enrolled at Georgetown University, which has strong connections with Washington's environmental political leaders.

As a freshman there, she had another life-changing experience when was invited to a meeting at the United Nations on the state of our oceans. "I was well versed in climate change, but this was the first time I'd heard any discussion about the role the ocean plays in the larger climate ecosystem. And I quickly realized I was the only young person in the room, learning about what's happening to our oceans. I also noticed a few things that the older people wouldn't. One was that there were not many communication channels. There was no livestream. And no social media getting this information out to my generation. I also realized that everybody was talking about problems, sharing these doomsday statistics; but no one was talking about solutions. No one had any hope about the innovations that could move things forward. I left that meeting feeling completely devastated because I had learned that our ocean was dying. And I also felt a sense of urgency to let the world know, to let my own generation know, that this was something that we had to pay attention to, because no one was talking about it."

On the train ride back to Washington after the meeting in New York, Daniela had a eureka moment. She realized that she could do a lot more as an entrepreneur than as a policymaker. With this thought in mind, she picked up a pen and pad. "I just started sketching out this model. It was literally two bubbles. In one bubble I wrote 'young people.' In the other bubble, I put the names of influential people, like various businessmen and high-level politicians. Then I put a concentric circle in the middle and thought, this is what the Sustainable Ocean Alliance (SOA) needs to be. A platform where young people can interact with high-level leaders so they can learn from them. But on the flip side, young people can also contribute to the solutions that these high-level people are looking for, that they're not finding. That's how the SOA was born."

Back at Georgetown, she hosted the first ever Sustainable Ocean Summit, and 500 students from across the country attended. Daniela incorporated her forward-looking ideas into the agenda for the meeting, with the help of U.S. Secretary of State John Kerry and the U.S. State Department. The meeting was streamed to all the U.S. embassies around the world: some even had Embassy watch parties, so young people from other countries could be involved.

"This was the catalyst that really kicked SOA into high gear. After that meeting, I had countless students from around the country asking me, How can I bring this back to my own university, country, city? So, I built a toolkit to help others replicate what I'd done. It made such an impact that after graduation, Georgetown gave me a two-month stipend to raise the funds to create this nonprofit."

Daniela quickly became one of the leading youth activists in the sustainable oceans space. She moved her headquarters to San Francisco, for proximity to an innovative startup culture, and started building out various aspects of her organization.

"There's a lot of innovation here," she says. "Our Ocean Leadership program provides resources and mentorship for young, aspiring leaders to build hubs in their regions. We partner with high-level conferences, like the Our Ocean Conference. And recently, we've started the Ocean Solutions Accelerator Program, which was set up for entrepreneurs who have ideas, and need help learning how to scale."

In the two years since its inception, SOA's accelerator program has helped launch 29 ocean tech startups. SOA has even started a venture capital fund to further support these companies, and the many more that they expect will be created. SOA has made such a splash that it received support from Marc Benioff, the founder of Salesforce.com. This has helped support SOA's newest venture, the Ocean Academy, a bridge program between SOA's leadership and accelerator programs, to provide incubation and ideation support for more young people. "What makes this so unique is that the learning is done through our Ocean Learning Labs, which are virtual learning experiences," Daniela explains. "The goal is to teach specific content for various learning skill sets, and about the professional industries and paths that are related to working in support of a sustainable ocean."

Despite her many successes, Daniela has faced countless obstacles on her journey to becoming a youth leader in the ocean tech space.

"I grew up as a first-generation student without a lot of money, in a single parent household. It was tough. Even when I was getting started with SOA, I got constant rejections from foundations. I faced a lot of naysaying. People tried to dissuade me from pursuing the path I was on. Thankfully, I had enough self-awareness to trust my own instincts and to believe in myself. And I had a good community of mentors. Most importantly my mom, who encouraged me to continue on this journey regardless of what other people said."

For young people who have similarly grand aspirations, Daniela's message is simple. "Never apologize for dreaming too big. That's something I had to learn the hard way. I always felt like I had to hold myself back. But in hindsight, I'd tell the youth, 'It's up to *you*, what your vision is to become.'"

Youth empowerment is critically important to Daniela; but she feels like the current approach of some of their adult allies could use some work. "When it comes to adults leading, it's important that they don't try to have young people execute *their* vision. Let the youth come up with their own ideas. That's a lot of what we do at SOA. We're not going out and telling young people how to solve these problems. Rather, we're empowering them to figure out their own methods to address these complex issues."

In a few years' time, there will be countless youth leaders emerging from the many educational, vocational, and entrepreneurial programs at SOA, and working on solutions to the issues we are facing. As Daniela continues to work toward her goal of creating sustainable oceans, she has already made the greatest innovation of all – empowering youth to contribute to those solutions, all around the world.

For most of history, man has had to fight nature
to survive;
in this century he is beginning to realize that,
in order to survive, he must protect it.

Jacques-Yves Cousteau

Call to Action: Join with Sustainable Ocean Alliance https://www. soalliance.org .

RISE AND GRIND
Fergus Moore
Revive Eco
Scotland

Fergus Moore had long dreamed of becoming an entrepreneur. His grandfather, a successful small business owner and venture capitalist, had instilled in him a desire to build something out of nothing. He saw from an early age that being a businessperson has its perks: like the ability to set your own hours and your own priorities. But it also gave him the ability to create things and see them take shape. He always knew that he wanted to make something that would have an impact -- whether that be on environmental, social, or economic issues.

He didn't know it at the time, but his neighbor Scott Kennedy shared the same dream.

Fergus and Scott grew up in the same neighborhood in Glasgow, Scotland -- a ten-minute walk from one another. They attended the same high school, though they didn't know each other too well at the time. It wasn't until they both attended the University of Strathclyde that they discovered how much they had in common.

When the two young men were placed on the same team for a class project as part of their entrepreneurship program, it turned out to be a fortunate pairing.

In addition to their passion for entrepreneurship, the two shared a few other things. Both young men were working in coffee shops to pay for school. After making thousands of coffees -- and throwing out filter after filter of spent grounds at the end of their shifts -- they had both started to realize something. It wasn't just one "aha! moment," in particular, but many smaller ones over time. They realized that coffee grounds, like cups and straws, represented a major source of waste that the industry hadn't really taken into consideration. Each year, in the tiny country of Scotland alone, between 40,000 and 50,000 tons of coffee grounds are thrown away. Across the UK, it's half a million. Worldwide, that number is exponentially higher.

Most of the coffee grounds in the world end up in massive, smelly landfills, where they emit methane -- a major greenhouse gas that is contributing to nearly half of global warming. By 2050, as many as 3.4 billion tons of food waste will enter the global waste stream -- and coffee grounds are a small, but nonetheless important, part of this.

Fergus and Scott knew it didn't have to be that way. "We were seeing firsthand the amount of food waste in general that was going out in the trash at the end of every single shift, and it was something that didn't feel right to us," Fergus says. "It felt like there was definitely more value there. It seemed to be something that people could use."

And so, at the age of 23, they teamed up to try to develop a solution to all that coffee-ground waste. Overwhelmed with the scale of the issue, they began with some online research. They discovered many ways that used coffee grounds could be reused and recycled: as fertilizer or compost, as a natural face scrub, even as insect repellent. Someone just needed to figure out an effective and business-savvy way to turn this waste product into something useful. As thrifty Scotsmen, the idea was compelling. As enterprising entrepreneurs, they decided to give it a shot.

What started as a class project has now turned into a full-scale company called Revive Eco. After three years of work in the lab, Fergus and Scott are testing out their creation. They weren't the only people who believed in the project. A grant of a quarter of a million euros from Zero Waste Scotland helped them develop the technology and test it in a lab before taking it to the real world. And they're still just 26.

In Scotland, coffee shops play an important cultural role. They're hubs for intellectual and philosophical discussion. They pulse with a unique energy, and provide a cozy space where people can take shelter from the country's harsh elements: wind, rain, and fog. Young people especially flock to them -- in Glasgow, Edinburg, Aberdeen, Inverness, and elsewhere too.

There are more than 20 coffee-roasting companies in Scotland, and each year Glasgow hosts a renowned international coffee festival. The coffee culture is thriving, but that comes with an unfortunate byproduct: massive amounts of waste. "The initial shock was just the volume of waste," Fergus says. "When you go into Starbucks and get your cappuccino, you don't see the waste. Even if you do see it, it just seems like such a small, little puck of waste, you don't really think about how much that all adds up when you take the millions and billions of people drinking coffee every single day."

"You hear about carbon emissions, but once you actually start looking into the numbers, it's difficult to comprehend: the number of hectares of forest being chopped, the number of tons of coffee waste, the number of tons of palm oil, the number of carbon emissions. It's really hard to even fathom," Fergus says.

Fergus and Scott are leading the way to a better world, and so is their country. Scotland was the first country in the world to set a goal of running 100 percent on renewable energy by 2020 -- and they have actually reached it. Offshore wind farms like the Beatrice Offshore Wind Farm and the Seagreen Wind Farm provide clean energy to hundreds of thousands of Scottish homes.

Now the country is bringing its waste goals in line with its renewable energy ones. By 2025, the Scottish government has pledged to send less than 5 percent of all waste to landfills, while ensuring it recycles 70 percent of the rest. The government plans to remove all plastic packaging from products by 2030, and to reduce food waste by one-third in the coming years. For Fergus, the most important thing was to tackle food waste in a reasonable and down to earth way. To take things one step at a time. "For us, what we are doing just makes sense," he says. "We're driven by logic."

Despite being a small startup, they're already speaking with some of the biggest players in the coffee industry. What if these companies got on board? What could they accomplish then?

In February 2020, they completed the prototype of an invention they been testing -- an industrial sized machine that can convert coffee grounds into environmentally-friendly products. If they can get the next round of investments, they will find a way to scale the project even further -- and that could change the world.

Just as two young entrepreneurs in Scotland can play a role in tackling food waste, so too must an entire generation. And they won't just need help from the titans of the coffee industry, but from also from other change makers, and -- perhaps most importantly -- from consumers.

"Our generation seems to be far more interested in sustainability and leading a more impactful life, rather than simply making as much money as possible," Fergus says. "I think change does have to come from a shift in mindset, and I would hope that our generation can be the one that can push them more toward that direction."

What humans do over the next 50 years will determine the fate of all life on the planet.

David Attenborough

Call to Action: Turn waste into something useful. Use your imagination to create innovative, positive action. Follow Fergus https://twitter.com/revive_eco?lang=en and learn about ReviveEco https://revive-eco.com/

ROBOTS FOR FIGHTING PLASTIC POLLUTION
Sainath Manikandan
Jane Goodall Institute UK
United Arab Emirates

Sainath Manikandan once read a story about the famous environmentalist, Dr. Jane Goodall. She'd helped him to see that no matter how small a step might seem, the tiniest effort can eventually make a huge difference. He was just a young boy in school, but he had paid attention when she said that it didn't matter how old someone was; what mattered was the action they took to move the world into the right direction.

So Sainath decided to start where he would be able to make a change -- in his own school. He'd seen that a lot of his classmates in the United Arab Emirates (UAE) used single-use plastics in their everyday lives. He found this extremely concerning.

He'd first noticed the impact of single-use plastics when he had visited his family's hometown in India when he was 8 years old. "It's normal for people in India to use single-use plastics, like straws, cups, and plastic bags in their day-to-day lives," he remembers. "But there just isn't enough room to dump all of the waste. There were small pieces of plastic everywhere." So the plastic ends up being tossed in the streets and then ends up in the rivers and lakes.

Sainath was bothered enough by this that when he got home he did some research. "This is a problem all over the world," he says. "An estimated amount of *eight million tons* of plastic ends up in the world's oceans every year." If that continues, it is estimated that by 2050 there will be more plastic in the oceans than there is marine wildlife. These shocking numbers made Sainath wonder what he could do about it.

To start, Sainath created a campaign to collect plastic trash and old electronics from his classmates. Once every three months he would hand over all the trash he had collected to the Emirates Environmental Group for recycling. "At first, it wasn't such a big deal," he says. It was a just a project he had started with some friends, placing some trash cans in the school to collect plastic waste, and convincing other students to stop using single-use plastics.

Then one day one of the teachers overheard Sainath talking to his friends about the project. That's when his PEPC (Papers, E-waste, Plastics, and Cans) campaign moved to the next level. "She wanted me to give presentations about our project to students in other classes," Sainath says. "Soon more people realized that they needed to get involved."

It took some time, but eventually, as more students joined the effort, the scope of the project grew. Together they started collecting plastic trash outside, educating others about the importance of sustainability, and even planting plants and trees around their school. Some students started bringing waste from home that wouldn't have been recycled otherwise.

"It was really inspiring, and it gave me the energy I needed to move forward," Sainath says. He realized that what was happening was exactly what he'd learned from the story about Jane Goodall: it just took one person to take one small step in the right direction to create a much larger wave of change.

Around this time Sainath joined other young changemakers by becoming a member of Jane Goodall's Roots & Shoots Programme in the Emirates. "It's about raising awareness, reaching others, and taking small steps that will create a big difference in the future," he says.

By now he realized that it wasn't going to be enough to tackle the issue of plastic pollution by just collecting trash before it gets to the oceans. After all, there is already an astonishing amount of plastic there. So he started to think about how the plastic already in the ocean could be collected.

Because the United Arab Emirates has both desert and coastline, it is a country with a strong interest in fighting environmental pollution and climate change. Therefore, technology is often used there to tackle important problems, like the lack of water for agriculture.

Sainath started thinking about how there might be a technical solution to the problem of marine plastic pollution. He had started going to robotics classes when he was 9 years old. Now he started wondering if his knowledge of robotics might be used to address this problem.

He decided to apply what he'd learned about robotics and put his skills to work. And with the support of his teachers and his parents, he worked tirelessly to develop a robot that would be able to collect plastics from water sources. There were many technical problems to solve: how to make the robot float, how to collect the plastic from the water, where to store the collected plastic, and how to protect the robot's sensitive electronics from the water.

"I used recyclable materials, like plastic bottles, popsicle sticks, pencils, and sheet glass to make my robot float on the surface of the water," he explains. His robot -- which he calls Marine Robot Cleaner (M-Bot for short) -- has three little motors: two of them act as paddles, and a third motor in the front is used to push the plastic trash into a basket attached to the robot's back.

With his robot Sainath aims to protect marine habitats and work toward the UN's Sustainable Development Goal 14: Life Below Water. The robot is only a prototype at this point, but Sainath has already showcased it on various occasions, like UAE Innovation Month, the Dubai Makers Faire, the Masdar Festival, and the Abu Dhabi Chamber's Future Entrepreneurs.

Once he produces the robot on a larger scale, he hopes to build an even bigger version of it that will be able to collect up to 15 tons of plastic before returning to shore. The batteries can then be changed with solar panels, making the robot completely carbon neutral. A Global Positioning System (GPS) can be installed in the robot for navigational purposes, and a rotatable wireless camera and sensor can be fitted. This will sense whether the water is clean, and if it is, will send a signal to the robot to stop the process.

Sainath's invention has earned him multiple prizes, awards, and international recognition. He is even in discussions with a large company about programming the robot to clean up rivers and lakes, and someday maybe even the oceans.

While developing his robot, Sainath realized the importance of learning from past mistakes. "I always take feedback from people on how I could improve my robot," he says. He then goes over his design choices to figure out ways to make his invention work even better.

For Sainath, this is also an important lesson for adults around the world to think about. After all, the huge problem of plastic pollution that we are facing today was caused by the choices made by previous generations. But if we can learn from our past mistakes, and change our behavior to reflect the lessons learned, we can repair the damage. "We need to start working together toward saving our environment," Sainath says. "Better late than never!"

From working on his own projects, implementing his PEPC campaign, and developing his M-Bot, Sainath also learned another important lesson about the power of taking action, that he urges other young people to remember. "Keep yourself motivated and never feel small," he says. "It is our responsibility to conserve the earth for future generations; and together we can create a wave of change."

There is a powerful force unleashed when young people resolve to make a change.

Dr. Jane Goodall

Call to Action: Start from where you are now, and you will have started a wave of change! Dr. Jane Goodall's Roots & Shoots: www.rootsandshoots.org Jane Goodall's Roots & Shoots UAE: https://uae.rootsandshoots.community.

SUSTAINABLE FARMING FOR OUR FUTURE
Vincent Kimura
Smart Yields
Hawaii

Born in Honolulu, Vincent Kimura grew up listening to his grandfather's stories. He'd been a risk-taker, who had pursued his own romantic version of the American dream. After a major earthquake in Tokyo, he left everyone and everything in Japan to join his uncle on the Hawaiian island of Kauai. There he would find work in the sugarcane fields. The work was hard and the days were hot. But as tough as the work was, the land provided, as it does for those who respect it. Soon, he'd realize his dream of owning and operating his own business.

Vincent's father had a similar drive to see the world. And so he moved the family back to Asia for a new life and a better path. Growing up, Vincent experienced the worlds of Hong Kong, Beijing, and Malaysia, and learned to appreciate the beauty of each. But wherever he was, he always remembered his grandfather's stories of working in the sugarcane fields. He felt a pull toward the tradition of working the land. And so he decided early on in life that he was going to pursue his own daring dream. He was going to go against the cultural tide of fast money. He wanted to heal the broken patterns that the world—especially the world of agriculture—had fallen into. He decided to dedicate his life to protecting the environment, and the small farmers who've always known how to care for it.

Vincent made the necessary sacrifices, and moved to the mainland United States. He wanted to learn everything he could, so his first step was to earn his bachelor's degree in environmental science at Oregon State University. After graduation, he worked first at the Pacific Basin Economic Council, then at the accounting firm KPMG, and finally at the Institute for Triple Helix Innovation, where he able to see how academia, industry, and government can work together for social and economic advancement. He studied innovative approaches to sustainability around the world. Gradually, with guidance from his mentors Bernice Glenn and Robert Lees, Vincent was ready to make his mark in the world of sustainable farming.

Since then, over the years he has built multiple green businesses to help small farmers. Inovi Green develops alternatives to toxic indoor cleaning products. AgriGro's line of green products adds beneficial microbes to the agricultural cycle. And his most impactful venture, Smart Yields (SY), gives farmers access to up-to-date data on their land through the use of a mobile app that provides real-time monitoring and analytics of their crops. With this powerful information, small and mid-sized farmers can plan ahead and achieve a greater degree of precision in their agricultural practices. This high level of precision means less waste, lower costs, and a more sustainable cycle.

But as a data man, Vincent knows just how unsustainable our current agricultural systems are. "Small farmers are struggling," he says, quoting the most recent USDA data. "Since 1997, we've lost nearly 200,000 farms, over 50 million acres of land. And 100,000 of those farms have been lost in just the last seven years." Vincent is especially concerned that the number of family-owned farms has fallen by 170,000, while corporation-owned farms have increased by 26,000.

Vincent listens to farmers share their concerns; and they believe this rapid change should be seen as a warning. More big agribusiness adds up to increased financial pressures on small farmers. When farmers are struggling to survive against the power of agribusiness, it affects whole communities. Prices drop. The "little guy" can't compete. Corporations don't need to buy local, so they don't. Money generated from the land doesn't stay in the community. Local shops are no longer supported, so they suffer too.

A small farmer struggling is a sign of an unsustainable community. Small farmers, who are on the front line of climate change, are just not prepared to face its threats. A system with less diversity. Fewer viewpoints. Lost traditional, local knowledge. And this unsustainable cycle is repeating itself in small rural farming towns across the United States. It is a serious threat to our country's food security.

Vincent is committed to helping repair this endangered cycle all over the world. Thanks to SY, small farmers now have access to the same technology as big corporations, at their fingertips. This makes for healthier, more competitive, and more productive farms.

Vincent first tested SY's advanced technology in Colorado in 2017. Steve Ela is a fourth-generation family farmer there who has 80 acres of orchards. SY's app allows him to micromanage his fruit trees, which is critical, especially when unpredictable bouts of freezing weather hit. "Climate change is going to shake up what we know as normal," says Steve. "Every year adds another data point." But, he adds, there is strength in numbers; when all farmers in the community pool their data, their region is stronger.

Edward Tufts, another Colorado farmer, has a 500-acre organic orchard in the Rocky Mountains. Thanks to SY, his business, Leroux Creek Foods, was able to save a crop of Honeycrisp apples during a late frost. "It can cost $500 an acre to heat an orchard through the frost season" he explains. "This system, which I can easily monitor on my phone, reduces my expenses by allowing me to operate more efficiently." For Edward, this savings was in the hundreds of thousands of dollars.

But the impact of SY goes far beyond dollars and cents. It makes the farming cycle more sustainable every step of the way. This technology has made such a positive impact in the world of sustainability that it was accepted in the first round of the Vatican's inaugural accelerator program, called the Laudato Si' Challenge. "When the Vatican officially recognized that climate change is real, it sent a unifying message around the globe," Vincent says. "As business leaders, we can't put profit first. We have to respond with what's best for future generations. This is the way Indigenous peoples lived…I've really redefined my perspective as a CEO. The journey isn't about the next billion dollars. There are larger things at play."

What Vincent really likes to talk about is bridge-building through mentorship, education, and professional development training. "I've always been a problem solver," he says. "It is part of my personality. I'm always looking for better, faster, more efficient ways of doing things. And that goes for mentorship, which has been core to my ethos. So I ask myself, what are we not taught about when we are embarking on an entrepreneurial journey?"

Some of the most valuable lessons Vincent learned along his own journey he learned by getting involved with local civic groups. "Right out of college, I went into Rotary Youth Leadership training. There, I learned how to manage insecurities and ego. Every journey can be fraught with mental health challenges. Burnout. Depression. Countless other things. Entrepreneurs need to understand this early on. When they see the signs of these things, they should take a step back," he says. "We need to be taught about these things to be able to recognize them."

Vincent has found that this wisdom is rare in the world of farming. "Nowadays, farmers are really struggling with mental health issues," he says. Increased pressures -- very long days, unpredictable weather, delinquent loans, rising debts, bankruptcies -- has farmers fearing they will lose everything, including their family's hard-earned legacy. Suicides are at the highest level in decades. "We need to change our perspective and talk about these things without judgment," Vincent says. "No matter where you are, you aren't alone. There's a tribe of people out there who can support you." Vincent finds that getting his hands in the soil is the best therapy. Growing vegetables is being used to treat PTSD in veterans, and others. "Once someone feels that connection to the earth, there's a pathway to healing," he says.

Vincent believes that if we act quickly, with some structural changes we can reestablish a healthy, sustainable approach to agriculture—and to our whole way of life. There are models to learn from all over the world, he says, and mentions innovative field design in the Netherlands as an example. Then he adds, "In Hawaii we can learn from our native systems. Years ago Hawaii fed over a million people from local, sustainable farms: now, we import 85-90 percent of our food. We need to support people in renewing our farms. We need to get back to those tried and true models of living. The knowledge is out there. And we can do it. We just need to pull together."

Agriculture is the most healthful, most useful and most noble employment of man.

George Washington

Call to Action: Buy local. Get your hands in the dirt. Support small farmers. Learn more about Vincent here: https://www.hawaiibusiness.com/20-for-20-vincent-kimura/ Visit https://smartyields.com or https://www.agrigro.com

TURNING WASTE INTO FUEL
Azza Faiad
Egypt

In Alexandria, Egypt, 14-year-old Azza Faiad was sitting in an idling taxi. It was July 2010, a looming energy crisis was taking hold of the world. Her driver was waiting in a long line of cars at a filling station, hoping to refuel before the pumps ran out. Which wasn't guaranteed–nothing was during the crisis. There was a massive shortage in oil supply, and this sort of wait had become normal.

As she waited, exhaust came through the windows, polluting the air she breathed. It clouded the atmosphere around the lines of cars as well. Everything felt cramped and suffocating. The streets were polluted. The expressions on worried faces all around her were difficult to take in. As Azza looked around at the seemingly hopeless scene, a thought struck her: *Why are we so dependent on oil?*

There had been peaks and valleys in the price of oil before. But this time it was particularly harmful. In the year from July 2007 to July 2008, the price of crude oil had risen from $60 a barrel to nearly $140. This impacted all sectors of the economy, and wreaked havoc in the daily lives of countless people around the world.

Many factors were contributing to this situation. Climate change. Political hostilities in the Middle East. Dwindling oil reserves. An increase in global demand for oil from developing regions. Financial speculation.

But as complicated as these reasons may be, the reality for the average person was quite simple: a crushing increase in the price of oil. And since oil is so entangled in global markets, an oil shortage makes the prices of many other goods and services rise dramatically as well.

This obviously affects lower income people disproportionately. The price of heating oil skyrockets. People have to make this-or-that choices at the market. Stress levels go off the charts. And of course, there is that one hallmark of any supply issue surrounding oil: long lines at every filling station in sight.

But sometimes, out of chaos, can come clarity. And in a somewhat ironic twist of fate, it was in one of those frustrating filling station lines that Azza's journey as a youth leader in alternative energy began.

"After that day, I often thought about how to approach our dependency problem," she says. Then one day at 14, she had a moment of revelation on another car trip, from Alexandria to Cairo.

"As we were driving, I saw this huge landfill. We passed by it slowly. It was so big I thought it was never going to end. At that point I thought, there's just so much raw material here. What if somehow we could use all this waste to solve the energy crisis?"

It all started moving really fast from there. Azza had a lot of questions. And so, with the support of her family, who are all very scientifically minded, she dove deeper into learning about plastic waste. "That's the second biggest category of waste, behind paper waste," she explains. "So there was no shortage of material to work with. In time, I started studying how waste can be converted to fuel." But of course, as just a teenager, she was limited in her knowledge.

Luckily, at 15 years old, she was welcomed by the Petroleum Research Institute in Cairo, to work with two of their scientists, Dr. Tarek Fahmi and Dr. Mamdouh El Melawy, on the project. "They were amazing mentors to me," she says.

Azza and her team ended up utilizing an existing catalyst in a different process that can break down plastic waste and turn it into fuel that can power vehicles. Even more amazing, this catalyst is significantly cheaper than the catalysts that were being commonly used prior to their discovery.

This discovery has huge implications on the climate change front and beyond. Because the process is cheaper, more people will adopt it. Waste will be reduced in more places, more quickly. This in turn, will lead to communities having a reduced dependency on oil. And, as with any discovery, new knowledge leads to additional advances and discoveries. And all of these component parts can produce jobs in a variety of new sectors for local economies.

In 2012, Azza won the European Fusion Development Agreement award at the European Union Contest for Young Scientists for her work. Still only 16 years old, she beat out more than 125 contestants from nearly 40 countries.

But while it's true that Azza is a gifted research scientist, she hasn't always succeeded academically.

"Going to Europe and winning this contest really changed my way of seeing things," she says. "It gave me an interest in traveling, and in competing in other international competitions. So, I decided to study abroad. I applied to a university in Canada, to study electrical or environmental engineering -- -but I didn't make it. I didn't get the required scores to qualify. That was a really devastating period for me. I'd won these competitions. Received praise for my accomplishments. And then, just like that, I suddenly felt like a failure."

But sometimes, fate has a way of pointing us in the right direction, even though it's hard to see sometimes, especially at the time.

"I continued to study electrical engineering at Alexandria University. But I wasn't motivated. I had dreams of studying abroad, and now here I was, right down the road from where I've lived my whole life. And for the first few years, I wasn't studying anything I wanted to. But then, out of nowhere, I stumbled into an opportunity in research. There was a spot open in with the energy materials research group at the American University in Cairo, and I was accepted. So, I traveled to Cairo, and once again I found my spark!"

The work was focused on the micro and nano structures used in solar energy, as well as water splitting for hydrogen production. It wasn't relevant to electrical engineering per se, but Azza realized that here were avenues to work on a variety of sustainability issues all at once. It was this holistic approach to scientific research that really intrigued her.

Knowing how discouraging hard times can feel for young people, she has some words of wisdom for those who might be struggling with similar issues.

"Having a setback doesn't make you a failure. You won't succeed at everything you do. But I'd urge any youth to explore their full potential, by learning about something that brings you fulfillment, no matter how many times you failed before. And then, when you gain knowledge, pass it on to others. Young people are always looking for someone to inspire them. They need someone to push them forward. Give them support. Perhaps you can take some time to teach your skills to another. Or maybe you can tell others about how you reached your own goals in life. We are all looking for that kind of support. It's a gift, to teach and be taught. It's what my many mentors instilled in me, and what I hope to instill in others too."

Then she explains how exploring a passion in one discipline can lend itself to many others.

"Although my work is in energy research, the knowledge I acquire won't simply be applicable to the energy sector -- - there are many places it can impact sustainability. More efficient power supplies can contribute to a smaller carbon footprint in many industries, such as electronics. And it can be used to create low-volt, higher-amp outputs in consumer products, and in industrial applications too. A research 'win' becomes a climate win. That's what's so exciting for me."

Azza has other plans to change the world of sustainability. Her dream is to one day work with her twin sister, who is a mechanical engineer. Together, she hopes they can address some of these problems, while having fun.

If at her young age, she could already figure out a more sustainable way to convert plastic waste into fuel, there's no telling what she and her sister will be able to contribute to creating a more sustainable world in the future.

"I hope to develop a product, or technology, that can contribute to pressing problems in energy or climate. I don't have a specific plan as of yet. But my sister has been thinking about efficient sources of power. So maybe some we can combine our studies and scale up a product that deals with sustainability. Yep. That is my dream."

The use of alternative energy is inevitable as
fossil fuels are finite.

Gawdat Bahgat

We have on this earth what makes
life worth living

Original quote in Arabic: علی هذه الأرض ما یستحق الحیاة

Call to Action: Ride bikes or walk to school/work, encourage your community to install more solar panels. To drive, use electric or hybrid cars.

V

DOING WELL BY DOING GOOD FOR THE PLANET

Sustainable Business

DOING WELL BY DOING GOOD FOR THE PLANET
Sustainable Business

Business can be a leader in building a more sustainable world. As a pioneer in the field of corporate social responsibility, I've seen it firsthand. In this chapter, I've featured a wide range of ways passionate business leaders are creating companies with sustainability at the heart of their mission - and challenging others to join with them.

Working alongside Lara Nuer and her mother Claire to bring their organization, from France to the U.S. was a life-changing experience for me. Learning as Leadership's mission affirmed my own belief - that it's possible to build healthy ecosystems; create a more culturally inclusive corporate culture; reduce executive burnout; and increase healthy relationships within families, while striving to build a more humanistic business model. Today LAL's leadership program prepares executives and their teams from Fortune 500 companies to make businesses more humane --and the people who work in them healthier, happier people.

I first met Elliot Hoffman while consulting for the San Francisco Chamber of Commerce. Through my teaching experience, I'd seen how public schools were in dire need of support. After getting my masters' degree in business, I consulted with Fortune 100 corporations, Chambers of Commerce and the Business Roundtable to engage business executives to support innovative strategies to address their issues of workforce development. They began to see that investing in today's young people in their community was a wise investment.

Always ready to get involved, Elliot had signed up for the Chamber's new School-Business Connection I had developed to get companies to build public-private partnerships to improve the quality of education in the city's public schools. With over 120 languages spoken in the homes of San Francisco, the city was a bellwether indicator for the increasing ethnic and cultural diversity in the U.S. And with the ever-growing influx of immigrants into the country, it was becoming clear that the education system was ill-equipped to educate these children. Our Principal of the Day program increased business awareness of the challenges facing schools, and the Job Shadow Day program connected executives like Elliot with students who were curious about his company, Just Deserts. By connecting with these young people, business leaders discovered the joy of sharing their own journey while at the same time investing in their future workforce. Elliot had grown up in a housing cooperative in the Bronx, so the idea of being "a cooperative human being" has always just seemed natural to him. In fact, every day on his way to school he saw a motto painted on the wall of the electric power plant he walked by: COOPERATION EQUALS POWER. So when he decided to go into business, he did so with sustainability in mind. "We just didn't want to waste anything," he says. "It was ingrained in us." Those values helped make his family's business, Just Desserts, not only socially responsible, but profitable. Now Elliot's with his company, REV Sustainability, he guides small and midsize companies how to transition to a more just and sustainable way of operating.

It was the first Earth Day when Ben Cohen first became aware of what was happening to the environment. When, years later, he became a successful business owner he knew that if he and his partner wanted to really change things for the better, they had to take a critical look at their own business's environmental impact. That's why Ben & Jerry's Ice Cream installed a solar array at their factory in Vermont, and a bio-digester that turns that waste into clean energy in their factory in the Netherlands. Today Ben invests in climate justice initiatives.

Ed Begley Jr. was also inspired by that first Earth Day in 1970. He began thinking about what the future could look like if the momentum from this event was leveraged to make an even broader impact. So he went to some of the leaders who had put it together and said, "It's fine to have this one day—but as a movement, and a community, what are we going to do for the other 364 days?" Ever since then, he has championed sustainable living in a variety of ways, including running a business that features a line of green indoor cleaning products called Begley's Best.

As a boy, Gary Hirshberg loved spending time on top of New Hampshire's Mount Washington. On clear days he could even see the Atlantic Ocean far off in the distance. But when he returned home from college, he noticed a big change: the air pollution was so bad that you couldn't see the ocean anymore. Later, he and his colleagues at Stonyfield Farms decided that 10 percent of their profits would be spent on initiatives to fight climate change. Since then, the company has spearheaded many measures to minimize its carbon footprint and to support environmental efforts.

Jonah Wittkamper was in high school when he learned about the principle of "radical inclusion" at a summer camp where kids came from all over the world. As a shy teenager who often felt out of place, that summer was transformative for him. As an adult, he's still practicing radical inclusion in a variety of ways, including founding NEXUS, a global network of influential philanthropists and social entrepreneurs who are tackling a wide array of social issues, including disaster relief and humanitarian aid, especially in the regions most affected by climate change.

And Henk Rogers was in a hospital recovery room flipping through a newspaper when he saw a tiny news story that said all of the coral in the world would be dead by the end of the century. "This should be front-page news, not jammed in the back," he thought. As a highly successful entrepreneur, Henk had had many profitable companies, but that morning he had found himself lying in the back of an ambulance, with a 100 percent blockage of the largest artery in his heart. "I'm not going, I still have stuff to do," he said. In the following days, he decided to dedicate the rest of his days to making the world a better place by doing what he could to making Hawaii have 100% renewable energy by 2045.

Each of the business leaders in this chapter whose life journey led them into developing sustainable companies arrived by a unique path. I invite you to enjoy their stories, and allow them to inspire you too to support sustainability, whether as a business leader, entrepreneur, or even as a consumer. We all need to work together on this!

The future will either be green or not at all.

Bob Brown

Call to Action: To keep up with the sustainable business ventures that Ed Begley is building and supporting, visit www.begleyliving.com.

A FUTURE FORGED IN RADICAL INCLUSION
Jonah Wittkamper
NEXUS
New York, New York

Growing up as a science geek, Jonah didn't have many friends. He often felt alone and isolated -- like he was different. And he struggled with accepting those he felt were "different" too. Thankfully, when he was 15, he went to Camp Rising Sun in New York, an international gathering of youth leaders who practiced the tenets of Radical Inclusion.

At Camp Rising Sun, each summer, 60 young men and 60 young women practice leadership skills in a supportive community of peers and counselors. There Jonah found himself mingling with youth from more than 35 different countries, celebrating their different cultures and ways–and practicing Radical Inclusion. He became fascinated by the wonderful diversity in all things – food, culture, language, you name it. "On Saturday nights, we'd sing a song called 'Everybody Loves Saturday Night'. Those who spoke a language others didn't speak would sing the chorus in their mother tongue." One by one, the chorus was belted out in French, German, Spanish, Yiddish, and a variety of African dialects--a rich diversity of accents, indigenous languages, in voices from around the world. Everyone was encouraged to repeat the words back in their same language, which created an exciting exchange of cultures. "In that moment, I really felt included," says Jonah. "I began to see the beauty in people who are different. But mainly, I lost my fear, and that allowed for real human connection."

When Jonah got back to high school, he made it a point to learn everyone's first and last name – particularly those students he thought might be feeling ostracized, much in the way he had felt before his camp experience. It was his first foray into a personal type of activism, in the tried-and-true practice of Radical Inclusion. Now, twenty years later, he's still stewarding support for global youth leaders.

In 2000 Jonah founded the Global Youth Action Network (GYAN) to connect, support, and empower youth globally. GYAN was formed with multiple aims in mind: to increase youth participation in decision making; to facilitate international collaboration of youth organizations; and to create a structure of support from established leaders in social entrepreneurship. With the support he has gotten from corporations, institutions, and governments, Jonah has helped to amplify the voice of youth in the policy and decision-making processes in more than 180 countries around the world. In 2001 GYAN merged with TakingITGlobal, a network of several thousand youth NGOs whose online platform is visited by thousands of people every day.

In 2011 Jonah went on to found NEXUS, a global network of influential philanthropists and social entrepreneurs who are tackling a wide array of social causes and issues, including disaster relief and humanitarian aid, especially in the regions most affected by climate change.

For example, in August 2019, Hurricane Dorian tore through the Grand Bahamas. A Category 5 hurricane with winds reaching 185 mph, Dorian caused nearly $3.5 billion in damage to this island nation. Nearly 70,000 people were left homeless in its wake, with nowhere to go, and local transportation and food supplies were devastated. NEXUS quickly responded to Grand Bahama Port Authority's Director Rupert Hayward's call for assistance, they reached out to their network of philanthropists to provide a lifeline of supplies. In the end, NEXUS members donated 19 planes, more than 50 boats, and nearly $2 Million of aid for relief efforts.

At the forefront of NEXUS's climate-related work is their support for innovation in the environmental and renewable energy spaces. NEXUS member Sam Teicher's organization Coral Vita is helping to rebuild damaged and vulnerable coral reefs around the world. With 30 percent of the world's coral reefs already gone, and 75 percent of what remains forecast to be lost by 2050, organizations like Coral Vita are needed now more than ever. Coral reefs are essential for maintaining the ocean's ecosystem. They provide a home for an astonishing 25 percent of the biodiversity we see in marine life. They act as protective barriers for mainland areas, by absorbing wave shocks. And when they are intact, they can serve as lucrative destinations for ecotourism.

Using an innovative technique called micro-fragmenting, scientists at Coral Vita have been able to create growth in coral restoration "farms" in a span of 6-12 months, a process that would normally take 25-30 years in the ocean. While this has incredible implications for reef recovery, it will still be an uphill battle. As the farms grow, the scientists invite people to visit them, so they have an opportunity to teach the next generation of scientists and conservationists about the importance of innovation and social entrepreneurship.

Through the NEXUS Impact Accelerator program, Jonah is striving to get resources directly to those social entrepreneurs who are working on the most critical global environmental challenges. An inaugural fellow in this program, Blayne Ross, is CEO of Shorelock, a company working to protect vulnerable coastlines around the world. Shorelock helps sandy beaches, shorelines, and coastlines resist erosion by wave action, winds, storms, and other natural phenomena. By applying a powdered mix of a sustainable bonding agent to sand, it creates a microlayer of water that helps waves run off the shore without bringing the sand along with them. This technology has been proven to be 100 percent environmentally sound, and has even helped restore the breeding habitats for certain rare species like sea turtles. Shorelock works with the Small Islands Resiliency Program in the Bahamas to protect the coastal lands of indigenous communities, while ensuring that the vital islands' infrastructures, which have been severely impacted by climate change, remain intact.

Galvanizing support for innovation in combating plastics pollution is also critical for Jonah. NEXUS's The SUpR Initiative launched by NEXUS in 2020 in partnership with Oceanic Global and Accenture works with professional sports teams to reduce and eliminate single use plastics in stadiums. Along with NEXUS community-led summits like the Ocean SOS Tech Summit in 2018, Jonah has organized the resources and knowledge to think creatively about ways to solve plastic pollution in oceans.

He is also helping to raise the visibility of social entrepreneurs in the political and financial arenas. In 2018, he founded the Healthy Democracy Coalition (HDC) to help mend the political divide in the United States, by bringing Republicans and Democrats donors together to address the societal problems that have been ignored, and exacerbated, as a result of the increasing divisiveness. Jonah believes that by creating communities to seek solutions together to problem issues like plastics pollution, environmental damage, or even the need for a green, global currency, it will bring people closer, while accelerating the speed with which we can solve these problems.

Jonah strongly believes that getting youth involved in decision making along with adults offers a variety of benefits, especially at a time when people are so divided. One reason why young people are such a key leverage point for any social change strategy, he says, is because they can see the problems that aren't being addressed. They can see problem solvers who've gone stagnant, and become out of touch. Investing in young people becomes a positive investment in the future. "Until we fix the ways we are managing the global commons, there will continue to be problems in the future," Jonah says. "Until we can overcome the accountability gap of our current global governance system, these problems will only get worse, not better. We must engage with the next generation of youth leaders, to look with fresh eyes at these persistent problems. To help us find a solution, and lead us out."

Jonah's message to youth is simple. Celebrate inclusivity and diversity. Educate yourself about what issue you want to get involved in. "If you are working on climate change, learn what the current policy debates are all about," he says. "And set a goal to realize a change or innovation."

And of course, don't be afraid to practice Radical Inclusion—to reach out across borders, real and imagined, to form communities, and to work together with those communities to find answers. Jonah has dedicated his life to innovating precisely in this way: with the strength of the diverse, global community of social entrepreneurs he's brought together, let's hope he can inspire the next generation of youth leaders to innovate in a similarly daring way.

> *Philanthropy is commendable, but it must not*
> *cause the philanthropist to overlook*
> *the circumstances of economic injustice which*
> *make philanthropy necessary.*

Dr. Martin Luther King, Jr.

Call to Action: Engage with the growing community of youth philanthropists and social entrepreneurs Jonah is leading with NEXUS. Find out how you can get involved at https://nexusglobal.org/.

A SUSTAINABLE LEGACY OF BLUE INNOVATION
Henk Rogers
The Blue Planet Foundation
Hawaii

One day Henk Rogers was in the hospital recovery room, flipping through a newspaper. Just before he got to the last page, a tiny snippet alerted him that all of the coral in the world would be dead by the end of the century, from ocean acidification, which is caused, among other things, by the burning of fossil fuels. "This should be front-page news in Hawaii, not jammed in the back," Henk thought. That's when he realized that there were a lot of important things going on with climate change that people are just not aware of. "And if we don't do something, these things are going to happen."

Up until then, Henk had been best known as being the man who brought Tetris to the world. As a successful entrepreneur, he had spun off many profitable companies, including Blue Lava, which he sold for $137 million in 2005. But he almost didn't have the chance to enjoy the fruits of his labor. A month later, the excitement of this life-changing business deal came to a screeching halt.

On that fateful day, Henk woke up to find himself lying in the back of an ambulance, with a 100 percent blockage of the "widow-maker," the largest artery in the heart. "I'm not going, I still have stuff to do," he said.

Over the next couple of weeks, he came up with a "bucket list" of sorts that asked the question, What are my missions in life? "Up to that point in my life, all I'd done was get people to play games and make some money," he says. "In the ambulance that day, I realized I hadn't really done anything to justify my existence. When I do leave this planet, I want my legacy to be as someone who made the world a better place. I didn't know exactly how to do that in the moment. But I decided to dedicate the rest of my days to doing just that."

And after reading that brief article about coral in the recovery room, Henk says, "I understood what my mission #1 was. And the rest is history."

Henk started the Blue Planet Foundation to drive change, empower youth, and inspire action to help power the transition to 100 percent clean energy in Hawaii. He believes that a future entirely free from fossil fuels is possible, and he hopes to act as a model for global change. Perhaps what makes Henk's contributions doubly important is the fact that he has the technical know-how to take longstanding inefficiencies in the energy sector that are contributing to climate change, and innovate green solutions to this problem.

When Blue Planet was first starting out, Henk sat on a panel to discuss the future of energy in Hawaii. "I announced that Blue Planet's plan was to achieve 100% renewable energy in Hawaii by 2045. An expert from the university sitting next to me said that it was impossible and gave some reasons. I said 'Well, I'm not as smart as this researcher, so I'm going to do it anyway.'"

They started with some simple local outreach efforts. They organized elementary school children who went door to door to exchange 300,000 old light bulbs with residents, for new, energy-efficient bulbs. They even had junior high school students draw pictures on sidewalk to show where high tide would reach in a one-meter rise in sea level.

Soon, Henk's work gained wide-ranging support from the Hawaiian community at large, and even gained attention at the state level. His work was integral in implementing Hawaii's mandate of achieving 100 percent renewable energy by 2045 - which has made Hawaii the first state to do so.

Now came the tricky part, Henk says: How do we do it? "I knew I had to clean my own room before I could ask that of other people. And Hawaii is my 'room.'"

Henk worked to pass a bill that incentivizes the solar industry and gives rebates for rooftop solar installations. It was estimated that this would produce about 30 megawatts of renewable power. But within a few years, the program had actually led to the production of 300 megawatts, which created another problem: the grid couldn't handle that much intermittent power.

"So, at my Energy Lab on my Pu'u Wa'awa'a Ranch, we got to work on how to become energy independent. Part of the solution was to make hydrogen using the excess energy our solar panels produce on sunny days," Henk says. "Hawaii spends $5 billion a year on oil for only 1.5 million people. If we can implement the energy independence strategies we have developed at my ranch, just think of how much money Hawaii could save by switching to renewable energy." Henk's associates are even working on building five hydrogen fuel stations in Hawaii, to further boost the state's energy independence.

Henk's journey to becoming a leader in Hawaiian sustainability can't be told without mentioning his daughters, Maya and Julie, who not only inspired him, but have taken up his legacy as their own. "Maya has always been the business- minded one, even before she got involved with Blue Planet Software, which is the company I set up," Henk says. He recalls going to Pepperdine, where he was invited to speak to Maya's business class. "I got there ten minutes early, listened to a presentation, and told the class I had learned more just then than I'd learned in my whole career. I knew nothing when I started. And it was then I realized just how far ahead of us the youth are today."

Being the oldest child, Maya had always shown that instinct to lead. "When I realized that she could handle it better than I ever could, I let her take the reins of the company," Henk says. What he didn't anticipate was Maya being able to take their shared passion for sustainability and spin off yet another profitable business. She now runs the incredibly successful Blue Startups, which is an incubator for blue technology companies. To date, it has launched more than 90 companies, including their first "unicorn" in Volta, which operates electric charging stations in shopping centers. It is set to go public with a valuation of over $1 billion.

Julie took a less traditional path. She spent a year in Bhutan working at the Gross National Happiness Centre, and in Bali at the Green School. A number of her experiences at these forward-thinking institutions led her to believe that she could help change the whole way we approach sustainability. "Climate change is important," she says. "But it's just one of the things that needs to be fixed."

Now, at the Akahiao Nature Institute, Julie is educating the next generation of environmental leaders how to inspire others to have passion, understanding, and appreciation of the natural world around us. The Institute has had great success with its immersion programs, which allow kids who don't have a connection to nature to come and see what it's like to live sustainably. "Julie's been years ahead of the curve with her back-to-nature approach," Henk says. "What she's doing to change our outlook on climate change and sustainable living is as important as anything we are doing technologically. If the kids don't have a connection to nature, why would it matter to them to try and preserve it?"

Henk's message of encouragement for youth is as empowering and hopeful as he always is. "You may not realize it, but you have the power to change things in a huge way," he says. "Today, the battle is climate change -- and you can stop climate change. You can fix anything in the world if you put your mind to it. Don't let us adults stop you!" He is working now on an app that deals with energy, waste, nature, and intervention, designed to help bridge the gap between older and younger people, and get them working together on issues of sustainability.

With their intergenerational approach to combating climate change, Henk, Maya, and Julie are working to shape Hawaii's and America's blue future. "Our target 2045 Sustainable Development goals are already set at the UN," Henk says. "But we believe that in 2030-2045 we have to focus on the Regenerative Development goals. It can't just be about sustainable living. We need to fix the damage that we've done. And I think we can."

Surely we have a responsibility to leave for
future generations
a planet that is healthy and habitable
by all species.

Sir David Attenborough

Call to Action: To get involved with the Blue Planet Foundation and its many innovative projects shaping Hawaii's blue future, please visit https://blueplanetfoundation.org .

BUILDING A SUSTAINABLE BUSINESS ECOSYSTEM
Elliot Hoffman
REVSustainability
San Francisco, California

Elliot Hoffman's motto, "Cooperation = Power," has been etched in his mind ever since he was a child growing up in the Amalgamated housing cooperative in New York City, in the Bronx. These words were scrawled on the wall of the local electric power plant that Elliot passed by on his way to school. "Being a cooperative human being is just built into my DNA," he says. It was a way of life for him and his brother and sister, who were raised by a single mom on a razor-tight budget after his father's life was tragically cut short when Elliot was seven years old. "My mother always told us that our lives should never be solely about making a lot of money. Life was really about building a community and being a good human being. It was about caring for your community and others."

Elliot found his soulmate in his wife Gail. "She was raised with the same philosophy. So when we decided to go into business with sustainability and social responsibility in mind, it was a match made in heaven." Together, they founded the dessert company Just Desserts in San Francisco in 1974. By reducing waste and increasing efficiencies in water, heating, and electricity, their company saved money. "We just didn't want to waste anything. It was ingrained in us."

As CEO of the company, Elliot established himself as a pioneer in the sustainable business movement at a time when few were thinking this way. Over time, his leadership has influenced other companies in the San Francisco Chamber of Commerce as well as other business associations in California and across the country.

Elliot and Gail were deeply influenced by the environmental, civil rights, and women's movements of the 1960s; they committed themselves to "being the change" for good they'd admired in those who'd been so courageous. "While sustainability was always the goal, we also asked ourselves what kind of a workplace we wanted to create. At our company, we embraced a whole different set of values. Chief among them was joining with others to enact social change."

With his mantra of Cooperation = Power, Elliot joined the Social Ventures Network to align with like-minded people nationally who were committed to investing in a more equitable and just society. "It was all about embedding positive social impact into your business and working for social and environmental change," he says. He learned a lot about melding business with social ventures from such thought leaders as Ben Cohen and Jerry Greenfield of Ben & Jerry's, and Matt Parsky of Trillium. Inspired by these dynamic business leaders, Elliot launched his own social venture project in the vacant one-acre lot behind Just Desserts. The Garden Project gave former prisoners an opportunity to rehabilitate themselves by growing food that fed the homeless. Over a period of nine years, Elliot hired more than 30 former prisoners for this project.

As Elliot's innovative ideas caught on, he was invited to help shape the country's first sustainable business management degree at the Presidio School of Management. "The Board really believed we could move the business world toward a more sustainable way of operating, and our students did too. We knew the environment was being destroyed, and that the climate would become a huge deal in the near term. We saw ourselves as training future sustainable leaders to lead the way not only in a business sense, but in regard to social issues. I really always believed that business could be a very positive vehicle for social change."

Always eager to engage others, Elliot and a team of business friends launched the New Voice of Business, to advocate on behalf of sustainable businesses. He led a group of influential CEOs in the San Francisco Bay area to rally together to lobby for much-needed solar legislation in California. And he combined his listening skills and visionary approach with his business savvy to frame the initiative in such a way that it would attract forward-thinking businesses. In what became the largest solar power initiative in the history of the country, Elliot helped launch a solar rebate program (California Solar Initiative - CSI) that installed 1 million solar roofs in California in seven years. Following on the heels of the CSI, Elliot helped to bring the same new voices of business to support passage of AB 32 - the California Global Warming Solutions Act of 2006. To date, it is the only legislated regulatory global warming initiative in the United States, and Elliot takes great pride in having found a way for the new voices of business that had gone unheard for so long to finally be heard.

Emboldened with this victory, Elliot felt that a healthier way of doing business had proven itself to be something the community at large wanted. But he knew that this new coalition of sustainability-minded businesses was only the beginning. Through AB32, CEOs had just made a huge impact on the environmental health of the state of California. Now he wondered, "What kind of an impact could 400 CEOs make?"

In 2013, Elliot founded REV, an enterprise meant to guide small and midsize companies how to transition to a more just and sustainable way of operating. REV strives to accelerate the transformation of the marketplace to a new mindset of sustainability, energy efficiency, resource productivity, and climate resilience by providing education in sustainability and supporting tools for businesses, organizations, and communities. REV's Sustainability Circle Program hosts employees from businesses over a six-month period and provides them with curriculum, coaches, experts, and action plans to implement sustainable changes. "We want to destroy the myth that sustainability is a cost. If I can show companies that they can do good for the environment and keep money in their pockets through the process, then we can have businesses start picking up the slack they should have picked up decades ago, on a large scale."

To date, more than 400 companies have completed REV's Sustainability Circle Program. Corporations that go through this program substantially reduce their use of electricity, water, therms, and also reduce their CO_2 footprints. The average projected savings REV has generated for businesses who opt into this program is more than $316,000 a year. Among those who have partnered with REV to help support the program are PG&E, SDG&E, Southern California Gas, and Southern California Edison.

For young people who are interested in starting a business, Elliot encourages them to do so with a sustainable outlook both because it's what's right *and* because it's what's profitable. "If you want to attract top talent to come into your company to grow for the future, you'd better be on this path," he says. "Young people know their future is dependent upon the quality and the health of our communities, our environment and our economic engines. If your company is not doing these forward-looking things, like seeking diversity and an inclusive culture, which are all connected with sustainability, it won't attract the best and the brightest."

As he always has, Elliot believes in being vocal about what you believe in and using that voice to build shared communities. "I urge young people to find out where there are others that care about sustainability and climate in your community and play together. Get together for lunch. Just talk about this stuff. And take action. People on this journey are very happy in general to share their ideas. Participate and learn as a community. Sustainability, climate, and regeneration are three sides of a triangle that are coming together. We are in a climate emergency. It's time we start working towards solutions with all three of them in mind." And if there's one message that Elliot hopes youth will heed more than any other, it's this: COOPERATION = POWER.

When we face a problem like global warming,
and you understand that the biggest impacts
on global warming come from business and
industry, business needs to take a leading role.

Ben Cohen & Jerry Greenfield

Call to Action: To get your business involved in the Sustainability Circles Program, check out REV Sustainability at www.revsustainability.com.

CREATING MISSION-DRIVEN COMPANIES
David Dietz
SUPR
New York City, USA

David Dietz likes to be where change is happening, and where he can make a difference. As a budding journalist in the early 2010's, he had the rare opportunity to be a witness to history in the making with the Arab Spring. When David embarked on a journey to the Middle East he was on the ground for critical moments as they were happening in Tunisia, Egypt, Libya, Lebanon, Syria, and Bahrain.

These six countries were desperately seeking relief from poverty, as well as freedom from the oppressive, corrupt regimes. Uprisings, antigovernment protests, and rebellions were spreading across the Arab world. David knew this assignment would require some grit, and would even mean facing some danger, in order to be on the ground where change was really happening.

Among the many stories David wrote, one touched him deeply, beyond the complicated geopolitics of the moment. He was assigned to write a "puff piece" on the Egyptian cotton industry, known as the finest, most luxurious cotton in the world. At first, it seemed like an unimportant story – a page-filler that on the surface seemed unlike the kind of political story he usually sought out. But as he began his research, he learned about the harmful industrial agricultural practices that were being used in the Egyptian cotton industry, and the devastating toll these practices were having on the health of the farmers. This discovery changed the trajectory of David's professional life almost immediately.

It's well known that the gas and oil industries are contributing to our current environmental crisis, but with cotton, there is no apparent evidence of pollution -- no puffs of smoke coming from exhaust pipes that we can easily see or smell. And yet, "75 percent of the farmers I spoke with had cancer from the incredibly toxic pesticides being used," says David. "As I dug into the story more, I discovered that cotton was the second dirtiest industry in the world, right after oil and gas."

Cotton is a crop grown from the earth like any vegetable or fruit, and it has all of the dangerous pesticides, herbicides, fungicides, insecticides, and other chemicals used in the agricultural production process. But it is not simply harvested and then sent to stores to be consumed, like tomatoes or carrots. Cotton also has a massive *manufacturing* footprint, processes during which dyes, solvents, and all other kinds of chemical treatments are used, which can make it particularly toxic. Some estimates state that the average T-shirt has more than 40 kinds of chemicals that the FDA considers harmful – and these chemicals have been found in alarming numbers in the breast-milk of new mothers around the world.

"When I saw the toll this process was taking on human lives, and on the environment; and that it was being ignored by everyone else in the region, I realized I didn't just want to report on this urgent story," says David. "I really wanted to *do* something about it. I wanted to make a change."

To understand the scale of the cotton industry and its environmental impact, in 2019, there were nearly 14 million acres of cotton fields planted in the U.S. alone. This yields roughly 800 pounds per acre, all of which has been chemically treated in the fields, and then will be treated again in the manufacturing process, as it is worked into textiles. In Egypt, in 2019, there were roughly 350,000 bales of cotton produced, each of which contains 480 pounds of cotton.

David's first article about the cotton industry caused quite a stir. And the more he wrote about it, the more entrepreneurs who had similar concerns about the cotton industry reached out to him. Mostly, they reached out to thank him for highlighting this issue. Frequently, they wanted to spread the word about businesses in the fashion industry that were using ethically and environmentally conscious practices.

For his next adventure, David decided to build a socially conscious company. So he returned home to the U.S. and started his first company, Modavanti, an online boutique for ethical fashion brands. "My Mom was happy I was coming home, since the Middle East was dangerous," David says. "However, when I told her I was planning to start a fashion company, she was pretty confused. I'd never been into fashion. And in the beginning, I really didn't know anything about fashion. In fact, I was known for my rumpled journalist look," he says with a laugh.

To David, it didn't matter *what* industry he worked in, or what people thought about his new venture. What mattered to him was that he could create a mission-driven company, one that would tell the story of entrepreneurs that are running businesses the right way.

After receiving a massive amount of support from ethical fashion companies around the world, he was invited to speak at the United Nations about the need for sustainable fashion. "Through this process, I really learned about the power of community," he says. "I learned that if you share your story, and you live with passion and conviction, people will come along for the ride with you."

For six years, David grew Modavanti; then he sold it because he wanted to expand his social entrepreneurship ventures. "I, and so many others, feel the need to push the boundaries and keep going," he says. "We must never get complacent with what we've accomplished. So many challenges lay ahead of us. With a strong community, we can impact change in a positive way for everyone." To explain his unique business ventures, David likes to quote a favorite television character, Sam Seaborn of *The West Wing*: "The history of man is hung on the timeline of exploration, and this is what is next."

At Modavanti, David had built partnerships with several brands that were addressing the issues of plastic waste, recycling, and upcycling plastic from beaches and waterways. He realized that with a little bit of entrepreneurial know-how, he could leverage this community for the next level of good. This is when David decided to join Nexus, where a vast network of like-minded, socially conscious entrepreneurs were on the forefront of enacting precisely this type of approach. David went on to lead the sustainable fashion segment at the Nexus Summit, where he was embraced by the community, offered support in a variety of ways, and was setup with mentorship opportunities from the veterans in the space. He was encouraged to continue tackling larger and more nuanced sustainability issues by this strong community he'd found, and he credits this support as having a great impact on his continued success.

As Director of Impact Initiatives at Nexus, David, with the increasing support of the community, decided to take on one of the most pressing sustinability issues of our time – plastic waste. So, in 2020 he launched his new venture, SUPR, with the purpose of making an impact on the reduction of single-use plastic products. To realize his ambitious goal, SUPR partnered with Accenture and Oceanic Global, to develop a master plan for how professional sports teams can transform their supply chains to become plastic-free.

All of David's ventures are done with a dual purpose: to introduce sustainability concepts to a wider, and younger, audience. Since so many people around the world are influenced by sports, David believes that if organizations like SUPR can get cultural leaders to get vocal about social responsibility, it can go a long way towards making a healthier, more sustainable world.

In 2020, the Miami Dolphins hosted the Superbowl for the first time in 10 years. David was thrilled that the Dolphins went 99.4 percent plastic free for the Big Game, implementing many of SUPR's plastic free solutions.

Since then five teams have made the pledge, and have committed to making changes in their supply chains and practices to reduce plastics. One team has even begun recycling Coke bottles and turning them into athletic wear for stadium employees.

David knows that we are reliant on the next generation to come up with the solutions to save the planet.

For youth who want to get involved with such work, he says, "It's not going to be easy. But nothing that's worthwhile is: it's important not be dissuaded by the challenges that lay ahead of us. They are both wide and far-reaching." He wants young entrepreneurs to understand that creating a mission-driven business isn't going to harm their chances of success. "In the near future, businesses with a social, environmental, or justice-related mission will be the ones leading the way," he says. "Saving the planet and helping others will be part and parcel of successful businesses. And since we are at such a tipping point, I not only believe it's economically the correct move –I believe it is our *obligation* to do so."

David knows from where he speaks. He has truly "lived the change" he wanted to see, by dedicating his professional life to walking a noble, restorative path. Anyone -- including his Mom, who is now a believer -- should be proud to follow him down that path.

Do your little bit of good where you are;
it's those little bits of good put together that
overwhelm the world.

Archbishop Desmond Tutu

Call to Action: Encourage your sports teams to take the SUPR's Plastic Free Pledge to reduce plastic pollution. Spread the word about SUPR https://www.pledgesupr.com/pledge .

CREATING A NEW SOCIAL CONTRACT
Sam Jacobs
Resource Generation
New York, New York

Sam Jacobs is a philanthropic activist committed to ending inequality. He has the highest of hopes – to truly change the way we think about wealth redistribution. Coming from a long line of philanthropists, this is something Sam understands well.

"My grandpa founded a multinational tech firm and accumulated a lot of wealth. My dad followed in his footsteps. That created a childhood for me with a lot of privilege. Every opportunity was available to us. I went to a great private school in San Diego. I grew up in a beautiful home with a view of the ocean. It was a picture-perfect childhood."

Through his travels, Sam learned early on that he was privileged, and his parents reminded him every step of the way. "I knew I had a privileged position in the world. And because of that, I had a great responsibility too," he explains. "That sort of wealth doesn't come from nowhere. It's only possible because of the community."

Sam's grandparents were influential philanthropists, and their giving planted a similar seed in him. They supported all kinds of cultural institutions, museums, universities, and arts programs. And one Chanukah, they shifted the focus of their giving to Sam.

"When I was 18 my grandparents gave me some money to give to charities of my choice," Sam explains. "This is when I really started thinking seriously about philanthropy. At first I was pretty overwhelmed. It was a lot of responsibility! There were so many questions. Who deserves my help? What causes are worthy of addressing? Mainly, I wondered, what were my values as a donor?"

At the same time, the Occupy Wall St. movement was unfolding. Sam's English teacher, Mr. Hendrickson, was teaching a class called the Art of Protest. He brought the class to downtown San Diego, where for the first time Sam could really see the way people were feeling about – and suffering from – income inequality.

"It really affected me," says Sam. "It made me wonder what were the root causes of this inequality. And how do we combat them?" Sam admits, "It took me a long time to get a hold on that," he says, adding, "I'd been shielded and protected. After a lot of deliberation, I realized something important. Despite my elite education, I wasn't actually in the best position to solve these problems. Actually, the solution should come from the people who'd been dealt the short end of the stick. That's when I realized that what I really wanted to do was to take the money I'd been given, and help lead people affected by economic inequality out of their situation. And I also wanted to invest it, and allow those resources to build lasting political power...So I decided to unite the wealthy, and towards a transformative common goal: upending inequality."

A few years later, Sam found the missing piece of this puzzle at Resource Generation (RG). RG is a community of young people with wealth and/ or class privilege who are committed to a more equitable distribution of wealth, land, and power.

"At RG I finally found people doing really powerful work in philanthropy," Sam says. "I met young people with wealth, in a similar situation to mine, which helped me combat feelings of isolation. And we were fighting on important fronts. This was important for me."

Now Sam works with RG hosting workshops, learning exchanges, and meeting groups where people can get together, and share feelings about their class and wealth. "It's important to have a shared space with mutual understanding," Sam says. "We nurture strong accountability relationships. It's crucial to be open and transparent with partners who don't come from wealthy backgrounds too. Honesty has to be key. We're so often discouraged from talking about these things that we get all twisted up inside about what wealth is for, and what it's supposed to do."

That's why Sam signed the RG's Giving Pledge. This is a commitment to giving a significant portion of your money to social justice movements over a set period of time. Sam hopes that by setting an example by giving to Grassroots International and Third Wave Fund, and creating funds like the Works in Progress Fund, he can inspire others with wealth to get on board and support these causes.

Sam's work isn't exclusively philanthropic. He's involved with a variety of non-profit organizations that fight against disparities in social, economic, and criminal justice. In the fight for housing justice, Sam has partnered with the New York chapter of the Right to the City Alliance

(RTTC). With RTTC, one of Sam's areas of focus is helping communities respond to gentrification, and to halt the resulting displacement of low-income people, people of color, LGBTQ people, marginalized communities, and others from their neighborhoods. "Everyone has the right to dignified and affordable housing," Sam says. "We work in support of tenants' rights. And we try to ensure that alternative housing is available, by buying land and building affordable housing. It's a problem a lot of well-off people overlook. But it's important."

Sam is works diligently to support green advocacy during Earth Week. In April 2020 he will be guiding rallies in support of the Green New Deal, leading acts of civil disobedience, and directing volunteers.

Sam has also been closely involved with the NBA (National Basketball Association). It started with a family connection to the Sacramento Kings, whose larger community was in turmoil. In March of 2018, the Sacramento community was deeply affected by the tragic shooting death of Stephon Clark, an unarmed black man who was shot in his own backyard. Sam decided that he could use his Works in Progress Fund to partner with the NBA, and help bring some semblance of healing to the community.

In the wake of this tragedy, Sam partnered with the team, who hosted the Team Up For Change Summit. The goal of this Summit was to address social injustice, and create partnerships with law enforcement and the community to aid in increase police accountability. The Summit resulted in more than $50,000 in scholarship pledges, to be awarded by the Sacramento Police Foundation Criminal Justice Magnet School Academy and the Sierra Health Foundation.

In 2019, Team Up For Change expanded to include the Milwaukee Bucks, and support of cultural figures, including Kida the Great, and seven-time Grammy award winning rapper, songwriter, and producer Antwan "Big Boi" Patton. With such a positive response, Sam hopes to continue his involvement with the Summit for years to come.

While Sam has accomplished some amazing things with his philanthropy and his community involvement, he doesn't want other young people to feel overwhelmed at the idea of getting involved. "People might say that you are inexperienced, or that you don't know the way the world works," Sam says, adding, "Just remember -- -we get to decide, together, how the world is going to work in the future. We, as young people, are really powerful, and always have been."

For young people with wealth, Sam had a similarly uplifting message.

"It's important to think about the messages we've received about managing money, and think forward. So much we're told about money is about safety, or security. Or the ability to use your money to get into a good school, to get a good job, and to make more money. Everything is in the service of money — not the community. That sort of story really covers up the fact that we are the most safe, secure, and able to flourish, when we are in deep community, and interdependent on each other. That's not to say that wealth is a bad thing: it's not. Neither is creating wealth. I just want everyone to have access to the same options that I did. And we can make that kind of American dream possible for anyone. It's just going to take those with wealth sharing that prosperity much more equally than we do now."

Sam will continue to give all that he can to issues of social justice, great and small. But he stresses that it's important to understand that giving isn't just about dollars and cents. It's a mindset. It's a way of life. And as far as Sam is concerned, being a giver is the only way to fully live one's life.

Wealth is not to feed our egos but to feed the hungry and to help people help themselves.

Andrew Carnegie

Call to Action: Invite your friends to join Resource Generation - and take the RG Giving Pledge: https://resourcegeneration.org/contact/

FOR TOMORROW'S CHILD:
AN ENVIRONMENTAL EPIPHANY
John Lanier
Ray Anderson Foundation
Atlanta, Georgia

John Lanier recalls an anecdote from his youth that has shaped his leadership of the Ray C. Anderson Foundation to this very day. "One day I was thinking about what to do, what path to go down, and I had this memory of my grandfather. I was just 18. On my way to visit my grandfather, I came up with a question I wanted to ask him, to show him I'd really been thinking about sustainability. When I got there I asked, 'If you could wave a magic wand and make one of the world's environmental problems go away, what would it be?' Without hesitation, he answered, 'Global warming.' Even then, in 2004, the science was clear -- and it's even more clear today. Today, 17 years later, the majority of my work is in the climate space. It was a seed that was planted back then, and it has become the purpose of my life to work on reversing global warming. And I have my grandfather to thank for that."

Ray C. Anderson, "The Greenest CEO in America," often shared the story of how he had *his* environmental epiphany. "What is Interface doing to help the environment?" a customer had asked one of the company's sales reps one day. "Complying with environmental law," he had answered.

But when Ray was told about this exchange, although he knew it was an *accurate* response, he realized it wasn't actually a very good answer. He felt that Interface could do better than that.

By that time, Interface was a multinational manufacturing powerhouse leading the modular carpeting industry. There was no real reason for Anderson to risk his position at the top, and he hadn't intended to -- until that question from a conscientious customer came to his attention, and caused him to think again.

Ray Anderson prided himself on being a thoughtful and intellectually curious man. He knew it was what had allowed him to have such success in business. So when it came time to look for a better answer to the customer's challenging question, he approached it with that self-same curiosity. He picked up a book, *The Ecology of Commerce,* by Paul Hawken. And by the time he had finished reading it, he realized that reading that book was going to change the trajectory of his life.

Anderson famously described his epiphany as a "spear-in-the-chest moment." He later said that reading *The Ecology of Commerce* had as good as convicted him as being a plunderer of the earth. From that point on, he worked desperately to drive the necessary innovations that would allow his publicly traded company to take a pledge of sustainability, and set the stage for a new way forward in the realm of sustainable business practices.

For him, the work was never about a personal legacy. He believed wholeheartedly that future generations *must* be able to benefit from businessmen solving the environmental challenges of the day. He was laser-focused on the importance of the *continuity* of the work he was doing. And his "North Star" was always "I'm doing this for the generation to come, for tomorrow's child."

Today, his grandson John Lanier carries on his grandfather's legacy through the Ray C. Anderson Foundation, which Ray endowed upon his passing in 2011. Anderson left his family without a specific directive, aside from the understanding that the endowment was to be used to serve the greater good. John feels that this open-endedness was a gift. "It put the onus on us as a family to carve out our own niche in sustainability."

But he started by studying his grandfather's approach to making Interface an environmentally friendly business.

Ray Anderson had started by working to change the company culture internally, which was an uphill battle. As he announced changes, employees often wondered if this was just another "flavor of the month" from the top. "Aren't we supposed to be in the business of making carpets?" they sometimes grumbled. The substantive changes their boss was introducing took a lot of convincing. But he knew that his job wasn't just to describe *what* Interface was doing: he had to explain *why*. He believed that if his employees understood the need for widescale change in manufacturing on a global scale, they would eventually come around. And slowly, but surely, they did.

After a few years, Interface was ready to do the work they were aspiring towards: but what that work was for, exactly, wasn't defined. Ray was adamant that Interface *would become* a sustainable company, *and* that they would "do no harm."

To do that, he knew that they needed to first ask the question, "What are the ways in which a manufacturing company does harm?"

Ray Anderson played a pivotal role in defining what sustainability in manufacturing actually is. In doing so, he tasked Interface with scaling what he called the "7 fronts of Mt. Sustainability."

1. Achieve zero waste.
2. Produce only benign emissions into the environment.
3. Be powered entirely by renewable energy.
4. Develop a closed-loop manufacturing process.
5. Achieve resource-efficient transportation of people and products.
6. Engage stakeholders, including the supply chains and customer base, to minimize negative impacts.
7. Look for ways to redesign commerce that incentivize positive environmental and social outcomes.

Amazingly, and to the surprise of the many skeptics in his own company and beyond, Interface actually became a significantly *more* profitable enterprise for taking this course of action. Ray's work had laid bare the persistent myth that a business could not pursue both profitability and environmental ends concurrently. The four components of his model for increasing profitability through the expansion of sustainability efforts, which still stand today, are: 1. Efficiency 2. Innovation 3. Culture Change and 4. Goodwill.

If there is a place to look at just how deeply Ray C. Anderson impacted the people who took up his cause, perhaps his legacy was best captured in a poem by longtime Interface employee Glenn Thomas, which was read by Anderson at his TED Talk in 2009.

Tomorrow's Child

Without a name; an unseen face
and knowing not your time nor place,
Tomorrow's Child, though yet unborn
I met you first last Tuesday morn.

A wise friend introduced us two,
and through his shining point of view
I saw a day that you would see;
a day for you, but not for me.

Knowing you has changed my thinking
for I never had an inkling
That perhaps the things I do
might someday, somehow, threaten you.

Tomorrow's Child, my daughter/son
I'm afraid I've just begun
To think of you and of your good,
though always having known I should.

Begin I will to weigh the cost
of what I squander; what is lost
If ever I forget that you
will someday come to live here too.

© Glenn C. Thomas 1996

Used by permission of the Ray C. Anderson Foundation

Intent on educating the next generation of environmental businessmen and women, the Ray C. Anderson Foundation's first major undertaking was to establish the Ray C. Anderson Center for Sustainable Business at Georgia Tech. "It took my grandfather until he was 60 to figure this thing out. We wanted to make sure our up-and-coming leaders don't have to wait so long," John Lanier says. Next, the Foundation developed a partnership with The Biomimicry Institute to support entrepreneurs who are utilizing biomimicry in their startups.

To honor his grandfather's legacy, John has also helped to launch Drawdown Georgia, an initiative inspired by Paul Hawken's seminal 2017 book, *Drawdown*. This initiative is addressing the most substantive climate solutions for the state of Georgia. Its ultimate goal is to achieve carbon neutrality for the entire state, and to bring climate solutions to scale.

And it's not just John carrying on his grandfather's legacy: the whole family is involved. Ray's five grandchildren and their spouses formed the Foundation's NextGen Committee to invest in projects geared toward making the world a better place for "Tomorrow's Child." The committee funds programs in conservation and climate change education, urban agriculture, agroforestry, and grassroots solutions to address climate change challenges in Indigenous communities.

For today's young people who want to carry on a legacy of sustainability,

John's message is simple. "Educate yourself with a passion," he says. "Our greatest hope is for the youth to understand that they have to be experts about the challenges they want to solve. It's a lot of work. But I think they are just the generation to do it. And I look forward to seeing their successes."

[The poem] Tomorrow's Child has spoken to me with one simple but profound message, which I share with you...we are each part of the web of life and we have a choice to make during our brief visit to this beautiful planet: to hurt it or to help it...it's your call.

Ray C. Anderson

Call to Action: To learn more about the Ray C. Anderson Foundation, visit https://www.raycandersonfoundation.org/nextgen/.

HEALTHIER SKIN WITH TRUE BOTANICALS
Hillary Peterson
Mill Valley, California

Growing up in Pasadena, Hillary Peterson was aware of the role that toxic environments could have on one's health. Living just outside of Los Angeles, she remembers the air pollution that often lingered over the city. "The smog was so bad that on many days, we couldn't play sports outside after school. I'd go home and have to stay inside, and I remember my parents saying that it was so harmful, wondering if we should move away. Living near the ocean, plastic pollution was also on the top of my mind."

When she was just 32 years old, Hillary's world came to a screeching halt when she was diagnosed with thyroid cancer. "I was perplexed, because I had always gone to great lengths to live a healthy lifestyle. I ate organic foods, meditated, spent my free time in nature and at the ocean." As a young mother of twins, she was desperate to discover what could have led to her health crisis so that she could protect her children. "I was so concerned," she says. "I knew that if this could happen to me, it could happen to anyone." Thinking back to her own childhood, she began to wonder if her unhealthy environment had contributed to her disease.

Hillary was shocked to hear on an NPR radio program about a study by the Environmental Working Group that had found that toxic chemicals found in women's personal care products were being found in their babies' blood. "When I researched endocrine-disrupting chemicals, I discovered they were in all of the products I was buying to look and feel beautiful. How could the beauty industry be selling products with these toxins in them to the people they are claiming to want to help look and *feel* better?"

With a sense of both indignance and determination, Hillary embarked on a mission to fill the gap that the industry was so callously ignoring. That is how, and why, she began True Botanicals -- a non-toxic beauty enterprise "to give people the chance to look and feel better because they were using a product that was actually making their skin *healthier*." With Hillary's rigorous dedication to using non-toxic ingredients and employing sustainable business practices, True Botanicals quickly became a guidepost for the cosmetics industry. Because of her unflinching standards, she has gained the support of a wide range of environmental advocates and celebrities like Laura Dern and Olivia Wilde.

"When I opened up my email to see a message from Laura Dern, I was floored!" Hillary says. "She loves our products, and our story, and what we stand for." As it turns out, Laura grew up near Hillary: she too had experienced the smog and other kinds of pollution and saw how they were impacting children's health. This is the reason she has always used her platform to lead on important environmental issues. "It really matters to have people with a reach stand up for causes that empower a sustainable future," Hillary says. "Laura has helped expand the reach of True Botanicals with all the dynamism I could've expected, and more."

For Laura Dern, the issues a leader and her company embody are just as important as the integrity of the product itself. "It's one thing for me to support this sustainable company as a customer, but it's another thing to then meet Hillary, and discover the origin story of the company, and the passion that comes with wanting to make products that are good for you, good for your children, good for the planet -- and to care deeply about it. I was interested in continuing the story," Laura says. "As women, and as activists, we're working to show people that you can use your voice to be true, to live with an authentic story and not hide behind shame -- which is a perfect parallel to wanting to serve people with a company. What we're all doing is leading with the truth."

Hillary credits the flourishing of True Botanicals to the authenticity of their people, process, and products, which she constantly puts to the test. Every product at True Botanicals is certified by Made Safe® certified, a nonprofit that screens products against a list of harmful chemical ingredients like behavioral, developmental, reproductive, and neuro toxins; carcinogens, endocrine disruptors, fire retardants, heavy metals, pesticides, toxic solvents, and harmful volatile organic compounds (VOCs). True Botanicals has the distinction of being the first entire cosmetic line of products to have the Made Safe® certification. Hillary is proud that her company is also Leaping Bunny certified, the gold standard for cruelty-free, non-animal testing in all stages of its product development.

Sourcing sustainable ingredients is another important guiding principal for Hillary, and to achieve this she works with a large network of entrepreneurs with a similar worldview, who lift one another up through collaboration and education. "Whether it's Birdsong Herb Farm from Vermont, and their organic calendula, or Hudson Hemp from

New York, and the oils from their regenerative farm, we source from a healthy, organic, regenerative cycle, and our products reflect that ethos. This is how you build communities. By supporting the businesses out there that are doing the right thing, and educating those that want to join. There are more than you might think. I urge everybody to pitch in. It all makes a difference."

Hillary hopes True Botanicals can continue to influence leaders in the cosmetics industry, as other sustainable pioneers have done in their industries. She draws inspiration from leaders like Zach Bush of Farmer's Footprint, who works to spread awareness of regenerative farming practices. "Zach says he is not concerned about fixing conventional farming, because it's a dinosaur going by the wayside," she says. "Regenerative farming is the movement of the future, and that's where he can make an impact, so that's what he is doing. At True Botanicals, we are about showing a better way forward and how it can be done profitably. That is our important work. If conventional beauty product companies don't want to be obsolete, over time they will have to adapt to what we are doing."

What makes Hillary so sure that her stance is sound is the demand for just and sustainable cosmetics from consumers themselves. "Our industry has a term for our highly educated consumer base: 'skintellectuals'," she says. "With such widescale concern about the health and safety of the cosmetics we use, there is no question that in the coming years, eventually 'clean' will be the new standard across the board. It will not be the exception, but the rule. And I will be ecstatic to have played a role toward creating a more balanced, and healthy cosmetics ecosystem."

It has now been 25 years since that life-changing event when Hillary was diagnosed with cancer. While she needs to take synthetic thyroid every day, she says there is no doubt that the biggest impact her diagnosis had was on her life path and the opportunity to create a meaningful role as the founder of True Botanicals. "My twins are now 26, and are both passionately working to have an impact of their own, my son as an officer in the Marines, learning all that he can about mentorship and leadership, and my daughter as a staff editor at the New York Times, telling stories that must be told. And our younger daughter is studying neuroscience in the hopes of attending medical school. My children and their peers give me so much confidence that a more thoughtful, sustainable future is within our reach."

For those looking to introduce sustainable measures into their businesses, Hillary offers some simple advice. "Wherever you are headed, it's always one step at a time. It's critical to just get started. Everything can't happen at once, and depending on the type and size of business you want to manage, your approach will be different. Even so, what is true for us is true for any business. *Any* business can analyze its processes and pursue the sustainable option: cut down on packaging, go organic, or root out the source of ingredients to ensure that the supply chain is just and regenerative. Every bit of good helps."

For youth who are interested in building a more sustainable future, Hillary knows the task at hand is a mighty one. "When you look at climate change, there are so many issues of great importance that face us today. I'm sure for the next generation, who are just getting their footing, this can feel completely overwhelming. I've learned that it can be easy to get weighed down by these challenges."

As great as the challenges might seem, she urges youth to focus on what they can do, because she knows they have the ability to do something extraordinary. "Whether it's through my professional work, or in my own personal journey, I focus on what's possible, and work to make it a reality. It feels like a really positive way to spend my time," she says. "So, when we find ourselves getting overwhelmed by challenges, it helps to shift our focus to possibilities. Seeing the possibilities is an important step that can lead us all to a more sustainable future."

For success, like happiness, cannot be pursued;
it must ensue, and it only does so as the
unintended side-effect of one's personal
dedication to a cause greater than oneself.

Viktor Frankl

Call to Action: Help Hillary inspire more businesses in the personal care industry to pursue sustainability by visiting https://truebotanicals.com.

ICE CREAM AND CLIMATE ACTION!
Ben Cohen
Ben & Jerry's Foundation
Vermont

When Ben met his friend Jerry in the seventh grade back in 1963, little did they know that together they were going to make the world a better place.

Born in Brooklyn, Ben Cohen grew up in a small town just east of New York City. In the twelfth grade he got his first job, and it held a clue to what his future would be: he became an ice cream man.

Ben went on to have a number of different jobs: he worked as a cashier at McDonald's, delivered pottery wheels to customers, and drove a cab. "I wanted to be a potter: I tried to make a living selling pottery," Ben says. "But no one would buy my pots."

Eventually he became a teacher at the Highland Community School, working with youth who suffered from mental illness. There he picked up his old passion. "Mostly I was making pottery with them," he remembers.

At about the same time, Ben and his old friend Jerry were making big plans. At first, they talked about starting a bagel business. Luckily for the world, the equipment needed for a bagel shop was far too expensive. So a new idea took shape: what about opening an ice cream business?

As he and Jerry were exploring this idea, Ben added a new activity to the curriculum at his school. "We started making ice cream together," he says. "I made a few batches with the kids; it was kind of an extracurricular thing."

Ben and Jerry realized that for their ice cream shop to be successful they should find a town with warm weather and college students. "But all the warm places already had homemade ice cream parlors," Ben says. "So we decided we'd go all the way up to Burlington, Vermont." They started their business in their garage, and they distinguished their brand by giving their flavors hip names and including extra-large chunks in the ice cream.

And their ice cream was a hit -- soon everyone in Burlington had heard about it, and wanted to buy it.

That was great, but as the company grew, Ben became increasingly aware of the environmental and social impact their company was having on their community. Social justice issues had been on Ben's mind since an encounter with the police he had in his college years. He had been arrested for smoking pot, but the police let him off the hook with a ticket for littering. A lucky turn of events that wouldn't have happened if Ben wasn't white.

"If I were Black, I probably would have been arrested, thrown into jail, and ended up with a criminal record," Ben said in a statement he made on the Black Lives Matter protests that erupted after the murder of George Floyd. "I never would have been able to get a bank loan or help from the SBA. The reality is there would never have been a Ben and Jerry's."

That incident back in college made Ben wonder who really has power in the United States. And how was that power being used? He came to an important conclusion: he who is silent consents. That is why Ben and Jerry's has always taken a clear stand on social justice issues. For example, in 2018 they introduced a new flavor called "Resist," with the claim, "This pint packs a powerful message under its lid: together, we can build a more just and equitable tomorrow."

The company is also engaged in calling for reform of the justice system: on their website, they urge visitors to sign petitions, and they also support movements on the ground. In St. Louis for example, Ben & Jerry's hit the road for one month, and sold 13,420 scoops of ice cream in support of a coalition that was working toward closing the St. Louis Workhouse Jail -- a jail where 90 percent of the inmates were not convicted of anything, but simply couldn't afford to post bail. In addition, 90 percent of these inmates were Black -- although people of color make up only 47 percent of the city's population.

In 2015, Ben & Jerry's also honorarily renamed their Chocolate Chip Cookie Dough ice cream to "I Dough, I Dough" to celebrate the Supreme Court's decision affirming the fundamental civil right of same sex couples to marry. But the company's commitment to equal rights for same-sex couples goes back to the very beginning of its history: as early as 1989, Ben & Jerry's was the first major employer in Vermont to offer health care benefits to the partners of their employees, including same-sex couples. Their commitment continues to this day: the Human Rights Campaign rates how well companies are doing with regard to protecting LGBTQ rights in the workplace, and in 2020 Ben & Jerry's scored an impressive 100/100.

There is, of course, a close connection between social and environmental issues. "Save our Swirled" is a delicious ice cream that was released in 2015 with a clear message, valid for both the ice cream and our planet: if it's melted, it's ruined!

"I became aware of what was happening to the environment when Earth Day happened for the first time," Ben says. Vermont prides itself on being one of the greenest states in the U.S. Ben knew that if they wanted to really change things for the better, they had to take a critical look at their own environmental impact.

So, to lower their carbon impact, Ben and Jerry installed a solar array at their factory in Waterbury, Vermont that produces enough energy to cover a third of the factory's demand. They also installed a bio-digester in their factory in Hellendoorn, in the Netherlands, that turns that waste into clean energy.

Back in 1984, when Ben & Jerry's established a public stock offering, their goal was to make the community the owners of the business; so they offered this opportunity to Vermont residents only. They also created the Ben & Jerry's Foundation. Ben made a statement of his personal commitment by donating 50,000 of his company shares to the Foundation, and challenged the board to donate an unprecedented 7.5 percent of their annual pretax profits to philanthropy. They started community programs, encouraged their employees to get involved in social change work, and supported grassroots initiatives on social and environmental justice around the country. Today their grant program awards about $2.5 million every year to organizations around the U.S. To make the process more transparent and representative, Ben and Jerry made another unusual decision: they decided their employees would be the ones to decide how this money was spent.

They also created the Ben & Jerry's PartnerShop program. They waived the normal franchise fees for Ben & Jerry's shops so that partner businesses that are independently owned by community-based nonprofit organizations could use the profits they made from selling ice cream to support youth and young adults by offering jobs and entrepreneurial training to those who might otherwise face unemployment. "We had this idea: have the nonprofit make the profit," Ben says.

Over the years, Ben & Jerry's has grown from a single local ice cream parlor into a global business. "When you are led by values, it doesn't cost your business, it helps it," says Ben. And he has some good advice for young people: "Do something that you are passionate about," he says.

For Ben, it is important to put worries on hold and take action. "The main thing is that people should start," he says. "So many times people don't start something because they feel like they don't have enough experience, or they don't know enough. I think it's just important to start really small; if what you're doing resonates with people, it will grow."

> *We don't have to engage in grand, heroic actions*
> *to participate in the process of change. Small*
> *acts, when multiplied by millions of people, can*
> *transform the world.*

Howard Zinn

Call to Action: Follow Ben & Jerry's https://twitter.com/benandjerrys Try their new ice cream: Pecan Resist! Pecan Resist supports four organizations that are working on the front lines of the peaceful resistance, building a world that supports their values.

LEARNING AS LEADERSHIP:
HUMANIZING BUSINESS
Lara and Claire Nuer
San Francisco and Paris

Lara Nuer was an ordinary teenager living in Paris with her family. She applied herself in school, had a close network of friends, and got along with her younger brother. Behind the appearances, however, Lara was resentful. "I was in the throes of a teenage crisis. I was easily annoyed by anything my mother said and felt oppressed by her sense of responsibility and sacrifice. I was on the shy and introverted side, so most of my rebellion was internal rather than voiced. But she knew it, and it hurt her."

Then, one day, everything changed in an instant. Lara's mother Claire was diagnosed with a terminal cancer and given three months to live. "When this happened, my teenage crises vanished overnight," Lara says. "I immediately became determined to help her conquer this cancer. It was a very pure, naïve sense of hope and possibility. I was only 14, but I was on a mission to keep her alive. My father and I became her copilots on her quest for healing."

Claire knew what it was like to lose a parent. When she was nine years old, her father had been deported to Auschwitz, never to return. When Claire was only seven, she had been sent into hiding, away from her parents. She had faced hunger, abuse, and disease during the dark years of the Holocaust. Now she ferociously wanted to see her children grow up – and to be there for them.

Her type of cancer was very rare and there were no treatments for it at that time. But with her husband Sam's, and Lara's help, she became determined to try anything, look anywhere, even in the most unconventional places, for healing.

One of those places was *inside herself*. Claire and Sam became obsessed with this thought: "If we only have a few months left, how can we make the most out of them, in our relationships with each other, our kids, our community?" This propelled them into an adventure of self-discovery, as they learned how to "show up as their best selves" with their family, since time was now so precious.

They devoured self-improvement books, travelled the world looking for the latest medical treatments, and in the process met pioneers in the field of human potential of the 1970s and 80's in the U.S., like Gerald Jampolsky and Dr. Carl Simonton.

They slowly became more conscious of all the internal barriers people create instead of living each moment in joy, aligned with a sense of purpose. A big one, they came to discover, is the underlying fears and insecurities that stem from painful experiences in our childhoods. Claire realized as a "hidden child", she had developed fears of being excluded, abandoned and betrayed. That led her to lose her temper when she perceived someone was not keeping a promise, or didn't tell her the whole truth.

Through these new insights - while she was still battling her cancer -- Claire's life's work was born: to give people the tools to discover this kind of self-awareness back to the world. Claire and Sam created workshops to help others to bring their best selves to their projects and their relationships. "Don't wait until you have a few months to live to work on yourself!" was her motto.

Awareness of one's own fears, the origins of those fears, and their impact on behavior are at the core of the educational seminars that Claire developed over time -- with Sam, and a growing number of volunteers. Reflecting back to these early days, "I was fascinated by how this work was allowing people to transform their lives, helping them become more who they wanted to be. It was very empowering."

From the very beginning, Lara attended every seminar she could. She too was eager to work on her own issues of shyness and her defensiveness. "I'd complained about how my mother always needed to be right," she says. "Turns out I had my own need to be right!" .

"Like my mother, I was convinced that if people could learn to bring their best selves to their relationships, their work, their lives, that this would curb their need to demonize the 'Other'," she says. "Ultimately, we hoped we could prevent another Auschwitz."

So now Lara was on a mission, not only to keep her mother alive, but to spread this work. Her friends in school, her boyfriends, her teachers, her boss and her manager in the marketing department of Evian: "They all attended, drawn by my enthusiasm," she says. "They were all transformed."

After graduating from high school, Lara attended one of the top business schools in France. "I saw how teams, though wanting to innovate and create great things, ended up in 'us vs. them' dynamics, 'I have to win over you' mentalities, and turf wars."

"After I graduated from college, I felt a calling," Lara says. "I didn't want to climb the corporate ladder of a major company; I wanted to help spread this work to the business community. Because if the business leaders can work on themselves, then we will *really* change the world, one ego at a time!"

It was then that Lara decided to join Claire's organization full time, where she was in charge of outreach to executive leaders. The programs continued to develop, infused by encounters with pioneers in related fields, like Dr. Maxie Maultby, the founder of Rational Behavior Theory, and Peter Senge, the co-founder of Learning Organizations, and author of *The Fifth Discipline*.

Claire was now being invited to speak at major conferences and offer her programs in the U.S., Canada, and Mexico. Because Lara was fluent in English she became Claire's translator, and she worked feverishly to translate her work, enroll and coach business leaders around the world, and help build media campaigns for special community dialogue projects.

Meanwhile, Claire's audience kept growing: she was asked to speak in prestigious venues like the Commonwealth Club in San Francisco and at Brenton Woods. Leaders like Deepak Chopra, Willis Harmon, and George McCown wanted to meet her. They were all curious how this petite woman who spoke only French and barely had a sixth-grade education could have such a powerful impact on so many people.

By the late1990s, Claire's curriculum had evolved into a one-year program that included several seminars, one-on-one and team coaching, and consulting, to help leaders in business, government, the nonprofit world and academia bring their best selves to their work, their families, and their communities.

"I discovered my ego's hot buttons, how they are rooted in ways I felt victimized in my past," one CEO admitted to Lara in a coaching session, "This became a lens I project onto the world, and now when those buttons are triggered, I react and become, inadvertently, the victimizer, thus perpetuating onto others the very pain I suffered from. I am committed to stop perpetuating this cycle. I now have a Noble Goal."

By now corporate executives, nonprofit leaders, consultants, and academics were all seeking out Claire's training programs. "I am so proud that my mother, this little Frenchwoman, deprived of schooling in her childhood, developed a methodology that has been taught to thousands of people around the world, and is the basis of curricula now taught at Harvard, Stanford, Darden, and other universities," Lara says. "It's having an impact in the fields of leadership and organizational behavior, social psychology, and inter-group relations."

Claire lived for 17 more years after that auspicious day that changed her life: when she was told she had only three months to live. She would come to call cancer her "dear friend" because of the changes it had brought about in her life and in the lives of so many others.

By the time Claire passed away, Lara was 31 years old. Her brother Noah, for years inspired by his parents' journey, gave up his film career to devote himself full time to the continuation of their work. "At first when my mother died, I was crushed," Lara says. "But little by little I found meaning to her departure. It pushed me, my brother, and others to suddenly grow to a whole new level. We had to find a way for the work to continue! We had to step up to the plate and facilitate the seminars, run the organization on our own. It was time for us, and for me, to step into a new level of responsibility." She pauses, and reflects, "My reverence for my mother might have prevented me from finding my own voice. But she had told me more than once, 'One day you will continue this work in your own way, and it will be different–and better.' That gave me the courage to continue on the path she had started."

Since Claire's passing, under Lara and Noah's leadership, Learning As Leadership (LAL) has become a leadership training of choice for Fortune 500 companies. Featured on NPR, and in the award-winning book *Ego Free Leadership*, the organization is committed more than ever to helping organizations shape a more humane culture.

Today Lara is married to Shayne who, as a rebellious teen had come with his parents to one of Claire's seminars. He is now president of LAL, and father to their two children. "I'll always be grateful for the model my mother set for me," Lara says, "for her boundless selflessness and generosity. For her passion for life, and for *Tikkun Olam*.

"Just as my mother confronted her demons with the onset of the cancer, her death has pushed me to confront mine. Just as she faced her fears in order to pursue *her* noble goals, I am finding the courage to confront mine. It is an enormous privilege to be a recipient of her legacy. And I am committed to carrying it on. It has become my life's work."

Today Lara's extended community is working together to support major corporations in becoming more humanistic - and in the process, more successful too. Together they are carrying on Claire's legacy... to humanize the world of business, starting with their executives, their families ... and one day, the world.

> *When you say 'so what' to your fears, when you*
> *reach for the stars, the magic of being human*
> *unfolds.*

Claire Nuer

Call to Action: Go beyond our Ego to create a context for humanity together. Learning as Leadership: www.learnaslead.com • Nuer Foundation: www.nuerfoundation.org

SEA2SEE EYEWEAR:
SUSTAINABLE PRODUCTS WITH A CONSCIENCE
François van den Abeele
Spain

François van den Abeele's idea for cleaning up plastic in the oceans emerged over time. As a journalist, he'd covered social and environmental issues in over 130 countries in some of the world's most vulnerable regions, like Sub-Saharan Africa and the Middle East. From what he'd seen, the crisis of plastic pollution in the waterways was devastating impoverished communities, and the scale of the neglect was monumental. Francois was troubled and often thought about this problem -- and about what could be done.

"You don't just get out of bed one day and say, 'I want to manufacture eyeglasses out of plastic waste'" he says. "I started to wear glasses later in life, so by then they were more on my mind." One day he thought, "Hey, glasses are something people all over the world wear. Frames are made of plastic. Then the gears began turning."

While Francois had no experience in fashion, he was a quick study. He discovered that fashion is a $100 billion a year industry, and that it is among the most environmentally damaging, ranking only behind oil and gas in terms of its negative impact. His vision was ambitious, but it was not unrealistic. He'd worked with impact businesses before. "I soon realized that this was a way to create a sustainable product that was profitable, and that could help clean up the oceans."

In 2016, he put together a team, gathered up 20 kilos of recycled plastic, brought it to a processor in Italy, and made Sea2See's first run of products -- 20 sunglasses. "It was a big idea and there were a lot of skeptics. Even my wife thought it was a crazy idea, using marine waste for frames. But there they were."

The product was a hit almost immediately. To keep up with growing demand, Francois began working with fishermen in Spain to gather plastic. He then expanded his operation to France. Now he works with African fishing communities in Ghana, Senegal, and Togo, and he is hoping to expand to other African countries as well. Together they clean up polluted waterways while providing a much-needed revenue stream for these once marginalized fishermen. "When I first went there, they thought I was crazy," he says. "They wondered why this guy was going to pay them for collecting waste." To his critics, François responded, "Waste has value. And cleaning it up has a value too -- it benefits everyone."

Over time François has leveraged the power of this new community of fishermen to address other regional problems. With the excess plastic that remains after the frame-making process, he launched a line of watches that supports the nonprofit organization Free the Slaves, to stop child exploitation in places like Lake Volta in Ghana, where children are forced to work. "The sale of one watch finances two weeks of education for each kid that is saved. Our campaign is called Time for Time, because we all have time; and I believe we should give meaning to our time by giving back to the most vulnerable among us." And not all of the waste collected by Sea2See goes into glasses or watches: they are also building a recycling plant, to provide recycled plastic for industries looking for it.

In 2017, François took his growing business to Chivas Venture, whose international contest invests in social entrepreneurs with start-up projects. Sea2See won Best Start-Up in the 2nd edition of the contest in Spain and went on to the finals in Los Angeles. While Sea2See did not receive the gold medal, in a tough field of sustainable innovators, Francois did receive a call some months later that made his intercontinental trip worthwhile.

When Spanish movie star Javier Bardem saw Sea2See glasses at the contest in Los Angeles, he was so inspired that he asked if he could join François and his fishermen for a day on the water. He wanted to bring his film crew along, so they could raise awareness about the problem of plastic pollution in the ocean and showcase Sea2See's successful venture. "When Javier came out on the fishing boat to support us, it really was a boost. He genuinely wants to use his voice to help make a change, and he really did," Francois says. Together, François and Javier created a film campaign that has raised awareness about the dangers that single-use plastic straws pose to marine life.

To thank him for his generous support, François gave Javier a pair of Sea2See frames. A few days later, at the Cannes Film Festival, Javier's wife Penelope Cruz wore the frames to a film premier, and *Hola,* one of the biggest celebrity magazines in Spain, featured a signature photograph of her wearing her Sea2See frames on their cover. "It's great that we got that exposure," François says. "I really hope more influential people with a platform decide to take up this cause."

As of March 2021, Sea2See had collected 443 tons of plastic for its glasses, all while adhering to the strictest standards of the Cradle to Cradle certified products program. This program is the benchmark by which sustainable businesses are measured, particularly as it pertains to the circular economy. Sea2See has received the Platinum distinction in material health, and the Gold certification overall, meaning it has achieved excellence in each of the five categories: material health, circular economy, renewable energy, water stewardship, and social fairness. Francois is very proud of these distinctions. "It proves the purity of our recycled raw material," he says.

"We are proving that there is another way," he says. "By now, most people understand that the linear model of business just doesn't work. That's why we bring a cyclical point of view to plastic waste cleanup. We are the only business that is vertically integrated all the way from waste collection to the final product. We hope we can inspire others to do more of the same. It's important, because by giving value to waste, we have an environmental impact on the coastal environment but also a social impact, thanks to the new source of income the waste collectors have."

And François has in fact succeeded in inspiring others: for example, he was invited by sustainability experts in Brussels to speak at a conference on SIDS (Small Islands Developing States), where he met diplomats who were intrigued by Sea2See. He was then invited to attend the United Nations World Ocean Conference in New York. "When I got there, I was talking with the Minister of Foreign Affairs of Brussels, who shocked me by saying, 'I know you.' At first I thought he must be mistaken." But then the Minister pulled out his papers and showed François how he had written about Sea2See in his remarks. "I am going to talk about you at the Assembly today," he said. "We need to help start-ups that are raising the issue of ocean contamination and reusing plastic waste."

At the conference, Sea2See was showcased as an example of how to reduce marine contamination while creating value for consumers worldwide. "I was thrilled to see people catching on to the idea of a circular economy -- especially those who were advocating for it so passionately. It gave me a lot of hope for what's to come."

François believes that the future of *all* business must become sustainable business, and this is where the youth can really lead the charge. "If you want to start any type of business, it's my belief that it should have an impact beyond whatever product or service you are offering. There are so many things you can do. I know it's tricky. It takes time. But if you have the resolve, you can do it. Try to have an impact. That's what I've tried to do. And if I can inspire people to try and have an impact in the same way, I've done my job. So, do it! Get involved. Sweat. Work. Bring your ideas to reality!"

In order to attain the impossible, one must attempt the absurd.

Miguel de Cervantes

Call to Action: Learn how you can turn a problem into a new business: Check out the Sea2See sustainable products: www.sea2see.org.

SERVICE IS JUST WHAT YOU DO
Gary Hirshberg
Stonyfield Farm
New Hampshire

As a young boy, Gary Hirshberg loved every minute he spent on top of Mount Washington. He went hiking and ski-racing, breathing in the cold, fresh air and feeling the warm sunlight on his face. He especially enjoyed the breathtaking view from the mountain top: on clear days he could even see the Atlantic Ocean far off in the distance.

When he was in college, and he returned to the summit of the mountain he knew so well, he noticed a big change. "You couldn't see the ocean anymore," he says. The change was for a well-known reason. "Air pollution and atmospheric changes from climate change."

As a child, the importance of giving back to others had been deeply ingrained in him by his mother. "She lived by that example," Gary says. "She worked in soup kitchens, volunteered for presidential candidates, helped at the local hospital, or at the Boys and Girls Clubs," Gary says. He pauses, remembering. "I can't remember a dinnertime conversation where my mother wasn't saying that it's up to us to give back."

Dr. Martin Luther King Jr. was another big influence on Gary. The King family were friends of Gary's family, and when Coretta Scott King and her children visited the Hirshberg's vacation home, Gary spent a lot of time with them, just hanging out, talking over meals, listening to Coretta. Then, in 1968 Dr. King was assassinated. "I was just 14 at the time, so it really became cemented in me, that service wasn't an option. Service was just what you did."

When Gary was in college, he worked in an environmental education camp for high school students in Maine. He and his fellow camp guides were responsible for managing 26,000 acres of wildlife refuge, and teaching students about the importance of environmental preservation. But sadly, all around this amazing forest, they could see that the timber industry was cutting down trees.

"While we were putting our hearts and souls into wildlife and conservation, all around us we could see these clear cuts, with herbicides and everything else," he says. "The refuge was surrounded by about a million acres of pulp and paper land. I got the message that 'This is bad. We need to work on alternatives.'"

Coming up with ideas for viable, more sustainable alternatives was something Gary had to do often at the family dinner table. His grandfather was a successful banker with rather conservative views. "More often than not he would slay me with some economic argument; I really didn't have the answers then," Gary says. "But I learned that business is where all the polluting happens, and that while business wasn't the only problem, it was very definitely not part of the solution. So I was really seeking alternatives."

Gary understood that if there was going to be change, it needed to come from within the business community; and it needed to come in the form of viable alternatives. So when he was 23, he joined the think tank New Alchemy and immersed himself in the emerging renewable energy industry of wind power.

New Alchemy was a small start-up: it needed lots of investments to get off the ground. Fortunately, very quickly Gary discovered that he was a gifted fundraiser. Within two years, at the age of 25, he became the executive director of the company.

Gary put his fundraising skills to good use for small organic farming school, the Rural Education Center in Wilton, New Hampshire. It wasn't easy. In the 1980s public funding for environmental projects had dried up under a new administration, and competition for the little funding that was available was fierce.

Gary enjoyed the fringe benefits from the school's farm. "My partner was producing this incredibly delicious, wonderful yogurt, which we would sit around eating," Gary remembers. "And then one day somebody -- we're still not sure who it was -- said, why don't we start selling this yogurt?"

That was the beginning of Stonyfield Farm, which would become the world's leading producer of organic yogurt under Gary's leadership.

Turning Stonyfield from the little farming school it was initially into the national organic yogurt company it is today, took a lot of hard work and dedication. They started out by selling their yogurt at only five stores.

"Night after night, even after milking and after making yogurt, one of us -- whoever wasn't milking -- would go and do a demo at the store," Gary remembers. "We would stand there, and we'd talk to consumers, and we'd simply not let them say no."

Soon, they were able to sell their yogurt in 10 nearby stores, then in 35. Eventually, they were the third largest brand in all of their stores. From the very beginning, Gary and his business partner, Samuel, used the packaging of their products to educate customers. "It was very simply our way of being able to tell our story," Gary says. "The early packages were like mini lessons in where people's food comes from."

As their brand grew into a real company, Gary and his colleagues at Stonyfield Farm started using their profits to support all kinds of special projects. Early on they decided that 10 percent of their profits would be spent on initiatives to fight against climate change. Since then, the company has spearheaded many measures to minimize its carbon footprint and to support environmental efforts. Some of Stonyfield's newest initiatives include the OpenTEAM project, the StonyFIELDS #playfree initiative, and a new goal of reducing carbon emissions by 30 percent by 2030.

As CEO of Stonyfield, it was important to Gary to incorporate the values that had been instilled in him during his childhood – and to reconcile his entrepreneurial spirit with service to his community. "I realized that we needed a real strategy, an economic strategy," he says. "Creating an actual economic enterprise whose mission is to save family farmers, and try to slow down the urbanization of rural land, providing healthy food, all of that: it was very appealing."

Gary used every imaginative way he could think of to educate the public about sustainable farming.

In 1989, the company introduced the Have-a-Cow Educational program, through which customers were invited to "adopt" one of the Stonyfield cows. Then they would receive regular updates about the cows they had adopted, along with information about the issues that small-scale farmers were facing.

But Gary and his team realized that it wasn't only the public that needed to be educated -- farmers, too, needed information and training on how to run their farms sustainably. Stonyfield also noticed that the population of organic dairy farmers in this region was aging. More and more farmers were getting close to the age of retirement with no plans for who would take over the farm when they retired. So in 2015 Stonyfield partnered with Wolfe's Neck Center for Agriculture and the Environment to establish a first-of-its-kind residential organic dairy training program where younger generation of farmers could learn about regenerative farming practices in a two-year apprenticeship program. Additionally, over time, starting in 2014, Stonyfield built up a network of direct supply organic dairy farmers, and they were able to start supplementing their milk supply with milk from other local organic farmers. So, first they supplied local farmers with the skills and technical assistance they needed to make their businesses grow sustainably: then they bought their milk. It was a win-win situation.

With his hard work and dedication, Gary has managed to grow Stonyfield Farms into a national enterprise that is also giving back to the local community -- just like he had learned to do from his mother and his childhood friends.

"I always say to folks that determination is the most important and underappreciated characteristic needed to be an entrepreneur," he says. "Nothing takes the place of hard work and passion."

> *It really boils down to this: that all life*
> *is interrelated. We are all caught in an*
> *inescapable network of mutuality,*
> *tied into a single garment of destiny.*
> *Whatever affects one destiny, affects all*
> *indirectly.*

Dr. Martin Luther King Jr.

Call to Action: Find the nearest local farmer's market to your home -- it's fresh food, locally produced, and 100% good for the environment. Or find a CSA (community supported agriculture) to support: they'll deliver fresh organic food right to your home.

SPEAKING TRUTH TO POWER
Maria Ressa
Rappler!
The Philippines

Maria Ressa has been fighting for her voice to be heard all her life. When she was just eight years old, the Philippines' President Marcos declared martial law; and that affected everyone's freedom of speech. Maria's family fled their homeland to start a new life in the United States, in Toms River, New Jersey.

It was challenging for everyone in the family to adjust to this new world. In order to make enough money so that Maria could go to a good school, her parents took the bus into New York City -- two hours every morning, and two hours back every evening, through the heavy traffic of highway I-95.

For Maria, adjusting to life in the United States didn't happen overnight. She was the only person of color in her classroom, and also the shortest. "When we arrived in Toms River, I was the short, quiet kid who could barely speak English," she says.

It was her music teacher, Don Spaulding, who gave her the courage to overcome her doubts and to grow in self-confidence. "He nurtured me and others like me: kids looking to belong, looking for our place in the world," she wrote later. "I first found that in music, and then that became the foundation for the many other extra-curricular activities and academics that shaped my world." By the time she graduated from high school, she was voted "Most Likely to Succeed."

Maria went to college at Princeton University to study molecular biology. When she returned to the Philippines in 1986 on a Fulbright scholarship, she began her studies in journalism at the University of the Philippines Diliman. Finding herself once again in the country she had left at an early age, she began to feel a thirst for creating change outside of the laboratory. She wanted to right wrongs and reveal the abuses of power she saw around the world. *What better way to accomplish this than as an investigative reporter,* she thought.

For more than 20 years, Maria investigated environmental catastrophes, human rights violations, and political scandals for CNN. She's led CNN's Jakarta bureau, and traveled throughout the region on reporting trips. She made a name for herself as a hard-nosed reporter -- someone who was never afraid to speak truth to power, even when it might put her in personal danger.

But because she is an entrepreneur at heart, despite all she had accomplished, Maria still felt something was lacking. She wanted to create something of her own. The answer came in the form of Rappler, which she started in 2012 with three other women. The idea behind Rappler was found in a simple equation: rap (to talk) plus ripple (to make waves).

Maria started Rappler because she didn't want to just report the news, she wanted to shape the world into something better, and more human. She believes in the power of technology to create change; and as climate change and conflict intensify around the world, a little bit of optimism achieved through technology can go a long way.

Their aim was to give a voice to the Filipino community and undo stereotypes that she had seen as a reporter for CNN and other Western media outlets. And in the Philippines, where human rights violations and climate change both pose existential threats, this combination is more essential than ever.

Rappler isn't like every other media organization, though. The Rappler-mobile looks a bit like one of Doc's inventions from the movie "Back to the Future." It's a small white truck, equipped with an almost comically large satellite on top -- its antennas facing skyward. With those antennas, it's able to beam signals across the Philippines -- a collection of more than 7,000 islands in the South Pacific Ocean -- and spread news around the world. Still, the vehicle cost a pretty penny, especially for a Philippines-based media startup like Rappler: about $100,000.

But on a human scale, the investment in that little white truck made a lot of sense.

When Typhoon Haiyan, otherwise known as Super Typhoon Yolanda, touched down in the Philippines in the fall of 2013, Rappler's truck was one of the first vehicles to make it to the storm-affected areas. The truck drove through debris, allowing a small team of reporters to get a better sense of the human impact of the storm. Its power strips also helped people to recharge their phone batteries when the power had gone out in their homes, so they could make calls to emergency services, and to family members, to let them know that they were alright. In other words, the little Rappler-mobile became a lifeline.

Rappler was just a small news media startup with a staff of about ten people at the time, but when they beat many of the biggest news outlets in the Philippines to the scene in the aftermath of the typhoon, the small team of journalists knew that they were filling an important void -- one where journalism doesn't just inform readers and viewers, but truly serves them on a human level.

Maria's job hasn't been simple. The Philippines is the country that is most affected by climate change in the world. More than half of the ten deadliest storms that have ever hit the chain of islands have done so in the past decade and a half. Sea levels are rising, and the country's infrastructure isn't ready for these kinds of changes.

Now, under President Rodrigo Duterte, it is also a place where human rights are increasingly violated. Since he launched his brutal drug war in 2016 more than 5,000 people have been killed, including five journalists.

Rappler detected a number of privacy violations on Facebook, against women who were speaking out to oppose the "war on drugs." Where other news outlets stayed relatively silent, Rappler went on the offensive, publishing investigations and reports that showed the crimes being committed by the government in its quest to eradicate drugs and poverty. When Maria published an article on the topic, she earned the wrath of an army of online bots who supported the president. Later, when she reported on the shady business dealings of a powerful businessman, she was arrested and accused of libel -- defaming someone's name.

Maria's battle is an uphill one. She has been arrested and bailed out of jail eight times in 2019 alone. For leading the war on fake news, she may be jailed for 12 years on libel charges. President Duterte has labeled Rappler itself a "fake news outlet." She is grateful that the British-Lebanese human rights lawyer Amal Clooney is championing her case. "We will pursue all available legal remedies to vindicate her rights and defend press freedom and the rule of law in the Philippines," Clooney has promised.

Maria has spoken out about climate change since well before the marches and manifestations led by Greta Thunberg kicked off. At the Reuters Institute's 35th Anniversary of the Journalist Fellowship Program, she spoke about how Rappler was working with the Filipino government to create a real-time map of climate threats and resiliency systems. "That's the closest to what I feel like we can do," she said. "Because we did help save lives. The reason why the community comes [to us] is not just because the platform is transparent to everyone, but also because they get information they can trust."

As climate change sets in, countries like the Philippines suffer the most obvious consequences of it. Maria calls Facebook "friend-enemies," as she strives to find ways to use this powerful social media tool to educate ordinary people, rather than being used as a weapon against them. At Al Gore's first global Climate Reality Leadership Corps training in 2016, she inspired thousands of people to become climate change champions where she urged attendees to use the power of social media to apply a "whole of society" approach to responding to natural disasters. "This is something that's in your hands," she said. "Largely, social media is free. It's about giving the information needed to build communities of action."

Despite the challenges she is facing, Maria strongly believes in the importance of exercising freedom of speech, and of journalists speaking truth to power. She has said that when the truth comes under fire, journalists need to be activists. For her courageous reporting, Maria was named by Time magazine as one of the journalists recognized as Person of the Year in 2018. In 2020 she was named by Time - "100 Most Influential Women of the Century".

And when she was awarded the Madeline Albright National Democratic Institute's highest honor, she said, "We are journalists, and we will not be intimidated. We will shine the light. We will hold the line."

Maria's fight to be heard, and to speak truth to power has led her from her childhood home in the Philippines halfway around the world, and back again. Now we all just need to work together to make *her* work matter.

Courage, as they say, is contagious.
People who have the courage to change their
societies
inspire each other and create rights for future
generations.

Amal Clooney

Call to Action: Be awake, aware, use social media responsibly. To join or support Maria's Rappler Plus: https://www.rappler.com/plus

SUSTAINABLE BUSINESS, SUSTAINABLE LIVING
Ed Begley Jr.
Los Angeles, California

Ed Begley Jr. was a 20-year-old struggling actor who was deeply impacted by the first Earth Day. That historical day, April 22, 1970, launched what would become a global environmental movement. "I was watching the future being made in real time," Ed reflects. "It was a very humbling experience to be a part of it."

It really got him thinking: imagine what the future could look like if the momentum from this one-day event was leveraged to make an even broader impact. Ed reached out to the leaders who had organized Earth Day, like U.S. Senator Gaylord Nelson, and posed a question: "It's fine to have this one day," he said. "But as a movement, and a community, what are we going to do for the other 364 days?"

Many responded with ambitious plans to expand efforts to clean up the land and water around the country. "I knew this was important," Ed says. "I lived in smoggy LA, and could see how needed these programs were. So I committed to doing my part to live sustainably." And he has ever since.

Ed got an impressionable nudge from the man he admired most in the world. "My father said to me, almost as a challenge, 'I know what you are against, Eddy. The smog. Well - what are you for?' I knew what he meant. And he was right. I'll never forget those words. My father remains a great inspiration for me."

Ed describes his father as "a conservative who liked to conserve." "Growing up, we turned off the lights. Turned off the water. Saved tin foil. We never used the word environmentalism. We just knew this was something we all needed to do. I still feel this way. Republican, Democrat, Independent, Green Party. We can argue about different things. But I say, let's all agree on this: Do we want to clean up the earth? Put more money in your pockets? Have intact forests and oceans for our kids and grandkids? Great. Then we're all environmentalists! Let's do it."

Ed has lived sustainably for over 50 years, carrying that legacy from the time he was a struggling actor to now, when he is a celebrated actor who has starred in hundreds of films and TV shows.

He started small, recycling, composting organic matter, eating vegetarian and buying an inexpensive solar vehicle, a Taylor Dunne. "It was great supporting a sustainable business," he says. "And I felt good about driving around Los Angeles and not contributing to the smog."

It didn't take long for Ed to realize that these personal decisions that supported sustainable businesses were not only good for the environment, but were also cost-effective. "Soon I realized that going green was actually cheaper. It's the same today. It's still cheaper to plug a car into the wall than to pay at the pump." With his savings, Ed continued to increase his commitment to buying and supporting sustainable businesses, with a particular affinity for companies that were pushing the boundaries in electric vehicle (EV) technology.

Ed then began experimenting with projects of his own. "I went from that Taylor Dunne and bought a used 1973 Subaru for $1750 and converted it to electric, which took another $2500. Ultimately, I had a really cheap freeway-worthy electric vehicle. That was back in 1990 - and there weren't many out there at the time." Ed went on to convert a Volkswagen Rabbit to electric. After tinkering on his own projects for a time, he decided to trust the business leaders, and went back to driving EVs from companies leading the industry. "I leased an EV1 from General Motors, which was way ahead of its time. I went on to a Toyota Rav 4, a purely electric vehicle, a precursor to their amazing Prius. Then a Nissan Leaf. And now I'm driving a Tesla, which is innovating in ways I could've never imagined."

Ed's passion led him to dabble in wind energy. "Early on I worked with PacWind, which built turbines around 75 kilowatts. From 1985-2015, I owned a wind turbine footprint in Palm Springs Desert as part of the Painted Hills Wind Energy Repowering Project. Then I transitioned to the Dutch company Zond, whose amazing turbines produce around 1.5 megawatts. It took me 20 years of saving to be able to afford solar power on my home - and I've never looked back. There's a long list of things you can't do, but there's a lot longer and more interesting list of the things you can do."

Practicing what he preaches has become a whole way of life for Ed, and even the subject of a reality TV show, Living with Ed. He is now a big believer in the power of education and outreach to raise public awareness of what each of us can do to be environmentalists. "It's why I write books. It's why I speak to young people. I contribute in my small way. What Greta Thunberg is doing—to take a sailboat across the Atlantic—I couldn't do something like that, so I do what I can. But thank goodness she is! The way that people young and old are responding to her is amazing. She's inspired me to get out there and do more. A lot of us from the earlier generation felt like we were in low gear for a while. She got us reinvigorated."

Both living and teaching sustainable living is essential for Ed; he knows that personal action alone won't solve this problem. Whether it's his actions or Greta's, there needs to be an infrastructure supporting this change. "It's not just about me recycling my bottles," he says. "Legislation and corporate social responsibility (CSR) are major parts of this equation—three parts of a triangle, really."

On the legislative front, Ed points to a long list of environmental crises that he's seen remedied in his lifetime. The Hudson River in New York City was so polluted that you couldn't safely swim in the waters. Now it has burgeoning fisheries thanks to the Clean Water Act. The Cuyahoga River in Northeast Ohio that caught fire in 1969 does not catch fire anymore. "Los Angeles gives me hope," Ed says. "Even though there's four times the number of cars here, and millions more people, we have a fraction of the smog today than we did in 1970. This is because of the Clean Air Act. That's a real success story."

Ed himself runs a sustainable business, featuring a line of green indoor cleaning products called Begley's Best. His formulas include floor and counter cleaners, waterless pet shampoo, dish soap, wrinkle remover, and more. "I wanted to show that a business can have a conscience," he explains. "We can be ethical and drive these healthy habits while being profitable at the same time. Look at what Jeffrey Hollender has done with Seventh Generation. Take businesses like Ben & Jerry's, or innovators like Ray C. Anderson of Interface. There's lots of people doing well by doing good. And I want to encourage more of it."

As is the case with everything Ed does, he lives the change he wants to see in the world of sustainable business. Through his family foundation, he gives tens of thousands of dollars of profits from Begley's Best each year to support green initiatives he believes in.

For all of the sustainable business leaders doing great things, Ed wants to make sure they balance their outlook with a sober take on the situation at hand. "We still have plenty of areas in crisis. Most importantly, we have people from low-income communities who are struggling, and they need our help the most. I encourage more businesses and individuals to take on these challenges, because every bit makes a difference."

For young people, who have inherited the climate situation we are in, Ed has a candid message, "I'm sorry. I make a sincere apology to those that will come after me. We certainly tried. I wish I could have done a better job."

With his voice of sage wisdom and experience, he adds, "We need to be honest, and we have to accept that there is going to be some continuing loss and some damage. But don't stop because of that. There's so much left that we can save. And Mother Nature is resilient. So, I believe it's incredibly important to be hopeful. We've seen what happened with all the doom and gloom. So, let's remind ourselves of the good news from time to time."

Ed believes we owe a great debt of gratitude to the current youth environmental leaders who have brought the conversation into the mainstream once again. "Thanks to Greta Thunberg and other youth charging us into the future, I'm filled with more hope every day. They have challenged us to do everything we can, precisely because there is hope. Yes, the situation is dire, but many things can be fixed, and made right, and protected. They've showed us the way forward. Now it's time for us to come together as one and step up to the challenge."

The future will either be green or not at all.

Bob Brown

Call to Action: To keep up with the sustainable business ventures that Ed Begley is building and supporting, visit www.begleyliving.com.

VI

PASSING THE TORCH

Intergenerational
Legacy

PASSING THE TORCH
Intergenerational • Legacy

At the Stone Soup Leadership Institute's Celebration of Heroes with Walter Cronkite in 2002, we pledged to carry on the legacy of Mahatma Gandhi, Eleanor Roosevelt, Cesar Chavez and Dr. Martin Luther King Jr. to improve the conditions of our neighborhoods, our countries and the world through individual action and working with others. Together, we have forged new directions for the global economy, bridged the gap between the haves and have nots and striven to build a more peaceful world. This Pledge is woven into all the Institute's educational tools, trainings, and youth leadership initiatives. Our young people read it aloud at our Sustainability Summits to honor their legacy. One of the Institute's hallmarks is connecting young people with their elders in order to build bridges, cross-fertilize intergenerational ideas, and stand on their shoulders -- as well as to reenergize the elders with the creative, enthusiastic energy that young people exude.

I'm honored that this chapter features the grandchildren of Mahatma Gandhi, the civil rights leader Cesar Chavez, the media mogul and philanthropist Ted Turner, the musician Peter Yarrow, and Sri Lanka's Dr. A.T. Ariyaratne, as well as the children of Robert F. Kennedy, Frances Moore Lappé, and David Suzuki.

Kerry Kennedy was only eight years old when her father, Robert F. Kennedy, was assassinated. But she had already learned some very important lessons from him; perhaps the most important was that each and every person can make a difference. Hafsat Abiola's parents instilled in her the importance of sharing, and of helping others. Her father, who became the first democratically elected president of Nigeria, empowered people by helping them buy farms, start small businesses, and receive an education. Her mother taught her that simple things told a lot about a person's character. Today as president of Women in Africa, Hafsat is developing initiatives to help women respond to the challenges and dangers of COVID-19.

Arun Gandhi faced racial prejudice growing up in South Africa. When he was 12, seeing the understandable anger that was building in him, his parents sent him to live in India with his grandfather, Mahatma Gandhi, to learn the principles of nonviolence, and put him on a better path.

Long before the technology was ready, Cesar Chavez wanted to create a network of radio stations for his people, to keep them connected with up-to-date news. Today as director of digital strategy at Radio Campesino, Cesar Chavez continues to carry out his grandfather's dream. "We've become a useful tool for the whole community to better themselves, to keep the UFW struggle going, and to keep my grandfather's legacy alive," he says. Protesting for social justice and environmental causes runs in Valentina Ossa's family. Her grandfather, Peter Yarrow, was a leading voice for Civil Rights and against the Vietnam War in the 1960s, and her mother, Bethany Yarrow, is also a devoted activist. Valentina is proud to carry on the family tradition: her first protest came when she was just five years old and she wrote to the governor of New York about her concern that fracking would contaminate the water in her community. Niven Ganegama and his sister Tiara grew up admiring their grandfather, Dr. Ari Ariyatne, founder of Sri Lanka's Sarvodaya movement, a humanitarian organization whose work is known throughout the world. When they were teenagers, Niven and Tiara decided they wanted to carry on Dr. Ari's tradition of service to others by helping kids in remote rural villages learn English. "Awakening, caring for others, sharing our gifts" is his grandfather's message, says Niven. It is a legacy they are carrying on.

Growing up, John R. Seydel loved the cartoon series *Captain Planet*, which was cocreated by his grandfather, Ted Turner. At the end of every episode, there was a Planeteer Alert, where a diverse team of global heroes would talk directly to the audience about ways to find solutions to the environmental problems in their communities. "It taught us how to be part of the solution, not part of the problem -- and to inspire others along the way," he says. John R. is carrying on this legacy through serving on the boards of a variety of Turner family foundations, including the Captain Planet Foundation. Of all the environmental projects the Turner family has supported, perhaps the most historic was Ted's $1 billion gift to the United Nations Foundation in 1997.

Demi Weitz imagined a very different kind of 17th birthday than what it turned out to be. When the COVID pandemic got in the way of her party plans, her father organized a Zoom party for her, with some of his recording artist friends. This gave Demi an idea: why not organize Zoom concerts to benefit charities? That's how Quarantunes, an amazing success story, began. They've since raised more than $20 million for charities.

These stories reveal the wonderful gifts that parents can pass on to their children, as well as the gifts their children can in turn send into the world at large. At the Institute we seek to provide additional opportunities to nurture this rich cultivation of intergenerational legacy, to make a better world for tomorrow's children.

A CITIZEN OF THE WORLD
Leila Ndabirabe
Maison Shalom
Burundi/Belgium

Leila Ndabirabe began to notice that the climate was changing even as she was growing up. Few may have heard of the small African country of Burundi. But the country, located at the intersection of Africa's Great Lakes region, the plains of East Africa and the Great Rift Valley, has a special place in the continent. Burundi is known as the "heart of Africa."

It was here that Leila spent the first 10 years of her life. She lived with her family in Bujumbura, the largest city and a key port for goods like coffee and ore. She remembers the central market and the church her family attended. Everybody in her neighborhood knew one another well and there was a strong sense of community. Neighbors spoke with neighbors and supported one another.

However, the drier weather was making it harder to grow crops and people were being forced migrate to the cities. "The dry season it getting so dry, it doesn't rain enough, so people don't have enough food to eat," she says. "The soil is bad, and the pollution is bad. Everybody is moving into the city because they don't have enough food to survive."

The increasing lack of food undermined her country's peaceful coexistence, where was an unsettling feeling of instability that would soon spread across the small country. That instability -- spurred by a whirlwind of politics, prejudice and poverty -- eventually erupted in the 1990s, when Leila was just a child. The heart of Africa nearly stopped beating, ripped apart by a brutal civil war.

The Civil War didn't happen overnight and it didn't spread to Bujumbura immediately. "You would hear gunshots and you knew you weren't always safe, but we kind of got used to it," she says. "We slept with our clothes on in case we had to run in the middle of the night. We just made fun of it. The war was always something in the back of our minds."

By the time she was 10 years old, in 2000, her parents decided it was no longer safe to live in Burundi. So they moved to Belgium as refugees. Moving to a new country, and a new continent, at such a young age wasn't easy for Leila. Even though her new classmates were friendly -- she remembers them smiling at her and trying to connect with her -- it still took her a while to make friends. And though she had long dreamt of Europe as a sort of promised land, she learned that the reality of it was not that simple.

"When I arrived in Belgium, I had spoken Kirundi my whole life, and learned French only at school, but not enough to feel confortable in a conversation. Plus, I was the only black girl in my classroom," she says. "It's a lonely moment when you realize, oh, wow, you thought it would be a dream, but when you get there, you have to overcome a lot of things and learn a new culture, learn a new language," she says. "The temperature is different, the social environment is different, everything is different."

Being a curious child turned out to be her greatest asset that kept her positive through this major life change. Keeping an open mind and asking questions helped her to get to know this new, unfamiliar environment. "Instead of seeing things as a difficulty, you just try to see it's a good opportunity to learn something different," she says. "Don't be afraid and don't stay in your corner. Be open and just make the best of each situation."

Soon Leila began to become more confident and with confidence came success. She eventually learned several more languages -- including French, English, Dutch, and Swahili -- and she was accepted to law school to pursue her passion for social justice.

All the while, Leila was blossoming into a lovely young woman. At nearly six feet tall, with high structured cheekbones and dark eyes, she began to catch the attention of modeling agencies, in Belgium and Europe. People told her she looked like Naomi Campbell, the British model and entrepreneur.

At first Leila brushed aside the requests to model. Her mother was suspicious for her to start a modeling career. Back home in Burundi, there were strong gender norms and social mores that prevented girls like her from pursuing modeling. It just wasn't a "thing" for girls like her, she was told. Where her mother saw a dead end, Leila saw an opportunity. Not just to lead a successful career, but to inspire other girls like her around the world. Eventually, with a little help from her sister, she was able to convince her mom to let her give it a try.

Then her fashion career caught fire. She appeared in shoots for *Vogue* and *Harper's Bazaar* among other magazines. This started her on a new journey, to NYC where she lives now. "That's another dream that came true for me," she says. "But once again I had to start all over by adapting, and learning about the fashion industry, with its set of values. That led to building my career; having a voice; and becoming the woman I am today: a blend of three cultures -- African, European, and American."

Now, as Burundi's first top model, she's walked the runway wearing the dresses of some of the most well-known fashion designers: Oscar de la Renta, Marc Jacobs, Gucci, Hermes and others. From Fashion Week in Paris, to Milan and New York City, her career takes her around the globe, where she's become, in her own words, a "citizen of the world."

Her mom has now become her number one fan. "She's so proud because she realized that it's just a job -- no different from any other job," Leila says. "It's just a different path."

Over the years Leila's life path has inspired young black girls in Belgium, Burundi and across the African continent -- showing them there is a place for them in the modeling world. With a growing influence and platform, she looked for ways to be a force for good, helping girls who are struggling to find their way in conflict-affected countries like hers.

Growing up Leila had seen Marguerite "Maggy" Barankitse on TV sharing about her work with Maison Shalom. "In her speeches, she talks about humanity, about forgiveness, about hope," says Leila. She was touched by how she helps orphans gain access to a better future through loving support and education. Founded in 1993, Maggy adopted 30 orphans in Burundi during the civil war, and has gone on to help thousands more. She won peace prizes and would tour European countries and reach out to the Burundi diaspora to raise awareness and ask for support. "What she has done is just amazing!" says Leila.

Inspired by Maggy's work, Leila began to use her model platform as a force for good. She knew that her life could easily have gone this way. Had one of the bombs or gunshots she'd heard going off as a child, she or her family could very well have been in the line of fire. Five years ago there was another crisis and 300,000 people left the country. Maggie had to flee the country to the neighboring country of Rwanda, where she opened another house for Burundi's refugees.

In 2018 Leila wrote to Maggy asking how she might help. Since then, she has leveraged the power of the media to bring attention to Maison Shalom. She's given interviews bringing light to the crisis in Burundi, and visited a refugee camp in Rwanda where she met with some of the young people displaced by the war. "If I can be that channel to just open up people and even the young generation, I want them to just do something because it's not something that only international community can do. It's like everybody as an individual should do something."

Then for Christmas in 2019 Leila visited Maison Shalom's house in Rwanda's capital city of Kigali. "I imagined it would be sad, like an orphanage," she says. Leila was pleasantly surprised to see all children dressed up in their uniforms -- performing: singing, dancing, and smiling. "They really made me cry -- it reminded me of when I was little. It was just really beautiful."

Maggy gives the children all these opportunities in life -- to go to school, to learn how to cook, and to get a job. Some choose art and others choose career paths. Most importantly she gives them dignity. "She wants them to feel like this is just a moment in their life, that it doesn't define the rest of their life," says Leila. She wants to build a strong generation of young people who can then become the leaders their country so desperately needs. "If you give a hand in life, that's really what matters."

As climate change increases the instability in countries across East Africa, Leila feels a sense of urgency about increasing support for Maison Shalom. Conflicts over scarce resources are multiplying as climate change barrels its way across the agriculture countries of the region. The global outbreak of the Coronavirus has made her even more keen to join the fight against climate change. When the environment is threatened, people aren't able to get the necessary nutrients and with their weaker immune systems, they are more likely to catch the virus. "While this disease is now affecting everyone, some don't have access to how to eat healthy," she says.

Leila's new mission is not just to educate people about physical health, but about mental health and getting over trauma too.

"Your first condition in life, it doesn't define when you're going to become. So really, I hope that people will see that through hard work, good health habits, and through curiosity and hope and love, they can overcome."

When you have conviction, nobody can stop you.
I don't want to hate. I want to believe in human
beings.

Marguerite Barankitse

Call to Action: Follow Leila: https://www.instagram.com/leila.nda/?hl=en Support the Maison Shalom and help refugee children in Burundi and Rwanda live their dreams of a brighter future. https://www.maisonshalom.org/

AN OPPORTUNITY TO GIVE BACK – VIA ZOOM!
Demi Weitz
Quarantunes
Los Angeles, California

Demi Weitz's seventeenth birthday was unlike any other. It was the first day of spring break for her high school, Campbell Hall School in Studio City. She'd been looking forward to celebrating with her friends by hiking the nearby trails and having a picnic. Then the COVID-19 pandemic hit the U.S., and her hometown of Los Angeles, like almost everywhere else in the world, was in lockdown. So for Demi, a normal birthday party was just out of the question.

The night before her birthday, Demi's friends surprised her with socially-distanced picnic. Then, for the actual day, her father had an idea. As a partner at WME, a major talent agency, Richard Weitz represents well-known musicians who'd been affected by the pandemic. Of necessity, everyone had stopped going to live concerts, or listening to jazz at their favorite clubs: cancelled concerts and engagements meant lost income for them.

Demi's father had just gotten a text from a friend, a piano player in Chicago, asking him if there was any way they could lift people's spirits. An idea was born -- with a virtual birthday party for Demi at their kitchen table, with 40 friends and family connected via Zoom. "My dad invited his friend Debbie Gibson," says Demi. "And someone else invited John Mayer who sang my favorite song, *Don't Stop Believing.*" Then together, these two recording artists harmonized singing Happy Birthday to Demi, and everyone joined in. "It was the coolest day of my life," Demi says. "I was like, 'What has just happened?!'"

While she being serenaded by Debbie Gibson and John Mayer, a thought occurred to Demi. This was such a great way to gather people, to create a sense of community, and to let them enjoy music without leaving the safety of their homes. Why not organize Zoom concerts, invite people, and ask them to donate money for a good cause? Thus was born Quarantunes. "I realized that with Zoom, we have this amazing platform," Demi says. "It's a really great way to connect people!"

Growing up in L.A. as the daughter of a successful agent, Demi is well aware of her privilege. She is careful not to come across as spoiled, to drop names, or to feed off of someone else's work. "I'm the opposite of a flashy person," she says. "I try to understand my privilege and my good fortune."

In order to make her idea happen, Demi had to learn a whole new skill set, so she got busy. She started by setting up a GoFundMe page. Then she wrote a short description about the first organization she chose to benefit. Every Christmas, her family had supported their local community's free clinic: they would bring holiday cheer by "adopting a family," buying gifts for the children and food for the whole family. Sometimes they helped out with rent and medical expenses too. Over the years, they'd adopted the same family, so Demi had been able to see for herself the kinds of challenges they faced.

As she planned for the first Quarantunes concert, Demi set a goal of raising $10,000, then her father encouraged her to up the ante to $30,000. Demi was thrilled when they surpassed their goal, raising $33,000. She knew what a difference it would make to the clinic. "This was an opportunity to start something that is my own -- and to give back," Demi says. "I'm using this, and the things that I've been given, to make a change."

In high school, Demi had been an activist - joining her friends in protesting gun violence, and working for women's rights. In the fall of 2019, she made posters for the Global Climate Action Strike with some of her environmentalist friends. "They have inspired all of us to do the little things we can," she says. "Like switching from using single-use plastic water bottles to reusable water bottles."

Living in Beverly Hills, Demi could see that under all the sparkle of celebrity life was a serious crisis: 60,000 people were living on the streets in the "City of Angels." She could also see that low-income people were the most vulnerable to the effects of climate change. Global warming is blamed for the five-fold increase in areas burnt in California over the last five decades: and in 2019 the housing crisis in Los Angeles was exacerbated when 7,860 wildfires burned more than 250,000 acres of land.

Then came the pandemic, and everyone was scrambling to provide shelter for those 60,000 people. Clinics were in desperate need of support to provide services and PPEs for all the homeless. "It's a really bleak time," Demi says. "People are losing their jobs; they can't even put a meal on the table for their families."

This was an injustice that Demi was unwilling to accept. So, for the third Quarantunes concert, she researched her options, and decided to partner with the United Way Greater Los Angeles, the largest agency working with the homeless. Someone offered to match all donations up to $50,000. And on April 4, 2020, for two hours, while musicians entertained 200 of her friends via Zoom, Demi worked her magic. She received enough donations to meet the challenge, and the amount she brought in was doubled. "We ended up raising $100,000 in just 30 hours," she says. "It was amazing!"

Demi was really happy that with the funds they had raised, hundreds of homeless people were given safe shelter in motel rooms, and Wellness Kits with hand sanitizer, gloves, and face masks. Encouraged with their success, Demi and her father decided to organize additional fundraising concerts. And after organizing just 10 Zoom benefit concerts, she has raised over $3,000,000. And as of April 2021, they've raised $20 million and counting!

Her success is no surprise, considering the high-profile acts she gets to play: John Legend, Rod Stewart, Sting, and James Bay, among others, have performed for Quarantunes events. "You can see these artists in their homes, and me and my dad in our kitchen -- it's a very welcoming and inviting space," Demi says. I feel like everyone's on the same playing field. It's like, we're inviting you into our home; and these artists are inviting you into theirs."

Meanwhile, on some level, Demi's days are like those of any other teenager in quarantine. Her education is her #1 priority. To keep up with her schoolwork, she is home schooling by Zooming with her teachers and classmates. "Then, in between English and Math class, I go to my dad's room, and jump in on a call," she says.

Behind the scenes, Demi is becoming a businesswoman. "My father's life is music," she says. So, he's in charge of inviting his musician friends to participate. Demi and her father work together to set goals, and respond to donors' requests. Each week she researches potential beneficiaries and prepares interview questions for the representatives of the organization, searching for the right match. "I'm learning so many aspects of the business" she says. And while she was once fearful of public speaking, she now has lots of practice honing her speaking skills, as she shares her passion for each organization's work with her dad's friends.

"Usually I'll interview someone that runs an organization - and we've had some frontline workers on the Zoom call. It has been really great to connect to people, to have the chance to shed light on crucial issues and raise awareness this way."

Increasingly, celebrities from the musical world have been joined by civic leaders like Los Angeles Mayor Eric Garcetti. Getting to hear from those in charge of fighting the pandemic has been both educational and shocking, Demi says. "Every call has been so inspiring," Demi says. "You are hearing from people from all different walks of life, with different experiences."

Quarantunes's support for local charities has now grown to include national organizations, like the United Way's relief efforts in six other cities. Beyond raising money for the homeless, for clinics and food banks, Demi likes to educate people who join their events. "All of their stories were very inspiring," Demi says. "It's real and authentic -- that's the most beautiful part."

Given her father's national network of generous friends, Quarantunes has been able to help in pandemic hot spots like New City's public hospitals. They've also supported hospitals across the country and the L.A. Food Bank. As the number of COVID-19 deaths in the U.S. surpassed 100,000, it seems unlikely that things will go back to normal anytime soon, Demi says. "The pandemic has literally changed the world as we know it," she says. "These issues, and the people that are suffering now: it's not like it will go away in a second."

The quarantine has impacted everyone's lives on all levels. So, when the Hollywood Bowl was closed for the first time in its 98-year history, people were understandably upset. Every year this iconic outdoor venue is for many people a favorite summer activity. Breathing fresh air under the overarching trees and enjoying expansive views of the city, it offers people a welcome respite from their busy lives and noisy highway traffic. Listening to their favorite musicians, it was heavenly. And it is every musicians' dream to one day play there.

So, when it was abruptly closed, Demi and her dad came up with a "wild and crazy" idea. They made lots of phone calls and got permission to use it as the venue for their 10th Quarantunes concert. They extended the limit to 1,000 invitation-only guests -- and kept it a secret. The concert was cohosted by music legend and rainmaker, Clive Davis, who spoke of the power of music to unite, and shared personal stories about each guest. The guests included Kenny Loggins (who sang "Footloose") and Gloria Gaynor (who sang "I Will Survive"), as well as Barry Manilow, Santana, and Rob Thomas. Orchestra leader John Williams opened the evening with the overture to *Star Wars,* with the trumpet section performing on the Hollywood Bowl stage – all with social distancing, of course. And Kevin Bacon did zoom dancing.

Demi is very proud of the beneficiaries they had chosen for this event: Share Our Strength's Billy Shore spoke about No Kid Hungry, proclaiming "This is a problem we can solve." Members of the Youth Orchestra of Los Angeles members played a short piece. And Billy Ellish talked about her mother's vegan meal-delivery charity Support + Feed. One appreciative person on the Zoom call said, "You are changing the narrative -- from fear, anxiety, and isolation, to connection and community."

For Demi what started as an unusual birthday celebration has become a life-changing experience. Organizing the Quarantunes events has been both rewarding and personally transforming. She had originally planned to become a film director, joining her dad in the entertainment industry. Thanks to Quarantunes, the 17-year-old has found her true passion for helping others. And now that she has discovered just what she is capable of, she wants to use her position in the world to make a positive change. "When you strip everything else away, the whole purpose of this is just to help," she says. "And that is something that I always remember and will never forget, because that is the intention behind all of it."

A dream you dream alone is only a dream.
A dream you dream together is a reality.

John Lennon

Call to Action: Find ways to care for those less fortunate. Create a GoFundMe campaign to support local social services in your community. Learn more about Demi's project at https://quarantunes.unitedwayla.org.

A VOICE FOR THE VOICELESS
Betsabe Reyna
Pathways to Peace
New Jersey

One day while she was cleaning her room, Betsabe Reyna opened up her journal from her first trip to Mexico, seven years earlier, and rediscovered this entry.

I will do whatever I can, even if I risk my life for the sake of others.

While she didn't remember writing it, when she read it, Betsabe felt an echo of her earlier conviction deep in her soul. And she started crying. "Wow, this is it," she thought. "This is what I want to do with my life."

Betsabe had grown up with a unique cultural perspective. Born in the United States with dual citizenship in Peru, she was raised in a small town in New Jersey. From a young age, her parents had instilled in her a strong work ethic, and morals that were guided by their Christian faith. Her family is a warm and loving one, and she was particularly close to her mother. "My mother had a very traditional upbringing," Betsabe says. "So she has a wealth of insight to offer."

But at school, Betsabe was more like an outcast. She didn't enjoy school very much, and she wasn't sure what she wanted to do when she grew up. And as the only Latina child in her class, she felt uncomfortable.

But all that changed at the age of 16 when she was offered the opportunity to travel to Mexico with 30 other kids. In the summer of 2012, Betsabe traveled to a small village in Mexico near Tijuana with her church's youth group to volunteer in an orphanage and work with the local community. There she witnessed a great deal of violence in the streets, and heard stories about domestic abuse. It was both shocking and scary for her to see this happening. The culture was so different than the one she'd grown up in. It opened her eyes to the fact that some people live in a very dangerous world, even in their own homes: and it instilled in her a passion to do what she could to protect them and do what she could to help.

Ever since that life-changing trip to Mexico, Betsabe has found ways to immerse herself in other cultures and other countries. And wherever she travels, she tries to use her voice to speak out against the inequalities, and the injustice, that makes the lives of so many people around the world so difficult.

In college, Betsabe studied theology and went on exchange in York, England. While she knew that she wanted to do good in the world, she was unsure of how to go about it. She had passion and drive, but she also needed direction, and guidance. Then, several of her professors nominated Betsabe to travel to Greece as a volunteer to help refugees. Along with five classmates, Betsabe spent three weeks in Athens.

When she arrived in Greece, the mood in the Olympic stadium in Athens was far different than the glorious fanfare of the summer games that had been held there almost 15 years earlier. Then it was a spirit of celebration: now the stadium was filled with thousands of desperate Afghani and Persian refugees who were passing through Greece. The resources needed to help these people survive, let alone build new lives, were just not available. All there was for them was an empty cement building, bleachers, and a playing field. To make it worse, three times a day, buses would unload more refugees at the stadium, sometimes hundreds of people at a time. So it was overwhelming, and very discouraging.

Betsabe was assigned to distribute food, offer basic medical care, and refer people to doctors and nurses when necessary. She and the other volunteers did the best they could to help. It was hard work, and it was disheartening to not be able to do more. But the people were really suffering and clearly needed her help, so she knew she couldn't just run away from the challenges. She dedicated herself completely to her work and tried not to focus on all that she couldn't do. Together, this small team of 11 people helped several thousand people. Betsabe continued her service for another 14 days at another refugee camp to help to manage the program's finances.

After graduating from college, Betsabe was trying to figure out what she should do next when a thought came to her to travel to Turkey. At this time, Turkey had the highest concentration of displaced persons and refugees in the world. She knew she was needed there.

At first, her mother wasn't so enthusiastic about her going to that part of the world. She was afraid that it could be dangerous. But she could see Betsabe's passionate desire for positive change, and she didn't want to stand in the way. So she reached out to a friend who did mission work in Turkey, and who could provide Betsabe with connections on the ground; and members of her church helped raise the money to pay her way.

When she got to Turkey, Betsabe traveled with five others in a small minivan, arriving at a refugee camp just a short walk away from the Syrian border. Due to the sensitivity of the mission, she had hardly any details about where should would be stationed or what she would be doing before she got there. She'd had to put her trust in God and in the organizing group. Now she discovered that she was on the front lines of the refugee crisis. Hundreds of thousands of Syrians were fleeing from Bashar al-Assad's brutal regime in Syria, and Turkey was often the first border they crossed.

She had to put a lot of faith in God to help her through this time. All the pain and suffering seemed unbearable to her otherwise. Regardless of their religion or culture, Betsabe saw the people staying in the refugee camp as her brothers and sisters. "Everyone fleeing violence and persecution is a human being," she says. "No one chooses to be a refugee."

One day, a group of five men drove up to the refugee camp in a pickup truck. They opened fire and shot several of the men in the camp. Betsabe and her coworkers hid in their minivan, hoping to stay safe. And it was while she was huddling inside the van that she had a crushing realization. Her ability to escape the gunfire and hide away gave her considerable privilege. Those staying in the camp did not have that option. Once again, she promised herself that she would do whatever she could to protect them.

These refugees were people who had been living normal lives before -- people with families, and jobs, and pets, and romances, and favorite books, and aspirations. "I realized that at any moment, normal life can be taken away from anyone," she says. And with the problems caused by climate change creating an ever-increasing number of refugees in the world -- by 2019 the UN reported there were 70.8 million refugees worldwide -- Betsabe knows very well that this is a problem that is not going to just go away. In fact it is growing rapidly, even alarmingly. "As long as I can, I will continue to fight for those who are suffering, and not take anything for granted. Protecting the rights of people around the world is as important to me as protecting my own family," she says.

Now back in New Jersey, Betsabe is preparing for her future by studying political science at Rutgers University. She also works on helping people across the U.S. access clean power. Later, she plans to pursue a PhD in Middle East studies. Her goal is to be an advocate for the rights of refugees, Indigenous people, and people in need across the world.

In 2017, Betsabe was invited to serve as a delegate and representative for Pathways to Peace, an NGO at the United Nations. Founded in 1998 by Avon Mattison, this organization promotes peacebuilding and education around the world. As its delegate, Betsabe represents Pathways to Peace at UN meetings to raise awareness and propose solutions for religious conflicts. Avon coaches Betsabe to help design peaceful solutions to chaotic circumstances.

And it was through Pathways to Peace that Betsabe found in Avon Mattison the mentor she'd always longed for. Despite living across the country from each other, and being from two different cultures, the two grew close. Perhaps Avon reminds her of her own wise and loving mother. "I feel the warmth that she carries in her heart and soul whenever I speak to her," Betsabe says. "She is a woman of her word. She has never failed me in being a mentor, colleague, and friend."

As the refugee crisis in the world continues to become more dire every day, sometimes Betsabe gets discouraged. It is God that she turns to, to remember her purpose and her calling. And when she calls upon Avon, Avon listens to her express her pain and frustration; and then reminds her of how important her work is, and why it's important not to give up.

As the Pathways to Peace representative at the United Nations, Betsabe is honored to carry on Avon's legacy, and is determined to remain positive, encouraging, and courageous no matter what. Like Avon, Betsabe believes that intergenerational collaboration and conversation can spark new ideas and new ways of thinking. "Throughout my life, I have been inspired by the stories people have told me," she says. She believes that by listening to the stories of people from a diversity of backgrounds, professions, and communities, world change *will* become more feasible. "I am hopeful that through this exchange -- by telling our stories, and by listening, truly listening to each other -- we can build a more peaceful, equitable world."

We are called to speak for the weak, for the
voiceless, for the victims of our nation
and for those it calls enemy, for no document
from human hands can make these humans any
less our brothers and sisters.

Dr. Martin Luther King, Jr.

Call to Action: The refugee crisis is real, and it is worldwide. Learn how you can help by visiting Pathways to Peace. https://pathwaystopeace. org/

CARRYING ON HIS GRANDFATHER'S LEGACY
Cesar Chavez
Los Angeles, California

To millions of people across the United States, Cesar Chavez was "the Latin Gandhi." But to his namesake, the famous Cesar Chavez was just his grandfather. When Anthony Chavez had his first son in 1981, he had given the baby his father's name. By then, the senior Cesar Chavez was traveling most of the time.

Little Cesar often heard stories about his grandfather; about how he had awakened Americans nationwide to the plight of migrant farm workers in California and convinced them to join them in boycotting one of their favorite fruits -- grapes. It took five long years, but eventually they got the farm owners to make concessions -- to stop using deadly pesticides - that made a huge difference in people's lives.

Little Cesar often saw his grandfather on TV, as he went around the state, inspiring union workers, demanding fair contracts from farmers, and challenging state officials to care for *all* of their people. He always closed with the same message: "When you have people together who believe in something very strongly - whether it's religion or politics or unions - things happen," he would tell them. "We can choose to use our lives for others; to bring about a better, and more just, world for our children."

It was always exciting when Cesar, the "gentle giant," would finally come home from his travels. Most of the United Farm Workers (UFW) families lived together on a 200-acre ranch near the Tehachapi Mountains, which had once been a health center for people with tuberculosis. It had also once served as a movie set. Then the director of the film sold it to the UFW for just $1. Cesar called it "La Paz," for the peacefulness he felt there. Being in nature was always the best medicine to help him rest, especially after a long journey.

Cesar named their communal kitchen, where the community would share meals together, *Pan Y Vino* (Bread and Wine). "He had studied cultures where the people who worked together, ate together," his grandson explains. He loved to watch the children running around, sharing stories with his devoted community of comrades. "All the volunteers working with the union, they weren't just workmates -- they were our friends, people we trusted and depended on."

For most of his life, young Cesar lived next door to his grandfather. By the time he woke up at 6:00 a.m. to go to school, he'd see his grandfather already walking down the dirt road to begin his workday. Often, he'd come home late at night. "I always knew he was really busy," Cesar says, adding, "But he always took time for us."

After school, Cesar would stop by his grandfather's office. "He'd stop whatever he was doing, even during meetings," Cesar remembers. "He'd bring us in and introduce us to everyone, then hug us and tell us he was busy and that we should do our homework and come back later to visit."

What he remembers most are the long hikes they'd take together into the mountains. "He'd show me these beautiful trails, and places he called our secret caves," he says. "And we'd talk about grandfather-grandson things."

A devoted student of Mahatma Gandhi, Cesar Chavez often fasted to bring much-needed media attention to the farmworkers' struggle. In 1987, he started the Fast for Life. Little Cesar, who was just six, visited him every day and brought him water. He fondly remembers the long hugs his grandfather would give him.

To Cesar, it seemed like a normal childhood, except that they lived at the UFW headquarters. On Friday nights, all of Cesar's cousins would join with his father in the big hall to silkscreen the UFW's black eagle onto red flags. "It was great fun," Cesar says. "We'd run with each flag to the end of the hall, lay it out to dry, and run back for the next one." By the end of the night there would be thousands of flags laying all over the floor, waiting to be put onto poles. Cesar would go to bed exhausted, but happy knowing the next day he'd see everyone waving the flags, and that he had played a part.

Sometimes his grandfather would remind Cesar and his cousins of the deeper meaning of their work. Even though he had been born and raised in the United States and served in the Army, he had felt the pain of being treated like a second-hand citizen. He wanted his people to retain pride in their own heritage as well in the contributions they had made to their new home. "Symbols are important," he would say. "We chose the Aztec eagle for our symbol, because it gives us pride. When our people see it, they feel a sense of dignity."

Saturday mornings, Cesar, and his family and friends, would all pile into station wagons and caravan down to that day's march, strike, or demonstration in Los Angeles or San Diego; or sometimes at their local supermarkets. While their parents formed picket lines, the children would walk around the parking lot passing out fliers and asking people for donations. Young and old, they each did their part, in solidarity with those who were working away in hot fields without health benefits, or enough food to feed their own families.

Cesar always wanted the children to walk close by him in the front of the marches. He found joy and energy in their youthful enthusiasm and the songs they'd sing, like "De Colores." Along the way, the children often learned important lessons from him. "One time a van of children drove by flipping us off," young Cesar remembers. "We were mad—but my grandfather just waved to them and gave them a big smile," he says. "Later he talked with us about the importance of nonviolence, of just being nice to one another. And he would say 'There is enough love and goodwill in our movement to give energy to our struggle and still have plenty left over to change the climate of hate and fear around us.'"

Sometimes young Cesar and his cousins would become discouraged by the seemingly overwhelming odds against them. "Our opponents in the agricultural industry are very powerful; and farm workers are weak in money and influence," their grandfather would say. "But we have another kind of power that comes from the justice of our cause. If we are willing to sacrifice for the cause, and persist in nonviolence; and if we work to spread the message of our struggle, millions of people around the world will respond from their hearts, will support our efforts...And in the end, we will overcome." Then, renewed by his heartfelt words, everyone would smile, and shout out, *"Viva la Causa!"*

Cesar's grandfather had always nourished his love for learning. Since he himself had never had a chance to finish the eighth grade, he strongly encouraged his people to stay in school and get a good education. And even though they were making progress, he was troubled that Latinos were still dropping out of school at record levels. Some had to leave, to get jobs so they could help feed their families. However, too many were dropping out for the wrong reasons.

Cesar Chavez knew that oppressed people throughout history often missed out on getting an education. He also knew that the key to sustaining the movement was to educate people about the issues; to help them distinguish facts from myths, let them know what progress was being made, and learn about the battles being won by their brothers and sisters in other parts of the country. He was troubled that most books about the movement weren't available in Spanish, so his people couldn't read about how they were making history.

On many levels, Cesar Chavez was way ahead of his time. Long before the technology was ready, he had dreamed of creating a network of radio stations to educate and entertain his people. He was determined to find a way to keep them connected with up-to-date news so they could quickly respond when called to action. He wanted to build on their Latino oral tradition, by passing on their history through storytelling. He first tried to buy ad space on the local radio stations. "But back in the 60's and 70's, the stations were all owned by the growers," he told his grandson. "They threw us out and told us never to come back."

Undeterred, he pursued his dream in a most unconventional way. He designed a plan to invent a makeshift microwave telephone system and received a grant from the state of California to implement it. The phone system, with satellite dishes on the mountaintops soon became the second largest in California, next to Pacific Bell.

From an early age, young Cesar had shown promise in technology and had taken an electronics class in high school. He'd been helping his father run the UFW's audio-visual equipment and installing their phone and alarm systems. "I ran all the wire in the attics and basements, crawling through spider webs," Cesar says of his early adventures into the world of technology. So, he was a natural candidate to help his grandfather build this new communications system. Soon he was climbing mountains with his father, installing the satellite dishes and connecting people in cities all over California. In the early days, it was quite a challenging project. If just one of the dishes went down, half of the cities in the network would be disconnected. Sometimes in the middle of the night, they'd have to travel to the cold, icy mountaintops to fix one, returning the next morning just in time for Cesar to go to school.

Finally, the project was ready: Cesar's grandfather applied for their first radio license, housed it in the National Farm Workers Service Center, and named it Radio Campesino. By May 1, 1983, they were on the air for the first time. Cesar warmly welcomed all his listeners, his courageous words ringing out strong and true. By November 1990 they were transmitting all the way to Phoenix, Arizona. After many long years, Cesar's dream was finally starting to come true.

But he wouldn't live to see the day when Radio Campesino would be connected via the latest satellite technology, computers, and digital audio software.

Cesar Chavez died near where he was born, in Uma, Arizona, where he'd been helping to fight another fight for his people. Young Cesar knew that something must be wrong when his father came to pick him up at school early one day. After putting the younger children in the car, he put his arm around Cesar and whispered in his ear, "Tata has passed away." At first Cesar couldn't believe his beloved grandfather was gone. But as they drove home, he heard the announcement on the radio. Then it hit him, hard.

Cesar's grandfather would have been proud of all those with careers in law, medicine, and education, who brought their children to his funeral. Rudolfo Anaya, known as a father of Chicano literature, gave the eulogy. "Our morning star," he called him. "...that luminous light that greeted workers as they gathered around the dawn campfires." And young Cesar read aloud the Prayer of St. Francis Assisi, in honor of his grandfather's love of nature.

Cesar is now carrying on his grandfather's legacy as the director of digital strategy at the Cesar Chavez Foundation. "Everything my grandfather fought for is still worth fighting for," he says, and adds, "Every day I realize how much the world needs to change, so our people can have equal rights, and peace. I try every day to push myself toward that goal, the way my grandfather did."

Now every day from 5:30 am to 3:00 pm., Radio Campesino is broadcast to people in eight states. During the workday, it lifts workers' spirits by playing Nortena Banda top 40's music. Local experts are featured on a 30-minute talk show. A paralegal informs them of their immigration rights; a highway patrolman urges them to wear seat belts; a nurse tells them how to protect themselves from the effects of pesticides. Because of Radio Campesino, now apple pickers in Washington, industrial workers in factories and woodshops in Oregon, and farm workers from Salinas, California to Puma and Parker, Arizona are all connected to a network of people helping people.

Listeners call in to share their struggles. "My husband got fired and we don't know what to do," or "They're not paying us overtime." Radio Campesino guides people to the UFW, or in some cases, to a lawyer. "We're always here if people need our help," Cesar says. "Over the years, we've become a useful tool for the whole community to better themselves, to keep the UFW's struggle going, and to keep my grandfather's legacy alive."

California was the first state to have a holiday in honor of Cesar Chavez -- the Cesar Chavez Day of Service and Learning. Now nine other states

-- Colorado, New Mexico, Michigan, Texas, Arizona, Utah, Wisconsin, Washington, Minnesota and Las Vegas -- all have a Day of Recognition as well.

Cesar now shares his grandfather's message by traveling to schools and communities across California. He knows his grandfather would be pleased to know that 41 schools have been named in his honor. "My grandfather inspired me to dedicate my life to helping others in any way I can," he says. Then he paraphrases a Mexican *dicho* by Padilla: "Cesar was our pine tree, and we are his forest."

La Paz has been transformed into a retreat center with a beautiful memorial garden around Cesar Chavez's gravesite. His office is now a museum where visitors from around the world continue to learn about this great man. If you visit there someday, you just might hear his words echo in your ears, "Perhaps we can bring the day when children will learn that being fully man and fully woman means to give one's life to the liberation of those who suffer. It is up to each one of us. It won't happen unless we decide to use our lives to show the way."

True wealth is not measured in money or status
or power.
It is measured in the legacy we leave behind for
those we love and those we inspire.

Cesar Chavez

Call to Action: Find ways to use technology to educate and bring hope to oppressed people. Tune into Radio Campesino: www.radiocampesina. com. Support the Cesar E. Chavez Foundation: www.chavezfoundation. org.

CAPTAIN PLANET:
A PHILANTHROPIC ENVIRONMENTAL LEADER
John R. Seydel

Georgia Turner Foundation
Atlanta, Georgia

Growing up, John R. Seydel loved the environmental cartoon series *Captain Planet.* At the end of every episode, there would be a Planeteer Alert where the diverse team of global heroes would talk directly to the audience about ways to find solutions to the environmental problems in their communities. The Planeteers would end each show with the same uplifting message: *The power is yours!* "It taught us how to be part of the solution, not part of the problem -- and to inspire others along the way," John R. says. "It was really empowering for a young kid like me. I couldn't wait to get out there in the community and be a Planeteer myself."

As he grew older, John R. understood that his grandfather, Ted Turner, had cocreated this TV show. "When I was finally old enough to understand just how much he had done, and inspired others to do for the environment, I realized he was a real-life Captain Planet," he says.

In 1990, during the height of leading his media empire, John R.'s grandfather founded the Turner Foundation to carry on his legacy of environmental advocacy and philanthropy. Ted's children and grandchildren serve as its board of directors, and his grandchildren make up T3G, the foundation's junior board of directors; John R. advises on youth engagement, leadership development, environmental stewardship, regenerative agriculture and experiential learning in nature.

As a lifelong animal lover and advocate, one of the organizations that holds a special place in John R.'s life is the Turner Endangered Species Fund (TESF), which honors the Turner Foundation's motto of "Save Everything." It uses public-private partnerships to secure land that can be used as an incubator for creating self-sustaining populations of endangered animals, and then expand and reintroduce them to the environment. "My grandfather did this earlier in his life with bringing back the American bison population," John R. says. "Like I said, he's a real-life Captain Planet." TESF is incubating many amazing species, among them the bolson tortoise, the peregrine falcon, the Northern Rocky Mountain gray wolf, the lesser prairie chicken, the Chiricahua leopard frog, the Arctic grayling, the Chupadera springsnail, the gopher tortoise, the Westlope and Rio Grande cutthroat trout, and the black-footed ferret.

The Turner Foundation is one of the most dedicated environmental nonprofits in the world, assisting environmentalists across the U.S.. To date it has contributed more than $400 million to environmental causes and community/movement building. Keeping a strong and engaged community of environmentalists is necessary to drive all of this sustainable action forward. The Turner Foundation works on growing the movement by highlighting efforts in diversity, equity, and inclusion that will involve more vulnerable groups and people, in order to gain their valuable perspectives. It also provides support to educational and immersion programs to encourage youth participation in these crucial issues, which are the primary global issues of their shared future.

John R. has been especially impacted by the women in his family who, like his grandfather, are all fierce environmental advocates. His grandmother, Pat Mitchell, was the first female CEO of PBS, and author of *Becoming A Dangerous Woman*, which advocates for global women's rights issues. This fighting spirit deeply influenced his mother, Laura Seydel, who has advocated tirelessly for vulnerable environments, people, and youth through her work with the Captain Planet Foundation, the Children & Nature Network, Mothers and Others for Clean Air, Project Drawdown, Chattahoochee Riverkeeper, the International Union of the Conservation of Nature, the Waterkeeper Alliance, Recycle Across America, and the League of Conservation Voters Education Fund.

John R. has also been greatly inspired by another matriarch of the family, Grandma Jane (Fonda). A lifelong activist, she risked her personal freedom -- and was arrested -- for standing with the young leaders at a Fire Drill Friday event in Washington DC on October 11, 2019. "She watched these brave youth demanding action from adults and political leaders while building coalitions that said 'Listen to us. ACT!,'" John R. explains. "At the time, she'd been feeling climate anxiety, and then, thanks to youth leaders like Greta Thunberg, her spark was reignited. She became determined to get 'back on the horse' so to say, and do everything she can to fight to her last breath for environmental justice, clean energy for all, an inclusive economy, regenerative agriculture -- all of it." Jane was arrested six times and inspired so many other people of all ages including John R.'s sisters, Vasser and Laura Elizabeth, mother, Laura and even his other "dangerous Grandmother" Pat

Mitchell. Reflecting on how it was young people who had inspired her, John R. says, "What these young Planeteers have awakened is truly powerful!"

John R. is honored to now help carry on this amazing legacy by serving on the boards for various environmental organizations, including the Captain Planet Foundation (CPF), which inspired him so as a child. Through the CPF, he has empowered countless youth through a STEM curriculum integrated garden immersion program called Project Learning Gardens and works to awaken that inner Planeteer in future youth leaders. Through the pandemic, while schools were closed, these vacant Learning Gardens were turned into Giving Gardens and in partnership with the Atlanta Food Bank and Foodwell Alliance, employed local farmers who helped contribute more than 100,000 pounds of food to families in need. Further, CPF's Project Hero, a free, project-based learning tool engages young people in quests to help threatened species and ecosystems in their own communities while in-person learning was limited. John R. enjoys being a mentor for the Ocean Heroes Bootcamp, which trains, empowers and connects hundreds of young water Planeteers from 40 different countries to create campaigns, programs and even policies that fight plastic pollution, conserve precious habitat and protect endangered species.

Beyond his foundation and non-profit work, John R. serves in the Mayor's Office of Resilience as the City of Atlanta's Director of Sustainability. He is proudly working to combat issues such as food insecurity and climate change, while making Atlanta more affordable, equitable, and resilient. The City of Atlanta passed the 100% Clean Energy Goal and Clean Energy Atlanta Plan for 2035, and John R. is devoted to attaining this lofty goal while ensuring a just, equitable, and sustainable transition to a clean energy future for all.

Going forward, John R. wants youth to know that there are countless ways for them to get involved in sustainability. "Just get involved, no matter how great or small the contribution is. If you care about an issue, and you know what you are doing is right for your community, tell the doubters what my Grandpa used to tell them: 'Lead, follow, or get out of the way!'"

Of all the environmental projects the Turner family has supported, perhaps the most historic was Ted's $1 billion gift to the United Nations Foundation in 1997. "I think what my grandfather has done, what my grandmothers, mother, sisters, wife and my really whole family embody, and what I hope to carry on as a legacy is in line with SDG 17, which is to revitalize the global partnership for sustainable development," says John R. Global issues like climate change, poverty and the extinction crises are the unprecedented challenges of our time. It also represents the unprecedented opportunity for global cooperation. Like the Planeteers in Captain Planet, "by our powers combine" Earth's real-life Planeteers can work together to transform our energy, transportation and agriculture economies to be clean, inclusive and resilient.

"We must work with each other and Mother Nature instead of against one another," John R says. "There is no other way. I hope I can be a voice of change that helps get us there together."

I love this planet...I want to see the environment preserved, and I want to see the human race preserved.
And I'd like to see everybody living decently in a more equitable, kind-hearted, thoughtful, generous world.

Ted Turner

Call to Action: Looking to become a Planeteer? Check out Captain Planet and the Turner Foundation on Instagram, Twitter, LinkedIn and Facebook. Reach out to John on Twitter and let him know you read his story here: @JohnRSeydel

EMPOWERING WOMEN TO LEAD
Hafsat Abiola-Costello
Kudirat Initiative for Democracy
Nigeria

From an early age, Hafsat Abiola's parents had instilled in her the importance of sharing, and of helping others. Her father, Moshood Kashimawo Olawale Abiola, came from humble beginnings, but when he became a successful businessman, he vowed to give back to people in communities like the one he had grown up in. He promoted equality and empowered people from different ethnicities and backgrounds by helping them to buy farms, start small businesses, receive an education, and take care of their families. During his life, he gave more than 3,000 scholarships to Nigerian students.

For her part, Hafsat's mother, Kudirat Abiola, had taught her that she must always take care of others and show people that she cared for them. "For her, simple things -- like the way you greeted people and said goodbye to them -- told a lot about a person's character," Hafsat remembers.

In 1993, when Hafsat was in her second year of study at Harvard University, her father became the first president to be elected after nearly a decade of military rule in Nigeria. Shortly after, he was sent to prison by Nigeria's junta government. Although he had won 60 percent of the vote, the military annulled the results and charged him with treason. His imprisonment triggered a wave of uprising and demonstrations, led by Hafsat's mother. Then, in 1996, when she was traveling through Lagos, the capital of Nigeria, in a car, she was assassinated.

Hafsat and her siblings were all in the United States when they heard the news. "We stood in a circle, and held hands," she remembers. "We just stood there, crying; then I said to my siblings 'We won't let her down.' And ever since that time we've been trying to make sure that we keep our word."

Two years later, Hafsat's father died in prison. Now it was completely up to Hafsat to look out for her younger siblings. And with both of her parents gone, she became even more motivated to fight for the rights of people everywhere. She decided that she wanted to focus especially on the vital work of empowering women that her mother had devoted her life to.

She created an NGO in her mother's memory, called the Kudirat Initiative for Democracy (KIND), with the purpose of empowering women to become successful leaders. KIND trains and supports women who want to run for public office, and provides resources for women who are victims of violence. Over the years, through her work, Hafsat has championed many initiatives for the women of Nigeria. For example, because of the high cost of prenatal care, many pregnant women do not visit doctors: and the maternal mortality rate in Nigeria is 630 per 100,000, more than 20 times as high as the rate in Europe or the United States, according to the World Health Organization. So Hafsat created a cash transfer project that helps poor women find healthcare facilities that will help them have safer pregnancies. KIND also strives to incorporate women into local, national, and global economic systems, transforming the power structure of the economy and empowering women.

Today Hafsat is one of the most prominent civil rights activists in Nigeria, and her leadership has grown to include all of Africa. She is the president of Women in Africa, an organization founded in 2017. This organization identifies and supports female entrepreneurs in all 54 African nations by giving them access to resources and training, and helping them to invest in female-led economic initiatives. In just three years, the initiative has had a tremendous impact by enabling women to come together and coordinate economic initiatives to drive an agenda.

Every year, WIA nominates one female entrepreneur from each African nation, recognizing their work reshaping Africa's economies. Zoussi Isabelle Ley is a female entrepreneur and the CMO of Complete Farmer, a Ghana-based farming platform that uses technology to help support innovative and ethical farms. Through an online site, consumers can connect directly with farmers, disrupting the current supply chain and ensuring farmers are treated better. Madina Youssouf Ismail created her own clothing business, Recy'design. The brand gives a second life to discarded fabric and materials, turning trash into trendy clothes. Her initiative has helped decreased waste from the textile industry in Djibouti.

In her role as president of Women in Africa, Hafsat focuses on initiatives to help women participate more fully in the economy. "The economy is the engine that powers the modern world," she says. "When women are involved in economic systems, we see greater gender equality in all other spheres. Women who have their own money are able to make healthier and more independent decisions. And they are able to more easily walk away from unsafe situations or relationships."

Hafsat likes to tell the story of Eleni Gabre-Madhin, an Ethiopian woman who decided to do something when her country was suffering famine in the late 1990s and early 2000s. She went to the United States to pursue a doctorate degree in agricultural management. After she had received her degree, she returned to Ethiopia and set up the country's first agricultural exchange. This program helps farmers meet directly with buyers, who purchase their products in a series of warehouses. With this direct connection, farmers are able to receive money for their products within 24 hours. Eleni's work has transformed the food system economy in Ethiopia, and has had a profound effect on the well-being of Ethiopian farmers. "This is the kind of change that I would like to see for women: building economies in a sustainable way," Hafsat says.

The Women in Africa initiative is preparing a new project that involves connecting Indigenous communities, scientists, and government officials, to ensure that women's local and scientific knowledge shapes laws. This kind of coordination is especially important when combating climate change in African countries, since women are children are most affected. While it is generally accepted that it is important to listen to scientists, Indigenous people can also help by sharing steps they use to minimize the damages caused by climate change. Enabling better communication can help to ensure that climate solutions take account of the different forms of knowledge within countries. "Within a given country, each community has a wealth of knowledge," Hafsat explains. "By connecting women's local and expert groups to their national governments, we can help ensure that climate legislation draws from all available sources and follows from an inclusive process of engagement." She adds, "Women are often good at having these kinds of conversations and at engaging communities, but in politics we're often sidelined."

As the president of Women in Africa, Hafsat has developed several targeted initiatives to help women in African nations respond to the challenges and dangers of COVID-19. "Africa's challenge is going to be very different than it will be in the rest of the world," she explains. "The economies are weaker. There are fewer hospital beds, less medical equipment, and insufficient tests." She is working to counteract these deficits, by encouraging people to adopt the practices that prevent disease, like hand washing, through public awareness campaigns. "This pandemic is going to bring about monumental change in African countries because people will realize that the cost of complacency on corruption is poor public healthcare systems, which in a pandemic means death," she says.

Hafsat's work continues to focus on ensuring that future leadership in African nations will include many more women. She believes that female leaders offer the possibility of being a counterweight to the current unequal balance of power in many African nations, and a force for economic improvement. And she believes that pushing hard for this kind of change is important. "It's better to push hard," she says. "That way even if there is push back, at least we would have made progress."

Hafsat has never forgotten the lessons she was taught early in her life by her parents: by her mother, who taught her to care for others and fight for equal rights, and by her father, who showed her how economic equality could both transform individual lives, and generate systematic change. Through her work she is carrying out their legacy, and she expects future generations to continue whatever work she is not able to achieve during her lifetime.

"By uniting women and creating a force for change, future female leaders will be able to continue the work of today's activists," she says. And she adds, "I really believe that women offer a different kind of leadership. We're in a world now that is finally ready for female leaders."

If you want to go fast, go alone. If you want to go far, go together.

African proverb

Call to Action: Support female leadership and empowerment, support Women in Africa https://wia-initiative.com/en/ Follow Hafsat https://twitter.com/HafsatKIND

PLANTING THE SEEDS FOR PEACE
Sami Awad
Holy Land Trust
Palestine

In 1983, when Sami was 12 years old, his uncle Mubarak Awad moved back from the USA to Jerusalem. For his leadership and his inspiring example of peaceful, nonviolent resistance, Mubarak has been called the "Gandhi of Palestine."

Sami's mother grew up in Gaza, on a small patch of land along the Mediterranean Sea. His father grew up in Jerusalem, in a neighborhood where Jews, Christians, and Muslims lived together in relative peace. And while the peace they experienced was sometimes tenuous, it proved that peace was possible.

When Sami's grandfather was killed in the 1948 war, his grandmother and her seven children became refugees. Like more than 700,000 Palestinians who were displaced from 1947 to 1949, his family was part of a massive crises called "Al-Nakba," the catastrophe. Sami was born in the USA but was just six months old when his family moved from Kansas to Palestine in 1971. Israelis and Palestinians struggled in a tug of war to claim this tiny piece of land for their own. Yet, despite having never seen peace for himself, Sami still believes it is possible. In fact, achieving it is his life goal.

Growing up in Palestine, Sami says, "the occupation was always constant." From an early age, his situation didn't feel right to him. The feeling of being under Israeli domination made him feel helpless, and sometimes angry, wanting to lash out. He wasn't the only one. Many Palestinians got caught up in the resistance movement, some becoming fighters with groups that wanted to overthrow Israeli rule through armed resistance.

But from his uncle, Mubarak, Sami learned powerful lessons, about protesting peacefully in the streets, and inspiring people -- both Israelis and Palestinians -- to join him. They planted olive trees to prevent the confiscation of Palestinian lands by encroaching Israeli settlements. They organized marches, and called for the boycott of Israeli products. "It started clicking for me, even at a young age, that we could do something about the situation -- even as children we were very involved," Sami says.

But things changed again for Sami when he was 17, during the first Intifada, or the Palestinian unarmed uprising. His uncle Mubarak was arrested by the Israeli authorities and deported out of the country. Many Palestinians turned to violence. But, following in his uncle's footsteps, Sami chose to carry on his uncle's legacy and choose a nonviolent path. "I committed my life to the study of nonviolence," Sami says.

Sami's studies took him first to the University of Kansas, and later a graduate program in International Relations at American University in Washington D.C. He returned to Palestine in 1996 during the Oslo Peace Process, with President Bill Clinton. With his deepened awareness and his new passion for peace, he wanted to include Israelis and Palestinians equally in the peace process, and teach them how to think differently about how to achieve peace together.

For the last thirty years he has continuously worked on shifting the dialogue about the past, present, and future among all peoples. "The past affects us and all the decisions we make in the present," he says. "It limits the possibilities of the future when we only use our past to make decisions." He adds, "I can instead make a decision in the present based on the *future* I want to build for my family, for my people."

In 1998, Sami founded the Holy Land Trust, a nonprofit dedicated to nonviolent community action." In addition to training and activism in nonviolence and nonlinear thinking for both Palestinians and Israelis, the Holy Land Trust organizes alternative tours for internationals.

Building on what he learned from his uncle Mubarak, Sami engages people in practicing nonviolent resistance, as well as healing trauma and developing the next generation of leaders. "Women and girls are key in this work," he says. "So too is a new generation of young people who are willing to break down borders and plant seeds for peace, instead of dwelling on the past."

"I'm seeing the next generation of young people who are involved in a new global consciousness, a new global understanding," he says. "How they perceive their own identity is changing. The younger generation are less focused on political solutions and national state structure," he says. "They want to live, travel, engage, and connect around the things they all have in common."

Today the future of younger generations is at greater risk than ever. Today, young people in Israel and Palestine, like young people everywhere, have their work cut out for them. This time, however, they face a common threat: climate change.

Sami names the challenges climate change will bring to the region, and which of them will be exacerbated by the Israeli occupation. Rivers, springs and water sources diverted by settlements means less water for Palestinian agricultural lands. Trees uprooted by the separation wall result in sewage flowing into farming communities in the Palestinian territories. The rise in global temperatures means that warm, dry places are becoming deserts. The Jordan Valley, the heart of Palestinian farming, is already drying up at a rapid pace. Sandstorms are increasingly sweeping across Jerusalem and other cities in the region. "Heat stress" at night makes summers nearly unbearable. The poorest will be hit hardest by the water shortages and droughts. The United Nations has warned that in the coming years the Gaza area will become unfit for human life.

Sami's organization is working to bring activists from Israel and Palestine together to tackle these challenges. The Holy Land Trust has launched a three-year project focused on increasing environmental consciousness across the region, beginning with awareness building and moving into activism and action.

"Every little action helps -- from picking up trash from the ground to installing solar panels in your neighborhood," Sami says. Over time, he hopes these little actions will turn into a groundswell of change.

They aren't alone in this work. Since the late 1990s, a number of groups in Israel and Palestine have begun to tackle climate change. Green Course, based in Israel, leads more than a dozen environmental campaigns each year. In Palestine, the Palestine Heirloom Seed Library is working to protect the agricultural diversity of the Palestinian territory by reintroducing local farming methods. Standing Together brings together activists across the border to resist the occupation and protect the environment.

Sami -- now in his late forties -- knows that change won't be easy. Despite his greatest efforts, it's hard to say whether peace between the Israelis and the Palestinians has come any closer during his lifetime. He's watched as his generation has failed time and time again not only to bring peace to the Middle East, but also to protect the environment and reduce global warming.

"We promised young people that it would be a better world and it's not,"

Sami says. "We need to create spaces where they're not just rebelling against us, and begin to ask what is the future we want."

Non-violence is the greatest force at the disposal
of mankind.
It is mightier than the mightiest weapon of
destruction
devised by the ingenuity of man.

Mahatma Gandhi

Call to Action: Support Sami and the Holy Land Trust in building resilient communities through nonviolent resistance in Palestine. Follow Sami https://twitter.com/Sami_Awad?s=20 https://holylandtrust.org/

RIPPLES OF HOPE
Kerry Kennedy
Robert F. Kennedy Foundation
Washington DC

Summers were a time of exploration and discovery for Kerry Kennedy when she was a child. Her father, Robert F. Kennedy, would take time off from his active public life of political, civic, and civil rights advocacy, and take the family on trips around the United States.

Robert F. Kennedy was attorney general during the Civil Rights movement, so the concepts of equality and justice were very central to Kerry's experience growing up. In fact, they were of the utmost importance in her home. "I remember, for instance, that when I learned how to tie my shoes, if I put my left shoe on first, I was taught to be sure to tie my right shoe *first;* because it was important that things always be fair. I mean, where does a child pick up an idea like that? It's got to be from their parents. And it certainly was in my case."

On their summer trips across the U.S. they'd stop in wilderness areas to raft, camp, or hike, so she and her siblings could experience firsthand the many natural wonders that this great, expansive country had to offer – which she still advocates for to this day.

But for Kerry's father, there was always more than that. He was always campaigning at least part-time, even when they were on a family vacation. Ever an advocate for the most vulnerable, he brought Kerry to some of the poorest areas in the country, where people were suffering in incredibly difficult conditions, to show her how "the other half" lived.

When they were out west, they would often stop at remote Indian reservations and speak with members of the tribe about the problems and issues they were facing. When they were in the eastern part of the country, they'd campaign in similarly downtrodden locales like rural Appalachia, and her dad's approach was always the same: he always tried to find out what the people needed, and how he could help them. And always, Kerry was close by his side, and watching carefully.

When he ran for president in 1968, she was only 8 years old, but she helped in the campaign in any small way she could. "He was always full of laughs and fun, and we just loved being around him," she says. "But he also taught us to understand all of the hardships people face in our country." She remembers that above all, her father thought it was important that she understand what public service is about. "There are many Americas," she says. "And it's a truth that one can never be too young to begin trying to understand that."

After listening to searing testimony about conditions in Mississippi by Marian Wright -- a 27-year-old Yale Law School graduate who was working with the NAACP's Legal Defense Fund in the state -- to his Senate Subcommittee on Poverty in April 1967, Kennedy followed Wright through the heart of the Delta, a region in northwest Mississippi known for its entrenched racism and suffocating poverty. He was joined by fellow senator Joseph Clark of Pennsylvania.

As he often did, he had brought her siblings along to the meeting. Kerry remembers him commanding the room where she and all her brothers and sisters were seated. They were a rowdy bunch, but when her father began to speak, a rare quiet came over the room, as everyone listened to hear what he would say. He looked around the room, shook his head, and then he said, quietly, "I've just been to a part of this country where three families live in a room the size of this one, and I want you to do something to help these children."

For Kerry, everything about her dad was interesting, and inspiring. Because of his example, she grew up believing that public service was what you *wanted* to do, because that was what made life meaningful. It wasn't a feeling of obligation, or a feeling that was burdensome. It was more a sense of an honorable duty. "But that particular instance [at the meeting of the subcommittee on poverty] is the only time I remember him saying, "You *have* to be involved." She adds, "That moment, as much as any, set me up on my journey into advocacy - and particularly on a journey toward exposing the many abuses that go on around this world, in all of their forms."

Tragedy struck Kerry's family shortly thereafter, when in June 1968, after winning the California presidential primary, her father was assassinated. Though she was only 8 years old, Kerry knew that she would dedicate her life to carrying on the legacy of the noble ideals that her father had believed in so deeply. And she would act in accordance with her favorite quote by her father; it laid out a pathway for her own future work, and for the life she was going to lead.

"Each time a man stands up for an ideal, or acts to improve the lot of others, or strikes out against injustice,

he sends forth a tiny ripple of hope, and crossing each other from a million different centers of energy and

daring those ripples build a current which can sweep down the mightiest walls of oppression and resistance."

To carry on the work of a humanitarian and advocate as great as her father was wouldn't be easy. But Kerry always kept those words in mind. She remembered them, and believed that each small act of hers would "send forth a tiny ripple of hope" into the world, that would build toward a more just future.

When she was in 6th grade, Kerry took her first public stand in service of an ideal. It was 1972, and Watergate was dominating the news cycle. For school, she had to write a biography of a famous person. "I chose Cesar Chavez. And my best friend said, 'Who's Cesar Chavez?' and I said, 'Well, how come you've never heard of him? He's as famous as Richard Nixon.' And she said, 'No, he's not. I've never heard of him.'" They argued about the merits of who was more famous and who deserved to be more famous – but the important thing for Kerry was her belief that Chavez should be a household name. Certainly in her home he had an enormous presence. Her family boycotted grapes and lettuce in solidarity with the farmers' struggle. So Kerry knew that Cesar Chavez had a story that needed to be told.

Some 16 years later, in 1988, her father's words echoed as true as if they had just been spoken; as Kerry took a small stand in support of an ideal, and that small act in support of Chavez' struggle led her on a course that brought her into contact with the great humanitarian himself. Chavez was embarking on his last great fast, and when doctors advised that he must end it or risk death, other leaders around the country picked it up and traveled with it. A network of human rights advocates and celebrities joined together to bring Chavez's uplifting message of solidarity forward, and Kerry took part in in too. "I had the honor of carrying the message forward from New York to Boston," she says. "It was a powerful thing to be a part of."

Over the more than 50 years since her father's tragic death, Kerry has lived up to being the fearless humanitarian and advocate for the disinherited that he inspired her to be in more ways than he could have possibly dreamed. What started in her kitchen one day, having an argument with her best friend, has blossomed into a life of service few can rival – both in the scope, and the breadth of the issues she has fought for.

"Human rights defenders teach us not how to be saints, but how to be fully human," she says. And in all of her work, this is precisely what Kerry has done. She has published a number of books, including *Speak Truth to Power*, which tells heroic tales of advocacy; and her writing has been featured in many newspapers. She has spoken out in favor of bail reform and other issues that stem from systemic racism. She has worked with Break Bread Not Families, to bring awareness to the current situation for refugees at the southern border of the United States, through fasting and prayer. And as the chair of Amnesty International's USA Leadership Council, she has fought in defense of people whose fundamental human rights are being abused and denied to people all over the world. To date, she has led more than 40 human rights delegations in the Americas, Asia, Europe, and Africa.

Currently, she serves as president of Robert F. Kennedy Human Rights, a nonprofit organization that uses legal means to stand up for political prisoners, uphold the rule of law in volatile nations, and act as the voice of the voiceless. She also oversees the Ripple of Hope Award given in her father's honor.

When asked why her father is remembered in such high regard by political leaders around the world, Kerry says, "I think he made such an impact on people because he appealed to the best in everyone. He appealed to people who believed that we could actually make a difference; that each person could make a difference. And I think that that it is rare in American politics, and is really powerful. I think that's really one of his great contributions."

Like her father, Kerry appeals to the best in people–and urges them to exercise compassion, and to fight for justice and equality. For any of the countless people, places, and organizations she has advocated for in her uplifting journey, there's no doubt she has faithfully carried on her father's noble legacy -- and then some.

Few will have the greatness to bend history
itself, but each of us can work to change a small
portion of events.
It is from numberless diverse acts of courage
and belief that human history is shaped.

Robert F. Kennedy

Call to Action: Learn more about Kerry's work, and explore the extensive humanitarian network supporting equal rights for everyone around the world at Robert F. Kennedy Human Rights https:// rfkhumanrights.org/people/kerry-kennedy

TACKLING THE ROOT CAUSES OF HUNGER

Anna Lappé
Small Planet Fund and Institute
Berkeley, California

Everything changed for Anna Lappé in middle school when she took a trip with her mother to rural Ohio. There, for the first time, she met some of the farmworkers who harvest the food that finds its way to our plates. While Anna had been raised to think about where her food came from, until that trip, the ideas had always been abstract for her.

Growing up, Anna split her time between her parents' homes, both of whom were passionate activists with a common goal: to make the world a healthier, safer, more equitable place. Typical family dinner conversations revolved around issues of world hunger, social injustice, or the dangers of toxic chemicals. That trip to Ohio brought home to her those many conversations over the years.

Since the 1970s, Anna's mother, Frances Moore Lappé, had been exploring the root causes of hunger and inequality in the United States and beyond. Through her mother's work, Anna learned firsthand about the impact of United States foreign policy, development aid, and farm programs. She learned about inequality in the United States and the exploitation of the people who grow the country's food and how farmworkers are regularly exposed to toxic pesticides. On that trip to Ohio, Anna was deeply moved as she listened to one woman tell how she had been diagnosed with a cancer that was probably caused by pesticides she came into contact with while working the fields.

While growing up middle class, the plight of farmworkers in rural Ohio may have seemed a world away, but she was aware that all of us are implicated in their situation. She knew that the lettuce, grapes, and tomatoes that come to dinner tables from thousands of miles away also come with grave human and environmental costs.

Anna knew she had to do something. Luckily, she had her mother to guide her. Frances Moore Lappé had sparked a revolution with her book, *Diet for a Small Planet*, which has sold over three and a half million copies since it was published in 1971. The book radically reshaped the conversation about hunger, helping people see that the real cause of hunger is not a scarcity of food, but a scarcity of democracy and how our industrial animal agriculture squanders abundance in raising factory farmed livestock. The book urges people to adopt a healthy, plant-centered diet to minimize the environmental costs of our food consumption and provides recipes for such a diet. But more than that, the book encourages its readers to see themselves as actively shaping the world around them, through everyday choices like what they eat to big choices like what they do with their lives.

Her mother had always been a role model for Anna: she sparked Anna's curiosity about social justice and the food system. Some of Anna's most vivid childhood memories are of spending time at her mother's office at the non-profit she cofounded, the Institute for Food and Development Policy known as Food First. She remembers afternoons on the office couch reading institute newsletters and evenings stuffing donation envelopes for fundraising drives with her mother's coworkers. Like her mother, her father also had committed his life to rooting out injustice, as a scientist and medical ethicist. These values inspired Anna to study international affairs and political economy in graduate school, where she learned about the political and economic concepts behind the injustice she had learned about growing up.

Around the 30th anniversary of her mother's first book, Anna had an idea. She proposed that her mom write a sequel: If the original book's premise was that hunger was caused by a scarcity of democracy, where around the world were there social movements and civic leaders tackling those roots to create thriving communities? The book, too, would include recipes, bringing to life meals that celebrate earth's bounty. Her mother agreed to do it on one condition: that Anna work with her.

Together, Anna and her mother travelled the world, covering five continents; meeting passionate leaders and investigating ways to build real food democracy. They spent time in India, Bangladesh, Poland, Kenya, France, and Brazil. The result of their journey is a book called *Hope's Edge*.

After the trip, Anna continued to work with her mother. The two founded the Small Planet Institute and the Small Planet Fund, to raise money for some of the groups profiled in *Hope's Edge*. Since then, the fund has expanded: it now supports other organizations working to protect the planet and reduce global inequalities. To date, the Small Planet Fund has given away nearly two million dollars and two of its grantees have won the Nobel Peace Prize.

Working with her mother, Anna realized the importance of generations working together for change. Anna sees the work of social change to address our challenges as a kind of "relay race:" people learn, work, and pass the baton from one generation to the next. As an activist, she always remembers the generations before her whose work she is building on and she envisions how future generations will take over from what the activists of today.

"Young people offer fresh ideas and perspectives, while older activists can share what they have learned through many years of experience," she says. She adds, "A leader is someone who takes responsibility for the world. We need leaders of all generations to solve the world's most pressing challenges."

Today, Anna is an advocate for better food systems that will protect the environment, promote health, and provide quality jobs with dignity. She has published two more books and contributed to more than 12 others. Her most recent is *Diet for a Hot Planet,* which focuses on the link between the global food system and the climate crisis -- and how food can be a key climate solution. In the book, she reveals the climate impact of industrial agriculture, particularly meat and dairy production. And she shows how sustainable farming and ranching can help reduce the climate impacts of the sector, even pull carbon out of the atmosphere to lock it in our soils. "Farmers and ranchers need to be part of any feasible climate solution," she says. "Unless we stop agribusiness driven rainforest destruction and push for a radical transformation in how we farm, the greenhouse gas emissions from this sector will continue to rise and contribute to climate change."

With these ideas in mind, Anna founded Real Food Media, which exposes food industry misinformation and shares the stories of food movement leaders around the country. She also founded and leads a grantmaking program for a family foundation that supports grassroots change around the world. Today, her work aims to help people reflect on the environmental and social implications of the food they eat and to see how they, too, can be part of building a food system that promotes health, animal welfare, sustainability, and worker wellbeing. "Taking on food is of critical importance if we are to create a sustainable future for people living on this planet," she says.

Equity, transparency, and accountability are Anna's key principles. Today the 21.5 million food workers in the United States are some of the most underpaid and most exploited employees in the economy. Women, people of color, and immigrants are especially vulnerable. Many of the practices used in the industry remain opaque, and powerful lobbyists often stand in the way of change.

But Anna will not give up hope. She calls herself a "possibilist." Neither an optimist nor a pessimist, she says a possibilist sees herself as someone who is ready and willing to adapt to the constantly changing world we live in.

Anna's unwavering curiosity, and her passion for the work she is doing, help her keep going even when the way forward is discouraging. "The fight will be long and hard, but you never know what is possible until you try," she says. She adds, "Activism can be a great source of solace and energy."

Through her activism, Anna helps continue her mother Frances' legacy, working towards a world where people everywhere have access to nutritious food that is produced ethically and sustainably.

> *In a world of plenty, no one, not a single person, should go hungry. But almost 1 billion still do not have enough to eat. I want to see an end to hunger everywhere within my lifetime.*

Ban Ki-Moon, Former United Nations Secretary-General

Call to Action: Make a difference by being conscientious about where their food comes from and choosing products from farms that take care of your workers and the planet. **Visit:** Real Food Media **&** Small Planet Institute **&** Small Planet Fund

THE CHILDREN WILL LEAD THE WAY
Valentina Ossa
New York

For days, 12-year old Valentina Ossa had been organizing with a couple of friends. They'd met secretly, hung up posters, and handed out flyers. It felt a little like a conspiracy -- their teachers hadn't noticed their efforts to organize a collective school walkout, in solidarity with the Global Youth Climate Strike.

"We did all this right under our teachers' noses," Valentina says. "When we first started getting the word out, I told everyone, if you need any information, come meet us on the playground."

For Valentina and her little band of young organizers, their plan was a success. On March 15, 2019, more than 180 students simultaneously walked out of class to protest global inaction in the face of the quickly escalating climate crisis.

For Valentina, it was one more example of how activism can empower people and bring them together.

Activism is a longstanding tradition in Valentina's family. Her grandfather is Peter Yarrow, of the legendary folk music group, Peter, Paul and Mary. As spokesperson for the most prominent folk group of the 1960s, he used his voice to rally the nation's young people to get involved in the Civil Rights movement, and protest the Vietnam War. Valentina's mother, Bethany Yarrow, followed in her father's footsteps as a musician, and as an activist.

And the tradition carried on to the next generation: when she was just five years old, Valentina had her first experience protesting. "I have been an activist my entire life," she says, proudly.

Valentina has spent much of her life in the rural community of New York's Schoharie Valley. She loves her backyard there, where a 120-foot waterfall splashes into a little swimming pool, the deep blue water turning into a shimmering green as it flows downriver.

But when she was five years old, the little paradise in the mountains was suddenly under threat.

426

"We are on top of a huge shale reserve, and they wanted to frack for gas," she explains. "I didn't want the water to be contaminated. I was afraid the river would die."

Valentina learned that fracking is a process through which companies extract gas or oil that is trapped in rock formations underground; that the gas collected from fracking causes a higher level of emissions than conventional gas; and that fracking sites can cause significant spills of poisonous chemicals, and earthquakes.

For Valentina it was clear that something needed to be done. "When my mom told that they were going to go ahead with fracking in 'sacrifice zones,' I started crying," she remembers. "The very next day I wrote a letter to Governor Cuomo, asking him not to frack the water."

Dear Governor Cuomo,

My name is Valentina. I am 5 years old. I don't want the bad people to frack our water. I spent all yesterday crying because I don't want them to poison our water. I want the water to be clear because I don't want anyone to be in pain. So if anyone wants to frack the water tell them they can't. Governor Cuomo, I hope you are the best Governor ever and save our water."

"I told my mom that I wanted to go to a protest in front of the governor's office in New York City, so she took me, and I got my whole preschool class to go too," Valentina remembers. "We made a banner that said DON'T FRACK OUR FUTURE. That was the first protest I went to. And we still use that banner at climate marches."

Valentina and her mother tirelessly continued to fight fracking and the pipeline infrastructure that was being planned throughout the region. "First fracking was banned, and then we stopped the Constitution Pipeline. That was a big accomplishment," Valentina says. "I was really surprised. I thought 'Wow! I really *can* do something about these issues.'"

When Valentina started school, she and her family moved to New York City, where she continued to go to protests and meet fascinating people -- environmentalists who were passionate about the dangers of fracking, as well as pollution, carbon emissions, and the increasingly violent and frequent forest fires.

Slowly, she started seeing the bigger picture. "I was really worried about all of these smaller things, and it kind of added up," she says. "So

I did my research; and then I decided to take a stand on climate change, so I could speak on *all* of these issues."

On March 15, 2019, the day of the first Global School Strike for the climate, Valentina organized her schoolmates again -- this time to join her in taking a stand for the planet. In her speech that day she said, "I am here to stand for all the people who don't have the courage, awareness, or opportunity to stand up for themselves. For all the kids my age who have been told, over and over again, that they are too young to make a change."

Valentina was grateful for the passionate support of her schoolmates. She feels it is so important for young people to raise their voices and share their concerns. "Every time I've voiced my ideas, I felt so proud that I had done it," she says about her activism. "I felt that I had contributed something."

Valentina has continued to stand up for what she believes in. After organizing the walkout at her school in Brooklyn, she and about 20 of her schoolmates joined millions of other young people in New York City for the Global Action Strike on September 2019. She was inspired by Greta Thunberg, and also by Alexandria Villaseñor, a cofounder of U.S. Youth Climate Strike. By the time Valentina joined her, Alexandria had already been striking for a couple of months in front of the United Nations. For the next several months, Valentina joined her: she went to the U.N. every Friday and she and Alexandria sat on a bench close to the big headquarters building. Valentina's signs had slogans like "SEA LEVELS ARE RISING AND SO ARE WE," or "THE CHILDREN WILL LEAD THE WAY."

Sometimes it was only Valentina and Alexandria; sometimes they were joined by others. Valentina always brought a few extra signs for those who hadn't brought their own, so that people driving by could see what they were doing, and know why they were protesting.

But she did more than just hold up signs. In May 2019, she travelled to Washington D.C., where she spoke at a protest in front of the White House. Valentina had been enraged by the Trump administration's destructive environmental policies. So, speaking through a megaphone in front of Donald Trump's office window seemed like a great opportunity to her.

"Suddenly it hit me that I was at the *White House*," Valentina remembers. "But then I thought, you know what? I don't care, I'm going to do it -- so what if it *is* the White House!" As she stepped onto the stage, she felt an empowering sense of calm determination. And when she raised her voice, she knew exactly what she would say.

"I am here, at the White House of the United States of America, sending out an SOS to the whole world. I am asking all the politicians, all the people in power, and every single person who hears me to stand with the children. Do everything you can. Get involved! Make sacrifices, big and small. It's going to take all of us. This is about the survival of the planet, and we are out of time!"

"We only have now," Valentina says. "We can't do anything to fix what happened in the past. We only have the present -- and we have to do something now, or we're not going to make the changes we need to make. People may say 'What can I do? I'm only one person.' But we've proven that when we come together demonstrate, and speak our piece, there is no way the power structure can avoid being attentive."

I think a hero is any person really intent on making this a better place for all people.

Maya Angelou

Call to Action: Speak up for what you believe in. Find a way to get involved -- join a protest or a climate change organization; or start your own project. Do something! Follow Valentina on Twitter https://twitter.com/valentinaossa11?lang=en Bethany Yarrow, on Instagram https://www.instagram.com/bethanyyarrowmusic/ www.bethanyyarrow.com

THE GIRL WHO SILENCED THE WORLD FOR FIVE MINUTES
Severn Suzuki
David Suzuki Foundation
Canada

As a child, Severn and her little sister started traveling with her parents to Indigenous communities. They wanted to gain a deep understanding of what was affecting these communities, and formulate a plan of action to help them. The most pressing issue facing the Indigenous people of British Columbia was the destruction of forests caused by clear-cut logging, the pollution of natural water systems, and the ramifications of these things on their traditional way of life. "Thankfully, my parents always brought us along when they were working with these vulnerable communities. I really felt like I was involved, and had a say. It was really empowering."

Since the late 1970s, the Suzuki family has been courageously fighting for environmental and Indigenous rights in B.C. For more than 40 years, geneticist David Suzuki has been a mainstay on Canadian television, hosting *The Nature of Things*, a documentary program on nature and society. This platform has allowed his family's message of environmental justice for all to reach a vast audience. But the heart, soul, and genesis of their enduring environmental legacy lies with the Indigenous peoples of B.C.

On a work-related trip to the Amazon, the Suzukis met a man who would change the direction and impact of their activism, from small-scale and local, to far-reaching and global. Paiakan was an Indigenous leader who was fighting against the construction of a massive hydroelectric dam in Brazil, that would flood thousands of hectares of pristine rainforest, and destroy countless Indigenous communities. "Of course, my Mom and Dad did what they always did; they got involved in the fight," Severn says. Her mother, Tara, an accomplished writer, activist, and organizer, led a fundraising effort that allowed them to bring Paiakan to Canada. There, she organized a meeting of Indigenous groups to confront the World Bank, which was funding the project – and they succeeded in getting the project stopped.

In the aftermath of this victory, Paiakan and his family received death threats, so the Suzukis brought them to Canada to escape danger.

When it was safe to return to their home the following year, the Suzukis traveled with them to ensure their safe arrival, and they were invited to stay in Paiaka's home in the Amazon. "It was transformational for me as a young girl. Fishing for piranhas from the banks of the river we had just been swimming in. Living in a sparkling green jungle. It was beyond my wildest imagination – *and it was real,*" Severn remembers.

After a few weeks in the jungle, it was time for the Suzukis to go back home. They got into a tiny plane that took them over the jungle toward the nearest town; but as they climbed into the sky, their windows quickly became completely covered in smoke. "As I got brief glimpses of the jungle below, I saw tons of fires burning everywhere. It was heartbreaking to see this incredible world being burned to the ground. Then I saw the farm and cattle operations scarring the land. I decided right then and there that I had to do something about it."

When Severn arrived home, she told her friends about what she'd experienced, and how she wanted to help preserve these pristine places. She quickly gained support from her peers, who understood the importance of her mission – but they didn't know where or how to direct their energy. Thankfully her Mom had an idea for them. "Why don't you start a club, and organize?" she suggested. So Severn and four of her friends started the Environmental Children's Organization (ECO), to advocate for intergenerational environmental justice.

At age 12, Severn successfully raised enough funds to travel with ECO to the 1992 UN Earth Summit in Rio de Janeiro, Brazil – the very country that had inspired her activism some years prior. ECO only planned to attend the summit as spectators. But when one of the speakers dropped out, Severn saw an opportunity to get the youth perspective on these issues out to the world. "We watched as all of these old people were sitting around discussing the future; but we were the ones who would be suffering from the consequences of their decisions," Severn says. "Who was speaking for us?" So she stepped up, and showed unbelievable resolve as she gave a powerful speech in front of many of the leading figures in the environmental movement including now Secretary John Kerry, former Vice President Al Gore and others. Seeds were planted then for environmental movements now.

A decade later, her speech became a viral sensation, called "The Girl Who Silenced the World For 5 Minutes." It reached more than 32 million people. "What was occurring, and what is still occurring, is that the people in power are ignoring their sacred duty to preserve the world for their children," she says. "It's amazing to see the world finally starting to wake up to the concept of intergenerational justice, after so many years. I'm proud of the young people, and ashamed that it has taken us so long to get on board."

After her speech, Severn was invited to sit on the Earth Charter Commission and help draft guidelines on how people should be engaging with each other and the planet in the 21st century. "We need an architecture for a different way of being, and it should be intergenerational. Young people have always been on the forefront of social change; they must be central to our guiding societal principles. A lot of people have been advocating for these sorts of things since the 1980s - it wasn't ever just me. I was falling in line with a tradition of young people being revolutionaries."

In this tradition, Severn, along with Our Children's Trust, has advised a group of 15 youth litigants from British Columbia, who are taking up the mantle. In October 2019, La Rose vs Canada was brought to the Supreme Court to contend that Canada has not been protecting the constitutional rights and liberties of its young people, who are being unjustly impacted by the ramifications of our environmental crisis. "It's heartbreaking that it has been left to our kids to take on this burden," Severn says. "But it's amazing to see the clarity and dedication they have. It reignites that passion in me." She, the David Suzuki Foundation, and Ecojustice, are all supporting the case.

With so many new ways to connect digitally, and to create communities through social media platforms, and with so many visible role models, Severn is sure that youth movements will continue to grow. Still, she believes that getting back to nature is necessary for the younger generation to gain a full appreciation of the natural world. "As a parent, that was my main focus for my kids. We live in an Indigenous community on an archipelago where the Haida have lived for over 14,000 years. I wanted my kids to experience the way of life their ancestors did. I wanted to ground them in their homeland. And now that they have that connection, we can shift our focus to defend it – and defend the Earth at large."

She also wants aspiring youth environmentalists to understand that a reimagined future isn't something intangible or out of reach. In fact, she hopes the movement will continue to support and understand the significance of Indigenous people, who have practiced sustainable living throughout human history. "The current way of life that we are experiencing is just one iteration of how a human society can function. There are all kinds of examples of Indigenous civilizations, past and present, that show us precisely how to live in harmony with the earth. Indigenous people remain the most marginalized, displaced, and attacked peoples around the world, yet they survive. There's a lesson there, and understanding it gets more urgent by the day. If mainstream society intends to do the same, it's this varied legacy of our Indigenous forebearers that we should be aspiring to going forward."

Though the obstacles we face as a global society are many, Severn is hopeful for the future. Now Severn Cullis-Suzuki, married mother and a trained biologist, she has seen how the information that's been amassed over the years regarding climate change is now irrefutable. This is reassuring, even though it has also made clear the precariousness of our situation. "There's no ambiguity about what we need to do," she says. "As a planet, we have to decarbonize, plain and simple. If we love our children, this is what we have to do. And I believe we will."

Change is never easy, and it often creates discord, but when people come together for the good of humanity and the Earth, we can accomplish great things.

David Suzuki

Call to Action: Learn more, get involved and show your support for any number of environmental causes at David Suzuki Foundation https://davidsuzuki.org.

WE MUST BE THE CHANGE WE WANT TO SEE IN THE WORLD
Arun Gandhi
Rochester, New York/South Africa

Born and brought up in South Africa, Arun Gandhi faced a lot of prejudice because of the color of his skin. "It filled me with a lot of anger," he says. "I wanted an eye for an eye. I began to go to the gym to learn how to fight back and defend myself."

Thankfully, his parents recognized the seriousness of the situation, and thought it wise to bring Arun to India to live with his grandfather, Mahatma Gandhi. There the 12-year-old could learn from the great teacher himself, before he let anger take control of his life.

Arun's parents knew that the temptation to respond to prejudice with violence and anger had occurred in their family before. In fact, the great Mahatma himself had had a very similar experience early in his life.

As a young lawyer, Mahatma Gandhi had been the victim of racial prejudice upon arriving in South Africa. He'd been thrown off the first-class car of a train, since people of his color were banned from traveling first class. This humiliation made him really angry. Initially he felt compelled to react to this treatment with anger. However, before lashing out, he stopped himself, realizing that using anger would only perpetuate a cycle of violence -- and would ultimately turn into something even worse. He vowed right then and there to dedicate his life to doing whatever he could to stop this cycle of violence, beginning with himself. And he famously went about creating a practice of using nonviolence to resolve sociopolitical and interpersonal conflicts.

He delved deeply into studying *Ahimsa*, the principle of nonviolence toward all living things. *Ahimsa* is a central tenet of many eastern religions, found in the ancient codes and texts of Jainism, Hinduism, and Buddhism. Little did this angry young man know that one day his life, and his message of the power of nonviolent response to oppression would influence the world's greatest civil rights leaders, including Dr. Martin Luther King and Cesar Chavez -- and would ultimately lead to a massive improvement in the lives of millions of people around the world.

When Arun arrived in India, his grandfather shared the teachings of *Ahimsa* with his grandson. And he talked to him openly about his own difficulties in controlling his anger. "*Ahimsa* extends far beyond physical nonviolence; it must include all forms of passive nonviolence," Arun explains. "It doesn't simply mean 'Don't hit, don't hurt, don't kill, don't harm.' *Ahimsa* extends to the negative things we say to one another. Our destructive actions. It even extends to our thinking, like the negative patterns of thought we find ourselves in, or the anxieties we fixate upon."

Arun's grandfather told him to write every day in an anger journal, to help him learn how to manage his anger and search for positive solutions. "This helped me understand my anger, and learn how to channel the energy of anger into something positive," Arun says. "That's the most powerful lesson he taught me: to use the energy constructively, rather than destructively."

Arun sees an analogy between the power of anger, and the power of electricity. "It's just as useful, and just as powerful, but only if we use it intelligently," he says. "It can be just as destructive too: so we must channel this energy to be in service of the good of humanity." He pauses, then adds, "I believe this type of training should be compulsory education for young people. So much pain and violence in the world could be avoided if youth understood how to channel their anger."

Arun fondly remembers walking by his grandfather's side as they traveled through the villages of India. There he could sense the greatness of this man he called Grandfather. After dinner each night he had a nightly practice of self-analysis with his grandfather. "He made me draw a genealogical tree of violence, like a family tree. In the tree, violence was a grandparent, and physical violence and passive violence were the two offspring."

Every night before Arun went to bed, he would do this self-analysis, thinking about what had made him angry during the day, and putting it on the tree. "Physical violence we know about and understand. We see it and we can see that it hurts," he says. "Yet we don't think about passive violence when we are young. There are many things we do that we just don't think of as being violent. Anything we do that hurts somebody or something, directly or indirectly, is violence. Hoarding resources. Overconsumption, when so many are going hungry. And of course, the way we treat the natural world around us; the environment." He adds, "All this analysis made me realize that passive violence fuels physical violence; so we must cut off the fuel supply, which comes from each one of us. It is just as my grandfather said: we must be the change we want to see in the world."

Mahatma Gandhi was one of the first to recognize the dangers of the global climate situation. He spoke out against violence against nature in all its forms. He stressed that when we don't live in harmony with the natural world, it's inevitable that we will destroy nature – and ourselves. For today's youth leaders in the environmental movement, Arun believes that his grandfather's message would be the same.

"My grandfather always tried to convince people to bring about a change," he says. "Our leaders preach, but they don't practice. If we want to seriously deal with the climate situation and get the people of the world to stand hand in hand, the leading countries must follow their own advice. Even children learn more from what they see than what they hear. It's the same message for adults in this movement, who are working either on their own efforts, or in support of their children: *you must live what you want others to learn.*"

As a self-described "peace farmer," Arun has taught countless numbers of people over the years how to abide by the principles of *Ahimsa.* In 1987 he and his beloved wife Sunanda were invited by the University of Mississippi to study racial prejudice in South Africa, India, and the U.S. Then in 1991 they founded The M.K. Gandhi Institute for Nonviolence. They spent decades traveling back to India to work with orphanages and homelessness in India.

Over the years Arun has been increasingly troubled by the destruction of the environment, in both South Africa and India. In impoverished communities, he was disturbed seeing mining operations with little or no regulation, and heavy deforestation. Wherever he goes, the main thread he sees linking this destruction of the environment is poverty.

"Everywhere I go I see the same thing. Wherever there is poverty, there is more pollution. If we don't eradicate poverty in the world, we won't be able to stop this environmental degradation. Millions of people in India and Africa live in such poverty that they are forced to use up any resource they can just to survive. Miners wear out their land to sell coal and oil to rich countries. When they don't have the money for cooking or heating oil, people go into the forest, and chop down trees to use as fuel. When the forest gets used up, they must burn things like plastics and garbage to keep themselves alive in winter, and this causes massive amounts of pollution." He pauses, and sighs. Then he adds, "This sort of problem can't be addressed without addressing poverty.

Unless desperately poor people have an alternative, we can't really save the environment. There has to be a balance between materialism and morality."

Arun's global travels have caused him to focus his energy on compassion as a necessary part of any healing.

"Some of the most devastating social problems in the world, like homelessness and poverty, can't be solved by government. Government does not have the capacity to deal with the issue of compassion. Simply pouring money into an issue does not eradicate it. It can only be solved by rebuilding self-respect and self-confidence in people – and that can only be done by people like you and me," he says. But he adds that those who are attempting to help need to maintain a sense of humility. "We must listen to the people with these problems. Sit with them, talk with them, and try to understand from *their* perspective how their problems can best be resolved. This is what nonviolence teaches us: humility, and compassion, and love. And understanding."

Today, 86 years old, Arun is still inspiring people. After his beloved wife passed, he moved to Rochester, New York to be near his daughter and her family. He is often invited to lecture and talk to people, and to write about climate change and nonviolence. In 2015 he traveled to Martha's Vineyard to be with youth leaders from around the world at the Stone Soup Leadership Institute's Sustainability Summit. They were awestruck by Arun's stories of his grandson. "Young people today are hungry for a deeper level of authenticity," he says. "They are longing for us to take the time to listen to them, and work together with them to solve some of these challenging issues facing our world."

Perhaps they are the ones who will be able to implement more of the noble tenets of *Ahimsa,* so that the world will truly be able to forge a path through this climate crisis with balance, perspective -- and most of all, humanity.

> *The day the power of love overrules the love of power, the world will know peace.*

Mahatma Gandhi

Call to Action: Become involved with Arun's work to create a better, safer, more humane world by visiting The M.K. Gandhi Institute for Nonviolence at https://gandhiinstitute.org .

YOUTHFORCE CARRIES ON DR. ARI'S LEGACY
Dr. Ari Ariyaratne & Niven Ganegama
Sarvodaya, Sri Lanka

Nestled at the foot of the Sinharaja Forest Reserve, about three hours outside of Sri Lanka's capital city of Colombo, is the small village of Kalawana. It is one of Sri Lanka's eight UNESCO World Heritage sites. With thousands of unique species of birds, flowers, medicinal plants, and animals, this island nation is one of the most biodiverse countries in the world -- and this is its most biodiverse village.

Kalawana's children grow up to know the names of the native plants and animals: it's part of their rich heritage. There are majestic eagles, hawks, peacocks, and jungle fowl; gorgeous Blue Lotus, tender pink Naa leaves, and 25 varieties of butterflies; giant squirrels and leopards, and even recently even a black panther. Local people are proud of the lush soil that grows their famous cinnamon and Ceylon tea, as well as powerful medicinal plants like turmeric, curry, aloe vera, and hibiscus, their "welcome" drink.

One day Kalawana's teacher reached out to the *Sarvodaya*, a charitable humanitarian organization, and asked for help. The Sarvodaya is often asked to help Sri Lanka's 2.1 million people, especially those in remote areas. And when asked, they do their best to do whatever they can. Since its founding in 1958, the Sarvodaya movement has spread to 15,000 villages in 26 districts, reaching over 800,000 villagers all over Sri Lanka. They have built 5,000 preschools and 7,000 bridges, held 100,000 peace marches, organized 100,000 water programs – and benefitted 7 million people. It all started when Dr. Ari Ariyaratne held the first *Shramadama* camp. His idea was simple: "We build the road, and the road builds us," he explains. He began his values-based teachings of teamwork, volunteerism, mutual respect, and action amongst the poor.

In this case, the teacher wanted her students to learn to speak English. Dr. Ari's wife Neetha shared the teacher's request with her teenage grandchildren, and they were eager to help. Tiara, 16 years old, and Niven, 13, were born in the U.S. They knew that speaking English could open doors to a whole new world for these children. Their grandparents had taught them to always help others, especially those less fortunate.

In fact they had recently joined the Sarvodaya's children's workcamp in the nearby village of Nimalagama, and were surprised to see that the children had smartphones and Wifi. "Just imagine if they could learn English," Niven thought. "It could be life-changing!"

Over the years Niven and Tiara had heard stories about their grandfather's amazing journey around the world -- from India, where he visited Gandhi's birthplace; to meeting with His Holiness the Dalai Lama in the U.S. and then India, to Europe, Asia, and the U.S. They'd seen photos of him at the White House with First Lady Hillary Clinton, as well as with Dr. King's wife Coretta, and other leaders. They'd watched videos of him proudly sharing Sarvodaya's work at major conferences with people like Deepak Chopra, Ram Dass, Joanna Macy, and Jack Kornfield. And they'd heard how he'd spoken to 650,000 people in Malaysia with Bhante Mahinda. They'd also heard stories about how others sought their grandfather's counsel. Before founding the Nobel prize-winning Grameen Bank, Dr. Muhammad Yunus had traveled from Bangladesh to learn from Dr. Ari how his microcredit programs were empowering local people. And in the early days of the Peace Corps, the founders had met with Dr. Ari to learn about Sarvodaya's impressive volunteer movement.

While he frequently walks among world leaders, Dr. Ari is a simple person, with a simple message for how to empower local people. When tourists visit Colombo, they wonder how the streets are so clean. Dr. Ari tells about how his first project there inspired local shopkeepers to clean their streets, and how that instilled in them a sense of pride. Niven enjoys the story of how his grandfather, at 14 years old, had started a cooperative to empower local coconut shuckers to eliminate the middleman and receive a fair wage for their hard work. No matter where he went, Dr. Ari's message was always the same: by awakening one person, it could lead to awakening a whole family; then an entire community; and then, one day, even the world.

Sarvodaya is now the country's largest community-based NGO: it has comprehensive programs in maternal and early childhood education, community health, rural technical services, woodworking, international volunteers, and partnerships with? the Institute for Higher Learning; in disaster management, and Deshodaya's self-governance program to engage ordinary citizens in consensual politics, and to promote democracy, good governance, reconciliation, and sustainable peace. At last year's 60th anniversary celebration, people from all over the world traveled to Sri Lanka to honor Dr. Ari's great work.

For Niven and Tiara, the Peace Marches Dr. Ari led are especially memorable, since they happened around the time they were born, in 2007. For more than 30 years a civil war had plagued their beautiful country. Dr. Ari and Sarvodaya had mobilized millions of people to take a stand for peace. They worked alongside the brave soldiers who gave their lives for this noble cause. For his constant message of inspiring people to live together in peace, Dr. Ari became known as "the Gandhi of Sri Lanka." Niven and Tiara moved back to Sri Lanka from the U.S., and lived safely with their families and friends.

Dr. Ari is happy to see his grandchildren enthusiastically embark on this project to help children learn English.

He is tickled with their resourcefulness, and he is proud of the new club they have started: YouthForce. Niven is president of the club: he knew he needed a good organizer, so he asked his sister Tiara to be vice president. His 15-year-old cousin Sanara is an aspiring author: Niven asked her to be the club's secretary. Established in 2019 YouthForce has now grown to 20 members. For a year they collected supplies - books, pens and pencils, stationary, coloring books - and raised funds to buy ecofriendly cloth bags. Then they traveled to Kalawana from Colombo to deliver them. Everyone was grateful for their support.

Next, Sanara recorded the cellphone numbers for all 35 children, and each YouthForce member picked two children to sponsor. Now they call every weekend to check on their progress. They ask them: What did you learn? How did you practice your English this week? And these 5-10-minute phone calls in English are changing their lives.

Like his grandfather, Niven has a twinkle in his eyes. When he was about 9 years old, people started to see his grandfather's spirit shining through him. The second-youngest of Dr. Ari's 12 grandchildren, Niven is now growing into a youth leader. At 13, he is helping to organize Shramadamas like his grandfather taught him. He organizes tree planting projects, partnering with youth groups like Interact. He leads the prayers and songs; most importantly he acknowledges each and every one who helped create the project.

YouthForce is now envisioning a major tree planting program. Niven, Tiara, and Sanara have seen how climate change is affecting their country, especially in the rural areas. Landslides, beach erosion, oppressive heat waves, and extreme and unpredictable weather changes are affecting farmers' crops. In Sri Lanka the forest cover has been reduced from 50 percent to just 20 percent in just 10 years. The children's favorite beach is gone, left with only rough rocks along the shore.

In 2004, Sri Lanka was ravaged with its first tsunami. Over 30,000 people died, and thousands lost their homes. Immediately after the storm, Dr. Ari texted Sarvodaya's 26 districts and set up partnerships between those who had weathered the storm, with those whose villages had been destroyed. For its rapid response and organized relief efforts, Sarvodaya won the U.N's prestigious Award for Tsunami Rehabilitation. As part of their rehabilitation program, they had built a comprehensive Eco-Village for homeless families that is now a model of sustainable living.

YouthForce wants to help protect these villages using its own resources. They've heard the legend about their grandfather's birthplace, where King Hanuman is said to have lifted a whole mountain to find the powerful medicinal herbs underneath. Dr. Ari's grandchildren are deepening their appreciation for their country's biodiversity - and they realize they must do whatever they can to help preserve and protect it. From scientists they've learned that "big trees" are the best - since they help regulate the climate, the *water cycle*, and provide precious shade in the heat, *while* creating vital habitats for creatures. "Every day, the Kalawana children walk among these big trees," thought Niven. "Why not invite them to collect the seeds from these trees off of the forest floor? Then we can bring the big tree seeds from the forest to Colombo for their next tree planting project."

Niven and YouthForce traveled to Kalawana for the Sinhala New Year in April. "We organized speakers, instructional games, and fun activities - all in English!" he says, enthusiastically. To encourage more people to join and support them, they created a short video describing their project. Niven is grateful to everyone at Sarvodaya for their support, especially Sarvodaya's liaison to YouthForce, Yamuna Balasooriya for their special support They've found a host family for a Sarvodaya volunteer from England, who now lives in Kalawana and works with the children. Last week the village teacher called Neetha to say how motivated the children are. They were getting good grades, too. The teacher predicts that soon the number of students being tutored will have doubled. The whole village wants to learn English!

Now 88 years old, Dr. Ari enjoys being at home, where photographs of his grandchildren's smiling faces adorn the kitchen wall. To them, he is "Seeya" (grandfather). His home is always open to any children who come by to visit. They too call him Seeya. "We must listen to our young people, and help to awaken their potential," says Dr. Ari. "They have some great ideas, and they need our support."

Niven loves sharing stories with his Seeya about his project, about the children in the forest who are learning English. He treasures just sitting by his grandfather: listening, watching, and learning. He hopes that one day he will grow into his grandfather's shoes. For now he proudly "stands on the shoulders" of those -- those in his family, and *all* those -- who have dedicated their lives to the Sarvodaya. "I'll never forget my grandfather's message," Niven says. "Awakening, caring for others, sharing our gifts, carrying on his legacy."

At the end of every Shramadama, they sing this song.

May there be seasonal rains

May the harvest be bountiful

May the minds of all beings be peaceful

May the rulers be righteous.

****

Let's spread boundless loving-kindness to the entire universe, towards all living beings including humans, animals and plant kingdom. Having universal thoughts of loving kindness to entire humanity irrespective of cast, creed or religion and acting with this universal vision is the only way to get through this challenge.

Dr. Ari Ariyaratne

Call to Action: Support Sarvodaya's work of building and sustaining healthy communities in Sri Lanka: https://www.sarvodaya.org/

VII

EACH ONE
TEACH ONE
Emerging Island Leaders

EACH ONE TEACH ONE:
Emerging Island Leaders

The emerging island leaders in this chapter tell the continuing story of the Stone Soup Leadership Institute's journey. They hold a special place in my heart. They have become my teachers. My first goal was to listen, *really listen to,* and learn from them. We invited them to share their dreams. And in spite of daunting odds, they dreamed of a better life. Today, 18 years later they are lawyers, doctors, business executives. And each and every one of them is an inspiration to their island community.

For more than 20 years I've lived on islands, trying to finish this book and have traveled to more than 60, from Martha's Vineyard to Vieques, Puerto Rico, and then island hopping through the Caribbean. And I've gone from the island state of Hawaii to the island nation of the Philippines; and in Europe, to Croatia's 1000 islands, and then to Sri Lanka in Asia. Each one of these has its own special beauty, culture, and peoples.

Then, in 2004 I went to Vieques in search of a quiet place on the water to finish this book. However, when the mayor of Vieques saw the beloved actor Edward James Olmos's name on the cover of the Spanish edition of the first book, *Pan Y Vino Para El Camino,* he asked the Stone Soup Leadership Institute to help him rebuild this island community. It was then that we turned the Institute upside down in order to work directly with young people. We invited Spanish-speaking people from the first book, *Stone Soup for the World,* to serve as faculty for the Institute's first Sustainability Summit. Edward James Olmos sent a welcome video to greet the delegates. Nane Alejandrez led an Indigenous 'passing of the torch feather ceremony'. And the grandson of Cesar Chavez inspired everyone with his family's stories of their work with farmworkers in California. Over the next four years we mentored these youth to build a new generation of leaders.

Just before embarking on this journey I had led Healthy Community Initiatives in Cleveland and Detroit. Consulting for business, government, education, and community leaders, we built public-private partnerships to address challenging local issues. It's been shown statistically that communities with less than 20,000 people have the greatest chance of success for this model. On island communities, there is less than 1 degree of separation between the people. Everyone knows everyone -- and knows everything! There is a natural cohesiveness: people know their neighbors and tend to help each other out in a host of ways, from building houses to caring for each other's children. When someone is in trouble, or a loved one passes, everyone offers to help, bringing casseroles or lending a hand. By luck or divine intervention, I discovered that islands, with their small populations, were ideally suited to bringing the Stone Soup metaphor to life. This universally known fable provided a simple and easy-to-understand way to get everyone to work together to improve their communities, especially for their children.

Living and working alongside young people in these island communities for 18 years has been enlightening, and a deep cultural learning experience. My life has been enriched by them and their simple ways of living -- and their beautiful beaches. But I have also witnessed the dark side of this paradise; the growing inequities between the "haves" (tourists, developers) and the "have-nots" (locals). It has been especially painful to see how little support there is for young people. Schools are ill-equipped to prepare young people for the 21st century. The best and the brightest leave their island homes for better education and greater opportunities. And without experienced leaders, these island communities are increasingly vulnerable to exploitation by those looking for a quick investment -- or worse.

Islands are a great place to write. I had first gone to the island of Martha's Vineyard to walk on the beach, and think about a question: "What was I being called to do?" Little did I know that this question would have a two-part answer. A magical stone that found me on Lucy Vincent Beach led to my writing a book, founding an international Institute, working with the island community's schools to bring the stories to life, being exposed to celebrities, creating amazing events. And then, when I was asked to bring our Stone Soup magic to others, we worked with national organizations like the YMCA of the USA, and other organizations in Baltimore, Boston, Cincinnati, and Oakland.

In today's world, with the increasing dangers of climate change, island people are now "the canaries in the coal mine." Every day they see their coastlines eroding, their fish supply depleted, plastics littering their beaches, and toxic waste and environmental hazards dumped into their pristine waters. On Vieques, after Hurricane Maria, there was literally no food, no water, no gas, no ferry, no working ATMs. In such circumstances, understandably, along with the loss and pain, have come illness and death, and sometimes apathy and despair. The limited availability of space on islands, and the lack of affordable housing, access to living-wage jobs, government services, and other key resources are threatening the investment these families have devoted to their island for generations, just so they can survive. Many of them are being forced to sell their lands in hopes of finding a better life. But where can they go?

I have deep respect for island people; they are models of resilience, survival, and resourcefulness. They live sustainably just to survive. At our first Summit in Vieques, there was no running water for more than a month, except for those who had a cistern in their backyard. So one of our resourceful youth leaders took the initiative to lead a workshop on how to take a bath with a gallon of water.

Given that the young people on Vieques speak Spanish (and I didn't), and they wanted to learn English from me, the situation was a little challenging. We had to quickly create a model that allowed local people to train each other. It was then that we adopted the phrase "Each one teach one" as our motto. Dr. Martin Luther King had often quoted this saying to inspire people to reach back and help others climb the ladder to economic equity. It is an African-American proverb that had originated in the U.S. during slavery, when slaves were seen as chattel and denied an education; so when one slave had learned to read or write, it became their duty to teach someone else.

The Institute grew right along with these young people, starting with our four-year bilingual demonstration project in Vieques and our cornerstone programs: Cultural Arts & Entrepreneurship; Leadership; Sustainability; and Technology. The youth leaders from Vieques then served as faculty and facilitators for the Institute's other island community initiatives, and became an inspiration to other island youth. From Josue Morales Cruz and Kassandra Castillo Cruz in Vieques to Feliza Fenty in the British Virgin Islands, who rallied her friends to the aptly-named Dream Come True Villa, and then to the Bitter End Yacht Club for the Institute's 2008 Sustainability Summit. When Josue and Kassandra traveled to Martha's Vineyard, we convened the Institute's Youth Leadership Summits and launched a year-round program for the next 10 years. Among the hundreds they trained to become local leaders were Mary Ollen, Lucy Norris, Shavanae Anderson, Chris Aring, and Taynara Goncalves - who then led the Institute's year-round program for other Brazilian youth on Martha's Vineyard and helps guide the Rhode Island Youth Leadership Initiative. With the launch of the Institute's Sustainability Initiatives in Hawaii, Josue and Kassandra mentored

Trevor Tanaka, who then mentored Elijah Anakalea-Buckley, Alex Siordia, Jackie Noborikowa, and many others. Today, these Emerging Leaders are the heart of the Institute's Facilitators Program using the TouchStone Leaders Platform to inspire the next generation of young people to build a more just, equitable and sustainable world.

Each One Teach One: Policy-In Action: 2020 Reports

These young leaders were invited to envision a sustainable future for their islands - and create a 2020 Report for Sustainable Development. Through an intensive visioning and community engagement process, they prepared well-researched, well-documented presentations that challenged their leaders to develop policies that balanced protecting their communities' fragile ecosystems, providing for their families, creating opportunities for their children, and building a prosperous future. They courageously presented their 2020 Reports to their leaders and communities.

In Hawaii Trevor Tanaka embarked on a quest to bring sustainability education to public schools. Trevor now works with the Institute to get it implemented -- including the Institute's Sustainability Forums with youth, business, community, and government leaders and the Hawaii Department of Education. Hawaii's youth proudly presented a report on strategic recommendations from the Hawaii Governor's Report on Climate Preparedness Resiliency to President Obama. He then secured a grant from Hawaii's Department of Tourism, Business, and Economic Development to create an online system, the Sustainable Hawaii Toolkit. All this was to ensure that all of Hawaii's young people would learn about sustainability in school. Trevor achieved this by standing on the shoulders of youth leaders from Puerto Rico and Martha's Vineyard, who had championed their 2020 Reports and Policy-In-Action projects.

Each One Teach One.

A MULTICULTURAL DREAMER
Taynara Goncalves
Martha's Vineyard Youth Leadership Initiative

Ever since she was a little girl, Taynara dreamed of being a doctor. Growing up, she and her family lived a simple life in the little village of Mantenópolis, Brazil. As she walked past her grandmother's house, she loved smelling the luscious mangoes that she grew in big pots on her porch. "Everything we ate was organic and seasonal," she says. "When it was mango season, we ate mangoes. When it was banana season, we ate bananas."

However, with Brazil's economy in tatters, there were few jobs. Life was hard. Try as they might, it was tough for her parents to make ends meet. Often Taynara's family went without much food. For years, her parents saved every penny they could so they could search for a better life for their little family. And every night they prayed together.

People in the village talked about the island of Martha's Vineyard off the coast of Massachusetts. A few local men had traveled the 5,000 miles there, and found jobs building big homes for wealthy summer families. During the cold winter months, they'd return home and work on building their own homes. Since Taynara's father was a carpenter, he was eager to see if he might find a good job there too, so he could provide for his family.

In December 2001, they left Brazil with just a few things, filled with hope for their future. As they boarded the plane, 3-year-old Taynara held her mother's hand and looked up at her. "Does this mean I'll get to go to college and become a doctor?" she asked. Her mother smiled and said, "This means a lot of things if you are willing to try your hardest."

When they arrived, they were one of the very first Brazilian families to live on Martha's Vineyard. Life wasn't easy, especially in the winter. This little island had a tight-knit community of 20,000 year-rounders. v struggled in the long winter months to eke out a living. During the ᵊr months, the island swelled to 100,000 people, including service from Ireland and Jamaica, who worked in the hotels. Then, ᵐmer, everyone went home. So, when Brazilians began to ᵊir whole families and to stay -- and send their children to school -- local people were nervous. They didn't think there would be enough to go around, especially in the winter months. Taynara remembers how it hurt when she saw how people looked down on her parents when they heard their accents.

Taynara's mother was relieved to discover that Elio Silva had opened a little shop with Brazilian foods, including the chocolate Caixa de Bombons that her father had bought her for special occasions. By the time twenty years had passed, there were several restaurants catering to the more than 2,000 Brazilians who now live year-round on the island. And Brazilian youth strengthened the high school's soccer team, which won the coveted statewide championships.

On her first day of kindergarten at the Oak Bluffs School, Taynara could feel everyone's eyes on her. There was only one other Brazilian child in her class. Taynara only knew four words in English: "Hi, how are you?" But with her warm smile, sparkling eyes, and gentle ways, she made friends. She practiced her English and picked up words watching movies on TV. To this day, Taynara greets everyone with this same message -- and with the same intention. She sincerely wants to know how you are -- which makes you want to respond in kind.

School wasn't easy for Taynara, but she pushed herself, studied hard, and always got good grades. "I constantly reminded myself that this was my big chance to achieve my dream," she says. "Whenever I was discouraged I reminded myself how lucky I was to be here and to have this opportunity." In high school, she was proud to be invited to join the National Honor Society. Step by step, with laser focus, and along with her daily prayers, Taynara pursued her dream of becoming a doctor.

Then one day her teacher nominated Taynara to be a youth delegate to the Martha's Vineyard Youth Leadership Initiative (MVYLI). When she arrived at the orientation, she was surprised to see that the codirector of the Summit, Josue Cruz, was from the island of Vieques, Puerto Rico. Josue had been just 14 years old when he went to his first Summit in Vieques. Now in college, he was pursuing his dream of becoming a lawyer. "It was amazing to listen to Josue; he had faced struggles, but he wasn't defined by them. He persevered," Taynara says. "I knew then that I wasn't alone. That I can do this too!"

On the first day of the Summit, Taynara was fascinated to meet so many multicultural young people from islands like Vieques, Virgin Gorda, and Hawaii. Taynara felt that she had a new family of friends who were all ready to support her in realizing her goal. "It's awesome!" she says. "It gives you another family, a safe place to talk about important things

-- and to bring back to your school setting too."

At the Summit Taynara developed a greater awareness about climate change and sustainability. On tours they took to the Vineyard farms, she saw different crops than those she'd known in Brazil. She saw firsthand how climate change was contributing to coastal erosion. Waterfront homes were being threatened, and the frequent flooding of the Four Corners intersection by the ferry held up traffic for hours.

A few years later, Taynara visited her family's village in Brazil. "It was culture shock," she says. "Somehow it didn't feel real. It's a whole different world. Sometimes I wonder what my life would have been like if I'd stayed." During that visit she realized that climate change was taking a toll on her family's village. Extreme weather -- first dryness from the lack of rain, and then torrential downpours -- was washing away the precious rich topsoil so important for farming their crops.

As the first in her family to go to college, Taynara was excited and nervous. Her high school guidance counselor had discouraged Taynara from applying to a four-year college. "That's too much for you," he said, and directed her instead to a community college. But Taynara knew that she'd never become a doctor unless she started at a four-year college. "I was a good student, involved with extracurricular activities, just like the other students," she says. "Why shouldn't I be able to pursue my dream?" She walked out the door, never to return. It was the first time that she had felt the sting of institutional racism.

But in MVYLI's college prep program, she got the help she needed: tutoring for the SATs and help for her parents in filling out the financial aid forms. She enjoyed visiting a few different colleges to see which one might be best for her. However, as a "Dreamer" Taynara knew that she wouldn't qualify for scholarships. Her parents couldn't help her either. Fortunately, the Institute found a benefactor who offered to sponsor Taynara's education. It was the answer to her prayers!

Taynara's dream of becoming a doctor continued to be shaped with MVYLI's Job Shadow Day. Each year she spent an afternoon with one of the island's doctors: she shadowed family physicians, pediatricians, doctors at the health clinic, and eventually in the hospital's emergency room. She loved it! Each time her dream was renewed, even as she refined her goals. Thanks to her mentors, Taynara was able to see the wealth of career opportunities for premed students, and her horizons expanded.

For her MVYLI Sustainability-in-Action project, Taynara worked with other multicultural youth to envision and create the Institute's Multicultural Assembly at the Martha's Vineyard Regional High School. "Hi, I'm Charlayne Hunter-Gault, and I'm multicultural," said the honored speaker when the day came. "We are standing on the shoulders of giants," she continued, quoting from President Obama's Inaugural speech. "I am, they were, you are where you are because we are standing on the shoulders of giants." Then high school senior Jacob Lawrence spoke of his African American heritage, with roots in Ghana and Nigeria. "Thirty percent of the MVRHS students are multicultural," he told the assembled students. "Take time to get to know your friends." Then Ana Carvalho shared her experience of being a Brazilian student at MVRHS in 2008. "When I was a student, there was a lot of tension," she admitted. Now a senior at Tufts University, she invited the students to be open to each other. "I hope you will learn to appreciate Brazilian culture. Your Brazilian peers have a lot to offer."

For the next Summit Taynara served as a "Visioneer," warmly welcoming the new youth delegates as they arrived. All through college, Taynara worked with Brazilian youth on Martha's Vineyard, encouraging them to pursue their dreams too. She now serves as a Facilitator at each Summit, training young people with the tools they need to pursue their dreams for their lives, their communities, and the world. She enjoyed working with the Institute's other Facilitators like Kassandra Cruz from Vieques, Puerto Rico, Namgyal Gyaltshen from Bhutan, Berta Pelaez from Guatemala and Patricia Pires Dias from Cape Verdes. "I love to get to know people that are multicultural," Taynara says. "Each person has a different story, and each one of them will impact you in a different way. This island is filled with multicultural people, even though not everyone knows it. We are all a big family, filled with amazing stories to share with one another."

Now a 23-year-old college graduate, Taynara was thrilled to get her dream job as a medical assistant and health educator at Island Health Care on the Vineyard. "I feel really blessed to be doing what I love, helping people, especially during the pandemic, when so many of my classmates are struggling to find any kind of job." When the new U.S. Congress passed the Dreamers Act, Taynara knew it was in answer to her prayers. Now she can finally dream again -- this time to go to medical school -- and finally realize her dream of becoming a doctor. "I've been praying for this for a very long time," she says. "And now? It's really happening!"

Every moment is an organizing opportunity,
every person a potential activist, every minute a
chance to change the world.

Dolores Huerta

Call to Action: Learn how multicultural youth are becoming leaders of a sustainable world: www.MVYLI.org

BE THE CHANGE
Chris Aring
Martha's Vineyard Youth Leadership Initiative

For Chris Aring, the island of Martha's Vineyard is home. For the summer people, celebrities, and even presidents, the Vineyard is a beautiful place to spend leisurely time with their families and meet old friends.

But for 16-year-old Chris, this year felt different. It was the first day of the Stone Soup Leadership Institute's Sustainability Summit on Martha's Vineyard. Young people from across the country had gathered together at a large up-island hilltop home overlooking Menemsha Pond. They had all been nominated by their communities to serve as delegates at the Summit, to learn how to become leaders of a more sustainable world.

After their morning ice-breakers, the very first speaker was Arun Gandhi, grandson of Mahatma Gandhi. All the youth were spellbound as he spoke. They'd often heard the phrase "Be the change you want to see in the world," and Arun was the embodiment of this powerful message. As Chris listened to him tell the story of his grandfather, he was transported to a little village in India. "Can you imagine being 12 years old and getting this powerful lesson from your grandfather, Mahatma Gandhi?" he thought. The anecdote Arun told had a very simple message about sustainability embedded in it: it was about the importance of not throwing away a pencil until the very end.

It was the quality of the people Chris met at this week-long intensive Summit that touched him the most. He fondly remembers playing football on the large lawn with Trevor and Elijah. This became the start of a very special friendship. Chris was impressed that the Hawaiian delegates had collected native tea leaves from their homeland to bring 6,000 miles to the Summit. As they taught him how to make Hawaiian leis, they shared stories of their culture, their language, and their world. Thanks to these young people and their aloha spirit, Chris came to understand the concept of sustainability in a whole new light.

At that Summit, Arun Gandhi asked the Institute to bring its transformative educational tools to the young people of India. Curious by nature, and a self-taught techie, Chris offered to help with this ambitious challenge. He had already won many awards, and had designed software and apps. While many of his classmates saw the technology career path as a ticket to a high-paying job, Chris was more intrigued with the idea of being able to use the power of technology for positive social change. His father, a longtime teacher at the Vineyard's high school had always encouraged his son to think outside the box. Now, empowered by what he had learned at the Summit, Chris was inspired to ground his ideals in serving humanity. He wasn't quite sure how this was going to happen, but he was willing to try.

That summer, while tourists and seasonal residents were vacationing, Chris joined the Institute's intergenerational team to dive into this very challenging task. Their goal was to envision a way to transfer 20 years of the Institute's trainings and educational tools to an online platform. First Chris looked at digital courses like Coursera and edX. "Too traditional," he decided. Next the team decided to use the Design Thinking approach, asking themselves the key question "How might we?...." to brainstorm ideas. Then Chris had a thought -- last summer he'd attended a Hack-a-Thon, where college-aged students immersed themselves for 24 hours to design innovative tech apps and software. "There's never been a Hack-a-Thon on the Vineyard," Chris said. "Let's do it!"

Chris thought it was a pretty simple idea. Little did he know what he was about to embark on. Reaching out to college students and inviting them to give of their time, and then travel all the way to the Vineyard by car, bus, and ferry took some doing. But they came! They came from Amherst College, Hampshire College, Mt. Holyoke College, and from the University of Massachusetts in Lowell. Later they said that the idea of responding to Gandhi's grandson's challenge had intrigued them.

Finding a home large enough to house this crew was quite an undertaking. It was now late November, and most large homes on the Vineyard aren't insulated. By luck, perseverance, and ultimately maybe even divine intervention, the owner of a 20-room Victorian mansion, inspired by the Institute's mission, offered her home. Overlooking Inkwell Beach in Oak Bluffs, the Villa Rosa was once owned by Joe Overton, a political organizer and the first head of a labor union in New York City. His home had served as the Summer White House, and leaders and organizers of the Civil Rights movement, including Dr. Martin Luther King, Jr. had stayed here. It was here, looking out over the vast horizon of the Atlantic Ocean, that Dr. King is said to have written his famous "I Have A Dream" speech.

The Design-A-Thon, as it was called, began with a sumptuous feast, with the owner of the house sharing stories about its history. Then everyone jumped into the immersive 24-hour experience. After the Institute's team gave an overview of their vision and goals, the visiting techies interviewed the Institute's youth leaders as well as the facilitators of the Summit to create a "user profile." Then everyone retired to their separate nooks to work on coding. They chose the attic as their hub, and set up the large screen where they could showcase their progress. All through the night they worked, sustained with lots of coffee, pizza, and junk food. It was an exhilarating time. As the youngest person there, Chris loved hanging out with these seasoned techies in the kitchen during their breaks and hearing them talk about user-design, prototypes, beta testing, and the ultimate goal: *user-friendly*.

A videographer documented the process, and interviewed Chris and youth leaders like Josue Cruz from Vieques, Puerto Rico and Alex Siordia from Hawaii. "This house is the right place to do this," Chris said. "I feel that in some ways what we are doing has a relation to what Dr. King was trying to do. Creating change and inspiring people to challenge the status quo, and how to be leaders. You can feel Dr. King's presence here. That what you are doing has a bigger purpose than just a computer program. I really feel that it can go somewhere."

In just 24 hours, the band of techies had created an impressive "pitch deck" presentation to present to potential funders. When it came time for the Reveal Event, Chris made the presentation to the Island's business and education leaders. He was pretty proud of what everyone had accomplished. "It was a really good feeling," he says. "It was the first time I'd had the experience of having a big idea, and helping to make it actually happen! To this very day, seven years later, every time I drive by that house, I tell the story of this life-changing experience to whomever is in the car."

That fall, as a junior in high school, Chris convinced his advisor that he should get credit to pursue this project as an independent study. Then he joined with the Institute's facilitators, Gia Winsryg-Ulmer and Grace Burton Sundman, to design a leadership course using the Institute's curriculum. Offered to the Martha's Vineyard Youth Leadership Initiative (MVYLI) youth, this 10-week pilot program became the beta site for the Institute's TouchStone Leaders Platform. "I learned that it's best to not sit back and overthink a great idea," Chris says now. "If you have an idea that you think would make a difference in your life, your community's life, or *anyone's* life, you should go through with it and act on it in a timely manner." Chris was convinced that his high school should incorporate this pilot into their leadership class. "We should share it with others so they can have an opportunity to learn the necessary leadership skills for life. This program teaches many skills not found in the classroom."

To continue his exploration into the tech world, Chris was matched with a business leader, John Klein for MVYLI's Job Shadow Day. And the following year, he was matched with virtual reality pioneer Galen Ho. As they explored Galen's state-of-the-art Immersive Worlds, Galen listened to Chris's dreams for his future, and encouraged him to apply to the little-known Olin College of Engineering, just outside of Boston. When Chris received a full scholarship to study there, Chris's father was thrilled. He had attended Northeastern University, but had had to drop out and get a job before he could complete his education. He knew what a difference it would make for his son to graduate debt-free from college.

At the next Summit, Chris was a freshman at Olin College of Engineering. He was thrilled to see Trevor again, who was now a senior in college. Chris especially enjoyed rooming with Trevor and sharing lodgings with the younger male delegates at the Summit. "They were so full of energy, so funny, and eager to hear about my experiences at college," Chris says. "I was happy to be able to be a true mentor to these high school youth. It was a good feeling."

For the past few years Trevor had worked with the Institute to design strategies to bring sustainability education to public school students. He was also searching for ways to use technology to help youth get jobs in the emerging field of sustainability. Chris was happy to help Trevor with this new challenge. Along with the Institute's tech advisor, Chris and Trevor once again dived into the question "How might we...?" "Let's create a new site," Chris said. He quickly searched for available ones. "Sustainability is Fun is available," he said, "Shall we grab it? What a great name - kids will love it!"

Throughout the following year, Chris worked virtually with Trevor and the Institute's team to create the new site so that it could be tested with youth at the next Summit. Then he brought his college roommate, Ilya, to the next summit, which was held in Newport, Rhode Island. With Trevor as their guide, they envisioned an online ecosystem that connects youth, educators, and companies to build sustainable economies.

They'd also made plans to create a Design-A-Thon to be held just before the Summit. This time it was with business, education, and government leaders of the Blue Economy in southern New England.

They designed surveys, gathered data, and facilitated an engaging user-design experience with these industry leaders. With Trevor as their guide for the week-long event, they drilled down on the data and designed a presentation for the Summit about the Sustainable Workforce Development Network: SustainWDN™.

"It was truly a pleasure to meet our next generation of leaders at the Design-A-Thon," says Robert Rak, of Bristol Community College's Blue Center. "It was inspiring to see these young people actively engaging in the development of meaningful communication with business leaders. They were not only seeking information for themselves, but also for the youth of today as a whole. Bringing together the many players in this emerging Blue Economy is very important so that we can work together, as a team, to bring a bright future to our region and the nation as a whole."

Just before Chris graduated from college, his beloved father passed. He had been so proud of his son, and his own passion for teaching had inspired all his students: he brought out the brightness in everyone. One day, Chris hopes to follow in his father's footsteps and become a teacher. Inspired by Gandhi's grandson, and standing on Dr. King's shoulders, Chris is grateful for the opportunity to help pass their legacy on through this platform so that other young people can work together to truly make the world a better place.

We must be the change we want to see in the world.

Mahatma Gandhi

Call to Action: Learn about how Chris's idea is changing lives: check out the Institute's https://www.sustainabilityisfun.com/about and SustainWDN.com

FROM RECYCLING TO RESALE: REBAG
Kassandra Castillo Cruz
Vieques, Puerto Rico/New York City

Kassandra Castillo Cruz grew up in what some would call a paradise. With its 100 beaches, Bioluminescent Bay, warm weather, and cool Caribbean breezes, Vieques is a popular tourist destination off the main island of Puerto Rico.

Isla Nena "Little Girl Island" was also home to 10,000 people, many of whom lived in abject poverty. When in 1941 the U.S. Navy set up testing for the worst weapons to be used in Vietnam, Afghanistan, Iraq, they suppressed the economy, and encouraged people to leave, or to go on government assistance. Many left, but others, loyal to their homeland and its people, stayed and managed to eke out a meager living. Kassandra's mom was hard-working and determined to provide for her family. Every Saturday morning Kassandra and her two younger sisters would jump up on her truck and travel around the island with her, collecting trash. As the eldest child, Kassandra felt a responsibility to set a good example for her sisters. She would always warmly greet her mother's customers with a big smile as she gracefully gathered up their trash.

Sometimes she found little treasures in the trash. One day she even found a Christian Dior saddlebag. It was almost new, probably left behind by a tourist. For 12-year-old Kassandra, it was a great first handbag.

Thanks to its rich diversity of cultures -- from the Indigenous Taino with their delicate features, to the descendants of North American, Spanish, and other European colonists, to Cuban and Dominican Republic islanders and the descendants of African slaves -- Puerto Rican women are known for their exquisite beauty. They have proudly claimed five titles for Miss Universe, and seven for Miss World. Many of the islanders who watched Kassandra walk down the street on her way to school, with her regal bearing, hoped that one day she would be the one to bring such a title home to Vieques.

On May 1, 2003, when the U.S. Navy finally left the island after 68 years of protesting and civil disobedience, the Island's people celebrated

- there were music and dancing in the streets. It was Kassandra's 10th birthday, and she loved the celebratory fireworks that day. Kassandra had loved working with her father to make buttons and T-shirts with messages protesting the Navy occupation of the island. When he died the following year, Kassandra was devastated. He had instilled in her a longing for a better life; so, she knew that he'd want her to push forward with her dreams.

When she was 14, a friend invited her to join a new youth leadership program, the Vieques Youth Leadership Initiative (VYLI). And when she was asked at the Stone Soup Leadership Institute's Sustainability Summit, "What is your dream for your life, your island, and your community?" she declared that she wanted to become a top model. Later, in a VYLI video, she said, "I want people to recognize my island for all the *positive* things here, and for our talented youth, not for the negative statistics; we are too often excluded."

While she was very shy, Kassandra was even more determined to pursue her dream. She set about finding out what it would take to realize it and signed up for her first beauty contest. To lend their support, VYLI's loyal band of youth traveled with her to San Juan for the contest. They marveled as she confidently walked down the runway. And they celebrated enthusiastically with her when she won third prize!

The next year for VYLI's Job Shadow Day, Kassandra was matched with Ileana Cambó, a former Ms. Puerto Rico and the VP at L'Oréal. That led to her first photo shoot and the beginning of her professional portfolio. At fundraising events, like VYLI's Taste of the Island, she was introduced to other leaders of the fashion industry. And from there, her modeling career skyrocketed! In just three years, she became a top model for UNICA, the #1 modeling agency in Puerto Rico, and was being featured on fashion magazine covers and receiving many awards.

However, Kassandra was not naïve; she saw the dark side of the fashion industry, which glorified prepubescent girls and often took advantage of their vulnerability. Wise beyond her years, Kassandra kept her head on her shoulders, and stay focused on her goals. She knew that modeling wasn't a *life* for her, just a stepping stone from which to pursue her bigger dreams.

Because she had achieved her first dream, to be a top fashion model, she was an inspiring role model for young girls on Vieques. She led workshops and provided guidance for aspiring models, organized professional photo shoots and fashion shows for them, and led college prep workshops to encourage local youth to strive toward higher education. With VYLI's

Entrepreneurship Initiative, she also led workshops where young people turned local natural resources -- seeds, beads, shells, glass, and stone -- into unique jewelry. On the weekends, they sold their wares to tourists and raised funds to invest in their initiative. They were thrilled when they were invited to be the youngest representatives at the 3rd Annual Caribbean Artisan Festival in the British Virgin Islands and were able to fly for the first time, to the neighboring island of Tortola, where they met artisans from ten different Caribbean countries, as well as entrepreneurs and re-foresters who were preserving their traditional cultures as well as their island environments.

Kassandra carefully saved the money she was earning from modeling so that one day she would be the first in her family to go to college, an even more important dream come true. At the Inter American University in Puerto Rico, she received her degree in Business Administration. And she spent a semester abroad at the Spain Business School in Barcelona, studying swimwear design at the Centro de Las Artes del Diseño y la Alta Costura.

In 2012 Kassandra continued to expand her horizons by traveling to Martha's Vineyard to share her experiences at the Stone Soup Leadership Institute's Sustainability Summit. And she traveled to the tiny island of Lanai, Hawaii and then the Puerto Rican community of Holyoke in western Massachusetts and to show young people how they could use their entrepreneurial skills to realize their dreams.

The next year Kassandra moved to Boston and became the first employee for a startup sustainable fashion company Rebag (Trendlee. com). In 2014, when the company expanded and moved to the U.S. fashion capitol of New York City, Kassandra moved with them. Rebag is now a $50 million luxury resale retailer that buys and sells luxury handbags. As its Head of Operations, Kassandra oversees teams of 20 people based in branches all over the world.

Rebag allows customers to refresh their closets as often as they like and choose from a selection of thousands of designer handbags. "You can purchase a bag, carry it for up to six months, exchange it for Rebag credit worth at least 70 percent of the original purchase price, and put the credit toward a new bag," Kassandra explains. During the COVID pandemic, the company launched a resourceful new app, "Clair AI," that allows customers to instantly determine the value of new and pre-owned luxury handbags and purchase remotely. "And you haven't had to directly interact with anyone to make it happen," she says. "We get to give these bags three to five 'homes' during their lifetime instead of having them end up in the trash after just one season," Kassandra says, as she reflects back on the Christian Dior bag she found in the trash as a 12-year-old. "That bag is still very popular," she says. "And it is worth $3,800!"

Kassandra is proud to be working in the sustainable fashion industry, along with companies like Poshmark and ThredUp. She's pleased to see that some large companies, like Levi Strauss, are adopting more sustainable practices too, and she keeps a discerning and watchful eye on the way sustainability practices are defined and applied in the industry.

When in 2017 Hurricane Maria devastated all of Puerto Rico, it brought Vieques to its knees. The island's famous Bioluminescent Bay was destroyed, along with its rich mangrove ecosystem. Without ferry service, people were without food and gas; and the environmental toxins left behind by the U.S. Navy had left people vulnerable to scary autoimmune illnesses. Without a hospital on the island, many people died, especially the elderly -- including Kassandra's beloved *abuela*. Kassandra did what she could to help her family, raising funds and sending them to her mother, and offering her sisters and their children shelter in her tiny Manhattan apartment.

But people on Vieques are survivors, and they are resilient. They have rallied, and together they are slowly rebuilding their island.

During the pandemic, Kassandra has continued to work with Rebag remotely, which gave her the chance to return to her homeland so her new son, Thiago, could spend time with her family. She loves seeing that the spirit of Vieques is still strong. She's especially inspired by how young people are leading the way with organizations like La Coleman Cimarrone, creating community gardens and big composting and recycling projects, as well as ecotourism companies that offer hiking and other island adventures. "It's refreshing," she says. She's glad to see that people on Vieques are striving to become more self-sufficient by growing their own foods and creating renewable energy projects. And she's especially glad to see that they are working together to improve life for *everyone* on the island. When she returns to her life in the Big Apple, she hopes that one day she can live part-time on Vieques so her children can appreciate its beauty and its community spirit.

Ever the entrepreneur, Kassandra may one day even create her own company, and the chance to make new dreams for her life -- and her community -- come true.

*The only limit to the height of your achievements
is the reach of your dreams
and your willingness to work for them.*

Michelle Obama

Call to Action: Invest in young people to realize their dreams. Vieques Youth Leadership Initiative: www.vyli.org. Check out Kassandra's company on Istagram: kavani_handmade.

HOW CAN I HELP?
Josue Cruz
Vieques, Puerto Rico/Texas

When Josue woke up, he was excited for the first time in a long time. His friend, Carmianne, had invited him to join her for a Youth Leadership Summit on their little island of Vieques, Puerto Rico. At first Josue was concerned he'd have to take a week off from his job at the local pizza shop. At 14 years old, this young man felt responsible for helping his family, who were barely surviving on welfare and food stamps.

Times were tough. When the U.S. Navy arrived 68 years ago, they had suppressed the island's economy: they told everyone to either leave or sign up for government aid. For three generations, people weren't able to even have a job. Now that the Navy had finally left, everyone was hopeful for a better future. Ever since Josue could remember, he'd heard the bombs exploding, testing the worst weapons for wars in Vietnam, Afghanistan, and Iraq. People tried to stop them with peaceful protests and civil disobedience, even putting their bodies on the runway so planes couldn't refuel. Over and over again they were arrested. Sometimes celebrities, like Edward James Olmos, joined them, to get the media's attention. The famous actor had even been the Mayors cellmate in jail.

Vieques Mayor invited the Stone Soup Leadership Institute to help train the island's youth for a better future. On the first day of the Institute's Summit, Josue watched the beloved actor share a video message to Vieques youth.

You've been chosen to be here as part of the Youth Leadership Summit. This is much needed not only in Vieques, and Puerto Rico but on the entire planet. You are the hope of the future. The future depends on all of you sitting listening to me today. I wish I could be with you there, and inspire you, as you would inspire me. Really, we belong together. Thank you for being here today to become the leaders we need you to be. God bless you and thank you all.

Josue arrived early to the Summit, eager to check things out. When he saw the Institute's organizers setting up, he asked, "How can I help?" Josue was honored to be asked to hang a poster of his heroes: Gandhi, Dr. King, Cesar Chavez, and First Lady Eleanor Roosevelt. Thus, began

Josue's life-changing journey: it would end up transforming his life, and many other lives too.

To begin the Summit, Native American Nane Alejandrez from Barrios Unidos in California led the youth in ceremonial chanting at the ancient site where a medicine man's 4,000-year-old bones had just been discovered. He asked for prayers for the young people to have the courage to lead their island to a better future for all their people.

"What is your dream for your life, for your island, and for the world?" For the first time, Josue was being encouraged to dream big. "My dream for my life is to become a lawyer," he said, determined. "For my island: to be the Mayor. For my world: Peace." Josue was passionate about giving young people the opportunity to better their lives. Every day he could see how Americans were coming to invest in his island - buying real estate, starting restaurants and setting up B&Bs and hotels. Tourism was booming. More than anything Josue wanted his people to reap the benefits of their hard-won victory and earn a good living to provide for their families.

For the next four years, Josue worked tirelessly to cofound the Vieques Youth Leadership Initiative. He was impressed that rock star Tito Auger continued to keep his promise to help Vieques. During the years of peaceful protests, Tito's "Song of Vieques" had been their anthem. Vieques youth were excited that Tito traveled from San Juan to Vieques to work with the Institute's team to develop the Cultural Arts & Entrepreneurship Initiative. They created a logo, a theme song, and a photographic display of their faces with their dreams. Everyone was so proud to see it hanging in the Vieques Airport so those who visited would see them as Vieques's future leaders. During weekly workshops, Taino artisans trained youth to make hand-crafted jewelry, climb trees to collect calabash, and carve Indigenous designs for unique lampshades. On the weekends, they set up a table on the Malecon and sold their wares to tourists. They practiced their English and developed math and money management skills. One winter they raised over $4,000.

More than anything, Josue knew that if his people were to succeed in this new economy, they needed to learn English. To protest the Navy occupation, teachers had refused to teach their students English. So now there were three generations of families who spoke only Spanish. Vieques was very isolated from Puerto Rico and the world. There was only one wi-fi hotspot on the whole island. With just a few computers, the paying tourists got first dibs. But lucky for Josue, Island Computers was right across the street from his home. The owner was kind and offered to help. With the Institute's support, they applied for a Microsoft grant for the first computer training on the island. First, Josue had to make his case to justify the request. From piles of papers stacked on the floors of government offices, he collected statistics to develop the report, "The Challenges Facing Vieques Youth." When the grant was received, this 16-year-old was the program's first trainer. Josue felt a deep sense of pride training his people to learn computer skills and explore the power of the World Wide Web.

Vieques had a long way to go to catch up. Josue was on a quest, searching for ideas, eager to discover best practices from other island communities. As the youngest person at the Caribbean Media Exchange conference in San Juan, he met San Juan's top meteorologist. She was surprised to meet such an inquisitive young man asking serious questions about climate change and how it might affect his island. Josue was fascinated by her presentation, with scientific facts and a declaration from 70 prominent scientists calling for a moratorium on building on Puerto Rico's fragile coastline.

Later that year, when it rained 24 inches in 24 hours Josue remembered the meteorologist's message. He realized then that he needed to find ways to help his people prepare for natural disasters. He set up one of the first Facebook groups to map where families, especially the elderly, lived. He wanted to be sure they weren't forgotten if - and when - future disasters hit again. Little did he know how prophetic this would be when in 2017 Hurricane Maria devastated Puerto Rico. Vieques was at the eye of that storm.

Josue continued his travels, next to Los Angeles. At the next Youth Leadership Summit on Vieques, he had met the grandson and namesake of the great Latino leader, Cesar Chavez. He'd read about his leadership for the farmworkers in California. Josue was happy to translate for Cesar and bring his inspiring message of hope to Vieques youth. So, when Cesar invited Josue to visit him in Los Angeles, he jumped at the chance. Within a few short months, he visited Cesar Chavez burial place, La Paz and his Radio Campesino, where he was a featured guest speaker. Cesar taught Josue how to create a website to share VYLI's message with the world. Upon his return, Josue created his own radio show, where he featured local experts to share their vision for Vieques' future.

Everyone on Vieques longed to see the world. So, when Josue returned from Los Angeles, he was famous. When asked for his advice, Josue would always encourage young people to stay in school, get good grades, and make something of their lives. He humbled himself by sharing that once he was a C-D student and now he had a 4.0.

Next Josue led his people on a mission to ask the government to help. Josue boarded a plane with 42 youth and parents from Vieques to fly to San Juan. Dressed in their VYLI T-shirts, everyone stood proudly in front of La Fortaleza, the Governor's mansion, with their friend Tito Auger. Inside Josue gave an impassioned speech demanding action from government officials. From that moment on, everyone knew this young man was destined for greatness.

Next Josue traveled with the Mayor's Economic Development team to Tortola to study how the small business model in the British Virgin Islands supported local companies instead of investing in the economic trap of the supermalls in San Juan. Since Josue was now fluent in English, he was asked to make the presentation on behalf of the Mayor to the BVI Prime Minister. The Prime Minister was so impressed he asked the Institute to bring the VYLI model to his country to inspire BVI's youth. Josue's friends from the Cultural Arts & Entrepreneurship Initiative joined him at the Caribbean Artisan Festival. As the youngest artisan/entrepreneurs to showcase their wares, they were fascinated by the eco-foresters from Trinidad and Tobago who grew trees and harvested the seeds to make exquisite jewelry. From the $4,000 they earned during the winter, they paid for their trip.

Josue continued his mission as an ambassador for Vieques youth, joining Vieques Mayor to meet with Puerto Rico's First Lady, then speaking at events in New York City and Washington D.C. On May 1, year, Boston's first Puerto Rican City Councilman, Felix Arroyo, hosted an event celebrating the anniversary of Vieques's freedom from the U.S. Navy. Josue had become an impressive orator. When he received the Institute's first Walter Cronkite Award, he said, " Walter Cronkite is an icon of the highest standard of democracy and equality. Being the Walter Cronkite award winner, was a door opening experience for me. I feel a responsibility to carry on the legacy of a man who represents responsible and human journalism."

Soon Josue was featured in prominent publications like *Caribbean Business* and the *Vineyard Gazette*. People started asking Josue to be the Mayor of their island. He reminded them that he first needed to finish his education and realize his dream of becoming a lawyer. For now, he was proud to be a 4.0 college student a full scholarship. As a law student, he was the only one from a family on welfare. At his graduation he received the prestigious honor for his contribution to the people of Vieques.

Then in 2010 Josue traveled to Martha's Vineyard to serve on the faculty of the Institute's 6th Summit. There he met youth leaders from other Caribbean islands of Bahamas, Jamaica, Barbados and from the newly formed Virgin Gorda Youth Leadership Initiative. For his presentation on Vieques he shared his dreams for his island community. Josue loved visiting the Vineyard, which is the same shape and size as Vieques. He especially enjoyed learning about innovative projects he saw on the Sustainability Tours. When he visited the school's gardens and heard Noli Taylor's presentation on the Island Grown Schools Initiative, a light went on. "If they can feed their people - with just a five-month growing season, just imagine what we could do in Puerto Rico!" he exclaimed.

Upon his return, Josue embarked on his action plan. He researched and wrote a grant to get federal funds for school gardens. He even worked with the opposing political party to get both sides to work for the good of their people. Josue is proud of the 100 school gardens they built, especially the one for handicapped students who now have a path towards self-sufficiency, selling their produce at the Farmer's Market. Unfortunately, Josue also learned about the underbelly of politics. When the press conference was held and awards were presented, Josue wasn't invited to the stage. While he was the one who did all the hard work, the credit went to those from the other party. Nonetheless, Josue was proud of his accomplishments. The second year the grant doubled, as did the number of school gardens. In his heart, he knew his people had the tools to feed themselves and become self-sufficient; that was reward enough.

Josue's next journey led him to Hawaii - 7,000 miles from his home. On the Big Island, he swam with the dolphins, witnessed the active volcano, and reveled in the snowcapped mountains of Mauna Lea. On the Institute's Sustainability Tours he learned about renewable energy projects like Hawaii Pacific Academy's Energy Lab. At the Waimea Elementary School garden, Josue shared his experiences in Puerto Rico and learned new tips for organic gardening. His favorite memory is of spending an afternoon with Nancy Redfeather in her luscious gardens. Nancy was Noli Taylor's mentor when she first studied school gardens. Nancy was touched that her mentee had inspired Josue to follow in her footsteps. In return, Josue was happy to share his connections so Nancy could receive grants to support Hawaii's State School Garden Initiative.

After Josue's classmates passed the Bar, they took high paying jobs and climbed career ladders that guaranteed them a comfortable life. With his newly minted law degree, Josue decided to first help his people get titles to their land. People had lost their land when the Navy confiscated and razed their homes to build new ones for its officers. Josue was Vieques first lawyer who could now represent them. It was a long, arduous process. Gathering all the legal documents to prove their ownership, then representing his people at the government's offices in San Juan was challenging. Josue spent many days there pleading their cases. For him it was just the right thing to do.

Josue then traveled to Texas to join his friend Carmianne, who invited him to join a law firm. For a while, he tried it out, but didn't like what he saw there. He was furious that Spanish speaking people were being robbed by some of the lawyers, who promised to get them U.S. citizenship. So, he explored other options before deciding to create his own firm. He put out a shingle and used social media to post videos showing how he was an honest person with integrity. People started coming. Word got out. People who had lived, worked, and paid taxes in the U.S. for 10, 20, or more years were being deported. Josue was outraged. While he had never liked going to court during his law school days, he now felt a passion to help these people.

Then the Border Wall fiasco began. People from Central America affected by U.S. wars and climate change were desperate. Josue saw it as his moral duty to help families who were losing all their rights, and being treated like animals, just for trying to give their children a better future. So today, Josue's days are long. He doesn't get to travel much or see his beloved island of Vieques. But he has peace of mind knowing that he's doing the right thing by helping people who desperately need his help.

Now 29 years old, Josue is proud to see his friends, VYLI alumni who are now successful doctors, lawyers, and business executives. He loves seeing all the young people he mentored at the Institute's Summits who are pursuing their dreams. The work he started goes on! To Josue, this is life's greatest reward.

*As you discover what strength you can draw from
your community in this world
from which it stands apart, look outward as well
as inward.
Build bridges instead of walls.*

Supreme Court Justice Sonia Sotomayor

Call to Action: Urge your congresspeople to vote for urgent funds to rebuild Puerto Rico after Hurricane Maria. Support Josue's social justice and legal practice: @abogadojcruz; www.josuecruzabogado.com

NATURE'S LITTLE SECRETS
Feliza Fenty
Virgin Gorda Youth Leadership Initiative
Virgin Gorda, British Virgin Islands

Growing up on the little island of Virgin Gorda in the British Virgin Islands (BVI), Feliza Fenty saw how people around the world loved to visit her homeland. Sometimes called "Nature's Little Secrets," the BVI's 60 islands, with their gentle trade winds are the sailing mecca of the Caribbean. With its rich ecosystem of coral reefs and abundance of little fishes, tourists enjoy discovering their magical world by snorkeling there. Tourism from its five-star resorts, high-end villas, and luxury yachts represents over 40 percent of the BVI's income, with an equal amount of revenue coming from offshore financial services.

Like many others who wanted better opportunities for their children, Feliza's parents had moved from Barbados to Virgin Gorda. They were well-educated, they found good jobs, and became leaders of their church and in their community. They made a good life for their family, living in a modest middle-class home next to Handsome Bay. Feliza loved walking on the beach with her father, collecting colorful conch shells and watching sea creatures scurrying across the sand.

Feliza's parents had instilled in her the importance of getting a good education. Always planning ahead, they made sure she had dual citizenship. While she was in labor, Feliza's mother journeyed by ferry to the hospital in the U.S. Virgin Islands capitol of St. Thomas to give birth there, so that one day her little girl would have the option to attend university in the United States.

The British Virgin Islands are a gateway for all British-owned Caribbean islands. It is a stepping stone "across the pond" for those who aspire to go to university and pursue a professional life in the islands' mother country of the United Kingdom. Feliza grew up with children from Dominica, Jamaica, Guyana, Antigua, Barbuda, and the British West Indies who made up the diverse Virgin Gorda community of 4,000 people. In Virgin Gorda, everyone knows everyone else. Feliza had seen how the less well-educated parents of some of her classmates travelled to work from their homes in tin-roofed shacks on primitive scooters, wearing the crisp uniforms required for their jobs serving tourists.

470

From an early age, Feliza wanted to find a way to help more young people strive for a better future. She was troubled by what she saw around her -- the vast inequity of wealth, and the lack of opportunities for local children. So, when she was 16 and she heard about a new youth leadership program that was going to be offered on Virgin, she jumped at the chance. She was fascinated to learn about how young people on the nearby island of Vieques, Puerto Rico had created the Stone Soup Leadership Institute's first Sustainability Summit and, following that, the Vieques Youth Leadership Initiative. "If they can do it, so can we!" she thought.

She invited some of her friends to join her for a meeting at the Road Town Café, where The Institute's team started the meeting with a question for them: "What is your dream for your life, for your island, and for the world?" she said. She loved hearing her friends share their dreams with each other. "Just imagine if we could make them happen!" she said.

Feliza has always had a gift for communication, and for bringing people together. She was eager to share her friends' dreams with adults, especially with the government leaders on BVI's capitol island of Tortola, who she felt could be more supportive of too-often-marginalized Virgin Gorda's youth. In order to be taken seriously, Feliza decided that first her group needed a name and a mission statement; *then* they could ask for letters of support from community leaders. And that is how the Virgin Gorda Youth Leadership Initiative (VGYLI) was born.

Feliza was happy that at the VGYLI meetings, The Institute's team actually listened to young people, and asked them what was important to *them*. Too often in patriarchal societies, children are expected to be "seen and not heard." But VGYLI youth had some good ideas for how their community could be better, and now they had a chance to put their ideas into action by organizing community service projects.

Feliza began to imagine herself as a TV journalist, and decided she wanted to create a VGYLI video. She thought it would be a good way to get the message across. So she found a filmmaker, picked out background music, decided on a location, created a script, rehearsed her voiceover message, and then cajoled her friends into sharing their dreams on camera. And she invited local business leaders, like the Bitter End Yacht Club owner, Dana Hokin, to talk about the importance of training and hiring young people to work in the tourist industry on camera too.

When the film was finished, it was a hit! Everyone loved it.

At one of their meetings, VGYLI youth watched an eye-opening movie by former U.S. Vice President Al Gore, **An Inconvenient Truth**. Everyone was shocked to discover just how fragile their island -- and our whole planet -- really are to climate change. They began talking among themselves, seeing things differently, and putting two and two together. They began thinking about why it was, for example, that it was always 10 degrees hotter on Virgin Gorda than on the neighboring islands. They could see that their daily lives were already being affected by climate change. For example, with very little rainfall, Virgin Gorda had had to create the first desalination plant in the BVI, just so everyone could have enough drinking water. And because it has very few trees to serve as a coastal barrier, their island was very vulnerable to hurricanes.

Felicia was concerned. Now that she'd seen the "inconvenient" truth, she wanted everyone else to see it too. She knew that nothing would change until people got together to make a change. She created a survey and shared it with her community -- asking people if they'd heard of climate change and if they knew what was happening to their environment. She was even more worried when she found that of the 80 people she surveyed, only a few had even heard of climate change. So she wrote a report and featured it on VGYLI's website. "While the truth is inconvenient, we must each do our part," she said. "Before you throw that soda can in the road, think twice. We can be a shining example."

Once they'd seen the movie, VGYLI youth were curious to learn more about their island. Thanks to a generous charter boat owner, they had the opportunity of a lifetime when he invited them to go on an Environmental Stewards Sustainability Tour. Like most Caribbean youth, they didn't even know how to swim! And they'd never been snorkeling. The experience was incredibly exciting for them. "When I jumped off the boat, I had to overcome my fears of heights - and be adventurous," one of them said. Another said, "I was so scared, but then I realized, I can do it! And then I had fun." These future youth leaders were thrilled to see all the magical creatures who lived under the sea -- right in their very own backyard! *So this is why all the tourists come to visit!* they realized.

During the trip, the captain shared with the young people the harsh reality of how these precious coral reefs were dying from uneducated boaters who had anchorage habits. To make things worse, in 2005, rising sea temperatures had bleached the coral reefs. This experience left a lasting impression on Feliza. "Knowledge is power," she thought. And then, "Knowing, seeing, believing – knowing is seeing, and seeing is believing!"

Eager to learn more, in 2007 the VGYLI youth created the first Sustainability Summit to be held on Virgin Gorda. Hosted by the Bitter End Yacht Club, Virgin Gorda youth learned from the Vieques youth leaders who shared their sustainability initiatives, as well as local business leaders, who challenged them to study hard and pursue their dreams.

Feliza's next adventure was to travel to St. Lucia to be a youth delegate at the Caribbean Media Exchange (CMEx) Conference on Sustainable Tourism. There she learned from government leaders about innovative sustainability practices that were being introduced on neighboring islands. And, emboldened by the enthusiasm that her video had met with so far, she presented it at the next CMEx Conference in San Juan, Puerto Rico.

Upon graduation from high school, Feliza decided to go to college in the United States at Texas Christian University to study journalism. Whenever she went home for a visit, everyone looked to her for leadership, and she always encouraged them to do better with their lives. And while many of the BVI's best and brightest leave for college and then stay away, where there are more career opportunities, Feliza was determined to return to Virgin Gorda after graduating from college.

Putting her communications skills to work, she began as an information officer at the BVI's Ministry of Natural Resources and Labour. Sargassum -- a floating seaweed that suffocates small ocean creatures was invading the BVI's beautiful beaches -- and it had a putrid smell! The Handsome Bay beach near Feliza's family home was covered with it! She wrote a report on the sargassum invasion for the BVI Conservation and Fisheries Department, and harkening back to her earlier years, she also took a lead role in preparing a report assessing BVI's ability to cope with a mass casualty event. It turned out to be a warning of things to come.

Working alongside BVI's Minister of Natural Resources and Labour, Dr. Pickering, next Feliza used her organizing and communication skills to shepherd what would become the Climate Change Trust Fund, the first financing framework in the Caribbean for climate change issues. This positioned the BVI as a leader among small island states globally in establishing the policy and financing framework needed to address the causes and impacts of climate change. But unfortunately, when the government changed hands, the project was shelved - just at the worst possible moment.

When Hurricane Irma hit in 2018, it devastated many Caribbean islands. Virgin Gorda was in the eye of the storm. With its few trees, the little island was demolished, and life changed forever. The precious coral reefs were decimated. Sargassum invaded the island, and then mosquito-borne illnesses. Feliza, like many others, contracted the life-threatening dengue fever, with its long-lasting symptoms. The impact of climate change was so sudden and dramatic, it turned life upside down for everyone. Then, just as Virgin Gorda was starting to slowly rebuild, the COVID pandemic hit, crippling the island's economic base. Feliza, like many others, lost her job.

In times of great challenges, Feliza has learned to be resilient and adapt to the new reality of life on her island. Now the proud mother of four-year old Ifunaya, Feliza is using her organizing and communication skills once again - this time to rally Virgin Gorda's women to create healthier, better lives for their families. She has launched her new company, UPLIFT as a self-improvement training development to help women balance their personal and professional lives, as well as the lives of their communities. "What does it mean to be a Black Caribbean millennial in today's world?" is the question she is asking members of her community now. "How can we be resilient and take care of ourselves and prepare for our children's future?"

Feliza has always been ahead of her time. One wonders what might have happened if Virgin Gorda's leaders had listened to Feliza the other young people. Maybe they would have been better prepared to deal with climate changes. It's never too late!

When Feliza accepted the Tortola Rotaract Club Award as the Young Professional Public Relations Officer of the Year, she challenged the organization to also bring Rotaract to Virgin Gorda, which they did; and she now proudly serves as a charter member. When asked what advice she has for youth, she says, "Don't allow yourself to be overwhelmed by circumstances. When I first left high school, I never imagined that someone like me would get to go away and study something so fun, interesting, and worthwhile." She adds, "I want the future youth of our territory to always put their best foot forward in whatever jobs they may have. Build a reputation of responsibility and reliability. Make it so that if there is anything people can say about you it is that *you always do the very best you can.*"

**You must never be fearful about what you are
doing when it is right.**

Rosa Parks

Call to Action: Learn more about Virgin Gorda Youth Leadership Initiative: www.vgyli.org and Feliza's project: www.preetbird.com

WHAT DOES SUSTAINABILITY MEAN TO YOU?
Trevor Tanaka
Sustainable Hawaii Youth Leadership Initiative
Hawaii

Trevor was excited that President Barack Obama was coming home to Hawaii to welcome world leaders to the Asia Pacific Economic Summit. "We are 21 leaders from across the Asia Pacific who represent close to 3 billion people...men and women of every faith, color. and creed," Obama said. "We're more likely to realize our aspirations when we pursue them together. That's the spirit of Hawaii."

In conjunction with the Summit, Hawaii's students had been invited to enter an essay contest answering the question, "What does sustainability mean to you?" And Trevor was struggling. He was a junior at a public high school, and a good student; and he thought he should know the answer to this question.

For Trevor, sustainability was a way of life. He had grown up on his family's farms, where the rich soil from volcanic ash produced fruit trees, taro and green vegetables, and Kona coffee. Trevor was instilled with a deep respect for *'aina* -- the land. Working with his family in the gardens was his *kokua*, his responsibility. In school, he'd learned Hawaiian chants to bless the land, and to protect the food and waters. But he'd never studied it in school.

As an island state, Hawaii is particularly vulnerable to changes in the weather. Three thousand miles away from the nearest land mass, Hawaii imports 90 % percent of its food. Even little children know their families would run out of food in just three days if the ferries didn't run. Since World War II, every Hawaiian family has made sure to stock up on nonperishable foods like Spam: their garages are always full of supplies.

Trevor did his best on the essay. However, after he had turned it in, the question stayed with him. He knew his friends at private schools had had courses in sustainability. "*Everyone* should learn about it," he thought.

As an officer of the student council, Trevor was invited to create a resolution. Thus, began what Trevor calls his "sustainability journey." The Sustainability Resolution he wrote would require every public-school student in Hawaii to take one course on sustainability. When he introduced it, people cautioned him not to get his hopes up. Others, much more knowledgeable and experienced than he, had tried for years to introduce such a measure, and had failed. But Trevor was determined. He thought it was only right that all of Hawaii's young people should learn about how to live sustainably.

When he was 16 years old, a local farmer and champion of school gardens, Nancy Redfeather, nominated Trevor to serve as a youth delegate to the Stone Soup Leadership Institute's Youth Leadership Summit for Sustainable Development. Trevor wasn't sure what to expect, but he was curious to see where this journey might lead. So, he traveled 6,000 miles, to the island of Martha's Vineyard off the East Coast of the United States, where he met young people with big dreams from other islands. During a week-long intensive training, he had many eye-opening experiences. He loved the sustainability tours, during which they visited some of the Vineyard's 42 farms, and kayaked the island's waterways, where they saw oyster planting projects designed to reduce nitrogen levels.

While he was there, Trevor was fascinated to hear how those with far less resources and opportunities than he had in Hawaii had learned how to make things happen. He was especially impressed by Josue Cruz, a college junior from Puerto Rico, who talked about his Five-Year Plan. At his first Summit, when he was 14 years old, Josue had asked himself some simple questions: *What is my dream for my life, for my island, and for my community?* Since then, Josue had gone from being a mediocre high school student to being a 4.0, full scholarship college student, who was now heading to law school.

Trevor had never thought about having a Five-Year Plan. As a basketball star who aimed for the state championships, he knew the importance of hard work and discipline in achieving goals. But his horizons had always been focused on just one semester, or one year, at a time. So, when it was time for him to create his Five-Year Plan, he had to stretch himself: but Josue's reassurance, support. and confidence in him made all the difference. Josue asked him some challenging questions, which helped him expand his idea of what was possible. Trevor started to see how he could make his dreams come true - and how he could make the Sustainability Resolution happen.

He returned to Hawaii with greater focus, and strengthened energy for the journey ahead. As a founding member of the Institute's Sustainable Hawaii Youth Leadership Initiative, Trevor now put into practice what he'd learned at the Summit. He made concrete action plans, and asked for help from members of the community. He knew that he'd have to learn how the government worked in order to make the Sustainability Resolution a reality, so he was grateful when his state representative, Denny Kaufman, agreed to meet with him. Rep. Kaufman asked his aide, Nicole Lowen, to help Trevor write the Sustainability Resolution, and agreed to sponsor it in the House.

Next Trevor needed to find a champion in the State Senate. Through the Institute, he met Ian Kitajima, a seasoned business leader who took Trevor under his wing. Trevor flew to the state capitol in Honolulu and walked the halls of power with Ian. He was thrilled when Senator Jill Tokuda said she would support his resolution.

Next he needed to show that other Hawaiians felt that the resolution was important. He reached out to friends and community leaders and asked them to write testimonials. Step by step, he built the momentum they needed. Then he traveled back to Honolulu to present his resolution in the Senate chambers. They were impressed with Trevor's passion and vision. After just six months, the resolution passed unanimously in both the House and the Senate.

Everyone was amazed at Trevor's accomplishment. The press made him a local hero. His Sustainability Resolution became his capstone project for his senior year. And, as icing on the cake, Trevor graduated as valedictorian of his high school class, and his team won the state championship that year.

Then came the hard part - making the resolution a reality. For the next few years, Trevor pursued his college education. He worked with the Institute's team to organize forums with Hawaiian youth, educators, and leaders of business and government. Using "Design Thinking" language, he explored how to implement the Sustainability Resolution. The biggest challenge was that it would cost the schools money to adopt a new course, and Hawaii's Department of Education just didn't have the resources. They were woefully underfunded. Teachers were underpaid. There was just no money to add new courses, nor were there funds available to train teachers, or develop state standards.

Then in 2014, Hawaii's Governor Ike took a bold stand: he declared that Hawaii would have 100 percent renewable energy by 2045. By now Nicole Lowen was Trevor's new state representative, and she chaired the powerful Grants in Aid budget. She worked with Trevor and the

Institute to get a grant in partnership with Design Thinking Hawaii. Trevor created a simple survey to engage local youth and educators, as well as business and community leaders, to determine what was most important to Hawaiians. He integrated the UN's Sustainable Development Goals with Hawaii's sustainability goals, and found that for Hawaiians, food scarcity and the cost of electricity were the top issues. Through the surveys, Trevor learned that companies were having trouble hiring people who had only a 5th grade level of math proficiency to monitor their water meters. He researched all the best programs in Hawaii, and worked with the tech team to design an online resource – the Sustainable Hawaii Toolkit.

At the Institute's 2018 Summit, Trevor presented the toolkit to youth delegates from all over New England. He'd discovered it was especially challenging to find information on local green jobs. Now a college junior, he was eager to find out how he and others could get jobs in the emerging field of sustainability. He shared his frustration with the Institute's tech team. All week, Trevor and Chris Airing, a fellow Summit alumnus grappled with this question. They decided to expand from focusing on just Hawaii to include other states: Massachusetts, Rhode Island, Puerto Rico, and California. They created an online tool, "Sustainability is Fun" that featured all the best sustainability resources, including games and interactive learning opportunities, as well listings of green jobs. They beta tested their prototype with the Summit delegates, and got ideas for how to make it even better. At the Summit graduation, Trevor was recognized with letters from a number of state and local leaders of government, including Hawaii's governor. One was from Rep. Nicole Lowen, who wrote:

> *Trevor Tanaka, a Konawaena High School graduate, is a beacon of excellence, inspiring those around him with his commitment to creating a healthier, more sustainable planet. Even though some challenges may seem insurmountable, the Hawaiian proverb 'A'ohe hana nui ke alu 'ia (No task is too big when done together by all), reminds us that we can accomplish much with dialogue and collaboration.*

Then Trevor learned about the Blue Economy Corridor initiative in New England. At the Institute's 2019 Summit, he and Chris Aring created a Design-A-Thon, working with representatives of the Corridor, and Trevor designed a survey to drill down into the issues they were facing. While there were pockets of innovation happening, there wasn't a plan for how to build bridges between youth, schools, and companies so that the economy in underserved communities could thrive. So, Trevor and

the team envisioned a Sustainable Workforce Development Network --
an online ecosystem that connects youth, educators, and companies to
build sustainable economies.

As Trevor continues his journey by pursuing an MBA in business, he
has been working with the Institute's tech team to build a beta site
to test at the Institute's 2020 Summit. "Step by step we can build our
dreams for our islands, and for our world," he says.

> *Change will not come if we wait for some other
> person or some other time.
> We are the ones we've been waiting for. We are
> the change that we seek.*

President Barack Obama

Call to Action: To learn more about opportunities to learn and
build a sustainable world visit: Sustainable Hawaii Toolkit: www.
sustainhawaiitoolkit.com SustainabilityisFun.com SustainWDN.com

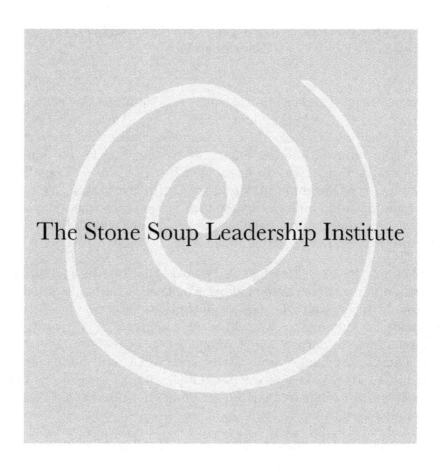

The Stone Soup Leadership Institute

THE STONE SOUP LEADERSHIP INSTITUTE
Background

The Stone Soup Leadership Institute was founded by people who were featured in the book, *Stone Soup for the World: Life-Changing Stories of Everyday Heroes*. They are concerned about the direction the planet is heading in, and the legacy we are leaving for our children. As community organizers, we knew that if we all worked together for the common good we could maximize our collective power. We use the Stone Soup model to invite everyone to share of their time, talents, and resources to support young people so that together we can build a more just, equitable, and sustainable world.

Founded in 1997 on Martha's Vineyard, the Institute is a 501c3 nonprofit organization whose mission is to develop multicultural digital educational tools, youth leadership initiatives, and provide technical assistance for sustainable workforce development. We've synthesized the lessons we've learned and developed a grassroots model to train local leaders, exchange innovative solutions, and build resilient communities. In response to the pandemic, we have transitioned all of our tools and trainings to a virtual learning environment that adheres to state standards.

Over the years we've developed partnerships, and increased media attention and funding. We've leveraged celebrity support to maximize media attention and the impact on those who are on the frontlines doing the work, often with limited support. We are now well positioned to leverage our collective resources to nurture and support brave young people around the world who are working so hard to create a just, equitable, and sustainable future for life on this planet.

Educational Tools

Stone Soup for the World: Life-Changing Stories of Everyday Heroes (Three Rivers Press/Random House) honors 100 people, organizations, and companies from 65 communities and 29 countries around the world. In his introduction to the book, Walter Cronkite called it a "handbook for humanitarians" and "a road map for building a better world." The book was premiered at the Presidents' Summit America's Promise in 1996, was featured in book clubs, and received worldwide media recognition.

Pan Y Vino Para el Camino: Bilingual Book and Curriculum:
Actor and activist Edward James Olmos asked us to translate our first
book into Spanish. In the introduction to the book Olmos writes, "One
of the most important gifts we can give our children is to read stories
about those who went before them." He believed that when Latino
youth read about these inspiring stories in the book, they are motivated
to stay in school, graduate, and pursue their personal, professional, and
planetary goals. We launched this book at the first Latino Book Festival
in Los Angeles, where we presented Olmos with the Institute's first
Cesar Chavez Award.

Companion Educational Curriculum: Piloted by the YMCA in eight
states, this curriculum offers lesson plans for multicultural literacy,
critical thinking skills and social studies, service learning, citizenship,
leadership development skills. The curriculum, which includes audio
and video elements, is a structured two-year program used by educators,
after-school programs, corporate mentors, volunteers, and churches. To
make it easier for educators to use in their classroom, each lesson plan
meets U.S. state standards. Educators have used it in 120 communities
to prepare the next generation of leaders to address the economic,
environmental, and social challenges of the 21st century.

***Stone Soup for a Sustainable World: Life Changing Stories of
Young Heroes*** features the stories of 100 climate change trailblazers,
environmental justice changemakers, educator champions, sustainable
business leaders, intergenerational legacy figures, green inventors
and entrepreneurs, and emerging island leaders from 38 countries
around the world, and 32 cities in the U.S. who are building a more
just, equitable, and sustainable world. The Institute's ***Young Heroes
Fund*** provides mentors, training, and financial support for these youth
leaders to scale up their organizations.

Companion Educational Curriculum brings these stories to life
with lesson plans for each story that highlight the values and basic
academic disciplines of Language Arts and STEM activities as well
as Sustainable Innovations and Sustainable Career Pathways to help
guide students toward blue and green jobs to help rebuild the planet.

Proceeds from the books support the Stone Soup Institute's global
initiatives. Over the last 24 years, the Institute has invested in training
young people around the world to become leaders in their communities
and the world.

Multifaceted Social Media Campaign. Each week we showcase one of the 100 stories from each of the books with a week-long series of posts that bring them to life, drawing on Story-a-Week -- a Hero Report video, narrated by Walter Cronkite. We feature an Honor Roll and Call to Action to invite people to support their efforts. We feature these posts on Facebook, Instagram, Twitter, and LinkedIn, and on our Virtual Education Toolkit for educators to supplement their classroom learning activities.

Youth & Community Leadership Initiatives: For the last 20 years, the Institute has been bringing these stories to life by working alongside ocean communities. During the Institute's Sustainability Summits and year-round youth community leadership initiatives, young people develop the skills and training needed to develop their personal, professional, and planetary goals. Taking initiative in one's life is especially critical for the survival of these island communities. These youth leaders created a 2020 Report for Sustainable Development and challenged their leaders to develop policies that balance protecting their communities' fragile ecosystems, providing for their families, creating opportunities for their children, and building a just, equitable, and sustainable future. We've inspired hundreds of underserved multicultural youth around the world to become leaders by taking initiative in their lives, their communities, and their world from Vieques, Puerto Rico to Martha's Vineyard, from Hawaii to Rhode Island, and from Virgin Gorda, British Virgin Islands to the Philippines.. Some of them are featured in the book, ***Stone Soup for a Sustainable World: Life-Changing Stories of Young Heroes.***

The TouchStone Leaders Virtual Platform scales up the Institute's 20-year real-world experience, using rich bilingual content and methodologies to educate young people to become leaders in their lives, their communities, and our world. It is a values-based, video-enhanced, content-driven, blended experiential learning environment featuring resources that educate, engage, and connect people with sustainable solutions that are empowering the next generation of changemakers to lead our world. It offers grassroots lessons learned through working directly with community-based programs. The program is action-oriented, making it possible for learning and social change to happen simultaneously and effectively. This personalized program trains people in the "soft skills" needed to address real-world situations, and to be effective servant leaders -- powerful communicators who are able to lead and work on teams, adapt to the demands of various settings, be creative problem solvers, think critically about various issues, resolve conflicts that arise, and use project management skills to get work done. The Institute's ***Performance Metrics*** measures the program's impact on skills essential to the 21st century job market, such as communication, teamwork, conflict resolution, problem solving, adaptability, critical thinking, and project management skills.

The TouchStone Leaders' Life Planning Tools. Dream Map™ is a framework for individualized learning, and self-directed careers for 21st century workforce development. The Dream Map™ is the gateway for youth to enter the virtual platform and track their journey with an individualized five-year plan for their personal, professional, and global goals. It is a "smart" tool that allows youth to *start to see themselves becoming their dreams.* Students use TouchStone Life Planning Tools to create personalized Dream Maps, a five-year plan with multiple time markers and personalized career pathways. These tools allow students to consistently work on their goals and self-reflect throughout the journey on what they have learned, and how it can affect their future endeavors. These tools allow students to proactively address their future plans, and highlight their best and strongest traits. It is a virtual space where people can discover their "true north," and is committed to the vital work of creating and leading innovative solutions to global problems.

Facilitator Certificate Program is a train-the-trainer program for teachers to maximize the impact of the Institute's educational tools in order to accelerate the development of 21st century skills. The Institute's *SustainWDN™ training program for guidance counselors* assists them to help their students navigate sustainable career pathways to help build a blue/green economy.

Multifaceted Engagement Initiatives: To launch **Stone Soup for the World: Life-Changing Stories of Everyday Heroes,** the Institute created a historic book launch with the World's Largest Book Signing in 40 cities. People featured in the book read their heartwarming stories, autographed books, organized special events, and signed people up for organizations. For the launch of the second edition of the book, we organized a Celebration of Heroes with Walter Cronkite in New York City. And we launched the Spanish version of the book, *Pan Y Vino Para El Camino* at the L.A. Book Festival with Edward James Olmos. Upon Walter Cronkite's passing, the Institute hosted the annual Cronkite Awards Ceremony to honor those who have used the power of the media for positive social change. Along with Cronkite's CBS colleagues Bob Schieffer and Nick Clooney, and leaders like David McCullough, Rose Styron, and Ted Kennedy Jr., we've recognized champions like Mission Blue's Dr. Sylvia Earle, filmmaker Bob Nixon, and CNN reporter and civil rights leader Charlayne Hunter-Gault, as well as the young filmmakers who produced the *Passing of the Torch* video featuring Harry Belafonte Jr. for Amnesty International's 50th Anniversary.

Our Pledge

We accept Walter Cronkite's challenge for a new kind of engaged activism, to be a force for positive change in the world.

We carry on the legacy of Mahatma Gandhi, Eleanor Roosevelt, Cesar Chavez, and Dr. Martin Luther King Jr.

to improve the conditions of our neighborhoods, our countries, and the world through individual action and working with others.

Together, we will forge new directions for the global economy, bridge the gap between the haves and have-nots,

and strive to build a more peaceful, sustainable world.

Celebration of Heroes with Walter Cronkite • November 13, 2002 • New York City

Stone Soup Leadership Institute

www.stonesoupleadership.org

THE INSTITUTE'S SUSTAINABILITY JOURNEY
The transition to a sustainable economy is the most challenging issue of the 21st century.

Young people want to get involved with sustainability - and are eager to learn what they can do. They are keen to get jobs and careers to rebuild the planet. The stories in this book have been thoughtfully chosen to showcase solutions to the most pressing issues of our time. Our companion curriculum makes it easy for educators to bring these stories to life in their classroom. The Institute is committed to bringing these educational tools to our schools. We hope you will join with us!

What We've Learned

For 20 years, the Institute has worked alongside young people who are on the front lines of climate change, social justice, and economic equity. Island people are now "the canaries in the coal mine." Every day they see their coastlines eroding, their fish supply depleted, plastics littering their beaches, and toxic waste and environmental hazards dumped into their pristine waters. In Hawaii, where they've set an ambitious goal of 100 % renewable energy by 2045, their systems are woefully lacking, especially their schools.

Education: The Challenge

As the news reveals every day, we need everyone to help rebuild the world in a sustainable way—one that provides opportunities to everyone, but not at the cost of future generations or the planet. However, while young people are hungry to learn how they can adapt to climate change in their communities, few students are obtaining even the basic STEM education they'll need to navigate that new reality. Few are learning how critical an understanding of sustainability is to their future. Ironically, at a time when we need more STEM education to help students prepare for the transition to a sustainable economy, schools are struggling to hire and keep STEM teachers. Some leave teaching for higher-paid jobs with companies. Some schools are even cutting their STEM programs to meet budget demands. Now with the COVID pandemic, many students must learn online with limited opportunities to develop their critical thinking skills, explore project-based learning, or even get the basic scientific understanding they need to help be part of this transition.

The Institute's Educational Tools

Over the years, the Institute has become a leader in developing sustainable education and sustainable workforce development tools -- by listening to and learning from young people and their community's leaders. Our multicultural youth are leading the way toward a reimagined future, where sustainability and environmental justice are at the forefront. The Institute's annual Sustainability Summit, and our educational tools, books, lesson plans, career mentoring, and workforce development programs through SustainWDN™, are custom-designed to prepare the next generation of youth leaders to build a more just, equitable, and sustainable world. Our programs align with the Green New Deal and President Biden's Plan for Climate Change and Environmental Justice.

Stone Soup for a Sustainable World: Life-Changing Stories of Young Heroes features the stories of 100 climate change trailblazers, environmental justice changemakers, educator champions, sustainable business leaders, intergenerational legacy figures, green inventors and entrepreneurs, and emerging island leaders from 38 countries around the world, and 32 cities in the U.S. who are building a more just, equitable, and sustainable world.

Our *Companion Educational Curriculum* is a dynamic, solutions-oriented program that brings these stories to life with lesson plans for each story that highlight the values and academic disciplines of Language Arts and STEM activities as well as Sustainable Innovations and Sustainable Career Pathways, to help guide students toward blue and green jobs to help rebuild the planet.

Our *Sustainability Summits* are the cornerstone of the Institute's work with hundreds of multicultural youth around the world who have been trained to become leaders, by taking initiative in their lives, their communities, and their world. We've hosted 17 Summits in four locations in two countries: from Vieques, Puerto Rico to Virgin Gorda, British Virgin Islands to Martha's Vineyard, and Newport and Bristol, Rhode Island. To respond to the pandemic and expand our reach globally, the Institute transitioned in 2020 to a virtual Summit -- which will expand exponentially in 2021 with the launch of the book *Stone Soup for the Sustainable World: Life-Changing Stories of Young Everyday Heroes.*

Sustainability Summit Speakers inspire young people to deepen their appreciation of science and pursue sustainable career pathways, blue and green companies, and global youth speakers from *Stone Soup for the Sustainable World: Life-Changing Stories of Young Everyday Heroes.*

Our Sustainability Toolkits

• *Sustainability Is Fun* connects young people with engaging, fun, and interactive educational opportunities like virtual sustainability tours; games; inspiring videos; and an educational curriculum. It can be customized by region or state to provide targeted resources.

• The *Sustainable Hawaii Toolkit* provides free resources, learning tools, videos, and green jobs in the sustainable workforce and contributes to Hawaii's goal of 100% Renewable Energy by 2045. Based on the UN's Sustainable Development Goals, it serves as a global model.

• *Virtual Sustainability Tours* The Institute's YouTube channel features inspiring videos that gives students a firsthand view of the fragility of our ecosystems, and teaches them how they can preserve and protect the planet for future generations.

• *Sustainability-In-Action Projects.* Students learn critical thinking and decision-making skills, how to troubleshoot challenges, make engaging presentations, and develop strategies to recruit youth and convince local decision makers.

• The *Sustainability Virtual Field Station* is a student-designed, web-based education and research tool with maps, tools, and sites. It is an invaluable resource for connecting young people with real-life science applications – leading to greater collaboration and sharing of data with nonprofits, as well as increased youth success with local/state Science Fairs.

• The *Sustainable Workforce Development Network: SustainWDN™* is an online ecosystem that builds bridges between young people, educators, and blue and green companies to build a 21st century blue/green workforce development pipeline. It offers educators and career counselors tools to guide students toward sustainable career pathways, and serves as an economic planning tool for communities to transition to sustainable economy. It helps companies realize a triple bottom line by preparing young people to contribute to a sustainable workforce, and a resilient community.

The SustainWDN™ Facilitators Certificate Program gives educators and career counselors the tools they need to prepare their students for the green/blue economy of the 21st century. This engaging resource serves as a network to build bridges between blue employers, educational institutions, community organizations, and young people who are seeking ways to rebuild their communities and the planet.

The Institute is partnering with forward-thinking allies across industries, from Ph.D.s and MBAs, to universities, green-blue companies, environmental organizations, educational institutions, technical and vocational programs, and most importantly, ***young people*** who are eager to build sustainable future. We are eager to scale this platform to reach more schools and businesses nationwide, so that together we can begin to really make a difference.

PRAISE FOR THE STONE SOUP LEADERSHIP INSTITUTE

The Stone Soup Leadership Institute is continuing the legacy of past environmentalists by fostering youth leadership throughout the world. Launching the "Green Revolution" from a grassroots base will be integral to future policymaking; it is up to these youth delegates to lead this movement. With a focus on sustainable building, sustainable economics, cultural sustainability, and sustainable agriculture, this year's Sustainability Summit will continue to tackle the most difficult problems our world community faces. Use this Summit as a tool to help hone your already-budding leadership qualities into a strength that can help you connect with people from all walks of life.

John Kerry
U.S. Special Presidential Envoy for Climate

Your dedication, compassion, and care for the island communities you work with is greatly appreciated and your efforts have not gone unnoticed. The work you have done for sustainable development across the globe is a valuable contribution to the future of our environment.

U.S. Senator Elizabeth Warren, Massachusetts

The Stone Soup Leadership Institute's work of inspiring, educating, and empowering young people to take initiative in their communities is a critical step in ensuring the success and longevity of our oceans, island sustainability and our planet.

Joe Kennedy, The Groundwork Project

I've had the privilege of working with some of the Institute's young people who are featured in the book, Stone Soup for a Sustainable World. I've seen the uplifting power they have on their communities and our world. If you like inspirational stories, pick up this book... if you want to be an inspirational story, pick a cause, and follow these trailblazing youth leaders into a greener future.

Nancy Slonim Aronie, Author, NPR Commentator,
Martha's Vineyard

The young people in Stone Soup for a Sustainable World are on the front lines of climate change. In times like these, their courage, bravery and perseverance in the face of overwhelming odds give us hope. They deserve our support.

Rose Styron, Author, Martha's Vineyard

The Stone Soup Leadership Institute's Virtual Education Toolkit and courses based on the book, Stone Soup for the World: Life-Changing Stories of Everyday Heroes is a treasure. It gives educators a powerful way to engage students through real-life stories with meaningful lessons that address the importance of SEL (social-emotional learning) values of caring for ourselves, others, and for the community. The Institute's noble work with students, teachers, and schools reminds me of how we created one of the nation's first SEL curriculum and founded two schools with SEL as a central pillar. We worked alongside educators, political and business leaders, and a group of Nobel Laureates to reflect on the educational needs of our society. We decided that the central foundation of a school is beyond students' knowledge. We must give them an opportunity to think, act, and lay the foundation for life-long learning. The Institute's curriculum and online courses gives teachers the tools they need to bring SEL into their classrooms. I encourage everyone who cares about our children, their future, and ours to bring these tools into our schools.

Karen Stone McCown, Founder The Nueva Learning Center, The Synapse School

I have had the privilege of working with Marianne Larned on a number of projects in Martha's Vineyard. She epitomizes what dedication and leadership really means to a cause, which in itself is leadership. She has nurtured so many young people to be strong role models in their communities and beyond. All the best for her continued success.

Gerri Laurino, Martha's Vineyard/Florida

The Stone Soup Leadership Institute has been a leader in sustainability education and youth leadership development for over two decades–it's time the Institute is recognized for its novel contributions to the cause.

The Rev. Dr. Carol C. Saysette, California

I was present when the real celebrity/dignitaries, Walter Cronkite and Marianne Larned, gave life to a concept that was to become Stone Soup for the World ... and led us here today. Having had the great honor to witness the beginning, I am thrilled to be part of this event to celebrate all of the 100 impressive heroes featured in Stone Soup for a Sustainable World: Life Changing Stories of Young Heroes, who are the manifestation of that dream. I applaud you all for your brilliance, ingenuity, and